A Song of

A boy grows up in a Staffordshire Village
1932-1951

by Percy Carpenter

Season of mists and mellow fruitfulness;
Close bosom friend of the maturing sun….
….Where are the songs of Spring? Aye, where are they?

Ode to Autumn - John Keats

Published in 2012 by Dr P B Carpenter

Dedicated to mom and dad

ISBN 978-0-9573434-0-5

Designed and produced by John Griffiths, printed in the UK.

CONTENTS

CHAPTER 1

'The start of life - c.1932 - 34'

It is the end of autumn and as the winter of my life begins, I find myself reminiscing on Spring as it was. At eighty years of age, memories abound of family and school, of mining and industry, of yet another world war and of beautiful countryside. It was essentially a joyful time of life, spent in a peaceful haven in and around Landywood in Staffordshire.

My mature yet fading brain still recalls the time and I soon churn out notes, endless pages of them. In next to no time I have resolved to chronicle this time of my life, warts and all. My discourse, I tell myself, will incorporate growing up in the 1930s and 1940s, using the real names of family and others I met along the way. It will include my recollections of exploits in and around local villages and elsewhere. I shall try to create an accurate timeline but, since I have never kept diaries, I beg forgiveness from others who may know better. With these as my rules of engagement, you my reader must then decide whether, in the end, my battle with a fading memory was won.

My first task is to develop the notes into stories before melding into their appropriate chapters. With these taking shape, I sit for the first time in front of my word processor, and it hits me how spoilt I am. Eighty years ago, I would have written them with a scratchy pen and blue black ink. If I made a mistake, the medium was unforgiving; at best necessitating a messy scratched out correction, at worst a whole page of text to be re-written. Simply looking around me so many things have changed, my computer, telephone and television set receive millions of items of information through an underground optical fibre thinner than a human hair. Eighty years ago, standing on Walsall Road waiting for a bus, pairs of tall telegraph poles as far as the eye could see carried about sixty wires bearing a similar number of simple telephone calls. Today, my television set flaunts high definition images, but eighty years ago our information came from a simple wireless (radio), the only electrical item in most homes, but the latest technology at the time.

With the scene set let me start at the beginning, with my beginning. I have no doubt that my seed was planted in a moment of happiness.

Mom was, at the time, managing Stanton's cake shop in High Street, Cheslyn Hay. Both Taylor's and Stanton's bakeries had outlets in most towns and large villages around Cannock Chase. Ida Baker was her name. She was 24 years old and no doubt a cracker as a young woman in the nineteen twenties. Like all young women, she adored the nice clothes of the day and had her beaus. None of the early ones left a mark quite like he who sent a verse when she shunned his advances,

Stanton's tarts break men's hearts,
That's what most folks say.
A Stanton's tart has broke my heart,
And lives down Landywood way!

It was a verse she was to repeat many times during her long life.

Dad, Harold Carpenter, like some three generations of his family before him, was an edge tool polisher at Gilpin's factory, a company established in the area in the eighteenth century, and by this time based at Churchbridge. He lived in High Street, Cheslyn Hay, directly opposite Stanton's cake shop. As a young man, he loved football and crown green bowls, winning cups in bowls tournaments with uncle Ray, his younger brother. Regardless of other suitors, dad obviously swept mom off her feet and my seed was planted, no doubt in a moment of unremitting and breathless passion as dad walked her home on a dark November night. As many before them had done, they are likely to have leaned against some five-bar gate to a field. It was a makeshift upright bed where they will have cuddled, kissed and groped to the point of no return.

I quake at the affect my implantation must have had when mom missed that first monthly curse. It must have ruined her Christmas in 1931. She will without doubt have panicked. She still had feelings for the beau who considered her a Stanton's tart. Who does she confide in? Dad, yes, but what good is a man in such circumstances. What will her mom and dad say? Whatever was said, whatever the varied advice, granddad will have had his way and she and dad married three months later on Saturday, 19th March 1932, as I subsequently found from granddad's family bible. It was the norm at the time. Sadly, the stigma and internal hurt of a pregnancy outside marriage stayed with mom for the rest of her life and she could never bring herself to talk about it. I am not sure whether she knew that both her mother and grandmother were at least three months pregnant when they married, as records show. Fortunately, the enforced marriage did no harm. Mom and dad remained in love for seventy years until they died in their nineties.

I was born on Thursday, fourth of August 1932, in a small semi-detached cottage, two-up and two-down in the mining village of Landywood, near to Cannock in Staffordshire. The cottage still stands at the end of Benton's Lane but has been subject to upgrades. Mom and dad were now twenty-five and twenty seven years of age.

My birth, it seems, was not an easy one. She knew this would be the case because a consultant obstetrician in Wolverhampton had told her so. He had measured her and felt her pelvis was not big enough to deliver a baby. She was distressed by his advice and did not want anything further to do with him. When the time came, she was in labour for two or three days, she was to tell me in later life. In charge of the lying in was Mrs Johnson who lived further down Benton's Lane. She was neither qualified in nursing nor in midwifery but she had done her apprenticeship at many births in the village, at a time when most babies were delivered at home. After the prolonged labour, accompanied I gather by blood curdling screams and with a great deal of pulling by the doctor, who Mrs Johnson had called in, I was delivered 'black and blue'. Unlike many babies at the time, I survived the trauma of the occasion with a seemingly minor injury. I shall expand on this in my school years, when it became apparent that pulling my head and neck to deliver the shoulders had torn my neck muscle. It was this that caused the severe bruising at birth, the 'black and blue' about which mom was to hold forth for most of her life.

That, and the fact that I rejected most kinds of milk during my first few months. Citrate it seems came to the rescue and I have survived to tell the tale, forever the apple of their eye. I assume that, after such a traumatic birth, mom decided that enough was enough and a sibling was out of the question. I was, therefore, an only child.

Percival (Percy), the name appended at birth, was never a name I would have chosen for myself but Percival was in the family and my father's second name and it seems I was lumbered by tradition. My second name Benjamin had also lived through two or three generations of the family. It must have seemed eminently sensible to mom and dad, but I lived my life hating my Christian names. Why couldn't I be David or Robert or John or any other name on earth than Percival Benjamin, noble as the name may be.

The small cottage in which I was born belonged to my granddad, Robert (Bob) Baker, who had rented it to mom and dad on their marriage. By this time he had moved with my grandma, Elizabeth (Liz), to a more recently built bungalow on marshland a quarter of a mile away adjacent to Shant's Bridge. Granddad owned about four cottages in the village and several parcels of land in the environs. Seven years before my birth, he had purchased the land on which had stood the first two Wesleyan Chapels in the village that succumbed to mining subsidence. Mom had in her earlier years attended this Sunday School. He sold the land for housing development a year or two before I was born. He had been a miner at two or three local pits and was, in his later working years, a shot firer. Granddad was not a miser but certainly watched his pennies since they grew into pounds, as he incessantly told me.

"Tek this, ode son, and keep it safe. If yer look after yer pennies the pownds'll teck care of 'umselves!", were his immortal words whenever he pressed a penny into my hand.

Granddad had a nose for a good bargain. The parcel of land to the southwest of Shant's bridge came cheap. Who else would buy it, it was boggy marshland?

In the late 1850s, the construction of the ramps and embankments to carry Landywood Lane over the railway line at its junction with Street's lane had resulted in entrapment of the water draining from the high fields, which over some seventy years had created a stagnant bog. It was nevertheless a fertile patch growing luscious reeds and, even worse, horsetail with which dad would battle with for years to come. Cheap as it was, granddad did not buy the land carelessly. He had found the buried and blocked drainage culvert beneath the embankment, incorporated during construction, and had realised that this was the cause of the swampy bog. It is likely that he knew of this before purchase. He was a man who had learned by experience and knew the importance of good drainage. He knew that clearing the culvert would have potential and it was to his credit that from his bargain purchase he created nearly an acre of firm dry land on which he would eventually build four bungalows for his family. Until the time of his death the drainage culvert and protective ditches beneath the high land were always correctly maintained to ensure his properties remained dry. The reclaimed bog proved to be extremely fertile dark loam and the budding gardens later grew prize-winning crops. Satisfied with his preparation of the land, he built a bungalow for himself and grandma and following this he intended to build bungalows for his children.

When I was about six months old, we moved from Benton's Lane into a newly built bungalow on the plot. It was built for £250 by Mr Paxton who had to contend with granddad's ways. According to mom, he ensured that every penny was spent wisely, time schedules were met and he frequently carped about the quality of the workmanship.

This conduct came from a man whom I, in later years, found so tight-fisted that he would never buy new materials for repair jobs to his rented properties.

Our bungalow was typical of the period, four rooms roughly twelve feet (3.6 metres) square which were used as a sitting (or living) room, parlour and two bedrooms. There was also a bathroom which included internal toilet and a brew house (locally pronounced brew'us), the kitchen of the day. The living room was fitted with a cast iron coal range with oven and hob where all cooking was done. The flat surface of the hob had circular covers which were removed to allow the flames or radiant heat beneath cooking pots or a kettle. It meant that pans invariably became caked with soot, needing regular cleaning. The other three rooms were fitted with coal fireplaces with tiled surrounds, but that in the parlour was of much higher standard, with more decorative tiles and a polished dark oak over-mantle. This was a room which would only be used on special occasions, as was the norm at the time. All rooms were fitted with a picture rail about fifteen inches (40cm) from the ceiling from which pictures were hung and, at floor level, eight inch (20cm) skirting boards.

The front door of the bungalow, some two feet (60cm) above ground level because of the land slope, opened into a quarried entrance hall onto which the other rooms opened. A recess in the hall created space for a dark oak palm stand bearing a blue and white jardinière containing a large aspidistra, seen in many houses. The bathroom was at the end of the hall. Washing hands after the toilet did not at the time have a high priority as no hand basin was provided for the purpose. When hands needed washing, it was done in the large ceramic sink in the brew'us which annexed of the living room, at the back of the house.

The brew'us like the hall was quarried with red tiles for ease of mopping after water spills. The ceramic sink was large and box-shaped with a cold water tap. In the corner, a coal-fired open boiler which held about twenty gallons (90 litres) provided sufficient hot water for wash days and baths. A twenty-one inch (54cm) lid with handle, which Mr Paxton the builder had fashioned from off-cuts of 'tongue and groove' floor boards, covered it. Hot water needed to be carried in buckets from this boiler to the bathroom since granddad had chosen not to install a back boiler in the range, providing hot water on tap. That would have been a few pennies too far!

The walk-in pantry off the brew'us had a cool concrete storage bench quarried to match the floor. Food at the time was stored without refrigeration, but a grill in the north wall meant that it was always cooler than other rooms and exceedingly cold during the winter. A built-in coalhouse occupied the other corner and opened on to the back yard. The brew'us was therefore an oddly shaped working area but it was adequate to allow access to water for various activities such as personal hygiene, washdays, food preparation, washing up and so on. Since we did not have hot water on tap, water for most activities was boiled in a large kettle on the range in the living room. A kettle of water was always kept on a hob so that it was nearly boiled and could be flashed up when required.

Mom had avidly planned for her new home and from the moment she took command, she proved to be extremely house-proud. Rooms had to be dusted and quarry floors scrubbed every day. She had set herself a particular chore for every day of the week. Monday was always wash-day, Tuesday was turning out the bedrooms and ironing and so on.

Mom and dad slept in a double bed in one bedroom and I slept in a double bed in the other. It was not furnished for a child, and was essentially a replica of mom's and dad's bedroom. They did not have a great deal of spare money for furniture and it was quite basic. The beds had mock oak panelled bedsteads and flock mattresses. Each bedroom had a wardrobe and dressing table purchased as a suite with the bedstead. Both bedrooms had built-in wardrobes at the side of the chimney breasts but for some reason mom would never use these for clothes. Each room had a blue basket weave chair. Mom had a few glass trinkets, presumably from her bottom drawer, which she displayed on the dressing tables. Curtains, probably made by grandma on her Singer sewing machine, were simple patterned cotton. Although both bedrooms were fitted with a fireplace for a coal fire, they were never used unless someone was ill. During a very cold winter the insides of windows were frequently covered with frozen condensation by morning! Our bed warmers were simply two house bricks which were kept in the oven throughout the day. Just before going to bed on cold nights, these were wrapped in brown paper, put in a cloth bag and placed in our beds. Bed coverings were normally a bottom and top sheet, two blankets and an eiderdown.

In the living room we dined from a solid pine table with four turned legs and four straight back dining chairs with twist legs and rexine (artificial leather cloth) padded seats, often referred to as 'poor man's leather'. The table was always covered with a patterned table cloth which was removed for rolling pastry, cleaning the brasses and other household chores. After using it, the pine top was thoroughly scrubbed with soap and water. We sat or lounged on a two-seater settee and two armchairs again covered with matching rexine. The floor was covered with patterned linoleum (called oil cloth), which dad laid from a roll purchased from D W Clarke in Cannock. A simple mat adorned the front of the hearth. To the left of the chimney breast, built-in cupboards with plywood panelled doors were used for storage of crockery and linen. The only electric power supply in the whole bungalow was one five amp two-pin socket into which was plugged a simple two valve radio that sat on the living room window sill. Any later electric appliances (in the 1940s) such as an electric iron, were plugged into the standard bayonet light socket above the table, after removing the bulb.

The parlour (front lounge) was not initially furnished since mom only wanted the best including a blue floral patterned carpet. As the years passed by, it was furnished with a nice fabric covered three piece suite, which we rarely sat on, and a walnut veneered sideboard on which mom could display her cut glass. Much later, her one craving for a blue floral carpet was fulfilled. It was a room she was very proud of but which was only used at Christmas!

This then was my home throughout my story and on granddad Baker's little acre lived all his clan except aunt Hilda and her family. Granddad's children, oldest to youngest, were aunt Hilda, uncle Bob, mom and aunt Ruby. Dad and aunt Sarah (nee Webb, of Upper Landywood) had married into his clan. In 1933, grandma and granddad and aunt Ruby lived in the first bungalow built on the site, to the left of ours, and uncle Bob, aunt Sarah and cousin Bobby in the bungalow to the right. Aunt Hilda was by this time already married with three children. She and uncle Jack (whose name was also Baker, though not related) had a house in Broad Lane, Essington. Me, well I was at the time the youngest member of the clan.

A concrete path, constructed around the back of the bungalows, was trodden at least twice a day by grandma who called on everyone to see how they were, sometimes to give matriarchal advice. Her first call of the day was always to borrow the daily newspapers so that granddad could have first read whilst the men were at work. On Friday every week, she came to collect a rent of ten shillings (50p) from mom and aunt Sarah, on which she and granddad survived since he had by now retired from the mine and was a full-time gardener. He himself only visited his offspring if he felt they or their spouses were not toeing the line, usually in a temper and slamming the door as he left. There were also times when grandma might have an argument with one of her family, most commonly short-tempered mom, and walked out in a huff. Some of the squabbles could result in her staying away for weeks at a time, passing by the offender's back door as she called in the other bungalow. Both aggrieved avoided each other until one day they might meet face to face as they turned a corner. Looking each other in the eye, they invariably laughed and made up as though nothing had happened. During these silly stand-offs, I still visited grandma and granddad in their bungalow and was always asked, "How's your mom?" They never involved dad or myself in their chastisement of their insubordinate daughter.

Aunt Sarah, uncle Bob's wife, was a simple kind lady who would always try to help people. She often did shopping for mom or helped with some repair or other. It was never a particularly good job, but she tried. She was a good source for village gossip and, after a shopping spree, usually off-loaded the latest to mom. Uncle Bob, on the other hand, I found frightening. It is difficult to say why he was so unpleasant, but he grew up the only boy in the family with aunt Hilda, aunt Ruby and mom as sisters. He never thought a lot of them, no doubt a macho man thing, but he was out-numbered and his views were invariably dismissed. All the girls were very strong-willed and would certainly take no nonsense from him. His dislike for them later reflected on their children and he never interacted kindly with his nephews and nieces. He never actually said anything caustic to me, it was just a vibe I had, but in his presence I was positively uncomfortable and knew he did not want me there. He was by trade a carpenter and as a hobby turned out quite nice modern casual furniture which he sold as a source of pocket money. His carpentry was first class and, even though not fond of him, I was still drawn to him by the quality of his work. He was meticulous in most things he did and even when digging his garden, the soil was raked to a perfect tilth and levelled as though done with a spirit level. Having said this, he had the loudest fart in the lane! Frequently, as he bent down to pick up a stone or pull a weed, his rear end would reverberate like the horn of the Queen Mary leaving harbour. He would stand up and look around innocently, bearing an expression of "not me!" I never dared laugh at him until I had turned the corner because he had an acerbic tongue and I knew what the response would be. When out of sight I invariably collapsed in uncontrollable laughter, my sides hurting, as any child would when a grown-up has humiliated himself.

Aunt Ruby was in her early twenties at this time, quite attractive, and her story unfolds later.

Dad's family, the Carpenters, lived in Cheslyn Hay. Sadly I never had the pleasure of knowing my grandparents Carpenter who had died before I could get to know them. Granddad Benjamin died of natural causes, possibly a heart attack, in 1921. Grandma Flora (nee Follows) died a year or two after I was born, allegedly from neurasthenia, but such terminology was not very accurate and the cause of death is not really known.

Whatever the illness her last year or so was spent in St Matthew's mental hospital, but I believe she did see me before she died. She gave birth to five children, one of whom, Decimus, died in his early years. The four who survived, oldest to youngest, were uncle Garland, aunt Nancy, my dad and uncle Ray and again we will meet these later.

CHAPTER 2

'Early memories - c. 1934 - 36'

Memories of my first three years of life are very hazy, one might even say non-existent. We are not to remember the trials of babyhood, the falls as we endeavour to walk, the exasperations of mom when she finds yet another dirty nappy or the joy we experience as dad holds us over his head and buries his nose in our tummy. At this time, the brain has created few links with recallable memory, but those which connected have allowed me some access to my early life.

My first image in the second year of life paints the splendour of an orange blossom bush *(Philadelphus)* in full bloom adjacent to the back door of the bungalow. Pure white blooms with orange centres had suddenly appeared to adorn what had previously been an insignificant and drab bush. I have but one thought, to pluck them! I do so, oh what joy! But why is dad not entirely happy with the carpet of white flower heads adorning the back yard?

"Yo munna do that, son, that bush's theere to make the garden look nice", was his gentle chastisement as he pulled me away from the bush.

No doubt he was hurt because it was the first blooming of one of the first shrubs he had planted in his new garden. He found contentment in his quarter of an acre, even though horsetail was the commonest single species. He had worked exceedingly hard with his spade over the first two seasons to create some semblance of a garden with paths constructed from clinker from the boiler house of the Plant pit. He had had no significant garden as a child living in High Street in Cheslyn Hay, simply a bricked back yard. Many households had an allotment away from home where they grew vegetables as did some of his family and he probably helped. Dad's new garden, though still immature, was the start of what became a lifetime's dedication, and here was I, tearing apart his first shrub as it burst into bloom. He was a loving father and laughed when he saw the disarray and, since I could only reach part of the canopy, there was still a display of the upper blooms. Then all too soon, about a day or so, the remaining flowers were shedding and I was back, playing in the white confetti collecting beneath the bush, throwing it into the air so that the wind caught it and dispersed it like confetti over the back yard. Mom was always irritated by mess, and flower petals were mess, and she yelled at me as she aggressively worked her broom to restore normality.

Sundays at the time were considered rest days and everyone was at home. Forgotten was the interminable noise and hard graft of the pits and industry. Some might go to church, others relax at home or work in their gardens, whilst wives prepared Sunday lunch. After lunch during summer, weather permitting, the clan congregated next door, on granddad's front lawn. The front doorstep like ours was about the height of a bench and was used as such. Chairs were brought from the house and a family group collected and chatted about all and sundry. Any comments made over the front garden hedge by passing neighbours were acknowledged and it frequently initiated a group conversation, on both sides of the hedge, in which gossip was passed on or the politics of the day discussed. This could also be seen down the lane as other families leant on their gate, raising a hand to a passer-by, but if truth were told, desperately awaiting the latest tittle-tattle.

Granddad's front lawn had a circular bed in the centre, around which I could run as though riding an ever turning roundabout. It is July and my attention is fixed on a beautiful standard tea rose planted to the side of the central bed. Although dad had created a large lawn in front of our bungalow, there were no endearing roses and the largest plant was a patch of Japanese knotweed under a bay window, with green leaves and streaked red stems. Its insignificant cream flowers certainly did not smell of roses, in fact they were quite unpleasant on the nose. Here, on granddad's lawn, the rose bush is adorned with large white blooms with a heady scent and dad pulls down a branch so that I can fill my nostrils. When heavy with blooms the branches arched nearer the ground and I reached them myself, swiftly experiencing a hefty prick and learning first hand that rose bushes have large thorns! I yelled at the top of my voice, even more so when dad tried to grab my hand to pull out the thorns. Once the deed was done and the bleeding prick kissed better, I begged him to chase me around the central bed and I laughed and screamed aloud, darting one way then another to stay opposite to him, never allowing him to catch me. I am not sure he was trying too hard but I ran and ran, until I collapsed prostrate on the lawn. I was both laughing and gasping for breath until alerted by mom's voice, shouting at me,

"Percy, gerrup off that damp grass, yole ketch a code and that's a damn clayne shirt this afternoon!"

It was Sunday and, of course, I had to be dressed in my best clothes, a white shirt with navy bow and short trousers. I am sure mom was simply showing her son to the world, but then everyone wore their best clothes on the day of rest, except granddad who wore the best of his patched trousers with braces and a clean flannel shirt.

After a light afternoon tea, usually a slice of Victoria sandwich, a walk around the lanes was the norm for many families. They inevitably stopped when passing one another and formed a huddle in the middle of the lane to pass on the week's events. Mom and dad went for a walk most Sunday afternoons. I never really enjoyed it because, for someone with short legs, the walk seemed inordinately long, often of the order of two to three miles. By halfway, I was usually lagging well behind and becoming evermore grizzly. It inevitably had the desired effect since dad would pick me up and put me on his shoulders, something I enjoyed because I could see over the hedgerows. The walk could go in any direction, down to Great Wyrley along Station Street into Cheslyn Hay and home, or to Cheslyn Hay and via Wolverhampton Road to Warstone, Essington and home, or down Jones' Lane to Norton Canes village and back. Every Sunday we alternated the route.

One walk to Warstone has left a lasting memory. There, on the triangular grass verge at the junction of Hilton Lane and Warstone Road, sat a large patch of harebells, far too pretty for a small boy to pass by without paddling among them. It was a sea of delicate blue bells on very thin dark wiry stems, wafting in the summer breeze and the local wind eddies were creating waves like the sea. They had not been there three weeks earlier and were so much more delicate than the bluebells I saw about two months ago in Wakeman's wood, a little further along the road. Then, I had also been overwhelmed by a dense carpet of bluebells beneath the trees as far as the eye could see. I ran through them, sat in them, rolled in them, picked them and thoroughly enjoyed the moments. Although I lived among a profusion of flowers in our own garden, nothing seemed to compare with this – and yet the next time we walked there, it was all over, a dull green carpet with no flowers, only dappled sunlight through the canopy to add colour to the scene. The harebells, on the other hand, were there for several weeks. Usually when we did this particular walk, we called in for tea and biscuits at the home of uncle Ray, aunt Doris and cousin Terry, who lived in Wolverhampton Road. This entailed getting out the best crockery. It was the practise in most homes to have a set of matching tea pot, cream jug, sugar basin, cups, saucers and tea plates for visitors, especially for Sundays and special occasions. Some may even run to matching comports to lay out cakes and sandwiches. Aunt Doris always welcomed us for tea and usually made a fuss of me. Uncle Ray was totally deaf and sadly could not join in the conversations but always had a most expressive smile.

I usually enjoyed the walks with mom and dad if they were not too far. I suppose, as my legs grew, walks became easier, but I quickly became bored if mom met a friend since I knew a long canting session was inevitable. When we were in the country, I could use the time to pick a bunch of wild flowers or, if we were walking down Jones' Lane, to poke a stick into the reeds along Gains' brook to disturb a stickleback or lift a stone to expose a crayfish. But, all hell was let loose from mom if I got mud on my clothing. We frequently saw foxes, stoats and rabbits and mom and I were sometimes distinctly alarmed by some of the encounters. It was the way the animal unexpectedly leapt from a hedgerow and darted off, rather than any real threat, but it was enough to make my heart pound as mom and I clung to each other for support.

A similar heart-stopping event happened one day at home as I was playing in the garden. Enormous chestnut horses with red-coated riders leapt over the hedge at the top of the garden making a hideous cacophony. The horses, presumably of a hunt from Hilton estate, leapt the three feet hedge but since there was a three feet embankment on our side, the six feet drop startled them and stopped them in their tracks. The riders fought to gain control, kicking up dad's garden in the process. I didn't see a fox and at the time had no idea what it was all about, except that it was noisy and very frightening. Fortunately dad had dug but not yet planted the top of the garden. Granddad raced to join mom, who had come to see if I was alright, and gave the riders an almighty rollicking. A rather plump man in red coat and black riding hat apologised profusely to my mom. I think they had leapt the hedge on past hunts but were unaware that it was now a private garden with a large drop and wide drainage ditch. Knowing granddad, I suspect he will have made a copper or too from their misdemeanour to pay for the disturbed hedge and mess. He was great at this, but in general never seemed to use the money to repair the damage done. The repair was made with a branch cut from the adjacent oak tree and threaded into the hedge to fill the gap.

Of my early toys one stands out above all others, my little red and green tricycle which I gather I was given at about two years of age. I have no recall of receiving it or of learning to pedal it, but have a clear recollection of riding it and of the day it lay in tatters. It had had a hard life. I incessantly pedalled it to the top of the garden and down to the front gate, a distance of some forty to fifty yards (45 metres). It was not the most stable of toys and the ninety degree bends on my race track were a significant hazard, certainly not to be taken at high speed, as my howling utterances sometimes made known. The rendering on the bungalow was quartz spar which was very unkind to hands or legs if I accidentally brushed against it. It was the source of many childhood grazes, the pain made many times worse when the injury was scrubbed and Vaseline or Germoline applied by mom. My dad frequently had to perform repairs on the tricycle, which did not take kindly to the stresses involved. Then one day, calamity! As I pulled on the handle-bars to accelerate they sheared from the vertical supports. I was distraught but mom was unsympathetic, it was to be expected the way I had been riding it! I should not expect another one. I spent several days still trying to ride it, one hand above the other on the front wheel strut but it was difficult to grip, somewhat unstable and almost impossible to turn a corner. It was dumped under the garden hedge and essentially forgotten.

Two or three weeks later I went, as always, to meet dad at the front gate as he returned from work. Over his shoulder was my beloved tricycle, fully repaired. I was overwhelmed with joy and with pride for my dad's achievement. The upright had been freshly drilled below the broken section and the handle bar passed through the holes and tack welded. This had resulted in the paint burning off which spoilt the appearance, but it was strong again, really strong and took anything I threw at it. As I belted around my race track, I looked down at the new holes which had been drilled through metal of all things and pondered how that could have been done.

At just under four years of age, I suffered a very unpleasant experience when mom was given a dog. I am not sure where from. It was a mongrel, about six months old, with some inbuilt Staffordshire bull terrier, an ugly and never a particularly friendly animal. For some reason, I may have made some gesture towards it, the dog took a serious dislike to me and bit my arm, drawing blood and an ear-splitting screech. The recoil and my fear seemed to make the dog even wilder. Dad ran to my rescue and lifted me high into the air with the dog jumping up to his shoulder level to get a purchase on my leg. I was terrified by the vicious snarling of the beast which had caused such pain and a river of blood which was running down my arm. My reaction terrified mom and dad and they struggled to get control, with the help of granddad who had by now joined them. Once the dog was grabbed and I was consoled, it was condemned to immediate execution. It was put into a sack and taken away by granddad to be shot by Mr Walley, the local farmer. Since that day, I have found myself disliking dogs, preferring the company of cats. A few years later, I witnessed another dog being dispatched in this way by the same farmer. The dog was again put in a hessian sack and shot through with a shotgun at about two feet range. It was killed instantly without knowing too much about what was happening other than the fear of being put into a sack. The blood stained bundle was simply buried on the spot in a corner of the field. Such scenes were part of rural life and did not concern me at all.

Granddad kept about two dozen chickens which supplied eggs for the family. As a toddler, I was allowed to go into the chicken coop with his soft cap as a receptacle to collect the still warm eggs from the row of laying boxes. I was quite puzzled by the fact that these eggs which mom fried were the same eggs from which cuddly little yellow balls of fluff appeared after granddad had incubated them. This he did about once a month by placing two dozen eggs in his galvanised box with lamp-oil heater (paraffin was called lamp-oil at the time). Every day thereafter I entered the small shed to peep. The air was filled with warm paraffin fumes and I could see the eggs through the observation window in the incubator. For a while nothing changed; then one day, as I opened the shed door the incessant chirruping signalled change. I looked in and witnessed nature's gift of unbelievably beautiful little yellow creatures surrounded by broken eggshells. Some granddad sold at a day old to callers at the door who had brought along a shoe box punctured with holes to buy six or a dozen for about two shillings. Others he sold at about two weeks old.

At feeding time, I was allowed to scatter corn into the chicken run but only after dad or granddad had carefully measured it from the large steel corn bin in the cowshed at the top of our garden. An old milk saucepan acted as the scoop and the corn was levelled at the rim with a blade. There must be no heaped saucepan or granddad would quickly point out that the hens were being overfed. A level saucepan of corn and a level saucepan of wheat was the daily ration for two dozen fowl, the rest they foraged for on his field. Most of the wheat he used for feeding was grown on site. After hand digging a large area of his field with a garden spade, he sowed it with wheat seed, walking along with a satchel of seed around his neck and swishing a handful of seed to each side as he walked the freshly prepared ground. He had sown wheat this way all his life as a smallholder. In late August the ripened wheat was harvested with a two-handled scythe, which was regularly honed with a spindle-shaped stone. The wheat was gathered by grandma and mom and tied into bundles or sheaves and set out in stooks to dry. When ready, and usually on a windy day, the sheaves were laid flat and threshed using sticks as beaters. After the straw was cleared away, the resulting pile of wheat was swished into the air with a fork to allow the husks to blow away in the wind. The wheat grains were sacked and the straw kept to make bedding for the chickens over winter. In the adjacent fields, local farmers with reaping machines pulled by shire horses were also setting out stooks in their fields.

Beyond home, mom and dad regularly took me shopping to Cannock or Walsall, usually on Saturday afternoon. In Cannock we always visited Stanton's cake shop in Wolverhampton Road for afternoon tea, usually canned peaches and ice cream with a pot of tea. Since mom had worked in Stantons before she was married, she knew many of the staff. I was always expected to be very proper in the way I sat at the table, displaying good table manners, so that her friends would be impressed. It was a small price to pay for peaches and ice cream which I adored. I much preferred to visit Woolworth's store, which was enormous in comparison to the local shops at home, so many counters, so many different items on sale and, of course, numerous toys and sweets. Usually I was carried by dad so that I was able to see the wares on the counters. On one occasion, in the Walsall store, I was walking with dad, guided by clutching his trousers. It was Saturday afternoon and at one point I obviously let go. Saturday afternoon in Woolworths was a jostling log jam of human bodies and I lost mom and dad. Looking up, all I could see above me were the chins of strange faces. It is more than likely that they were unaware that I was below them. I howled and screamed and whichever direction I turned and pushed through the crush of legs, I came upon strangers and was mortified. Mom had by now realised her loss and also panicked. Fortunately a kindly stranger, who terrified me by picking me up, lifted me high above the heads of the crowd and dad was soon on the spot to rescue me. It was a frightening experience and thereafter I clung onto mom or dad like a limpet. Shopping at Woolworths was like viewing a treasure chest of goodies. Mom could not afford to buy me the things I craved, but I still enjoyed looking.

Dad was always given pocket money each week from his pay packet and the rest of the wages was used for house-keeping. Mom was always the purse holder and usually made the decisions on family spending. He mainly used his pocket money for cigarettes but always seemed to be able to find a few coppers for a small present for me, often from Woollies. Every Saturday lunch time I sat on the railway bridge above home, awaiting his return from work. After leaving Gilpin's, he had invariably cycled the mile or so into Cannock in order to buy me a small gift, before pedalling the three miles home. The present was perhaps no more than an exercise book and pencil but it was a high point in my week, and I eagerly searched through the bag on his handle bars. It was like making a dip into Santa's sack every week and I loved him for it.

Dad was becoming an accomplished gardener and, to a gardener with a large garden, a greenhouse is an essential commodity and I was just four years old when mom and dad thought that they could afford to purchase one on easy payments. Dad looked into what was available and in November 1936 chose Samuel Jellyman, Cannock Foundry and Engineering works, on the Walsall Road just before Cannock. The factory was renowned for greenhouses and cast iron heating fittings. The specification of his pride and joy was to be a fifteen feet by nine feet (5 metres by 3 metres) wooden-based greenhouse constructed with three by two inch (75mm by 50mm) joists, one inch thick (25mm) tongue and grooved cladding and two and a half by one and a half inch (65mm by 40mm) glazing bars. It was to say the least a very robust structure and was to give fifty five years of service. The cost was ten pounds, but what use was a greenhouse without heating to protect the tender seedlings from frost and to give a start to the young plants. Dad chose a heating system based on a cast iron coal-fired boiler feeding five inch flow and return pipes around three sides of the greenhouse, adding another eight pounds four shillings and ten pence to the invoice. The total cost (£18.24) was to be paid by monthly instalments of ten shillings (50p) per month for four years, a cost of twenty four pounds in all. I had earlier been aware of mom paying monthly instalments to a furniture shop in Bridgetown for the furniture they had purchased when setting up home, because she walked there every month, wheeling me in my pushchair. From now on, our monthly jaunt would be a little further to Jellyman's. She never missed a monthly payment, paying off a debt was very important to her.

During the winter months, dad laid house bricks for a foundation and the sectional greenhouse was erected at the bottom of the garden and the heating equipment installed. He chose bright green paint for the base with white glazing bars and a white interior. It was an amazing structure and worth every penny and as the sun reflected from the glass, the whole thing glistened. He was the proudest man in the world and as a result was to make friends with well-established gardeners who worked alongside him at Gilpin's edge tool works, the likes of Mr. Belcher of Wedges Mills.

It was now time for dad to order his seeds. He enthusiastically browsed the Sunday newspaper for suppliers and settled on Dobbies, seedsmen of Edinburgh. Long winter evenings were spent studying the seed catalogue and compiling a list of vegetable and flower seeds for growing next year. He had to calculate what size packet he needed, a small packet, quarter ounce, half ounce or one ounce (8g, 15g or 30g) of the smaller seeds or a pint or half pint (450ml or 225ml) of the larger seeds such as peas and beans. The completed order was eagerly posted to Dobbies along with the appropriate postal orders. About two weeks later a box, the size of a shoebox, arrived by post. Dad was like a child opening a Christmas present as he worked through the wrappings, revealing dozens of seed packets. He was sent a free gift for his 'esteemed order', a couple of packets of balsam and godetia, rather anaemic pink flowers that he would never have ordered in a million years. At the bottom were several very large packets of peas and beans, ordered by the pint measure. Dad was in his element!

During the weeks before the due date for sowing the seeds, I frequently took them out of the box to look at them, sometimes using the packets to build a house or garage for my tin-can wind-up car, before neatly repacking them. Although sometimes getting the urge, I was never tempted to open the packets. Dad however held them up to the light to check how many seeds his sixpence (2.5p) had purchased.

"Yo doe get many o' them cucumbers fower yer money. We ought 'ave 'ad two packits if arma gunna 'ave some spare plants ter sell, Ida", he would hold forth to mom, "but look at the number of lobelia seed, there um thousands!"

Come late January it was time to sow the seeds for bedding plants, and it was the start of dad's year in the greenhouse. I shall detail this later but, suffice to say that after germination and about two week's growth, dad transplanted the seedlings and potted on to reach the planting out stage. It was a very busy time for him. He started in the greenhouse every night after returning from work and continued until darkness fell. Before coming into the house, the boiler fire was stoked up and the chimney belched black smoke, sometimes into the house if the wind was in the wrong direction. Plants and boxes were covered with newspaper as additional protection against frost and the door of the greenhouse locked. It was bedtime for the plants and he then settled down to listen to the radio.

During the evenings, if mom and dad found nothing of interest on the radio, we played card and board games before going to bed. The earliest I recall was 'Happy families' a card game given to us by aunt Sarah. Players simply collected members of a family, Mr Bunn, the baker, along with his wife, son and daughter, much as tricks are collected in whist. The same cards could also be used for playing 'Snap', a game where cards were placed as quickly as possible picture-side up on the table and anyone depositing the same picture card needed to shout "Snap!" before the card was covered by the next player. If it was called successfully, all cards on the table were picked up and added to their hand. Whatever the game, mom was always a cheat par excellence and became upset if anyone dared point this out to her. We also played the board game 'Ludo' but mom would soon tire of the game if she was unable to throw a six on the dice to begin her round.

Dad taught me draughts at quite an early age and often let me win. Later he played properly and it was quite common for him to wipe off six of my crowned pieces to complete a game. It was a while before I fathomed out that he had been setting me up for this grand slam. To be fair, he frequently gave me plenty of notice of impending doom if I did not change my last move but I knew best, and my obstinacy to learn in my own way often cost me the game. I made many more mistakes until the penny dropped and then it was 'Dad watch out' and we enjoyed many great games together!

In late March, dad started work outside. He had a large garden to dig and it was time for sowing seeds into the open ground. Even as a toddler, I was allowed to plant a handful of peas or beans in the six inch (150mm) wide trenches that dad had created in the garden. Very early in life I was aware that seeds grew into plants and from the plants mom and dad picked peas and beans for dinner. After laying the peas in the trench, they were covered with soil and a layer of lime and soot sprinkled on the surface to prevent the birds pecking out the seeds. It was then an impatient wait for the seedlings to appear but when the first seedling cracked the surface of the soil and pushed its way through, I felt a sense of immense joy. Hundreds more shoots appeared and it then seemed no time before they had grown large enough to be staked. I eventually had my own small garden patch in which I sowed salad seeds such as radish and lettuce.

During that first summer, as the tomatoes began to ripen in the new greenhouse, I stumbled across a hole in the wooden base. A large timber knot had fallen out and as I put my eye to the hole I had an excellent view of a rich red tomato about eight inches away. With little effort I was able to push my hand through the hole and grab the fruit. Retrieving the fruit was a different matter. My hand, tightly clutching the tomato, would no longer return through the hole. I struggled to no avail and, frightened by the possible loss of a hand, I screamed as I pulled harder and harder. Mom and dad raced out of the house to investigate and when dad had weighed up the situation he quickly went into the greenhouse to rescue my lost appendage. However, it was my tomato and this became obvious to dad as he tried to prise it from my clutch. The more he tried, the more I screamed and twisted my arm and the more mom panicked. He successfully released my hand and through unfocussed tearful eyes I saw him approaching with my tomato which he put in my grazed hand. The tears gave way to a big smile and a hug. For several years, the incident was a talking point and a joke for summer customers.

During these years as a toddler, the front gate to the drive was always kept latched to prevent me straying into the lane. It did not stop me climbing onto the gate where I sat and watched the world go by or, at an appropriate time, sat and waited for a deliveryman. We had the Daily Express newspaper every day and I regularly awaited the arrival of Mr Wootton on his bike, so that I could look at the Rupert bear strip before the paper was collected for granddad. At that time it was the only 'comic' strip I had access to but, within weeks, the first edition of the 'Beano' arrived in the shop and mom bought it for me. 'Big Eggo' an unruly ostrich was on the front page, and Lord Snooty and his gang inside. Cousin Bobby, next door, already took delivery of the 'Dandy' with 'Desperate Dan' and we were able to swap. In those early days I simply enjoyed looking at the pictures, usually making up my own story, but in the evening mom or dad read the speech balloons to me. In later years, the comics were an enjoyable way to learn to read. I only had two books at that time, a book of nursery rhymes and one of fairy tales including stories such as Little Red Riding Hood and The Three Bears, which intimidated me a little at the time.

Opposite our front gate was the London, Midland and Scottish railway line between Walsall and Rugeley and steam trains were therefore the norm for me. At the sound of an approaching locomotive, I ran and climbed the gate to watch it pass by. I knew most of the regular locomotives and, in those on the up-line, observed the fireman working furiously to keep the firebox topped up as the driver demanded more steam to make the incline. It was a very steep gradient and, almost daily, a goods train on the up-line would be brought to a standstill. The locomotive, already working very hard, would suddenly start puffing very rapidly with wheels freely spinning on the track, then coughing as the wheels gripped a little, followed by further rapid hacking and then silence. The guard was obliged to leave his van at the rear of the train and had to walk the quarter mile back to see the signal box man, so that later traffic was stopped. He then returned to report to the driver before the train was allowed to back-track down the hill to the level surface by the Plant pit. There the driver waited, sometimes twenty minutes, until they had built up sufficient steam for another try at the gradient, sometimes succeeding, sometimes not. I preferred the latter because the driver was then obliged to sit at the bottom of the hill until the next passenger train came along to push it up the hill as far as the Essington sidings. Sitting on my perch on the front gate brought a wealth of free entertainment!

I was always very fascinated by the two-carriage train on the down line, which passed our house empty, at 7.45 a.m. The locomotive was a small 0-4-0 side-tank which was pushing rather than pulling the carriages. At 8.30 a.m., it returned on the up line, now pulling the two carriages full of school children, many hanging out of the windows waving. It took a long time to fathom why the down train was pushing the rolling stock since it was unusual and, in any case, how did the engine driver see ahead for signals? It was several years before I sussed the control cable between the back of the train and the locomotive.

My first ride on a railway train was during the summer of 1936 when mom and dad bought cheap-day tickets for a railway excursion to Belle View (Manchester) to visit the zoo and fair ground. The journey was long and I soon I became extremely bored, sitting in a full compartment with about a dozen other people and nothing to do. The incessant 'da-da-da-da, da-da-da-da', got on my nerves and the journey never seemed to end. However, once we arrived at Belle Vue, boredom quickly gave way to excitement at the sight of the excellent fairground, particularly the big dipper. We looked at the animals in the zoo and had a delightful day. Most memorable was the firework display, held at dusk on the opposite side of the lake. Men in spectacular soldiers' uniforms were firing rifles into the air, seemingly creating very large coloured balloons, shaped as animals and other figures, which slowly descended to the ground. It was a magical scene. I had no idea how the balloons were created and, from that day, I have wondered whether I did see fantasy balloons bursting from rifle shot or dreamt it, since I have never seen the like again.

As darkness fell we made our way back to the railway station, all absolutely ravenous for something to eat, since we had only had a couple of sandwiches brought with us from home. Mom or dad smelled fish and chips along a side street and we followed our noses to a chippy with restaurant. We found a table and tucked into plates of crisply battered fish and chips, far better it seemed than any we had ever tasted before, but then we were gasping for food! The meal proved quite soporific and I woke up on a very cold railway platform on Great Wyrley and Cheslyn Hay station some two or three hours later.

I was sitting on my perch on the front gate one morning and was entertained by council workmen who had come to re-surface the lane. A lorry pulled up outside our gate with a trailer in tow. It was a tar boiler and was spewing forth distinctive smelling smoke and fumes. A worker manipulated a small crane built into the trailer and lifted a barrel of tar from the lorry and emptied its contents into the boiler. Another workman was busily stoking up the fire beneath. The grass verges which had overgrown the road surface were dressed back by the some of the gang to reveal the edge of the tarmac, whilst others swept the road clean. My eyes then caught sight of steam puffing along the lane from Landywood. I had not seen this before and immediately stood on the gate in the hope of identifying the source. It was only as it climbed the bridge, puffing hard, that I recognised a steam roller, my first view of such a beast in action, now making its way to the work site. When the tar was hot and smoking, it was pumped using a long handle on the appliance, and sprayed onto the road surface from a spray hose. Once an area had been covered with hot tar, two men filled shovels with chippings from a lorry and swished them onto the hot tar, covering the surface evenly. It was now the turn of the steamroller and I watched mesmerised as the enormous machine traversed the area, crunch, crunch, backwards and forwards, pressing the chippings into the hot tar. The driver worked frantically at the steering wheel, needing about twenty turns it seemed to make the enormous beast turn. What I would have given to be up there with him. In later years, we frequently threw tree branches, cans or anything to hand just to witness the crushing power of the massive roller, but it is that first sighting of a steam roller climbing Shant's Bridge that stays with me.

At around four years of age, I was living in my own little world, playing by myself within the confines of the garden, occasionally wandering to see grandma and granddad. I was totally oblivious to events in the wider world and I suppose did not even know that it existed. It had been a period of turmoil for the nation with great excitement as the Silver Jubilee of King George V was celebrated only, six months later, to be followed by sadness and mourning on the announcement of his death. Mom would have been glued to the radio and newspaper and shared the joys and sorrows with everyone she met. As if this was not enough, Edward VIII acceded to the throne but abdicated the same year over the woman in his life. I have no recall of any of this being explained to me, if it was, and was certainly not told that on our very own doorstep similar distressing events were playing out. It was I suppose the sort of thing that children should not know about.

During the previous year, aunt Ruby had become involved with a suave, well-educated man, an accomplished architect. Unfortunately, unknown to her, he was married with children. An obviously passionate assignation by the seaside led to her becoming pregnant by him. The family angst over aunt Ruby was, I gathered in later years, a drama that over-shadowed all of the national events. It was a crisis in the family and granddad, as patriarch, was running around like a headless chicken, trying to normalise the situation and reduce the terrible stigma which was about to befall his clan. To make matters worse dad, always the gentleman and perhaps a little naive, had taken aunt Ruby to the railway station to meet her lover, carrying her suitcase on the crossbar of his bicycle. Her man had greeted dad warmly and had later written from their rendezvous to thank mom and dad for the help they had given. His impressive courtesy and professional handwriting had impressed them and they were in no doubt that he was a very polite and sincere man.

Granddad was not happy that mom and dad had not seen what was going on, and held them at least partly responsible for the mess he was in. Headless chicken he may have been, but he did make arrangements of a sort, certainly at least to his own satisfaction. Aunt Ruby subsequently married uncle Joseph Morgan, a farm hand from

Shareshill. We were never to know the pact that granddad had negotiated but, for the moment, all seemed well again and in his eyes a socially acceptable family unit was restored. We know that part of the arrangement was that granddad would build himself a new bungalow and let Ruby and Joe take over his bungalow as their home. On 29th February 1936, leap year day, cousin Ron was born. As a baby, he became an apple of my mom's eye and, throughout her life, she was extremely fond of him.

My final intrigue as a toddler related to the voices that came from the wooden box on the window sill, which mom and dad avidly listened to. It was called a wireless and was talking to us day in and day out and playing music, but without gramophone records. Somehow I could accept that music came from the disc placed on the gramophone deck at granddad's house, but when I climbed onto a dining chair and looked in the back of our box, it had two glass bulbs, but no moving parts as with the gramophone.

At the front of our wireless was an illuminated one inch (25mm) square tuning dial with which dad changed programme. A shadow cast in the bottom of this small window exactly matched the curve of the back of our settee and for a long time, I assumed the voices were coming from people sitting on a settee within the box and, in my mind's eye, I visualised them sitting there, chattering away. On many occasions when mom moved the wireless onto the table to clean behind, I looked into the back, hoping to get a glimpse of the settee and the people speaking to us. I never did and remained puzzled. Mom and dad could not satisfy my curiosity, simply telling me that it was a wireless set which brought programmes to us. I knew it had an aerial, something dad always checked if there were problems, a wire stretching from a pole half way along the garden. He told me that the voices came into the radio set via that wire but when I studied it closely, it was a very ordinary length of wire tied to porcelain insulator on a pole. I frequently stood in the garden, looking at it, baffled how voices were created in a wire. To complicate matters, dad informed me that the people speaking on the radio were in London, a hundred miles away. How could that be, since the wire ended in our garden? So often, I puzzled why things were as they were but simply had to accept it and sometimes not ask questions.

CHAPTER 3

'Starting Landywood school - c. 1937 - 38'

I started school in September 1937, just after the coronation of King George VI. Although this was a very significant period in British history, I remember little of it apart from mom buying a commemorative cup bearing an image of the new king and queen which for many years had pride of place on her sideboard in the parlour.

On the first day of the new school year, mom took me to Landywood Primary School in Holly Lane, where I was registered. I had never really been in the presence of so many children before and found it bewildering. I am sure I had a fear of being away from mom, but it had been impressed on me that I must attend or mom and dad would be in trouble and could be sent to prison. It had also been instilled into me by mom that I must sit quietly in class and listen attentively to what my teacher had to say, and this I did.

My first teacher was Miss Thomas, a quietly spoken and very nice lady who I never recall shouting at us. This was far from the case in the classroom next door where Miss Jones, a very loud butch lady, could clearly be heard teaching her class. Only a flimsy folding partition separated the two classes and she was frequently bellowing at her charges. In a way it was the cacophony coming from next door which seemed to spell out that school was going to be a place of discipline, though our class seemed to behave itself in the gentle embrace of Miss Thomas. We sat at desks made for two pupils and constructed of cast iron, much I thought like the pedestal of grandma's Singer sewing machine, but with a sloping oak top. A groove at the top prevented pen or pencil rolling to the floor and a round hole provided a space for an inkwell. The seat folded up so that when the need arose we could stand within the confines of our desk. Such would be my work station for the next five years or so.

I was soon enjoying school to the full and happily listened and followed Miss Thomas' instruction. When it came to learning how to write we were handed a slate and a stick of chalk. The slate had horizontal white guidelines roughly an inch apart between which a letter of the alphabet could be practised. The outline of each letter was described by teacher several times on the classroom blackboard, giving a careful explanation how our chalk should move along the slate. The lower case 'a' we were taught should be drawn as a perfect circle in an anti-clockwise direction starting at three o'clock and when completed the chalk should rise vertically to the upper guideline then drawn down to the lower guideline to complete the letter. It was not acceptable to draw a circle, take the chalk from the slate and draw a separate straight line. After Miss

Thomas had demonstrated the letter 'a' several times, we were allowed to put the chalk to our slates. Starting very shakily between the top lines and trying very hard to keep the round shape between the lines, the letters would slowly improve and by the bottom of the slate, a dozen or so 'a's had been created. We did this over and over again until we were as perfect as possible, and our individual efforts approved by teacher. Each of the commonly used letters of the alphabet were treated in the same way. This was followed by writing small words such as 'mat' and 'cat' and then sentences, 'the cat sat on the mat'. After a month or two, slates gave way to pencils and a specially lined writing book on the front of which we wrote our names. This module of work led on to special reading books with a picture of a black cat sitting on a mat beneath which was the sentence, 'The cat sat on the mat'. We sounded out the individual letters to articulate a word, "'c', 'a', 't', 'cat' ", leading to the early reading of sentences.

In this first year at school we also started to use numbers. Small coloured bricks created the medium for counting, red being a single brick representing 'one', and blue a double brick representing 'two', which was exactly the same size as two red bricks. We added up the total of bricks and were able to say that six red bricks equated to three blue 'two' bricks or a yellow 'four' and a blue 'two'. I became very good with sums, as we called the subject, and also developed a reasonable hand when it came to writing letters, words and sentences.

One afternoon each week we had a singing lesson and joined the class next door for singing lessons, since Miss Jones played the piano. This entailed pushing back the sliding doors between the two classes. The first song I recall and, represented on the classroom wall by an illustration, was

> *"I had a little nut tree, nothing would it bear*
> *But a silver nutmeg and a golden pear.*
> *The king of Spain's daughter came to visit me,*
> *And all for the sake of my little nut tree."*

Miss Jones was never happy with growlers, children who were essentially tone-deaf, and unkindly pointed them out to the rest of us who had more melodic voices. Fortunately I was blessed in childhood with a very nice soprano voice, something I had obviously inherited from mom. My friend Eric would have been better providing the sound effects of an over-laden lorry, a struggling undulating monotone, and was frequently told to stop singing and get out a book to read. Miss Jones had a powerful alto voice and was very effective in leading a group of nervous singers, bringing some volume to their voices. The problem was that her voice in a different scenario, along with her large stature, put the fear of God into us all.

During the latter part of my stay in Miss Thomas' class, I was unfortunate enough to develop a sore throat, fever and a pink rash which proved to be scarlet fever. Once Dr Middleton had visited me at home and made the diagnosis, mom was told that I must be kept permanently in my bedroom with the door closed. Only she was allowed into the bedroom and if she touched me, she was to wash her hands in a bowl of water containing Dettol within the room. If I wanted to use the toilet, mom brought me the enamel washing-up bowl from the brew'us to use as a bed pan. The same bowl also doubled up for personal hygeine and bed baths after it had been carefully sterilised with Dettol. I had a visit from the doctor about twice a week. I was not allowed certain foods such as meat and eggs, but I was allowed sweets, such as barley sugar, biscuits and vegetables. I could eat a barley sugar as and when I wanted one and this was certainly a lucky feature of this illness as far as I was concerned. I was never particularly ill and yet the doctor was always very strict with his instructions to her and she was strict with me. I think the doctor had put the fear of God into mom with regard to possible complications of the illness. Any plea, even to look outside my bedroom door for a change of view, was totally rebuffed.

It was a very boring time and, apart from reading or drawing, there was little I could do. Through my bedroom window I could see the spoil mound at Harrison's Number 3 pit, referred to locally as 'the Sinkin'. It was a large conical shale hill very much like a volcano in appearance. In fact, it frequently smoked like a volcano, usually from the sides of the mound. Every few minutes, a tub rose to the apex on a railway track and tipped the contents onto the mound. I watched and counted the number ascending during a given time spell, anything to relieve the boredom. Being incarcerated in the front bedroom meant that I also had an excellent view of the lane and railway bridge. I watched people I knew going about their daily business, telling the time by their punctuality. Occasionally a locomotive, fully laden with coal trucks, stalled on the incline and created theatre for an hour or so. I could not have imagined when I started my isolation just how tedious it would actually be.

It was three weeks before I was allowed outside my room and that same day a man came from the local council to fumigate my bedroom. He taped around the doors and lit a candle in a can and, as we looked in from outside, the room quickly filled with dense yellowish smoke. After an hour or two, the fog had cleared and mom was able to remove the tape and open the door. The room had a choking sulphurous smell and windows and doors were immediately opened to the outside to allow in fresh air. I was at last now free and I did a victory run around the front garden. As the days passed, the skin peeled all over my body showering everywhere with coarse flaky scurf particularly when I undressed for bed. Mom's demeanour quickly changed from a caring nurse to normal,

"Wait a minute, let me get a damned newspaper to put under you, look at the mess you are making all over the floor! I shall never get the place clayne again."

After the long summer holiday I entered Miss Jones' class, in September 1938, and by now I had started to read simple books, usually as I have said, the words were a caption defining a picture. I had conquered the calculating bricks and could express that two threes made six. We now started on the Reading Books which were numbered One to Six. One had to be fluent in reading the book to Miss Jones as she sat at her desk, in order to be granted the privilege of moving on to the next volume. I remember walking with pride to the book cupboard, collecting Book Two and seeing how many pages I could read before the end of the lesson, at which point the book monitor collected them and placed them back in the cupboard in neat piles. I was about average in my reading but Eric Gibbs, who lived a few houses from me and was becoming a close friend, was up to two books ahead of me. He also had a better understanding of long words, since he was an avid reader at home. I never was and it took much longer for me to build a vocabulary.

In so far as arithmetic was concerned, we now started to convert the coloured counting bricks of Miss Thomas' class to numbers written in chalk on our slate. Mom had already started to teach me how to write numbers and I was probably ahead of some classmates. Miss Jones took the same care in demonstrating how to write Arabic numerals as had been taken in writing letters of the alphabet. She also introduced the signs for addition, subtraction and multiplication.

The multiplication tables, 'times tables' we called them, were next introduced. As a class, like raw drill recruits in the army, we had to sound out the multiplication tables,

"One two is two,
Two twos are four,
Three twos are six,"
and so on,

until we reached 'twelve twos are twenty four'. Then followed interrogation by Miss Jones looking sternly at someone,

"What are seven twos, Brenda?"

"Fourteen, Miss!"

"And Alan, what are nine twos?" A long silence ensued whilst he worked through the table, and then a light on his face,

"Eighteen, Miss!"   "Good boy, and now hands up, eight twos!", she would boom.

Several hands eagerly shot up to give the answer. By the end of the year, many of the class were well versed in the two, three, four, five and ten-times tables. It was a year when boys and girls became able to express themselves in the written word as well as reading and understanding it. At home I was able to read the easier nursery rhymes from the book I had been given for Christmas. A favourite was 'Who killed cock Robin?' which I read and sang repetitively.

Mum was very good with mental arithmetic, no doubt related to the calculations she made in her head whilst a shop assistant. Dad might fire a question at us to see who first came up with the answer. Any relating to money, she was mustard and beat me hands down but on simple arithmetic tables, I frequently answered first. I thoroughly enjoyed the exercise and was soon working on the more difficult tables such as sixes, sevens, eights and nines.

On Mayday each year we danced the maypole, a white pole erected in the playground and bedecked with multi-coloured ribbons. We each took a ribbon and danced around the pole to the piano playing of senior Miss Jones, weaving a pattern like a spider's web. As we danced, our Miss Jones was bellowing instructions,

"No, David, inside Mary and round Percy! That's it - Brenda, inside John!"

We danced round and round the pole creating some semblance of a pattern but inevitably as we unwound again, we created knots and Miss Jones was again given cause to impersonate an army sergeant major and ruthlessly take hold of one or other of us, pushing us one way then another to unravel the knot

Later in May came the annual school trip, this year (1939) to Rhyl in north Wales. On the day of the trip, five or six motor coaches parked nose to tail in Holly Lane, outside the school. We each had a ticket with a coach number and a teacher checked us onto the coach. We carried a small bag with a packed lunch prepared by our moms, who were there to wave us off. I eagerly waved to mom as the coach pulled away, extremely thrilled by what the day had in store for me.

It was an exciting journey and I felt like a fledgling must feel when it first realises that it can fly. I saw places and majestic things I had never experienced before. The coaches stopped for a short break at the Swallow Falls at Betts y Coed in North Wales, which was outstandingly picturesque and overwhelming. There was nothing like this at home. How could there be, the mountains around home were shale heaps not rocky hills covered by luscious vegetation and trees. Before we arrived it must have rained in the mountains and the noise from the cascading water was awe-inspiring. We raced the torrent to the bottom of the falls, leaping from boulder to boulder, and then back up again. We screamed superlative comments at each other but the thundering water drowned our voices. Every face reflected joy and exhilaration but time was called and we reluctantly climbed into our coach. We arrived in Rhyl at about lunchtime. It was the first time that I had been to the seaside and miles and miles of sand stretched out before me. At the time the tide was out and it was not really possible to paddle, but the fresh bracing air was quite an experience, even for someone who lived with fresh country air. We ran on the sands in delight, stopping occasionally to pick up seashells or beached seaweed. I collected a piece to take home which for several years hung on the orange blossom bush by the back door, giving clues about the coming weather.

During the afternoon we were allowed to go into the town, where I was immediately attracted to Woolworths, the shop I knew well at home and looking almost identical. It was here that I was to make a gaff about which I would be reminded for years to come. I had one shilling to spend and had decided to buy a present for mom and dad, rather than spend the money on myself. On sale in the store was a pearl necklace for three pence or a double string of pearls for sixpence which I knew mom would like. For dad I noticed a 'silver' cigarette case for sixpence, but for nine pence I could purchase the same with a nicely enamelled coat of arms of Rhyl. I was really drawn by the Rhyl emblem and although I wanted to buy mom and dad presents of equal value, the hypnotic attraction of the cigarette case with coat of arms meant mom simply had to be satisfied with a single strand of pearls! My shilling was duly handed over and the gifts purchased.

The journey home was long and tiring and we sang songs previously taught to us by Miss Jones. It was getting dark when we arrived home and our moms and dads were waiting for us. I gave them their presents as we walked home, which they admired. I was asked the inevitable question, "How much did you have to pay for these?" Mom laughed as she remarked on the difference with a comment that dad was obviously worth more than she was. I felt very guilty and embarrassed and I wept as I lay in bed that night. No amount of comforting allowed me to forget the enormity of what I had done and I was frequently reminded of it, albeit in a teasing way.

I enjoyed school because I seemed to be quite good in all lessons and therefore never became subject to the wrath of the teachers. I could write neatly and had no problems with numbers. I was not a particularly fluent reader but I got by and was usually in the top three for the highest overall marks in class.

School had its downside however, particularly when we had to see the school doctor, nurse or dentist. The schools' doctor only visited every two years or so and examined me and to mom's delight, pronounced me fit and healthy. Nurse Radcliffe was very stern but at the same time quite gentle when practising her art. She looked at our hair, at our skin and at every crease around our body. Mom kept me pretty clean and I rarely had skin infections. I was subject to flexural eczema particularly in winter months, which was very painful when the skin cracked, and she gave mom advice on treatment. I hated creams applied to my skin and invariably declined quite vociferously when mom tried to apply them. After nurse's visit, some boys were made to wear a nit cap whilst at school, a tight fitting denim blue skull cap. It was a stigma which led to us believing that they were dirty and we kept our distance. It must have affected the cap-wearers quite badly and, when I look back, they might just as well have been given a sign to hang around their neck saying 'leper'. One boy, in particular, spent much of his school life in a nit cap and for him it virtually became school uniform. This was one thing which mom always dreaded and she regularly groomed my hair, looking for the blighters.

The school dentist visited annually. It was the norm for him to remove at least one tooth from most of us, but some children might have six or seven teeth removed. I was not particularly good at cleaning my teeth and would try to get away without doing so if mom was not watching. It was laziness really since the toothpaste, Gibb's Dentifrice, a solid pink disc in a tin, did not taste too bad. Sweets caused havoc with our teeth and most milk teeth showed caries when they eventually dropped out. If the dentist needed to remove a tooth, he painted the gum with oil of cloves which deadened pain and before I knew what was happening, he was holding up a tooth in his forceps. I had not felt a thing and when nurse was happy that the bleeding had stopped, it was back to school classes.

Walking the half mile to school everyday meant that I became close friends with the boys from Street's Lane who were in my class, Eric Gibbs, Colin Parsons and David Loach. We were eventually trusted to walk to and from school together without our moms. After school, at week-ends and in school holidays thereafter, the four of us were a tightly knit band, regularly playing together. I had no siblings but now I had playmates and it was a wonderful life.

David and Bernard Loach lived in a large Edwardian semi higher up the lane. Their father, Jack Loach, seemed to be peripatetic in his jobs. He regularly purchased second hand cars, motorbikes and household items from auction or house sales. We spent many happy days as children playing with some of his acquisitions, particularly a motorbike with sidecar and a 1920s Wolseley family car which was parked in the lane beneath the large mature ash tree, opposite their house. Like others, it sat there unused for many weeks, until a second hand spare part became available to repair it. It was an ideal play ground for us, sitting in the old banger pretending to drive, and we might even try to start it with the starting handle. The heady smell of petrol and oil which pervaded the air gave an authenticity not found in ordinary toys. It was a bit dilapidated and almost certainly bought at a knockdown price but, to a man in his late twenties, it would have potential. So long as the engine came to life, it was considered a viable vehicle, no matter how bad the tyres, brakes or general condition. We keenly watched Jack Loach work under the bonnet and joined his excitement when, after an initial touch of bronchitis, the engine came to life and roared like a lion. The lane was enveloped in smoke from the exhaust and it was our turn to cough. It was all part of the fun. Old cars at the time could be death traps because they were never regularly serviced. They were simply repaired with parts from scrap when they broke. A year or so later, a car similar to Jack Loach's crashed into the railway fence and a deep ditch opposite our house when a worn king-pin (part of the front suspension) snapped as the car baulked at turning the slight bend in the lane. The driver was badly injured as he slammed into the steering wheel and his head smashed the windscreen and was taken by ambulance to hospital.

As a small child, David Loach caught diphtheria and was also whisked away by ambulance to an isolation hospital where he stayed for about two weeks. It was normal practise where a child had siblings but, as an only child, I was allowed to stay at home when I caught infectious diseases. Bernard, at this time about 2 years of age, suffered the most horrendous impetigo, large weeping sores around his mouth which caused him a lot of distress. His mum regularly dusted the areas with boracic powder, until the scabs dried up. Frances (Fran) Loach, was a delightful lady and dearly loved children and always had David's friends in her house. Their garden and the large greenhouse created a very desirable playground for David, Eric, Colin and myself, particularly in inclement weather. Unlike dad's greenhouse which was always in use, Jack Loach's lay uncultivated and we could play in it at any time.

Colin Parsons lived in a more modern semi on the opposite side of the lane with two much older sisters, Ivy and Eva, and mum and dad. His mom, Eleanor, was in the Women's Voluntary Service (or a similar organisation) and became a local 'officer' after war was declared. Colin's dad, Harry Parsons, was a miner at Harrison's No 3 colliery. I was always transfixed by his large Adam's apple, since no-one else I knew had one as large as his. When relaxed at home, he played the harmonium that sat alongside the fireplace. He certainly let 'Onward Christian soldiers' rip, and I frequently found myself singing to it. I think his repertoire was otherwise quite limited since the News Chronicle Song Book was always open at this page. When he was at work, I occasionally tried to play something and the experience somehow gave me an inner satisfaction, albeit I was playing rubbish. I quickly learned that when pedalling the bellows too slowly, it produced an unpleasant noise like someone moaning in acute abdominal pain, whereas fast pedalling created a steady sound which was more pleasant to the ears. Although I could play little or nothing, the exercise of sustaining notes on the harmonium was going to prove useful in later life. The Parsons' were not a particularly tidy family but Colin's mum also welcomed us into her house. She would chat with us when she returned from work and Colin's home was another in which we could freely congregate when it was raining. (My mom would certainly never welcome dirty feet across her floors even if we took our shoes off.) The garden expressed the same untidiness as the house. The front garden was filled by untamed laurel bushes and the rear, which backed onto the railway track was not really cultivated. This may not have registered with my friends but comparisons with our garden, and my granddad's, exposed Harry Parson's garden as unkempt and it was not difficult to draw the conclusion that he was not interested.

Eric Gibbs became one of my closest friends and our lives were to run parallel for many years, including attending grammar school together in our teenage years. He lived in a semi, two doors down from Colin. His mother came from Evesham and spoke with a Worcestershire accent. His father was a signalman on the London Midland and Scottish Railway, the line between Walsall and Rugeley which ran at the bottom of their garden. Jack Gibbs, a tall heavily built man, had the most interesting shed where he constructed models of all kinds, mainly in wood, using hand tools. It was immaculately tidy and his models were always finished to the highest specifications. During the second world war, he built a very large range of army vehicles including lorries, jeeps, personnel carriers, guns and tanks. I spent many hours in this shed, absolutely mesmerised by his models and the tools he used to construct them. When I could I studied very closely as, puffing away on his briar pipe, he worked on the models. His vegetable garden reflected this same level of care in marking out and planting, and although my dad and granddad could grow larger vegetables, there was always something highly appealing about Jack's tidiness. The tilth after he had hoed looked as though every grain of soil had been individually placed.

Both he and his wife, Winifred (Winnie), were relatively quiet people who did not mix a great deal, though would always chat with Eric's friends. I liked them very much and, though we mostly played in the shed, I was at times allowed into the house to see the 'O' gauge Hornby locomotives, rolling stock and track owned by Jack Gibbs. They were extremely valuable specimens which I thought must have cost zillions when compared with the locomotives we purchased in the average Hornby train sets. His locomotives had wonderful driving gear and were in their own individual boxes. They seemed to weigh about a ton each! He had points for changing track, which I had not seen in model form prior to this. We could take them out of their boxes and gently handle them but Eric was a teenager before he was allowed to take them out of the house or lay down a track so that we could see them in action. After play all pieces were carefully cleaned and in some cases lightly oiled before being returned to their individual boxes.

I should mention an interesting fact about the names of some of the lanes around me in the 1930s. I have referred to my home in Street's Lane. In fact, it was always called 'Modder River' and tradesmen and everyone in the village referred to and delivered to Modder River. By the same token, Gorsey Lane was always 'Spine' Cop. These obviously alluded to the Boer War (around 1901) and the battles of Modder River and Spion Cop but I have no idea why these nicknames were used instead of Street's Lane and Watery Lane (which in later years became Hilton/Gorsey Lane). There were terraces of miner's houses in both areas and perhaps it was a tag given to these mini-settlements by the local miners. In earlier years when our lane was probably still a dirt track, maps show that it had a fast stream running along its western side which possibly led to the reference to a river. Flooding of lanes with adjacent streams was not uncommon in my childhood. The Boer war appendages certainly continued into the 1940s and only really disappeared when in 1944 sign posts removed during the war for security reasons, were replaced by Winston Churchill as a signal to us of impending victory. Brand new and modern street nameplates appeared at the ends of the lanes and from then on the correct addresses of Street's Lane and Gorsey Lane came into use. Houses at the time were not generally numbered. It was commonplace to give them a name, often reflecting some idyllic haven. Our house was named 'Hill-side' because it was on the side of Shant's bridge! Dad carefully cut the letters for the house name from two-ply wood and glued them to a wooden back plate before painting it blue and white. Another house flashing 'Hill-side' was the cottage in the middle of Jeff's knob and as I cycled past I frequently conjectured whether dad had purloined the name from there.

'The Cop' did not have a particularly good name during my early years, though I am not sure why. Possibly it was snobbery by those living in their own homes, which was becoming the norm by the mid 1930s. They possibly felt a cut above those living in property rented from mine owners (Harrison's Buildings, Plant's Buildings and so on). Some of the boys in my class at school lived in the Cop and were often considered rebellious. I never witnessed this and, in any case, during childhood I had my share of run-ins with bobby Morris without being considered so, as my story will tell. We were all, wherever our home, prone to committing boyish pranks. I spent six years at school with Alan Holdcroft, Freddy Hughes and Rex Wiggin and, if I chose to walk home via the Cop, I accompanied them as far as their homes. I remember one of them (I think Freddy) using a hedgehog as a football. It was lying in the lane freshly killed by a vehicle and his kick resulted in the abdomen bursting and the intestines wrapping two or three times around his ankles, essentially shackling him. He was petrified by the sight of the long fleshy ribbon of bowel, which resembled something from a horror film. We laughed and taunted him as he tried to unravel it with a stick, retching with every move and obviously terrified by his ordeal. I doubt he ever kicked another animal!

CHAPTER 4

'Early years at home and play - c. 1938 - 39'

My first encounter with bobby Morris came on a day when the band of four of us were playing innocently together. David, Eric, Colin and I were frequently to be found at the top of David Loach's garden where his father had parked his disused motorcycle and side car, now well corroded by the elements. Uncle Bob had a similar rusting motorcycle on his backyard. It was a vehicle used commonly in the early 1920s by macho young men and simply kept to look at when it needed an expensive repair. I suppose pride would not let them sell or dispose of it. In our play on Jack Loach's old bike, one and then another would take over the driving seat, whilst the rest sat on the pillion or in the side-car. The noises we made, revving the engine and screeching around the imaginary corners, were probably an annoyance to the neighbours, but it was great fun. At some point, the driver would pretend to lose power and we set about the process of repairing the engine with improvised tools, everyone having their own view on the problem. The only words we seemed to know were spark plug, carburettor and magneto and a vociferous argument ensued on which was the likely culprit. Since, as he often reminded us, the motorcycle belonged to his dad, David usually had the final say!

On the day I refer to, we were in our den which encompassed the motorcycle and we had had our fill of running a TT race. David suggested we change to playing 'farms'. We were conversant with most things that happened on farms, ploughing, sowing, reaping, threshing, slurry in the farmyard, rounding up and milking the cows and these are the things we mimicked in our play. If someone was not practising a farming skill correctly, someone knew better, and an argument ensued. We squabbled a lot about any subject but eventually would accept the majority view. As I look back, we were all budding politicians!

It was this innocuous farming game which led to the visit from the law. David, the farmer, had decided that it was time to milk the cows. To make the game authentic we, the cows, would remove our clothes since cows were not clothed. We were let into the field and, on hands and knees, pretended to graze the lawn until we were rounded up for milking. Boys, of course, have natural udders which were pulled and squeezed by the farmer as he milked us. A neighbour had seen us from her bedroom window, obviously witnessing four frightful children pulling each others dicks, and she went to the police station. Oblivious of this, four naked boys continued playing innocently together in the warm mid-morning sunshine.

By the time I reached home for lunch, bobby Morris, a tall well-built man, was at the door telling mom what had been witnessed. His size alone was menacing and mom was cowering like a frightened animal. I knew that taking my clothes off in public was not something people did but how had bobby Morris seen what we had done in the confines of our den. I blushed profusely and mom gave me a severe dressing down. Over lunch she explained that Mrs Waite had seen what we were doing and reported us to the police.

Edward and Mabel Waite, an older childless couple, lived in a large detached house named 'Ashdene', two doors from David's house and we were later to find that they had no time for children of our age. The house stood about five feet above the level of the lane like a fortress with net curtains, high fences and a dark green solid wooden gate which was always kept bolted. The sombre facade looked down menacingly on the lane. It had a notice 'beware of the dog', but we never heard a dog bark. Mabel Waite had no doubt been observing us from her upper storey windows and had been disgusted by our antics. It was certainly a police matter she had convinced herself, though any sensible person would have had a quiet word with our parents. From a very early age we were scared of the house and its residents and would never have knocked the door for any reason. Occasionally a stranger or two might visit, but they were ushered in and the gate closed behind them. We mused on whether they would ever come out again.

Some years later, we were playing cricket in the lane using a golf ball and smashed the large centre pane in the Waite's bay window. This brought the couple out and, as might be expected, they were none too pleased. It was the first time we had really heard them speak and they had a fairly posh accent. We were given a forceful though blaspheme-free lecture on where to play cricket and told that our parents would be getting the bill for the replacement glass. We were frightened but quite pleasantly surprised by their lack of menace, not at all what we had expected. Our parents duly divided the cost of replacing the glass.

Games on the Jack Loach's motor-cycle continued, but stopped abruptly when I suffered a severe injury to my little finger. I had my left hand on the side-car when one of the gang slammed the door very hard, crushing my left little finger. It was a nasty injury with a long split, exposing the bone. Bleeding was measured in bucketfuls, or so it seemed, and should without doubt have been treated at hospital and my finger properly stitched. Unfortunately mom went to pieces at the thought of me going to hospital and, with the help of granddad, trained in first-aid, the finger was bandaged with some clean muslin. It caused me a great deal of pain and many spilled tears over several weeks, particularly when the dressing had to be removed and changed. It was soaked in hot water but still stuck to the granulating wound and caused searing pain as the dressing was lifted off. It took several months to heal completely and many years before sensation and normal shape returned to my little finger.

At any time of the day when not at school I might wander into aunt Ruby's house next door on a casual visit. Cousin Ron was now beginning to walk and into everything. Her house always looked dishevelled, a bit of a tip compared with ours which mom kept neat and spotless. I suppose I was attracted there because I could relax without commands from mom, not to displace a cushion or disturb a floor rug. It didn't matter if I jumped on aunt Ruby's settee or spilled my drink. If I wanted a cake, I could have one, without mom's inevitable pronouncement,

…"and doe drop the crumbs on the floor I have just clayned it!"

Having said this, aunt Ruby was not a good cook and, after eating one of her freshly baked fairy cakes, I was positively sick. As I bit into it, the taste was appalling, certainly nothing like any cake I had eaten before. I ran out of her house on the pretext of going home, violently retching on the way, and deposited the mouthful of the cake under the garden hedge. She had a habit of using the wrong ingredients, which was the butt of many of mom's jokes. The flavour was that of badly burnt beef fat and I assume she had used salted dripping out of the meat pan instead of lard or butter. Normally I enjoyed nothing better that a fresh beef dripping sandwich with plenty of salt but, in a fairy cake, the taste was indescribable. Mom only laughed when I told her.

Cousin Pat was born in October 1938. Aunt Ruby breast-fed her but from her howls was certainly not enjoying the experience. When a hungry Pat clamped on to the nipple she yelled in pain and her eyes filled with tears. I was somewhat bemused by the sight and really hadn't a clue what it was all about. If it was hurting so much, why was she doing it? Over time her nipples and the areola had become red like raw meat, badly cracked and must have been excruciating to touch. Feeding time was always a cacophony of screams from aunt Ruby, the incessant yelling of a hungry child and interspersed with melodic words of comfort from those in attendance. Everyone, including grandma and mom, were passing on their own choice cure to ease the pain. In the end, a three inch square of lint, with a small hole for the nipple to protrude, was coated with Vaseline and gently applied to the angry orbs. It produced a result of sorts. The room certainly became quieter and Pat was now a more contented baby as she snuffled and filled her tank. Within days of this episode she was taking bottles and aunt Ruby had visibly come down from the ceiling. It was the only time I had witnessed breast feeding and I distinctly disliked what I saw.

But to return for a moment to aunt Ruby's culinary efforts, she had a mediocre repertoire. Her mint sauce, to accompany lamb, was on one occasion made as a roux-based white sauce containing chopped mint, instead of the traditional vinegar base. Mom came home and fell about as she relayed the story to us. Poor uncle Joe, bless him, just took the punishment, painfully clearing all before him. Painful since he had appallingly bad teeth and chewing the meat could not have been pleasant. Aunt Ruby could not roast a joint of meat but she could carbonise it so that it came out of the oven roughly a third of the size it went in and looking like thick tobacco twist. Since Uncle Joe was a miner, free coal was plentiful and there was always a roaring coal fire. She seemed oblivious to the fact that such a fire was the cause of the walls of her oven glowing dull red inside. She never controlled the oven temperature with the dampers provided on her range and a medium oven was thus not a choice. Large cakes invariably came out half charcoal and half uncooked and, as a result, the dog and chickens received an unexpected meal.

In her youth, grandma had been in service in a large house and was an excellent cook. She had passed on her skills to mom but aunt Ruby had obviously not chosen the route of domesticity. Even though grandma's coal range had no controls, other than one damper, everything seemed to come out of the oven cooked evenly and perfectly and, as the smells from her oven tantalised my nostrils, I longed to try some of her bread, cakes or meat pies. She could turn her hand to anything culinary, which was obviously taught to a woman of her generation. She made highly flavoured pressed meats from the cheapest cuts she could obtain from the butcher. She also made her own butter, collecting the cream for a few days from the surface of their milk. Using a large seven pound (3 kg) glass sweet jar from a local shop, she sat in her sitting room, listening to the radio, shaking the jar incessantly until the globules of fat in the cream slowly coalesced into larger and larger lumps. After well over an hour an irregular pat of butter, about the size of a fist, appeared in the liquid. I never liked the taste which to my palate seemed tainted or rancid. But then, there were no refrigerators and storing cream for a few days, to collect sufficient, would without doubt mean the cream had turned a little, particularly in the summer months. Granddad loved anything that was fat and did not seem to notice anything untoward in the flavour. His supper was invariably a very thick slice off the end of a crusty loaf, caked thickly with grandma's butter, accompanied by a large slice of boiled fatty bacon. He relished his food and smiled with delight as he scoffed it. I was frequently overwhelmed by hunger as I watched him devour it but could not have eaten a smidgen of the fat on his plate.

Granddad was a shabby dresser, usually wearing an old shirt which looked as though it had been slept in all night and a well worn grey cardigan with fraying cuffs and holes at the elbows. In the back seam of his everyday trousers grandma had inserted a triangle of mismatching material to increase the girth of the waist band, because he would never consider buying a new pair. He was not a heavy man and the three inch increase of the waist band simply reflected that the trousers had been with him most of his life. They were held up by braces, some of the buttons replaced by one inch nails, until grandma could sew on new ones. On his feet he wore a pair of very sad boots, the laces long since replaced by common white string. They had been soled and heeled on many occasions, usually by dad, since he would not pay the price to take them to the cobbler. In this garb, better suited to a scarecrow, granddad took a daily morning walk of about two or three miles. On many occasions, he will have passed and greeted Old Tumpter, the local tramp, and together they must have felt very much in concert, dressed as identical twins. Grandma, using her great skills, did her best to make him presentable but could never persuade him to buy new clothing.

Most mornings when at home, I accompanied him into the garden to collect the vegetables for lunch, watching him wash them in a bucket and then, sitting on the upturned bucket, prepare them for cooking. He was never wasteful regardless of his large crop. The potatoes were scraped or peeled extremely thinly with a very sharp knife, freshly honed on the doorstep. Runner beans were thinly stringed and meticulously sliced. Peas were shelled and picked through to remove the occasional one found to contain a maggot. Shells and peelings were not wasted and were either thrown into the chicken run for them to forage or composted.

Granddad and dad were men who had learned nature's cycle and always put back as much energy and goodness into the soil as they had taken out. Compost heaps were the norm, and in Spring, after over-wintering, the rotted vegetation was dug into the ground to augment the soil's nutrition. To this was added horse manure, a load delivered every year from a local farm, and supplemented by droppings I collected from fields or from the street, after the horses of delivery men had relieved themselves. At the first sighting of a heap of droppings I was dispatched into the street with all haste to rescue the still steaming manure, before someone else did. They both put a lot of effort into digging the garden, which was an art. The soil was always dug to a full spade depth which was turned and broken coarsely to admit plenty of air. Occasionally for deep rooting crops, such as parsnips, it was dug to two spade depths. Remarkably the land had best loam to such depths.

In the first spring that uncle Joe came to Landywood, he was digging away in granddad's garden when uncle Bob looked over the hedge and laughed out loud at his efforts. For a start, he was not all that pleased by granddad's diplomatic arrangements around aunt Ruby's antics and often said so.

"What the bloody hell have you done to that garden?" he retorted in the pseudo-Oxford accent he had developed.

"It looks as though it has been kicked over by a bloody cart-horse!

God Almighty, what a pitiable sight! Ha! Ha! Ha!"

Uncle Joe walked away like an offended dog with its tail between its legs. He was a quiet man and never confrontational. He had been a farm worker in Shareshill before he married aunt Ruby and was now a miner at Hawkins' colliery in Cheslyn Hay. For him, life's past experience was of ploughed fields along which he had walked to sow grain and his understanding of gardening seemed to reflect this. In fact it has to be said that after he had dug over a patch, it did bear an uncanny resemblance to a ploughed field before harrowing. Nevertheless the soil had been properly turned and was so rich that almost anything would grow well, and did.

Along the lane next to our bungalows were the 'allotments' which occupied about an acre and a half of land. There were eight plots which were utilised by people living in the lane. Two outstanding plots worth a mention were those of the Bob Talbot and Bill Farrington. Bob lived in Plant's buildings in the house next to Loach's and was a foreman wayman on the London, Midland and Scottish railway track. He worked from a hut on the track just opposite our front gate. He was very strict about children climbing over the fence onto the trackside and would almost certainly give us a clip around the ear if he could catch us. At coffee and tea breaks, he was usually seen sitting on a pile of railway sleepers puffing away on a pipe with the largest barrel I had ever seen. It must have held a quarter ounce (8gm) of tobacco! He worked the end plot, next to aunt Ruby's bungalow and was a first class gardener. He grew the same crops as my dad, which were always good, but he was meticulously careful about the appearance of his plot, all rows parallel, not a pea stick out of alignment, runner bean frames a work of art and weeds impossible to find. Several other plots on the site were more like cultivated weeds, interspersed with rather scrawny vegetables. Bob usually left his job on the railway in mid afternoon and thereafter spent an hour or two conscientiously loving his plot before waddling home, for this was how he walked, and at all times puffing away on his monster briar.

Bill Farrington's allotment plot grew one species only. He was a miner, but was renowned for his top class dahlias. He not only showed them at local horticultural shows but also supplied quality blooms to many other showmen for their proposed displays. He would often tell neighbours that many of his blooms went to national shows which led to him being called a romancer by locals, including mom and dad. However, the quality and quantity of his blooms and large numbers of visitors, strangers to the lane, were such that, looking back, his claims were probably true. His knowledge of the perfect show bloom was exceptional and when we occasionally went to watch him, he explained the skills of presenting to us.

"The pom-pom must be completely open with even petals all over, the outer row curving back and just touching the stem behind the flower", he would explain, plucking a flower to demonstrate.

Any flower past its horticultural best, though still beautiful, Bill would cut and give to passers by. I was always transfixed by the beauty of his cactus dahlias and the enormous size of the giant decoratives. His season started during the early Spring when he dug in an enormous quantity of horse manure into which the dahlia tubers, that had over-wintered in a large frost-free hog, were seated. The planting was timed so that the first shoots appeared above ground in the third week of May, after the last frost. During June, all had to be carefully staked and within a month flowers were breaking.

Bill and Ethel Farrington lived in a semi-detached villa next to the Loach family, with their children Tommy and Margaret who were older than me. Tom in fact was by now a young adult, but Margaret was younger and occasionally joined in play with us. She was not the brightest of souls and was frequently ribbed by us or dared to do something which we knew to be beyond her capability. We tried to teach her to ride a bicycle but she had no sense of balance. At one attempt on top of Shant's bridge, she climbed onto the bicycle, which we were holding. When we let go, she accelerated down the hill to some twenty miles per hour, wobbling erratically, before flying over the handlebars head first into the deep ditch opposite aunt Ruby's gate. Fortunately she was not hurt, but could have been. She wiped herself down and ambled back home. I am not sure that Margaret ever learned to ride a bicycle.

Another gardener of distinction in the lane was Jim Bullock who lived with his wife and sons in the first detached house opposite to us. He was a coal miner, a short man and of relatively slight stature, with a moustache. He always dressed in a waist coat with a silver watch on a chain hanging from pocket to pocket. From the beginning of the gardening season he worked hard on his patch, again with good results which were a credit to him. Once his crops were staked and maturing, he would sit every day on a chair in the middle of his garden, smoking a pipe as he watched the world go by, sometimes gazing into space and visibly contemplating. In general, the men around us who smoked pipes, always seemed to be pondering on something, lost in the twilight world of tobacco. He soon came to life with the arrival of the newspaper at around 11 a.m., and sat there reading it from cover to cover, occasionally flicking an insect hovering around his face. Only if attracted by a passer-by did he leave his seat and go the five bar gate at the end of his garden. Here they would compare gardens or put the world to rights as they leant on the gate. This accomplished, he walked nonchalantly back to his chair, pulling a few weeds on the way, and sat there until his wife Ethel called him for dinner. His two sons, Bertie and Norman, were teenagers in my early years, certainly too old to communicate with me in any meaningful way.

There were many good gardeners but Granddad's garden was, without doubt, the highest cropper in the lane. Even though he had greatly improved his land by clearing the culvert, there was still a low area at the bottom of the garden just below the bridge which became saturated in wet weather. After lying awake at night and pondering, he made his mind up that the only way to deal with the residual bog and further enlarge his patch was to raise that area of land by several feet. Granddad, you will have gathered, never spent money if he could get something free and he came to an agreement with Wilf Hemingsley of New Street, Landywood, who was contracted to the local Council for house refuse collection. They agreed that Wilf's waste vehicles would tip sufficient refuse to raise the garden adjacent to Landywood Lane by about ten feet. Dustbins mostly contained the ash from coal fires, but there was also food waste, tin cans, bottles and so on and it usually stank. Not many people would allow the tipping of hundreds of tons of refuse adjacent to their home but such was typical of granddad.

Every home had a refuse bin, a galvanised metal container with lid which was purchased from a local hardware store or from the Co-op on Walsall Road. Bins were emptied every week by the bin collector's into lorries with six sliding tops (reminiscent of the top of a writing bureau) which retained some of the smells within. The bin was humped by the driver and his mate onto their shoulder and tipped into one of the compartments. When full to capacity, the driver made for the 'tip' in Holly Lane, between Landywood Primary School and the railway bridge, where he tipped the contents. The land was an old mining area and of little use for anything else. It was from this tip that we found the bits and pieces, such as pram wheels and axles, used to construct our wagons. The tip itself never seemed quite as smelly as the bins, probably due to the fact that the vegetable content had rotted and meat waste picked out by wildlife.

Using only shovel and wheelbarrow, granddad prepared for his deliveries by removing top soil from the area, creating two or three large heaps which would later be replaced on the surface. A new entrance was created to allow the lorries to gain access to his 'tip' and, over a period of six months, load after load of garbage was dumped there. No sooner had a lorry left than granddad was seen on the heap, sifting and sorting, saving some finds and throwing cans, bottles and larger rubbish down to the base of the heap, leaving mostly coal fire ash on top. Around the drainage culvert he built a semi-circular retaining wall to allow him to regularly check that it was draining freely. After about a year, he was able to replace the top soil creating a new raised garden. For the next two or three years, he grew irises on this land which were sold as bunches to local homes for three pence and sixpence a bunch. Almost by miracle, after two or three years of turning the 'soil' and growing simple crops, the tip became an area of quality garden which gradually matured with compost and manure until it grew quite good crops. The exercise had increased his garden by some fifty per cent and after a few years there was no evidence that it had been a refuse tip. I look back and applaud both his vision and foresight when he purchased the cheap marshland and also the amount of hard graft he put in to achieve his aim. Since I am modelled with some of his genes, I know he will have lain in bed at night planning his every move and never concerned about the labour involved, the only golden rule being that the project should cost him next to nothing and, apart from the cost of delivery of tons of manure, this was the case.

At home, mom (a chip off the old block) also counted her pennies and wanted to make the garden pay for itself. Dad was now growing sufficient produce to provide for the table and an excess which could be sold to pay for seeds and other gardening costs. During the spring, he sold bedding plants and tomato plants and in the summer months, mom sold bunches of flowers to callers at the house. All earnings from garden produce she put aside in a fancy Huntley and Palmer's biscuit tin and this would pay for next year's requisites. Only after all these had been purchased would she register the annual profit and use this money for other purchases, often new clothes.

By this time I was being given pocket money, a twelve-sided bronze thruppenny bit (1.25p), every Friday evening which was dad's pay day. This new coin had just replaced the small silver coin, referred to as a joey, which was very easy to lose or to swallow if buried in a Christmas pudding as was the national tradition! Mom was insistent that I save my pocket money. In fact I followed her practice and put the money away in a one ounce tobacco tin, counting it every week like Scrooge and from time to time boasting how rich I was becoming. As the weeks passed, the thruppenny bits were changed into silver and every time I was able to put a half crown (12.5p) in my box, I felt like a millionaire. The day that I was able to change the silver for a ten shilling note (50p) was a sensational feeling. As I shook the tin, what had yesterday sounded like a football rattle was now silent and I boasted to mom that I liked silent. I proudly shook the tin when grandma came in and the 'emptiness' alarmed her, but her face soon lit up when I revealed the secret. I was very much brought up to respect money and not to spend it unwisely. So long as this was my practice, granddad gave me an occasional silver coin to add to my tin. This habit quickly dried up when in later years I started to spend my wealth!

Apart from my three pence pocket money, mom did give me a halfpenny (0.2p) for sweets about twice a week. I was by now allowed to run small errands to our nearest shop which was just along the lane in Plant's buildings. Eliza Dutton, a small rotund elderly lady possibly in her mid seventies, ran a neighbourhood shop from a large cupboard in her living room. There was no shop counter or window display. Customers knocked her back door and entered the living room where she sat in front of a coal fire. She sold basic household items. My visits were often for sweets, five assorted toffees for a halfpenny which were served in a cone of newspaper. For a penny I could buy twelve toffees in a proper white paper bag, though rarely did. I always hoped that at least one toffee would be a 'black jack', a liquorice-flavoured toffee, but you asked for one at your peril since she could spit like a dragon.

"You have them as they come, my dear, no choosing!", she retorted in a stuffed up nasal voice as she put her hand into the large sweet jar and counted the five toffees onto her dining table. She shaped a small square of newspaper into a cone to serve them and took the coin from me which she put in a small glass bowl on the top of the cupboard.

Eliza lived with her family Howard and Jesse. I think it was the latter who suffered from haemophilia or other bleeding disease. He was frequently admitted to hospital with continuous bleeding following a simple nick such as occurs with shaving. He rode a motorised push bike and wore a crash helmet which was unusual in those days, but sensible in his circumstances. He died relatively young presumably of uncontrollable bleeding. Eliza Dutton died around the end of the war and was taken to her resting place in a black glass hearse drawn by two immaculate shiny black horses with silver feathered hackles. The first time I had witnessed such a cortege was as a very small child, standing by the front gate. Inside the windowed hearse was a large wooden box covered with flowers. I had no comprehension of a body within the box and certainly could not understand the weeping of folks walking slowly behind the hearse. Every house in the lane had drawn their curtains, including our house. It was a very wet day and a sombre sight. Everyone, even the horses, bowed their heads, but I did not relate the scene to death. In fact I do not think that I knew what death was until some years later since there had been no deaths in the family of which I was aware, in my few years of life. My grandmother Carpenter had died whilst I was a toddler, but I had obviously been spared the details.

I regularly visited Eliza Dutton for cigarettes for my dad, usually a thin paper packet of five Woodbines. On one occasion I was sent for a packet and a box of matches which would cost tuppence ha'penny (1p). I was given a silver sixpence and reminded by mom to bring home the change. Walking home I passed teenagers Dennis Wootton and Sonny Holloway (I think) sitting on the embankment by the allotment who asked what I had been to buy. I showed them the cigarettes and matches and they asked for a fag and a match. They were older boys and I knew that if I attempted to make a dash for home, they could easily catch me. I cautiously pulled out a match without opening the box too far in case they grabbed more. Unfortunately the match struck within the box and ignited the others, the match box quickly bursting into flames. I was sensible enough to throw it to the ground to avoid burning myself and ran home. After describing my ordeal, mom and dad seemed to find the story amusing and I am convinced they did not believe a word, assuming that I had been meddling with the box. They urged me to go back for another box of matches, with the assurance that dad would stand at the gate. He need not have bothered, my assailants had long since scarpered.

Dennis was the oldest son of the Wootton family who lived in Plant's buildings next to Bob Talbot. His father Len, a miner, was better known as the captain of the local cricket team which played on Harrison's cricket ground in Jones' Lane. His mother was Lena (Selina), an extremely industrious lady who never seemed to sit still for a moment. She usually spoke to mom whilst on the hoof, turning and walking backwards continuing the conversation until her voice faded in the distance. She was the hostess for afternoon teas at the cricket matches on Saturday afternoon. For many years she purchased dad's fresh salad items, tomatoes, lettuce, radish, spring onions and cucumbers for the teas. These were put in a large wicker basket alongside some three dozen fairy cakes which she had freshly baked during the morning. When loaded up, she was out of sight before you could bat an eyelid, her next port of call Liza Sambrook's shop on Walsall Road for loaves of bread and butter for sandwiches. Lena knew everything about everyone and was always a source of information, if mom wanted to have a nose. Their son Dennis and daughters Joan and Linda, were a little older than me and only played with us if we were playing rounders, cricket or other field games.

Sonny Holloway lived at the very old cottage, seen on old maps of the area, about half way between our house and Upper Landywood. It was separated from the rest of the houses by a shale spoil heap from past coal mining, which was one of our regular playgrounds. The cottage was a typical old country style, well over a hundred years old, with pebble dash cladding and quarry floors which were muddied by constant visits from the poultry kept by the family. When visiting for any reason, the first to the door was likely to be a hen which had wandered into the house looking for scraps. Mrs. Holloway was a kindly lady but often appeared tired and worn down, possibly the strains of housekeeping and part-time working. Mr Holloway was a miner. All the children were much older than me but Sonny, the youngest, did join in some of our games. Mrs Holloway was our local post-woman, based in Low Street, Cheslyn Hay. She used a very old bicycle which had somehow managed to stay the course and, when fully laden with post bags, she pushed it along like a trolley.

Aunt Hilda, mom's oldest sister, had a similar bicycle, perhaps in slightly better nick, and visited us every week. She lived in Broad Lane, Essington with uncle Jack. Sometimes mom and I walked to Essington on a return visit just to say 'hello'. We were always greeted warmly and mom got on well with Uncle Jack. He could be a little tetchy at times and silly things seemed to easily agitate him. He particularly disliked flies and during the summer months, when they were a nuisance in most households, he chased them around the room with a rolled up newspaper, splattering them on walls or windows. Just after we arrived on one visit, an enormous bluebottle caused a great flurry of activity, leading to out and out war. Both he and aunt Hilda chased the blue black monster around the living room, uncle Jack screaming,

"Kill the bugger, Hilda, kill it!"

"I've got it!   No, I've missed"

"Its coming your way again Hilda, get the bloody thing, kill it!"

His face was now highly flushed and eyes glaring furiously like a murderer about to strike his quarry. The fly was eventually atomised against a window pane. With a satisfied look as though nothing had happened, eyes now retracted into their sockets and bald head looking much cooler, he patted me on the head and quietly remarked,

"I don't like flies, old son, they're dirty, very dirty! ….and how are you keeping, Ida?"

Both uncle Jack and aunt Hilda were very generous both with gifts and the time allocated to seeing mom and dad. The Cheltenham Gold Cup, one of the big events in the race calendar every March, led to uncle Jack offering mum a day at the races. Dad could not get the time off work. It was 1939 and he arranged to take her, myself and Ray Worsey, his son-in-law-to-be, to Cheltenham in his car.

Uncle Jack's car was a fairly old clapped-out Morris and from the time he picked us up from home, it was apparent that it did not want to go anywhere, essentially pulling up at the first fence. It coughed and spluttered and was just not happy with hills. Had it been a mule, it would have literally sat down in the middle of the road and cried, "no further!". After ten miles or so, on the outskirts of Wolverhampton, the car was pulled over and he and Ray looked beneath the bonnet. They decided that the petrol pump was at fault, starving the engine of fuel. Come hell or high water, uncle Jack needed to get to the races for his gambling fix and they came to the conclusion that if Ray banged on the front of the foot well, to which the fuel pump was affixed, it might kick the pump into life and get us there. It seemed to work but it was a long way, some forty miles further to Cheltenham, and as we passed through the High Streets of several towns, shoppers were staring at us, no doubt wondering where the tom-toms were. It proved extremely tiring for Ray and on every hill as the car began to splutter uncle Jack would frantically shout,

"Give it more, Ray, hit it harder, go on, harder!"

At the best of times, uncle Jack drove at twenty five miles an hour. Lord knows how much thumping he would have needed to drive faster, but by some sort of magic we made the races. It was not a happy day from my point of view since it was wet, the ground very muddy, and I could see very little. Every half hour or so, the crowd came alive, cheering like mad and I could hear the loud drumming of hooves as the horses passed by. I was just about able to make out the many colours of the jockeys hats and shirts. Uncle Jack and Ray were somewhere along the avenue of bookmakers and mom and I were left very much to ourselves. I knew if dad had been with us he would have put me on his shoulders, but I was now too large for mom to help. Although I had a miserable time, uncle Jack apparently ran the bookies dry and was all smiles. It was now raining again and we had to find the car and listen to the incessant bang, bang, as we journeyed some two and a half hours towards home.

Half way home, uncle Jack decided to put some of his winnings to good use. We had stopped for petrol and fortunately the garage owner, like many self-employed of his time, worked all hours if there was money to be made. We had to wait whilst he finished another job after which he changed our petrol pump in about an hour and a half. We set off home and it was a heavenly journey, the car purring along and never once coughing. The miles passed by quickly and we reached home in no time. In reality the journey home had taken about six hours. Dad had worried the evening away since he had no idea what had kept us. He was fully aware that where uncle Jack was concerned, he would have taken a detour via Blackpool if mom had wanted to go there. I went to bed that night very late and far too tired even to have a nightmare of the day's experience.

Dad worked hard at Gilpin's to provide for us and outside work, as I have intimated, spent most of his spare time in the greenhouse or garden. Between January and March he sowed seeds in the greenhouse, transplanting the seedlings into wooden tomato trays, gleaned from the local greengrocer. In the same trays, he also laid out seed potatoes, Arran Pilot and King Edward, for chitting in a dark corner of the shed. Come April he turned his attention to outside. He had to dig about a fifth of an acre by mid April, sowing rows of seeds and potatoes every eighteen inches (50cm) or so. The last to be put in were the potato tubers and runner beans. They were sown directly onto a bed of manure, delivered from a farm by the load by Bert Kingston, a milkman from Cheslyn Hay. Both were planted about four inches deep and eventually threw up tender shoots which were highly susceptible to frost. All local gardeners knew that the last frosts of the year were in mid May. He taught me to time the sowings of these so that the shoots did not peep through the soil until the third week in May. Should the timing be wrong, a frost immediately turned the shoots black and if the worst happened, dad would come into the house looking somewhat dejected. In reality, the correct timing was all about who was going to have the first crop of the year when gardeners at work talked among themselves, and this setback would delay his crop. Some runner beans he started in a pot in the greenhouse, timed so that the plants were about six inches high and ready to transplant outside by this date which allowed him to pick early runner beans in late July or early August.

By late May the garden was looking in fine fettle. The peas were germinating in ten flattened limed rows, some with hazel twigs already in place to allow the new growth to climb and form 'pea hedges' about two feet (60 cm) high across the width of the garden. The runner beans had stakes, six feet (2 metres) high and arranged tent-like in four rows. A large onion patch was already prepared and scattered with soot from the chimney, to keep away onion fly. On this site would be planted about a hundred Ailsa Craig onion seedlings already four inches high in boxes in the greenhouse. This bed of large globular onion bulbs would be a sight to behold in early autumn. The hedgerows alongside the garden had put on their summer clothing, the hawthorn may was now blossoming and the sun was warming. What could be better! It was an amazing scene of life regenerating. Then, one morning, across the germinating row of peas, were six large mole hills bringing rank ugliness to an otherwise perfect scene. Moles in a field make a mess which can be tolerated, but a mole in a garden is another thing. Gardening is hard work and this beast can in a day or so nullify the weeks of toil and sweat. Dad immediately fetched the spade.

Catching moles is an art. He stood perfectly still and silently watched for ten minutes or more. Almost imperceptibly the soil lifted and then lowered on the end mole hill. Like the strike of a snake, dad thrust his spade into the ground alongside the moving heap, and rapidly turned over the spit of soil. The mole was now lying above ground totally disorientated and was dispatched with a blow from the spade. This process happened two or three times a year, the moles obviously coming into the garden from the wheat field above, preferring the soft soil and abundance of earthworms.

This was an exciting time of life. I couldn't wait to get out of the house to be with my pals but one day my eagerness led to my undoing when I ran from the front gate into the lane and into the path of a racing cyclist. I remembered flying through the air but the amnesia which followed took away any memory of hitting the road surface with some force. I was apparently carried into the house by the horrified cyclist, somewhat limp and bleeding from my nose and multiple facial abrasions. It was some ten minutes before I regained consciousness and mom was inconsolable. I hate to think what she said to the cyclist during that time, but freely confess that it was my fault. She would not hear of a trip to the hospital and I lay on the settee for the rest of the day, nursing a very sore face. I developed swelling around my eyes and it became recognised later that I had broken my nose in the accident. Since I was not taken to the hospital, it was not straightened and I have sported a crooked nose all my life. It did teach me never to run into the road again and with cars becoming more commonplace, this proved a good thing.

That is now two nasty accidents, suffered during my early years, which really needed hospital attention but, since mom hated hospitals, I was kept away. However, like many boys, I also suffered many more minor injuries. Both granddad and dad had a stoical approach to injury which meant that you let nature do the healing. If you could get up and walk after an accident, it was not necessary to involve the doctor. Doctors had to be paid for and to granddad, payment was the last thing you did, unless you could bargain and reduce the price. He did undergo surgery about two years earlier and when I was older he told me what this entailed. He had had trouble peeing and Mr. Vincent Patrick, general surgeon at Wolverhampton Royal Hospital, diagnosed an enlarged prostate gland at the bottom of his bladder. He advised surgery to remove the prostate but when he mentioned the price, granddad's heart sank into his boots. He could build another house for that! He declined the surgery but, as he was about to leave the consultation, Mr. Patrick made an offer. There was a new operation for this condition which he had never before performed and if granddad would be a guinea pig to allow him to try out the operation, he would perform it free of charge. Naturally, granddad jumped at the idea and underwent his operation, simply paying for his hospital room. Thankfully it proved to be successful.

For the most part, simple injuries were treated with linen dressings and minor ailments with grandma's favourite recipe. Probably the commonest was 'slops' which was freshly toasted bread broken up in freshly boiled milk along with a Beecham's powder for colds and flu-like illnesses. When available the milk might be spiked with a little whisky which certainly helped the sore throat. Poultices of hot kaolin clay were used for acute skin inflammations such as boils and carbuncles. The kaolin was thickly painted on a piece of muslin which was heated on the lid of a boiling saucepan and applied to the area whilst quite hot. It worked wonders with a very painful boil, both relieving the pain and, when the poultice was later removed, the boil had burst and its green pussy content was sitting in the dressing like snot in a handkerchief. Simple belly aches usually indicated the application of a hot water bottle, perhaps with an Aspro (aspirin) or

Beecham's powder. Grandma frequently advised a body-hugging corset of lint or brown paper around the chest for a bad cough which would not go away. I used to hate the fact that granddad coughed up phlegm and spat it onto the roadside. He would do the same with a stuffed up nose, hold one nostril whilst he blew out the horrid content of the other. Such islands of snot were commonplace since most miners seemed to do it and we had to be careful not to step in it. Looking back, it is not surprising that consumption (tuberculosis) frequently occurred.

No doubt because of doctor's bills, many people practised prevention, taking certain medicines weekly to ward off ailment. Scott's emulsion was considered a great preventative and I had to take a tablespoonful every week to ward off infections and fevers. It had quite a pleasant taste unlike cod liver oil and malt, which I hated. Both were similar and advertised as health-giving in that they also contained vitamins and calcium to strengthen our bones. Tea made from dried senna pods kept our bowels regular and we drank half a cupful every week. Failing this, a weekly dose of Syrup of Figs had the same effect. Any feelings of sickness or stomach pain and out came the vivid blue bottle of Milk of Magnesia. It was not unpleasant to taste, but afterwards the inside of my mouth felt as though it was coated with dry chalk and it remained so for some time. Regular shopping trips to Cowern and Hartshorne's chemist shop on the Walsall Road ensured mom was stocked up on these items.

In order to get professional medical care, mom and dad paid into the doctor's club. Every month mom visited Wyrley Wesley Church where Bill (William J) Garrett or Albert Handley collected one shilling and sixpence for Dr. Ralph Middleton's club. This meant that any significant illnesses affecting the three of us were treated by him, either by visiting his surgery at the end of Hilton Lane or calling him for a home visit. Feeling off colour, as a child, I sat in his waiting room looking at the green baize door waiting for the call to go in,

"Next!"

Being somewhat muffled, mom applied her ear to the door,

"NEXT!"

As we entered his sanctum he would offer a brusque 'Morning!' and without looking up, a hand pulled me forward to his side. Whilst mom was describing my problem, he was feeling around my neck and looking into my ears.

"Open your mouth", he asked as he pulled a steel spatula from a glass of pink disinfectant on his desk and poked it into my mouth.

"Say, aah!" was the next command. "Pull up your shirt!"

I jumped a mile as he put his cold stethoscope to my chest. Some gruff almost inaudible remark to my mom followed as he walked across to a small dispensary full of bottles at the back of the room. I was always overjoyed if I saw him pick up the strawberry coloured clear liquid from the shelf.

'Hooray', I thought to myself, 'Cherry medicine (linctus)!'

"A teaspoon three times a day" he explained to mom as he quickly ushered us out, to make way for another. As we were leaving, there was a loud "NEXT!" and the next victim obediently shuffled through the green baize door.

43

CHAPTER 5

'Noticing people and their ways - c. 1939'

In August 1939, for my seventh birthday, mom and dad bought me a bicycle from Jellyman's Cycles, a shop on Walsall Road in Cannock. It was black with sparkling chrome fittings and had twelve inch (30cm) wheels with pneumatic tyres. It displayed a gold 'New Hudson' crest on the front spar. I was over the moon and couldn't wait to bring my friends to look at it. I frequently parked it against the edge of the front lawn so that I could sit on it and pretend to ride. Every evening after work, dad supported me, holding onto the saddle as I pedalled around the lanes. It was the same route every time; Landywood lane, Upper Landywood lane (past Fisher farm or Walley's farm as we usually called it), through Upper Landywood and back down Street's lane home. I was secure in the fact that behind my back he was holding the saddle but was unaware that he had occasionally let go, his hand prepared if necessary a little way behind the saddle. About a week later, I was pedalling away and he showed me both hands. We were at this point in Upper Landywood and, since the rest of the journey was downhill, I was able to concentrate on balancing, steering and gently braking until I reached home. Dad was still walking home, about a quarter of a mile behind. The following evening I pedalled the journey, without support, and we practised stopping and starting from a raised grass verge. Mom was, as always, leaning over the front gate, awaiting my arrival and applauded and kissed me as I toppled off in the gateway. Before long I had achieved mounting and dismounting on the move and dad was now accompanying me on his own bicycle. I was cycling quite well, I thought, but there were occasions when I steered into him, as we rode side by side, with the inevitable collision. A grazed knee, much as it hurt, did not seem to matter. In about a month, I had become quite proficient and was cycling along the lanes with not a care in the world.

Although dad's commitments were heavy, he always found time to take me for a cycle ride, sometimes instigated by a request from mom to take something to aunt Hilda. The errand done we might cycle to Top Essington, journeying along Hobnock Lane, past the busy brickworks on the left. Opposite was a extremely deep hole from which clay was extracted and delivered to the factory up a steep hawser-driven funicular track, that passed under a road bridge. A gap in the hedge allowed us to get close to the rim of the quarry so that we could take in its vastness. I suffered a degree of vertigo with heights and held my breath lest even the slightest movement caused the edge to crumble dispatching me to the depths. It was a fear which became the subject of countless dreams which ended with me cycling over the rim, falling, falling, falling and then awaking on the floor of my bedroom, heart pounding like an express train. If not a dream about the quarry, I would dream of falling from the railway bridge at home, after workmen had for some reason removed the parapets, always with the same effect. With a sigh of relief that it was no more than a dream, I came to my senses and climbed back into bed.

August also brought 'Wakes week' every year, when Pat Collins opened the biggest entertainment fair in the Midlands, on his home ground in High Street, Bloxwich. The crowds in the streets of the town were always huge and, as soon as mom, dad and I alighted from the bus, we could hear loud music and the screams coming from the fair, still two or three hundred yards (metres) away. Our first view of the event was the spiral slide, towering above adjacent buildings, looking like a multicoloured lighthouse. The crowds were huge and we could only go with the flow, carried by the crush into the fairground. Immediately to our right as we entered, the mighty steamboats, two carriages about the size of a small bus, were swinging backwards and forwards, higher and higher, until the screaming occupants were virtually inverted. I expected them to fall from their seats, but they never did. Most rides were geared towards grown-ups but I was allowed to ride the various roundabouts and the carousel. These were fun but they bore no comparison to the excitement when dad took me on the bumping cars for the first time. It was a mixture of shouting, gasping and screaming with joy as he weaved our car in and out of the traffic, occasionally bumping into other cars. I yelled at him amid the noise to bump another car, and held my breath awaiting the collision which resulted in a guttural laugh when it occurred! A sudden almighty jolt from behind took my breath away, as someone returned the compliments, forcing me into the seat. It was a shock but dad chased the offender across the rink and I became more and more excited as we closed in. At the last moment our quarry was saved as all the cars lost power and came to a standstill. I begged for another ride but dad pointed out that crowds were waiting for a car and we should give others a chance. In lieu, mom bought me an enormous spiral lollypop about the size of a saucer, which I sucked on for the next hour or so.

I was particularly enthralled by the steam organs which were producing decibels of melodious pipe music, interjected with birdlike trills, drumsticks rapping rhythmically on pigskin and the cheerful clashing of cymbals. This delightful music brought the whole fair to life. I dragged mom and dad back to them over and over again, standing in awe, totally transfixed by the majestic sound and the military precision of the tympani. Behind the organs, a line of large steam engines were almost imperceptibly hissing and puffing, driving heavy flywheels which were belted to generators, feeding electricity to a fairyland of coloured lights throughout the fairground. During the day the lights were not yet at their best, but must have been a breath-taking spectacle after dark. Little did we know what would occur in the next few days and that this would be the last Wakes week for several years.

The sideshows, coconut shies, hooplas, air rifles, darts, roll-a-penny, fishing for goldfish and many others were lavishly decorated with dozens of large and small prizes that players could win. Mom proudly carried home a large pottery brown and white spaniel dog which dad had won on the air rifles. I think she adored being ogled by all those who had not won a prize and she lapped up the attention as we strutted down the street to our bus stop.

I loved mom regardless of her strictness, as any child would, but at quite an early age I was embarrassed by some of her antics. I suppose I had a shy disposition like dad, but mom was more outgoing and more determined in her prying into other people's business. I frequently blushed at the way she asked my pals questions about their new clothes, where they came from and how much they were. She would then have a good feel of the material to see whether she approved. At home during the afternoon, she usually sat behind the curtains watching, making comments about people and their clothes as they passed by, sometimes 'Oh, I like that!' but more frequently something derogatory. Grandma would do the same when she called in on her daily afternoon visit and one must presume that the habit had been passed on. In the absence of other entertainment, what else was there to do? It was I suppose the fashion parade of the day. From an early age, I felt very uncomfortable with some of their remarks. There was too much bitchiness. A few comments were actually quite funny and I joined in the laughter but always felt awkward about it, and even more so as I grew older. Even worse, when we were out at the shops, mom might whisper a disparaging remark about someone which I clearly heard and, since they were within earshot, I was mortified that they may also have heard.

Women at the time had more time to gossip within the community since very few went out to work. In the mid afternoon, they could be seen at the garden gate, household chores completed, waiting for husbands to return from work, but also hoping that someone was going to pass who might tarry awhile for a chat. Mom had a habit of weeding the front garden, but the area nearest the gate always received the most attention. Here, she was near enough the lane to engage in conversation. Many wives, Mrs Bullock, Mrs Gretton, Mrs Cliff, Mrs Corfield, Mrs Hawkesworth or Mrs Evans, shopped for small food items in Landywood or walked down to the Co-op at the end of Hilton Lane and on the way back were accosted by mom. They were an interesting group of women.

Ethel Bullock lived in the first house opposite and was the wife of Jim Bullock, the miner and amateur gardener, whom we met earlier. She had a somewhat musical drawl to her voice which was a delight for any impersonator. Mom was forever miming her, to the amusement of dad and I, and we frequently fell about laughing as she chronicled, in Ethel Bullock speak, the tales she had gleaned from her. Indeed, if at any time I felt the need for a laugh, I would ask mom to perform.

"Mom, do a Mrs Bullock!" I would goad her until she relented and went into character and performed, as well as any professional might.

No matter how much fun was generated at her expense, Ethel was a very industrious lady around the home, a typical housewife of the day, always seen in a pinafore, always doing something around the house. On Mondays, her washing line would be full from the top to bottom of the garden, on another day she might be seen hanging out of the upstairs bedroom window giving it a good clean. Mom often caught her at the front gate where they would spend half an hour chatting and no doubt mom topping up her script for a later performance.

The Gretton family lived next to the Bullocks. George and Millicent (Millie), had two children Donald and Joy, a little younger than myself. George had I think previously worked at one of the local mines but later purchased the field up the lane where he stabled a horse and cart, used for delivering coal between the pit and various homes. He mostly seemed to deliver 'the allowance', free coal which working miners received as a perk, though they had to pay the delivery man for the 'drawing' (the delivery of coal).

His horse was always reluctant to back up the heavy two-wheeled cart to offload and more often than not expressed this by rearing up, gyrating and whinnying in protest. George always gave the procedure a wide berth, standing well back, yanking at the long reins and screaming at it.

"Back up! Back! BEURK! BEUUURK!" he yelled, his voice rising to a piercing crescendo and his face becoming progressively more puce as he struggled to urge the unwilling beast into reverse.

Then at some critical moment he pulled at the cart lever, like a hangman at the trap door, dropping the load of coal to the ground. If it was tipped somewhere near target, he considered it an achievement. His face now lightened and displayed an expression of relief, only to be followed by one of profound embarrassment when he noticed we were watching.

Millie Gretton was a lovely lady, very prim and proper, nicely spoken and one felt would be better fitted to a middle class life-style rather than living in an industrial and mining community. Her accent was ultra-Oxford and noticeably out of place in a village where a broad Black Country accent was the norm. To her credit, her higher class upbringing, if that was the case, did not detach her from the rest of the community. She always passed the time of day, making conversation with people she met and frequently chatted to mom at the front gate. She was not always happy with the way we treated Donald, her son. Sadly he may have suffered trauma at birth, not uncommon in those days, resulting in mild spasticity so that his gait was rather awkward and stumbling. Though I understood his condition more in later life, his gait led to merciless teasing and even bullying during childhood by both my friends and I. It seems that through the ages children with an affliction have been bullied and even considered to be mentally sub-normal, when it simply was not true. It is one memory that I have looked back on and wished I could right a wrong by apologising to Donald for the misery we must have caused him, through no fault of his own. His younger sister, Joy, like her mum was also prim and, as a young girl, was rarely to come out to play with the likes of us though did play freely with children of relatives and friends who visited their home. Every summer their front garden displayed a huge patch of Aaron's rod (Solidago), a flower not grown by many people, and I have vivid memories of it in full flower for most of the school holiday. On occasion, Millie Gretton could be seen picking a bunch for the house and it seemed to reflect her persona, an armful of golden sceptres for a lady who might be a queen.

Residing in the attached semi' named 'Rockdale' were Joe and Margaret Cliffe who were looked up to, but childless. I am not sure that anyone ever used their Christian names. They were a couple who seemed conscious of their importance since Joe was in insurance and therefore 'Mr and Mrs' was apt. In those days such a tradesman displayed an air of importance, always clean shaven, soft skinned and wore a dapper suit. He was the only person in the lane who owned a car, a black Austin seven, which he kept in immaculate condition. In fact as the years passed we were to witness the emergence of a brightly shining red oxide roof as the black topcoat was devotedly polished away. It was never allowed to show road dirt. His wife Margaret, short and as wide as she was tall, was frequently seen swaggering along duck-like, a laden shopping bag in hand. She usually had a haughty expression on her face, looking straight ahead and seemingly pretending not to see someone who might be of lower status. Nevertheless, she always stopped and chatted to mom at our front gate. Even Margaret Cliffe may have some gossip which needed to be dragged from her by mom's guile! Joe Cliffe's garden generally exhibited a florid display of wild flowers such as ox-eye daisy, groundsel, poppies and common toadflax interspersed with a few straggly Michaelmas daisies. Occasionally one or other could be seen hoe-weeding the drive around the car but this may have been more to create a show place for it as it sat there gleaming in the sunshine.

Next door, Jack Corfield and Ivy, his wife, kept themselves very much to themselves. They were a pleasant couple but were rather shy and never, it seemed, found communication easy. For Jack, a simple though clearly well-intentioned greeting was about the normal level of communication with neighbours.

"Mornin' ", he would say in a gruff voice, eyes to the ground, as he went on his way. Never a word more.

They had two children, Christine the older was about three or four years younger than me and her sister, Janet, younger by six or seven years. The family kept a Scotty type dog, a bitch and probably a mongrel, which caused irritation by consistently yap-yap-yapping at anyone passing the gate. In fact, if I yapped back, the dog seemed to go into an uncontrollable frenzy, tying itself into a knot as it gyrated and snapped at its own tail. On one occasion when I was around seven years old, she came on heat and as we played nearby a passing Alsation took notice. Within the frenzy of sexual fulfilment he became well and truly impaled within the mini-dog. The Scotty began squealing, obviously in some distress. Jack Corfield heard the screeches from his dog and rushed into the lane to find Scotty swinging like a pendulum beneath the enormous stud. As we watched with incredulity, the monster cautiously walked up the lane, still impaled, wide-legged and with almost human embarrassment on its face. In a flash, Jack, rushed into the house and a bucketful of cold water was sufficient to dampen ardours and they parted company. The look on the face of the Alsation, a querulous 'what did I do wrong', was evident for all to see as it shook itself dry before slinking away. I was at the time too young to understand the mechanics of their predicament, simply assuming it was an episode of aggression between dogs. I puzzled how they had become so entangled and how different it was to a normal dog fight where dogs locked together, baring teeth and snarling. Nevertheless the episode was a sight to behold and we were deeply amused by the drenching that was needed to separate them. I went home laughing to tell mom but she did not explain.

Lily Molineux and husband Bob lived between my friends Eric and Colin. They were also very private people and I never knew where Bob worked, only that he cycled to work every day. Both rode good quality bicycles which had protection around the chains and a canvas cover over the rear wheels so that their clothing was not soiled. These higher quality cycles, along with a slight haughtiness expressed by Lily, led me to believe they were a family of higher status than other people, including my dad, who rode a normal rather tatty open-chained bicycle.

Lily Molyneux was one of only two wives in the lane who cycled everywhere. She had a wide beam and, as she pedalled away, her buttocks seemed to droop over each side of the saddle like panniers. Nevertheless, the exercise made her a very strong woman both in stature and in the assertiveness with which she spoke to people. Their daughter Joy was a little older than Colin, Eric and myself and she never joined us in play. If we did speak to her, she seemed to blush profusely as though embarrassed to be in our presence. I never understood whether this was severe shyness, or reaction to strict instructions from an authoritarian mother. Lily Molineux very easily became irate with people, sometimes during a conversation which had started with passing neighbours at the front gate. She seemed to hide behind her small Pickwickian spectacles which projected an air of wisdom. In a confrontation on some topic, she very vociferously conveyed her view and on occasions stormed furiously into the house, shouting as she went. Bob Molineux, on the other hand, was tall, slim and balding and a very shy man who wore a permanent flush from neck to scalp. He never displayed any degree of urgency in his actions and walked with a slow purposeful gait, almost a Guard's slow march. He never showed aggression and in this respect was just the opposite of his wife. Lily became pregnant with a second child, Marjorie, when Joy was about ten years of age and she didn't seem to relish the experience.

Granddad's youngest brother, Isaiah 'Zair' Baker, lived in the last house on the east side of the lane. He lived there with Nancy, his wife, and daughter Mary. He was initially a miner had who lost his leg in a mining accident in 1913 and wore an artificial limb which was not really detectable, except that he had a slight limp. Although handicapped, he still rode a bicycle to and from work. Now considering myself a qualified cyclist, I watched him and frequently pondered how he managed to propel his bike, since no way could I pedal mine with one foot. It was one of those many questions in life which tantalised me and I puzzled for answers to such quandaries. This one was resolved some time later when a school friend was riding a 'fixed-wheel' cycle and the penny dropped! Uncle Zair also had a rear wheel which was fixed not free-wheeling as was the norm. I was now happy and, as always, felt a degree of elation when something on my list of conundrums had at last been ticked off.

His wife, auntie Nance, was famed for her craftsmanship. She was particularly good with crepe paper and created very realistic artificial flowers which, in a large display, were very impressive, and wowed all who saw them. Year in, year out she decorated the Wesleyan church on special occasions, the quality of her paper flowers bringing perpetual spring and summer to these events, whatever the season. Their daughter Mary, was much older than me and married during my childhood.

Tom and Mary Hawkesworth moved into the first house beyond the allotments in about 1937. It was one of a pair of houses named 'Glenmore', built in 1901. These houses had outside lavatories which were dry cesspits. Ashes from the fireplace were daily thrown into the pit, covering the family excreta, to mask any smell. The lavatory seat was a well-scrubbed pine bench with a hole. Council workers periodically emptied the cesspit through an outside cover plate. As a child living in a home with a brand new indoor water closet, I remember feeling revulsion by the mucky chore undertaken by these men. I could only stand with my friends and stare as we held our fingers to our nose. They shovelled out the contents of the pit and conveyed it in wheelbarrows to a waiting lorry. Walking home, I was thankful that our lavatory used a flush of water to discharge its contents into oblivion and that we were not subject to such a grisly procedure. These dry lavatories were converted to outdoor water closets when I was about five years of age. My early recollection is of the Benton twins, children about my own age, moving into the house for a year or so before Hawkesworths took up residence. Tom and Mary were a childless couple and we did not really get to know them. However, mom frequently chatted to her at the gate and kept us updated. They were a couple who made their intra-marital arguments very public and we, and presumably everyone else, could hear every word some hundred yards away. Even so, they remained together for their natural lives.

Mom and dad also had occasional fights, I presume about marital problems. It is more than likely that she feared another pregnancy and the problems it might bring. On one occasion I was terrified when dad stormed out of the house with tears in his eyes, yelling at mom that he was going to jump in the cut (canal). Mom was also crying as she cuddled me and reassured me that he would be back. He did return after about an hour and they clung to each other.

In the other half of 'Glenmore' lived Tom and May Evans who, over the years of my childhood, produced a large family. Sylvia, Margaret, Tommy and Horace being nearer to my age and frequently played with us during our childhood. Their father, Tom Evans, was a strict disciplinarian, not infrequently threatening one or other with his belt, which certainly reflected on their behaviour. They would rarely take a risk if something we were about to do seemed wrong. Tom was a man of short stature, but a hard working deep pit miner, whilst May was a lady of larger frame, though too industrious to be fat. All his earnings it seemed were used to feed and clothe his large family which reached seven in number during my later childhood as David, Doreen and Kathleen came along. They were all a credit to their parent's care.

In the next houses, consecutively, were the Waite, Farrington, Loach, Talbot and Wootton families whom we have already met.

Liza Clift lived in Plant's Buildings next door to Mrs Dutton, the shop. She was probably around seventy when I was a child. Liza was as deaf as a post, or so she would have people believe. She had a mild speech impediment that frequently resulted in the listener being showered with saliva. She regularly gave us the impression that young boys were a pain she did not wish to tolerate, which led to a love-hate relationship between us. I am not sure of the reason for this attitude but it may have been that, as a result of her communication problems, she was badly teased earlier in life, particularly by young boys. We wondered about the authenticity of her deafness on many occasions, mainly because our parents had always been dubious. One morning, I was about nine, Liza Clift came to the bus stop where we were waiting and asked me whether the bus had gone. She cupped her hand to her ear and placed it close to my mouth for a reply. Without really thinking, David Loach whispered,

"Spit in her ear!"

This I would not have done, though his spontaneous remark did make me laugh aloud. Quick as a flash, Liza looked sternly at David and shook her fist at him.

"You cheeky little devil, I am going straight to your mother to let her know how rude you are and to wash your mouth out!" she retorted.

We were saved by the arrival of the bus and, as she mounted, she looked sternly at him again and repeated the message. David had obviously upset her and blushed and gave a rueful snigger as we followed her on.

When we found our seat, at a safe distance, David and I firmly agreed that a deaf person could not have heard what he had whispered to me. We disclosed the incident to other people and most were convinced that Liza could hear more than she confessed to. She was only deaf they said when she did not want to hear. Looking back, we had not known that some deaf people lip read and the comments may, therefore, have been unfair.

One day we tried out a trick on Liza which dad and his friends had played as a child. We tied a length of washing line her front door knob then to the knob of old Mrs Dutton next door. We then knocked both doors and darted for cover. The intention was that both would open the door but the first to open would be knocked out of her doorway as the second door opened. It failed, we had forgotten that Liza was deaf as a post and she did not come to the door!

Old Joe Plant lived as a lodger with Lisa Clift and was probably around sixty. He was a kindly, though possibly lonely, old man who passed our front gate every afternoon on his journey home from the pit. He always sported a bowler hat and waistcoat with gold chain, which dangled because of his posture, and to which was clipped a gold pocket watch. He had been a miner, but now had a surface job in the lamp house at the pit. He suffered a severe spinal rigidity which meant that his trunk was permanently bent forward and he was always looking at the floor. He was totally unable to lift his head to see where he was going and his gait was also affected so that he rolled from side to side, a little like a ship. People suggested that his spinal trouble had followed working in low coal seams where he had, day after day, picked and shovelled coal whilst bent double. The most likely cause was not his mining activities but ankylosing spondylitis, a chronic crippling condition of the spine which starts around the age of thirty and over time causes his type of rigidity and deformity. Joe will, without doubt, have worked on the coal seam for many years suffering unremitting back pain, until his whole spine finally seized in the shape of a letter 'C' as it now was. I am not sure whether I ever looked into his eyes, or he into mine in view of his problem, but there was something very endearing about his manner. If I was in the lane, he always stopped and spoke to me in a quiet whisper as though we were sharing a secret.

"Let me see what I can find you", he would say, grubbing around in his coat pocket until he found something.

He then pressed a toffee or boiled sweet into the palm of my hand. It was as though my hand had become the eyes which he could not see and he was thus communicating with me. Closing my fingers around the gift as though it was a precious stone, he patted my clenched fist and went on his way. One day he failed to appear and mom told me that he had died. I felt deeply saddened but mom said that, with his kindness, he would go to heaven. I dearly hoped that, when there, he would be able to walk tall again and greet everyone with a smiling face.

To complete the last three residents in the lane, the Gretton family lived next door to Mrs Dutton, the shop. Mrs Gretton was a hard working communicative lady (but never entrapped by mom to my knowledge!) and she had a pleasant family. The children, Audrey, Gordon, Sheila and Pauline were older than me and only occasionally joined in street games. In later years, when they moved to Landywood village, I could always rely on Mrs Gretton to buy a bunch of flowers from me when I hawked them around the village. Next door were the Evans family who were fairly quiet and their children George, Betty, Doreen and Eileen (I think) were older and did not really communicate with us. George and Louise Hollis lived in the end house of the terrace. They had no children and were nice but fairly reclusive people. On the other hand, they did regularly chastise us for playing ball games against the gable end of their house. I am sure it was far from pleasant for the people inside but, since it was the only plain wall in the lane, whilst waiting for friends, bouncing a ball off the wall was the only way to pass time. George

Hollis had a wood lathe in a spare bedroom and regularly turned out spindle and twist legs and other items for furniture. I am not sure whether it was a hobby or a part-time job, but I remember being very impressed by the quality of the items he produced.

Mom's need-to-know (sounds better than nosiness!) led to her excelling herself one day, as she dragged me into Bloxwich, I assumed on a shopping spree. She often used Bloxwich for shopping because she liked Taylor's cakes and there was the added convenience of using the Wyrley Whizzer, a bus which stopped on the bridge, opposite granddad's front gate. It ran hourly through Cheslyn Hay from outside Dakin's garage in Station Street and on to Bloxwich via Street's Lane and Broad Lane, Essington. It was a small twenty-four seated Bedford in Walsall pale blue livery, with a closing door. Unlike main stream buses it had no conductor, the driver collected passengers' fares as we boarded. The driving cab was inside the bus which allowed him to chinwag with his passengers on the journey.

The choice of Taylors may seem a little surprising for someone who had been a shop assistant for Stanton's, the opposition, but their cakes were good. I adored Taylor's Brighton buns (iced lemon cakes) and never baulked at making a trip there. On this day, there seemed to be a degree of urgency in mom's step as we alighted the bus at the terminus in Wolverhampton Road. She grabbed my hand and towed me at a pace along the High Street, to my horror passing by Taylor's cake shop. We turned off just past the church into Station Street, making towards the railway station. The level crossing gates closed ahead of us and the ground began to shudder as the half past ten express train to Stafford thundered through. I had seen this express train many times as it passed our house but standing by the crossing gates with the enormous locomotive three feet (one metre) away and towering above our heads, it was quite frightening. As the gates began to open I was dragged onto an area of common land I had never seen before and in a shallow dip noticed a pond towards which we were heading. It was only then that mom told me a woman she knew had drowned herself in the pool yesterday and her body had been dragged out by the police. There was nothing to see only an average pond with reeds and pondweed, like many nearer to home. The visit seemed to fulfil a desire in mom who was now happy as we retraced our tracks and set about doing some shopping. My reward, which I felt I had earned, was a Brighton bun which I tucked into as we rejoined the Wyrley Whizzer for home.

Every second week, mom shopped in Walsall and I was expected to tag along. The trip was essentially to buy black pudding and sausages from Marsh and Baxter's in Park Street. Their products were considered by mom to be the best in the world and she rarely bought sausage or black pudding from anywhere else. I thoroughly enjoying tucking into black pudding raw, with freshly baked bread and butter, but it was more often used as part of a mixed grill. Even after grandma told me in quite a graphic detail how it was made from a bucket of freshly collected pig's blood, my enjoyment was not diminished. Marsh and Baxter had created a dream meal as far as I was concerned.

Whilst in town, we inevitably visited Marks and Spencer to look at clothes and on market days, the market stalls, particularly those selling clothing where mom might see a dress or top she fancied. At lunch time, always dead on 12 noon, we walked through the doors of either the Co-op restaurant in Upper Bridge Street or Pattison's on the Bridge, for lunch. We were usually the first customers of the day and found a window seat so that we could watch the activity in the street below. We got to know several other early attendees who probably dined at the same table every day. A favourite of mine was the Co-op cottage pie, beautifully seasoned, which was far better than that mom cooked using the remains of a Sunday joint. She always expressed concerns about what our butcher might hide in his mince, and therefore gave it a miss. I adored the herby flavours added by the chefs and could easily have demolished second helpings. A slice of apple pie and custard rounded off an excellent meal. It was then time to head for the No 1 Hednesford bus for home.

CHAPTER 6

'War is announced and early days -
c. 1939 - 40'

As the summer holiday came to an end, my friends and I were suffering a little unease because at school we knew we would be entering Mr. Mountford's class. David called for me so that we could walk to school together. He was wearing a new grey suit for the new term and mom, true to pattern, asked him where his mother had bought it, followed as always by what it might have cost. I was very embarrassed by her prying since I knew it was a question David's mother would never ask me.

"It wuz from Worsal, miss, I think it was nine-umpse the jacket and six-umpse the trousers", David proudly replied.

This response appeared to tickle mom. Apart from the ridiculous prices of nine pence (about 4p) and sixpence (2.5p) she had never before heard of boy's suits being purchased as separates, and she chuckled as she oft-time relayed the story to others. My new suit was purchased as always as a complete suit, either from Wigley's, the drapery shop on the Walsall Road in Great Wyrley or from Buxton and Bonnet's in Walsall. A boy's grey flannel suit of jacket and short trousers cost about twenty two shillings and sixpence (£1.12p), about a third of dad's weekly wage. I think it gave mom some sort of uplift, spending a lot of money on clothes for her family. It was always very important to her that we looked good and she always went into a gent's outfitters with dad to make sure he selected the right thing.

David and I arrived at school on the first day of term and proceeded to our new class at the other end of the school building. Unexpectedly, we were greeted by Mr. Bickford who informed us that Mr. Mountford had been called into the armed forces and our class would be taken by Miss Liddle. We had not relished the thought of Mr. Mountford, whom we had been discussing for a day or two, since we had been led to believe that he was very strict. We were not unhappy therefore to hear about the change. To be more precise, we were overjoyed at the thought of Miss Liddle teaching us. We soon found, however, that she was already committed to the class above and could only cover our class some of the time. Mr. Bickford we were told would be covering the remaining lessons. 'Oh heck', I thought as I found myself a desk.

Percy Bickford was a small bald-headed man who lived, I believe, with his sister in Shareshill. He wore a grey suit, slightly shabby, usually with blue striped tie. He walked around his patch like a busy bee popping into one class and then another. Teachers always seemed to respond to his command. He maintained a log of school activities, scripted in his own very neat handwriting. It was the latter which always caught my eye if I had to go into his office to collect and ring the school bell, for which we had a rota. His voice was fairly quiet and, even though he had visible temper tantrums in that his face looked enraged, it was rare to hear him raise his voice. This also applied when he was delivering a punishment, usually in the form of hard slaps on a bare buttock or upper thigh after pulling up a trouser leg, which to date I had escaped. Boys frequently received a slapping but never the girls it seemed! He did have a cane which hung menacingly in his room but he rarely seemed to use it. As time passed I got to like him and his lessons, but I am aware that many did not. In the autumn we always looked forward to getting an apple from his orchard, even though many seemed to be windfalls. We were not given, nor could we choose a particular apple, we were only allowed a lucky dip from a large box.

School was much of a ritual and punctuality essential. We started at 9.00 a.m. and worked until a milk break at 10.45 a.m. A milk crate was collected from the corridor by the milk monitors, two pupils rostered for the duty each week, and brought into the classroom. We collected our bottle of milk and were expected to drink it in the classroom before going out into the playground. The bottle was a third of a pint and the cap was a waxed cardboard disc wedged into the neck of the bottle. In the centre of the cap a further small disc could be punched through to create a hole for a drinking straw or to allow a finger to be poked in to pull out the cap. After a break of fifteen minutes following a run around the playground and use of the toilet, the bell rang and we returned to our classes.

Lunch break was one and a half hours and many of us went home for lunch. Meals were not provided at school, but some children took sandwiches and stayed there. It took me five to ten minutes to cycle between school and home and I, therefore, had an hour at home for the meal. Mom usually cooked a dinner of meat and two vegetables, the latter depending on the garden produce at that time of year. I hated cooked dinners when the cabbage was in season and always refused to eat the greens. Mom became annoyed and I usually got a lecture about the need to eat to make me grow, and starving people and how lucky I was to have cabbage to eat. My thoughts were clear, 'they can have my cabbage or sprouts, any time they feel hungry!' She shouted at me and the more she did so, the more stubborn I became.

"You are not going to school until you have eaten that cabbage, and I shall tell Mr Bickford why!" she yelled, obviously furious at my tenacity.

Time was ticking by and the school bell only fifteen minutes away, but I was not allowed to leave the table until I had eaten the horrible fibrous heap. In the end with about ten minutes to go I think she had visions of a visit from the school inspector and I was allowed to make a furious dash to school. I was frequently in tears by then but the wind against my face had usually dried my cheeks before I reached the classroom.

On the day the war was announced, I was just coming out of Sunday School at Upper Landywood Chapel, where I had recently started attending. We were not aware of the major national events happening that day. Even when I returned home for lunch neither mom nor dad said anything to me and, in all ways, it seemed a normal Sunday. For some reason, mom did not want me to attend the afternoon class, which was unusual, but I was not going to complain! I presume they were trying to protect me. It was either next day or the day after, whilst walking along Shaw's Lane on the way to the bus stop, that I asked mom why I was not going to school (it had been closed for a few days as part of the war announcement). Mom then explained to me that war had been announced, which meant that our country would be fighting a war against Adolf Hitler and the Germans. I asked who Adolf Hitler was and she made some dismissive comment. She told me about it in quite a matter of fact way and did not explain what it meant or why we were at war. For days, she had a very worried look on her face and was obviously not herself, but never let on why she was so down in the dumps. She and dad sat by the radio set, listening intently to broadcasts, and whispering between themselves. They had been about my age when the First World War started and it began to sink in from comments I heard that dad might have to leave us and go to war.

Within days, life around us began to change. People in uniform, air raid wardens or the Womens Voluntary Service, frequently called at the door telling mom and dad what they had to do and handing out leaflets. The postman delivered an official looking envelope which did nothing for mom's nerves, but simply contained three buff cards with dad's, her's and my name and a special number for each of us. These were our Identity Cards and must be kept safe. For a week or two life moved on with no more than a little additional hustle and bustle, but then calamity!

Uncle Joe, next door, received his call up papers to join the army. Both mom, grandma and aunt Ruby were crying and trying to console one another. Mom was convinced that dad's papers would be in the next post and every day looked pale and nervous as she watched the postman cycle over the bridge, no doubt fully conscious of the fact that three quarters of a million men did not return from the first World War. If the postman came up the drive to deliver a letter, she looked terrified and was visibly shaking. Fortunately for mom, dad was outside the age range of men being called for military service. Like many of his age, he would keep factory production going, making requirements for the war effort. Women would make up the vacancies created by those called up.

Uncle Joe was essentially a country yokel who had never left home in his life. His demeanour was that of a very frightened and bewildered man who gave the impression that this was the walk to the scaffold. All the members of the family he would leave behind were equally disturbed. I am not sure whether his problem related only to the call-up into the army. He had to make a long journey, something he had never done before, to the depths of Somerset, to Yeovil in fact. I was a child but, along with our families, I deeply felt the coming loss to my aunt Ruby, cousin Ron and baby Pat. The adults, no doubt, had memories both of the horrors of the trenches and of the number of names it had put on the village cenotaph on the gates of the Recreation ground on Walsall Road and the cenotaph in Cheslyn Hay. Why should the second World War prove any different? Their reaction bore witness to the horrors which we might expect to unfold over the next few weeks or months.

Two days later, uncle Joe handed in his free rail pass to the booking clerk at Wyrley and Cheslyn Hay railway station and was handed his ticket to the war front. There were cuddles, tears and much waving, I believe, as the train slowly pulled away. Those of the family who did not make the journey to the railway station waved from the railway fence outside our house, as the train passed by on the journey to Walsall. Uncle Joe was at an open carriage window and waved back, but it was a sorrowful gesture.

We were obliged by government edict to attend the Primary room of the Wesley Church on Walsall Road to be fitted with gas masks. Four large trestle tables were set around the room and WVS ladies were assessing the size of rubber mask, whether small, medium or large, for each person. A small mask fitted me perfectly and as I inhaled my nostrils were filled with the smell of fresh rubber. Other ladies were taping extension charcoal filters to the ends of the masks with one inch white adhesive tape which were then boxed and handed over for distribution. It was impressed on us that we must always carry our gas mask with us. The cardboard box measured about seven inches (18cm) by six inches (15cm) by five inches (13cm) and had a loop of cord to hang it around our neck. Aunt Ruby was given a special cradle-like rubber box, with observation window, into which she was to put cousin Pat should gas be used at any time.

Within a week or so mom like many others, knitted a case with shoulder strap in which I could carry my gas mask box. Everyone came to school with a different coloured carrying case, some ornately decorated, and for some mothers it was obviously a fashion icon and they purchased very expensive looking cases. Market stall holders in Cannock and Walsall cottoned on and sold gas mask cases made of Rexine (artificial leather) and other materials.

Every week, in class, we were told to take out our gas masks and put them on. Miss Liddle or Mr. Bickford came round each of us to ensure that we were wearing them correctly, since any small chink we were told could let in gas which would kill us. We had a great deal of fun with this exercise since, when breathing out forcefully, the rubber side walls of the mask vibrated against our cheeks making a farting sound. The classroom reverberated ceaselessly with loud farts. If the side wall was made to vibrate more slowly it sounded like a cow building up a cowpat below her hind legs. The exercise was considered so serious by teachers that this noisy but un-gentlemanly source of amusement was tolerated.

Within weeks of the declaration of war, there was an appeal for any scrap metal which could contribute to the war effort. Aluminium in particular and iron and steel were required for manufacture of aircraft, tanks, ammunition and so on. Granddad had in 1926 purchased the ground and ruins of the old Landywood Wesleyan Chapel at the end of Benton's Lane following the opening of the new Great Wyrley Wesley Church on Walsall Road. He subsequently sold the ground to a developer but the iron railings of the old chapel were piled behind his bungalow for future fencing. They were cast iron and were the first to be collected for the war effort. With the urgent requirement for aluminium, one or two reasonably good aluminium saucepans were collected from family members. Everyone seemed eager to do their bit to help the war effort. We were left with a few chipped enamel saucepans which, over time, rusted and became leaky. Once a hole had developed it was repaired with a 'pot-mender', two discs of metal with a cork gasket, held in place by a nut and bolt passed through the hole. This extended the life of the pan for a few months but frequently the cork gasket burned or rotted away. Along with metals, scrap paper and cardboard were also called for and we took bundles of newspapers and cardboard to school where they were piled in large heaps in the playground awaiting collection.

As a result of the demand for steel scrap, a feature disappeared from Bloxwich park which I had looked at inquisitively and played around on many occasions when we were too early for the bus home. It was a large rusting first world war gun, called Big Bertha, like an enormous cannon with huge solid metal wheels and a substantial barrel. This sat for years against the brick wall alongside Walsall road, but the country now needed its raw material for new armament, and it was removed.

Meanwhile uncle Joe was training for war on an army camp in Yeovil. Every week he wrote a letter to aunt Ruby on a very poor quality writing pad, using a pencil. I presume the salmon-coloured lined paper was produced from reclaimed paper and available from the quartermaster, but it was no better than toilet paper. Mom and I were also allowed to read the letters and I was rather bemused by the fact that, week in, week out, they always started with the same sentence,

dear Ruby,
i hope this letter finds you as it leaves me this
week we have been marching...........
your loving husband,
Joe XXX

He wrote a similar unpunctuated letter to mom to thank her for supporting aunt Ruby and the children whilst he was away. I did not understand the opening phrase and asked mom what it meant. She thought it was silly and was because uncle Joe did not know how to write a letter. Mom always considered her writing as state of the art and somewhat developed, compared with other people! His phraseology was another of those silly things that bugged me and every time I looked at the letter, which mom kept for many years, I puzzled over it. Sometime later I learned that the Army at times censored the content of soldiers' letters for security reasons, and Uncle Joe's letter immediately sprang to mind. Perhaps, I thought, his opening remark was army jargon, reflecting that all he had written may not reach her due to censoring. Whilst my MI5 interpretation was an exciting one, and somehow put Uncle Joe in a super-league, it was more likely a case of 'I am well and I hope you are too'!

Instructional leaflets abounded at the time and were delivered to the house, informing us of actions we should take to prepare for war. We were for instance advised to tape the windows in order to reduce the likelihood of flying glass should they be shattered by explosions. This was to be achieved with brown sticky tape applied in a diamond criss-cross pattern, much like leaded windows. It was quite a job because we had so many window panes and the taste of the glue was ghastly on the tongue, but we all did our share of licking. At the time most houses had these false 'brown leaded windows' which was not too unpleasant to the eye.

Another directive concerned 'blacking out'. At no time must we allow stray light from our doors or windows since aircraft could then pinpoint our domiciles or village. Mom made a trip to Cannock market and purchased black material with which she lined the curtains. Any leakage of light around a curtain would soon have the ARP warden hammering at the door with a ticking off, which happened to us on two occasions. Cars and cycles were obliged to use slatted filters, so that the on-coming lights could be seen by drivers and pedestrians but no stray light must shine upwards into the sky. All street lamps were turned off and thereafter, unless a moonlit night, it became impossible to see anyone or anything. It was only if a voice was recognised during a passing 'good night' that the person might be identified.

"S'that yoe, Jack?", queried dad.

"Ar, it is Harold, how are yer? Looks as though we might 'ave a quiet night, doe it! There was a lot gooin' on last night, wore there!"

"Ar, let's 'ope its quieter tonight, eh Jack", says dad as they go into a huddle to put the world right.

We had just purchased a packet of Smith's crisps from the off-licence and I was desperate to get home to eat them. They were becoming a rarity and therefore were considered a luxury.

"Come on, dad!" I chip in and start walking hoping he will quickly bid the stranger good night.

So far tonight it was silent, but we knew that a siren might sound to warn of the approach of enemy aircraft, an intermittent sound for 'Air raid warning' and a continuous sound for 'All clear'. The first test run of our local siren during daytime had surprised me by its volume. It obviously came from the Cheslyn Hay direction and, being inquisitive, three of us set off on our bikes to find the source. It sounded so near that we thought it must be at the Plant pit about two hundred yards away. As we approached the pit, the sound was still some way away and must, we decided, be coming from Cheslyn Hay village. Try as we may we never found the source of the wailing and it was several weeks before a relatively small device (similar to an extraction fan) was noticed, built into the end wall of the Fire Station opposite Coppice Lane. The sound level which had emanated from this quite small device mystified me and I stood on the drive to the cemetery looking at it and puzzling how it was. After all, a train whistle at the railway station, the same distance from home was barely audible. 'Why?' I puzzled. It was another query that dad could not help with and sat for years in the 'mystery box' in my mind. The answer did come many years later during a physics lesson and brought back memories of that day when we had tried to trace the first air raid siren of the war.

The first Christmas of wartime came and went. It was little different from earlier ones apart from the wartime appearance of the bungalow. I received my pillow case of goodies from Santa Claus, mainly fruit, sweets, a compendium of games, a Rupert book and, as usual, a small mechanical toy. These small tin-plate toys probably cost two or three shillings (15p) and had a spring which was wound to bring the toy to life. This year it was a blue bear pedaling a tricycle. The front wheel could be turned and I had it pedaling in circles around the table top. Previous years I had been given a small tin-plate bluebird car, a brown bear beating a drum and a tin plate motor cyclist with sidecar. The problem with tin-plate toys was that I invariably opened the tabs with a dinner knife and took them apart to see how they worked. On the first occasion I could re-assemble it and close the tin tabs but after repeating the exercise, one or other tabs would break off and the toy was eventually ruined. As I played with my cycling bear, it never crossed my mind that, because of metal shortages, it may be the last metal toy from Santa Claus. Our Christmas tree was as usual a holly bush with berries cut from a local hedge and decorated by mom. For lunch we ate the usual seasonal fare, a roast chicken with all the trimmings and, spent the afternoon in the parlour, in front of a blazing fire, gorging on chocolates, sweets and nuts whilst playing cards and board games, such as Ludo.

News of air raids on England was appearing in the newspaper and on the radio and there was now a possibility that we could be bombed. We were aware that the sounding of the siren indicated the need to take shelter. Mom was insistent that we could get under the pine table in the living room. It was quite robust and would protect us from the roof collapsing. It was something she always did during a thunderstorm since she was absolutely terrified of loud thunder and lightning. Granddad had the bright idea that he could provide a large air raid shelter to protect the whole family. He would sink a large unwanted wooden poultry shed into the ground and cover the roof with corrugated steel sheets and about two feet of soil. Uncle Bob was not really interested since he preferred to keep his distance from the rest of us. Granddad and dad, therefore, slaved away, digging a very large hole in the refuse tip which had been created at the top of granddad's large garden. They unearthed old tin cans, bottles and other buried rubbish in the process. The hole was excavated down to the original field level. An old sectional poultry shed about ten feet (3 metres) by seven feet (2.1 metres) was dismantled and the sections carried into the hole. The floor and walls were easily assembled but the roof created a problem and granddad felt he needed the help of a lump hammer to seat it properly.

"Harold, const hold the roof up, wharl I get an 'ommer?" he asked dad.

He ambled off to his shambolic tool shed in which he could never find anything he was looking for. Minutes ticked by and dad was by now struggling to steady the heavy roof, afraid to let go in case it collapsed on top of him. His sweated brow and face was showing the considerable strain when granddad finally came back, there was no apology, simply a heavy blow with the hammer and instructions to let the roof down. Dad was visibly very annoyed but as always bit his tongue and said nothing.

Once all bolts had been tightened, the roof was covered with corrugated steel sheets and then with ash and earth, to the level of the road surface, a depth of nearly three feet (1 metre). Over the next week or so, the inside was painted with whitewash and it was kitted out with wooden bunk beds. The finished structure made a very cozy air-raid shelter. We entered along a gulley, much like a battlefield trench. I suspect that a very small bomb travelling at over a hundred miles an hour would easily penetrate the roof and the explosion was likely to blow everyone into oblivion, but this does not appear to have crossed anyone's mind. This temporary home would create some semblance of security and would at least protect us from flying shrapnel from anti-aircraft shells and bombs.

Uncle Bob on the other hand employed a builder to construct a shelter with domed roof, three bricks thick, sunk into his garden and covered with earth and turf for camouflage. It was very small, just sufficient for himself, aunt Sarah and cousin Bobby. Compared with granddad's shelter it was very substantial and, with thick walls between bomb and occupant, would be far superior if put to the test. However, both shelters had their problems, as time will show.

In the latter part of January of 1940 there was a major freeze up followed by a blizzard. Granddad elected to fight his way through some six inches (15cm) of snow, which was drifting in places, to get me to school since my friends were not going. Their parents seemed to have the sense to stay in the house, but mom insisted that I should try to get to school, and I also wanted to make the effort. Since I did not have Wellington boots, about three layers of brown paper were wrapped around my lower legs and tied with string, like army puttees. Granddad and I set out and struggled hand in hand against the elements and arrived there to find very few children had tried to get through. Some teachers had not yet arrived and the caretaker was unhappy about clearing the snow. To be truthful, I was glad that we were given the day off, but felt somewhat righteous that I had attempted to get through and succeeded.

In driving snow and inclement weather, granddad was always a brick and apart from taking me to school also brought me sandwiches at lunch time. He did so for many years so that I would not get wet cycling home in the rain. Mom was all for making sandwiches to take to school like other children but he would not hear of it. Sandwiches wrapped in newspaper he insisted would be stale by lunchtime and not fit to eat. My peers never came to any harm from eating 'stale' sandwiches, but this was granddad and his strange ideas. Looking back his selflessness towards his grandchildren was very much over the top. I did, at times, find it embarrassing in front of my friends and was always glad when we had a dry day so that I could cycle home for lunch.

Such a deep freeze may sometimes result in frozen lead pipes cutting off the water supply to our homes. In these circumstances, drinking water was carried in buckets from a house which still had a supply. Water for the lavatory or washing was easily produced by melting lumps of snow or ice in a galvanised bucket on the hob.

Granddad at this time still owned four houses in Landywood and frequently following the thaw, a lead pipe might split causing a flood in the brew'us or lavatory. Dad was very much a do-it-yourself man and had all the necessary implements for lead plumbing. Whenever a problem developed in any of his rented houses, granddad's first port of call was to our house.

"Harold, theer's a bost pipe at Perry's! Will yer goon mend it, theers a gud chap?"

Dad never said 'no' to granddad, patriarch of the family, which seemed to be the way in those days. Mom would also add her pennyworth since she collected the rents for granddad and had to face a tirade from the tenants if there were problems with the property.

"I aye gunna collect Perry's rent, 'til yo've fixed that bost pipe, so yo'de better do it!" mom interjected.

"Dunna yoe werrit, ode duck, arl do it at the wick-end", was the reply she was pleased to hear.

Come Saturday afternoon, after work, dad set out laden with his paraffin blow-lamp, a stick of plumber's lead, flux and various hand tools in a bag hanging from the handlebars of his bicycle. Now having my own bike, I accompanied him for the first time on one of his repair missions.

I stood close by him, as he pondered the burst pipe and then explained to me what he was going to do. Lead pipes invariably split an inch or two along the seam created during manufacture and, before soldering the pipe, the edges of the split would have to be tapped together with a hammer. Dad borrowed Mrs Perry's washing line prop which he always used to turn off a mains stop cock outside any house he was working at.

He then set about preparing the blow-lamp so that it was ready and standing by. An old piece of rag soaked well with paraffin was set alight and the blowlamp laid on its side with its barrel in the flames. It lay there until it was considered hot enough and then, with a thrust or two on the pressure pump, vapourised paraffin hissed from the nozzle and the blowlamp burst into life. Well, this was true on some occasions but, more often than not, it took several attempts before the process was achieved. A few more pumps to pressurize the tank and the lamp flame was roaring like a hurricane, ready to use.

I stood close by dad, watching, learning. Residual water in the pipe, he explained, was always a problem, usually due to a leaky stop cock, since the pipe could not be raised to soldering temperature. The trick was to pack the pipe firmly with bread to dam it and prevent water rising. This would hold back water for about ten minutes whilst the pipe was raised to temperature. He opened the crack further and forced bread through, packing it down the pipe as hard as he could. This done, the split was tapped together with a hammer and the pipe heated to temperature, which took several minutes. Solder could now be melted, applied to the area and shaped with a moleskin (cured skin of a mole) into a half inch thick bulge over the site of the burst. The job was done and the water could now be turned on at the stop cock. After a delay of a few minutes, half a loaf of water-soaked bread spewed, like vomit, from the tap. Dad was happy with a job well done and we waved goodbye to Mrs Perry, who was now wearing a happy smile on her face.

With the air raid shelter completed, we were now as ready as anyone could be for Hitler's threatened onslaught. Apart from making the preparations for war, life at first did not seem too much out of the ordinary. However, it began to strike home when during the next month or two, bacon, butter, sugar and meat were rationed. It meant that dad, mom and I would have to live on twelve ounces (about 350g) of butter, bacon and meat and a two pound (1 kg) bag of sugar between us for a whole week. We had each been provided with a ration book and had to register with retailers. Mom registered with shops in Cheslyn Hay, George Keeling in Station Street for meat and William Perks by the Cenotaph for groceries. We were able to eke out the allowed ration with non-rationed goods such as sausages and black pudding (from Marsh and Baxter, of course), faggots, corned beef and the like. We particularly enjoyed the ready-cooked faggots sold by Eliza (Liza) Sambrook at her shop on Walsall Road. They were probably delivered to her from Wilf Mear's butchery a few shops up the road and we certainly enjoyed them warmed through for an evening meal with some of our own vegetables. Fortunately at this stage, though meat was rationed, commodities such as bread, cakes and biscuits remained unrationed.

During the Spring of 1940, aunt Ruby received some good news from uncle Joe. The army didn't want him. His feet were causing him major problems on route marches due to large calluses. It seems he would have been more hindrance than use to his infantry battalion and I presume he did not have sufficient skills to be used elsewhere. He was discharged on medical grounds and became a miner at Hawkins Colliery in Cheslyn Hay. He also, with the rest of us, put his effort into digging to provide vegetables both in his own garden and on the allotment next door. Like granddad, he also set up a large chicken shed, mostly white leghorns, to provide eggs and birds for consumption. He was now in his element working the land and keeping livestock, it was back to his roots.

Just before the war started, auntie Hilda worked at a snack bar in Upper Bridge Street in Walsall, next to Ackers-Jarrett garage. Mom and I frequently visited her for a chat and a coffee when we were shopping there. I liked auntie Hilda and this was a pleasant experience, since we sat on tall stalls at the bar, something new to me. I suppose I enjoyed it all the more because I could not be reprimanded about table manners and I could relish the strawberry milk shake she had whizzed up on her machine. Whilst chatting, she incessantly worked at the coffee machine serving other customers, an industrious lady who never seemed to stop working. When it was time to leave, she tipped the wink that mom did not need to pay. Whether she herself put the money in the till I do not know, but I should think it unlikely.

At this point in the war, women like aunt Hilda were required to fill the jobs vacated by men who were called up and she joined the Walsall Corporation Bus service as a conductress. She was as always very hard-working, dashing up and down the stairs to collect her fares. She had a very dry wit and took no nonsense from her passengers, ushering them here and there to a seat, with some appropriate caustic remark where she felt it was indicated. She particularly kept an eye open for the passenger leaping on the bus and making for the stairs. For her, it was a climb too many to collect a single fare.

"Oi, granddad, if you're going on top, take your fare with you!"

The passenger inevitably responded to the order and shuffled back down, even if now nearly at the top. Woe betide him should he dare challenge her command, she would be waiting for him at the end of his journey and give him the length of her tongue! At other times she would be seen between stops, sitting on the back side seat of the saloon, holding her captive audience in stitches with her repartee.

On one journey, a lady put her shopping in the luggage hopper under the stairs and, when she retrieved it, the butter on top of her bag was now a dripping yellow liquid enveloping the other contents. She remonstrated with aunt Hilda for not telling her that it was hot in the luggage bay. Aunt Hilda bellowed that it was not her job to watch her bloody butter, she had enough to do running up and down stairs taking bloody fares.

"But what shall I tell my husband, it's our weekly ration?" the passenger plaintively asked, obviously very distressed and hoping for some encouraging remark.

"Tell him he's lucky! He's got butter with everything, the rest of us have to suffer bloody margarine!" was aunt Hilda's retort.

A few of the bus conductors were fun to ride with. An older male colleague of hers who was not particularly keen on passengers standing in the saloon, regaled them with,

"Come on, I don't want you standing in here, there are plenty of seats in the loft!"

Their humour kept passengers highly amused on the journey and many passengers were attracted to the saloon simply so that they could enjoy the theatre. The only times I sat in the saloon was when I noticed one of the conducter 'comedians' on duty. I enjoyed a good laugh.

With the arrival of Spring I suffered another childhood illness, this time 'yeller jarnders' as grandma and mom called it, more properly yellow jaundice (hepatitis). My eyes and body turned yellow and I felt and was very sick. I did not want food and if I did eat it very quickly came back. Once again I was committed to my bedroom with mom caring for me. Dr Middleton put me on a special diet and prescribed some revolting medicine, brown and cloudy in appearance. It stank and tasted and looked as though it had been made with cow manure. It was certainly no cherry linctus! Mom insisted that I take it and I always had a barley sugar ready to quickly pop into my mouth, sucking like crazy to wash out the repugnant flavour. I was allowed fish and mashed potato, but no meat. I was thankful that I could eat barley sugars and I think they kept me going.

A couple of weeks into the illness, I lay in bed feeling a lot better. The elation of this led to me singing at the top of my voice,

Jesus wants me for a sunbeam
To shine for him each day,
In every way try to please him
At home, at school, at play.

A SUNBEAM! A SUNBEAM!
JESUS WANTS ME FOR A SUNB.....!

I was oblivious to the fact that the bedroom window was wide open and the whole of Landywood must have heard me. I was also unaware that Miss Liddle had been standing outside the window listening to my rendition. She had called to see how I was getting along but had deduced that I was on the mend, as she laughingly remarked to mom. I was quite embarrassed because at school I was very shy and I am certain Miss Liddle had never before heard such a volume emanating from me. She congratulated me on my lovely voice. She was certainly the kind of teacher every child loved and she treated all her charges as though each and everyone was someone special. When we were sick, she would always enquire or visit. In class, she frequently updated us on Peter Turner, a boy from Wharwell Lane, who should have been in school with us but suffered from brittle bone disease (fragilitas osseum) which meant that simply picking him up might and often did break his bones. He was permanently resident in Coleshill hospital and was regularly visited there by her.

Miss Liddle was probably in her thirties when she came to Landywood School from Redcar, in Yorkshire. She was slim, a little taller than average and her hair was already beginning to turn grey. She frequently mentioned Redcar when chatting to us as though she may be homesick for her roots. She lived with Annie Garratt, post-mistress of Great Wyrley Post Office. She was softly spoken and exuded love for her charges, only occasionally being a little heated towards a naughty boy, pointing out that Mr Bickford was along the corridor. She listened to our questions and answered in a most caring way, ensuring that we understood. I was fortunate to spend three school years with her as my teacher and they were some of the happiest years of my life.

Miss Liddle taught us many interesting facts about England and its industry; illustrated stories about the hops grown and picked in the south east by pickers using stilts, fishermen on drifters out of Lowestoft fishing Dogger Bank, the herring boats of Cornwall, lifeboat men around the coast, kaolin from Cornwall and the porcelain made in the Potteries and many other interesting facts that we in a coal mining and heavy industrial area were unlikely to see. She brought the occupations to life usually with pictures and I sat fascinated as I listened to her. Every Friday afternoon she read us a section from a book, usually leaving it at a point that would whet our appetite for the next reading. A favourite of mine was 'The Wind in the Willows' by Kenneth Graham. She also moved us on from simple sums (arithmetic) to more difficult ones using two and three digits and calculations using pounds, shillings and pence. Since arithmetic was my favourite subject I never had any real problems with the complexities of adding, subtracting, multiplying and dividing money. Some of my classmates did run into serious difficulties with this level of arithmetic. As a child I was not aware that some of us are born with scientific brains and others with artistic abilities. This became more apparent later when cousin Ron proved to be an artist and had great difficulties with mathematics, as I shall describe.

The sums we were now doing had three columns and were quite difficult since we had to carry a sum from one column to the next using a different conversion factor for each column. There were twelve pennies to a shilling, but twenty shillings to a pound, or to take it further – two pints to a quart, and four quarts to a gallon – twelve inches to a foot and three feet to a yard. We were expected to remember these conversion factors and although I never had a problem it was no wonder some friends did. To make matters worse for them, Mr. Bickford might enter the class for a period of mental arithmetic.

No pencil or paper was allowed, just fingers under the desk, if necessary! He may ask anything from 'seven times seven' to 'how much will I have to pay for six pencils if they cost a penny ha'penny each', followed by 'how much change will I get from two shillings?' Those of us who knew the answer threw up our hands and gave the answer, when asked. Being top of the class in arithmetic, I thoroughly enjoyed the lessons, others understandably groaned when he entered the classroom.

It was during these lessons that I felt that Mr Bickford really liked me. He would put ten arithmetic problems on the blackboard and as we finished them, we took them to the teacher's desk at the front of the class. Mr. Bickford sat there as I placed my arithmetic book in front of him. With one hand around my hip and the other holding a red pencil he proceeded to mark my answers. For each tick I got my thigh stroked or a tweak of my bottom. He seemed to get satisfaction when he could put a tick by an answer, expressed in ways that were quite pleasurable to me, such as a warm hand wandering up my trouser leg and caressing my bottom. It was the sort of loving expression that I might get at home and added to my feeling of pride, having achieved ten ticks. With a gentle slap on the bottom, I was directed back to my desk.

One day, I was unfortunate to experience another side of Mr Bickford during an evacuation drill. If the school bell rang in the middle of a lesson we were expected to leave our classrooms in an orderly fashion, collect our outdoor clothes and gas masks from the cloakroom and line up in the playground. On one such occasion I was sitting in the dentist's chair, which was set up in Mr Bickford's study for the annual dental check. I heard the bell ring whilst the dentist was prodding my teeth but he continued to probe and I could do little. Given the all clear by the nurse, I went and collected my belongings from the cloakroom and wandered outside to the line up. Mr. Bickford was addressing the school and began to fume when he saw the leisurely way I had paraded outside, long after my classmates. He took me inside, pulled up a trouser leg and gave me a severe slapping of my bare thigh and buttock. It really was a severe thrashing which hurt considerably and my thigh was deep red for some hours afterwards. I was crying and told him that I had been with the dentist but to no avail, I had not followed the rules of emergency evacuation of the school. After that episode I saw Mr. Bickford in a very different light and was very wary of him. I still seemed to remain the apple of his eye with regard to my school work but I was hesitant how he might react to a wrong answer.

By now, I was quite proficient on my bicycle, doing wheelies and swerving around bends. I frequently made the sound of a motor cycle as I raced from place to place and I imagined myself in control of a powerful machine. One day, I witnessed an older boy riding his cycle which sounded very much like a motorcycle. The sound was coming from a piece of stiff cardboard which he had inserted between the brake calliper and front fork and was vibrating in the wheel spokes. I copied his creation and was very impressed by the result. The faster I cycled, the louder the 'revs' and the more the excitement. On my imaginary motorcycle, I felt empowered to take corners even more dangerously and revved my engine to full power as I accelerated down the bridge. It was an exciting development which made me feel very grown up and almost ready, I thought, to ride the real thing. One would have thought that I might have learnt the danger of high speed cycling, vis-à-vis my nose fracture, but here I was racing without a care in the world. I was thrown over the handlebars on more than one occasion but came out of the adventure more or less unscathed.

On some Saturday afternoons outside the gardening season, dad and I might go out for a cycle ride. We had several favourite routes. One, often used when returning home from Cheslyn Hay, was down Dundalk Lane, left along Moon's Lane and into the dog-legged dirt track by Spring Cottage, which rose very steeply onto the canal side. At the end of this path, a white counter-balanced wooden swing bridge could be lowered, like a drawbridge, to allow people or animals to cross the canal onto the track across the fields to Saredon. Cycling to the right along the canal towpath, dad extolled tales of this area, his childhood playground, where he and friends had played and swum as children. The canal terminated at the Nook Colliery at the end of Dundalk lane and we occasionally saw barges arrive to take on board a load of coal. They were pulled by a single shire horse with a long rope attached to a pole on the boat. A family including children lived in a small cabin at the stern of the barge. It was so small and yet they sat, cooked and slept in it, heated by a tiny coal stove. During 1938-1940, I saw about one barge a week, but canal traffic stopped altogether shortly thereafter.

We backtracked from the Nook, cycling the towpath towards Strawberry Lane in Upper Landywood and then down Street's Lane home. It was a route I cycled alone many times when dad was at work and enjoyed spending time on the canal towpath. During the summer months, the canal was full of life. There were invariably fishermen pulling out roach and perch, some quite large. The unused basins were quite overgrown with pondweed through lack of use. Large patches of yellow water lilies were usually in flower and their leaf pads created green fields over which water skaters and other insects constantly scampered. Large dragon flies dipped down for water and frog's eyes peered at me, their heads camouflaged with pondweed plantlets. Along the canal side, yellow irises and bulrushes were hiding places for moorhens and coots.

When all my friends had bicycles, we often took this route and might meet up with Gordon Challinor (in our class at school) at Gilpin's basin. He lived in the canal keeper's cottage adjacent to the basin. The parapet of the bridge over the entrance to the basin was quite low and made an ideal bench where we could sit and chat, tossing the occasional stone into the water to create ripple patterns. Cycling on, under the Strawberry Lane, Baker's Lane and Long Lane bridges took us towards Bloxwich and I sometimes used this route when on a errand there. Along this length of canal, branches of bushes and trees overhung the water and it was a haunt for several pairs of kingfishers. They nested in holes in the vertical embankments on the opposite side to the towpath.

By now, at eight years of age, I was cycling to places on my own and, when sent shopping to Cheslyn Hay, I could visit my uncles and aunts (dad's siblings). I knew their homes since, as a small child, mom had taken me in my pushchair to visit.

Aunt Nancy, dad's sister, lived with uncle Harold (Richards) and cousin Barbara in the terraced house at number 66 High Street, opposite Stanton's shop. It was the house in which dad had grown up and it is where he would have seen mom, as she worked in the shop. Aunt Nancy was a delightful lady with a quietly soothing voice, a loving smile, and always welcomed me with a big hug. Nothing seemed to ruffle her feathers and I never remember seeing her angry. On past occasions when mom and I visited together, she would make mom a cup of tea and they sat, passing the time of day, by a large coal fire in the small sitting room. When mom had finished embarrassing me with her comments about my achievements, I might wander into the enclosed yard where dad had played or go down onto the High street and sit on the pavement, watching people shopping. Anything, I suppose so that I didn't have to listen to mom spouting the same gossip I had heard at home. Aunt Nancy always looked sad when it was time to leave.

Directly opposite at number 57, adjacent to the High Street shops, was the home of Uncle Garland, dad's older brother and aunty Esther. Cousins Connie and Margaret were nearer my age and we occasionally played in the garden which fell down quite steeply from the house. After running around in the garden, the walk back up the incline into the house was like mountaineering, I remember. As I grew older I played more with my local friends and saw less and less of Connie and Margaret. Besides they were girls, and which boy at that age would play with girls if he had male friends!

Uncle Ray, dad's younger brother, who had been very close to him in their youth, lived at number 23 Wolverhampton Road with aunt Doris and cousin Terry, who was a little younger than me. We frequently visited them and vice versa. Uncle Ray was totally deaf following a motorcycle accident when he sustained a nasty skull fracture. With deafness coming in adult life (I think he was about twenty), he never learned to lip read and, sadly, contact with him was arduous. By the end of the day, aunt Doris had usually written messages all over the newspaper margins as she explained the gist of our conversations to him. Terry grew up with far better skills than anyone in communicating with his dad. Despite his handicap, uncle Ray always had an infectious smile for people he met. Like dad, he was an excellent gardener and frequently out-skilled him with his produce. He was my favourite uncle by far and as I grew older I frequently wished that a miracle would happen so that he might hear and we could converse better. Dad said he was very humorous and full of life in his youth and, but for the tragedy, would have brought even more joy to the lives of those he met. I know I would have learned an enormous amount from him. Their house was usually a stopping off place for a cup of tea if a Sunday walk took us in that direction.

CHAPTER 7

'Games, entertainment and services - all years'

In outlining early life, it would be so easy to omit a significant number of daily activities which were commonplace in all our lives, but I believe it would be wrong to do so. Our daily existence was obviously shaped by the environment and the times in which we lived. I shall, therefore, interrupt my chronicle at eight years of age to describe the games that we played, the leisure activities available to us at that time, the mobile services on the street, the deliveries to our homes and the many shops to which I ran errands. These topics I shall cover in named sections within this chapter.

The games we played in the street

We were always very pro-active in keeping boredom at bay by playing games and occupying ourselves in other activities. Some games, such as street games, had been passed down. Other games we invented ourselves and in the next few years, war games inevitably occupied a significant part of our play and will be described at the appropriate time.

Street games usually cost very little, certainly less than our weekly pocket money, and usually nothing at all. A few are worth a mention since they were commonplace and some could be played solo.

Hopscotch needed nothing more than a piece of blackboard chalk, sold in some corner shops, or failing that, any piece of limestone rock which would sketch on the road surface. We drew a pattern of eight squares, each with sides of about twenty inches (50cm). The layout was squares 1,2 and 3 singly in line, 4 and 5 as a pair, 6 a single square and 7 and 8 as a pair. We each searched for a nice flat stone which would not bounce or roll too much since we wanted it to stop within the furthest squares about eight feet (2.5 metres) away, after we had tossed it.

Standing in front of square 1, we tossed a stone into square 1 and it must land cleanly within the lines otherwise the turn was lost. If successful, the player hopped over square 1 and along 2 and 3 and landed feet astride into 4 and 5, then a hop into 6 and astride again into 7 and 8. Jump-turning around still astride within 7 and 8, he or she retraced their actions back to the start, tarrying in square 2 to pick up the stone before returning to the start. The stone must now be thrown cleanly into square 2 and if successful, the exercise repeated, jumping over square 2 (a foot in the square containing the stone was a foul). The object was to throw the stone into each square up to square 8 and back again to square 1, fifteen throws in all. The difficulty in the game was tossing the stone cleanly into the higher numbers. It was a game which could take an hour or two with three or four players throwing in turn. If the grid was successfully completed, the player started again. The winner was the person who had cleared most squares during the game period.

We frequently played with spinning tops since the lane surface was a level plane on which we they would spin freely. We could purchase a wooden spinning top for tuppence (0.8p) from any general store, such as Mrs. Challinor's shop on the corner of Benton's Lane. The top, usually made of beech wood, was shaped like a mushroom which tapered at the foot of the stem. The point of the taper was finished with a small steel stud which reduced friction allowing the top to spin for quite a long time. A whip was needed to work the top which we fashioned from a sixteen inch (40cm) stick from a hazel bush to which was attached a twenty four inch (60cm) length of good string. The latter was knotted at the end to prevent fraying in use. After wrapping the string several times around the stem of the top, it was held upright on the road surface, and with a sharp pull on the whip handle, the top was set spinning at high speed. In order to keep it spinning, the stem of the top was lashed firmly with the whip, usually making a loud cracking sound. The louder the crack, the faster the top seemed to spin. It was important to keep it on the road surface which was not always easy because a very hard whipping may throw the spinning top some fifteen to twenty feet. The winner was the person who could keep their top spinning longest, sometimes five to ten minutes. As a variation on this game, by using a selection of coloured chalks, we drew patterns on the dome of the top to see who had created the best effect when the top was spinning. We also added collages with coloured metallic toffee papers to create very stunning effects.

I have already referred to cycling, but we also had a great deal of fun with a cycle wheel or a car tyre. These we bowled, 'beating' them along with a stick about nine inches (20cm) long which was also used to guide them by pressing on the side of the wheel to change direction. We sprinted quite fast and sometimes raced each other from one point to another. I often used my tyre to run errands since it was less boring than running unaccompanied.

Tip-cat was easily set up and cost us nothing. The tip-cat was made from a small six inch (15cm) length of hazel, about one inch (2.5cm) in diameter, and sharpened to a point at both ends with a pen knife. A stick, about twenty four inches (60cm) long and half an inch (1cm) in diameter was the striker. The aim of the game was to strike one of the points of the tipcat with the stick as it lay on the ground. This caused the tip-cat to flip into the air and then, as in rounders, it had to be struck hard driving it as far as possible. The winner was the person who drove the tip-cat furthest. A strike of twenty five to thirty yards was not uncommon. Flying tip-cats were very painful if you were standing in the wrong place, as I found when one clattered into the side of my head!

A skipping rope, whether a posh one purchased from Mrs Challinor with patterned wooden handles or a length of washing line six feet long, could provide a lot of fun. We skipped whilst running and whilst stationary. Many of us could spin the rope under our feet several times for an individual skip, the rope moving so fast that it was virtually invisible. Most girls skipped to a nursery rhyme which they recited to the rhythm of their skipping, but that was a girlie thing which was not usually practiced by the boys, unless we had been challenged by them. Occasionally someone 'borrowed' a washing line from their garden, and it was then a case of how many could skip in unison within its twenty feet (6 metres) before someone snagged it. Three or four of us might sometimes pack into the space when the rope was long enough.

During the early autumn, one game in particular took over. Conkers! After the fruit had developed on the horse chestnut trees, we cycled for miles, even as far as Brewood, to find the largest and best shaped conkers. We were usually far too impatient to await the natural fall of the fruit and created missiles, boomerangs made from fallen branches, which were carefully aimed at the hanging conkers. We opened dozens of shells, looking for perfect shape. All too often they were paired in the shell and had one flat side which were rejected as not good enough for playing the game. When satisfied with our harvest we started the process of curing which varied from allowing the conker to dry naturally, sometimes hastening it by putting them in a warm oven, to forms of pickling, such as using vinegar. Everyone boasted a secret method for hardening their conker so that it would become the school or village champion. Boasts about hardening was a way of psyching out one's opponent.

When in season, playing 'conkers' was a sport played during every school playtime, but we also played among ourselves at home. In order to play the game, the conker was pierced so that it could be threaded onto an eighteen inch (45cm) string knotted at the end. It was important to make a good sized knot because the first blow could force the conker over the knot and off the string, a win for the striker! The passive conker was held by the outstretched hand so that it dangled on some twelve inches (30cm) of string. The striker wound his string around his index and middle finger leaving about ten inches (25cm), and then he forcefully swung the conker downwards, striking the opponent's with a furious blow. The essence of the game was to smash or significantly damage the opposing conker. A weakening crack was an excellent result, since the conker may smash on the next strike. Not infrequently a hit was scored on the opponent's knuckles, followed by a tirade of expletives. After each strike, whether a hit or not, the roles were reversed and the opponent could now wreak revenge. The game continued until a conker was smashed. The winning conker was now called a 'oner' and if successful in subsequent contests, a 'two-er', three-er' and so on. It was sometimes possible to go as high as six or seven wins, but in time even the passive blows damaged the striker's conker and it paid the price. It was a game which was played with a degree of passion and always a desire to win and own the best conker at school. If someone's conker proved to be well above average, he was inevitably pestered to reveal the secret recipe, usually to no avail.

At any time of the year we could flip 'fag cards' (cigarette cards) but it was a game won more by luck than by skill. All packets of cigarettes contained pictorial cards, which were collected to make sets of footballers, wild flowers, aeroplanes, makes of car and so on. The cards were in sets of fifty and collected by most boys and girls. An album could also be purchased for a few pence, specially designed to display the cards. At the time, smoking among working men was universal and relatively cheap and it was possible, in some families, to collect two or three cards every day. In my case, dad was not a particularly heavy smoker though I usually had a new card most days. Duplicate cards were frequently swapped between friends at home or school until a complete set was collected. The surplus cards, no longer needed for sets, were used for 'flipping'. Boys came to school with as many as a hundred cards and in a sheltered corner of the playground at

Landywood school, the game would begin. Cards were flipped or skimmed onto a patch of ground which was usually in a corner where there was little wind. Each player flipped or skimmed a card alternately and, when a player's card covered or partially covered one already played, he picked up all cards on the ground, sometimes twenty or more. It was not uncommon for someone to arrive with a hundred cards and go home gloating with two hundred but it was so much a game of chance that, next time, they may go home with none. The only rule was that the players must start together, someone with a few cards could not join in when the ground was already carpeted with cards.

Another game played in the corner of the school playground was 'Jacks'. For this we needed five steel jacks which were three dimensional stars with six points and about three quarters of an inch (20mm) in diameter. The five were tossed on the ground and one selected for the throw jack. The idea of the game was, using one hand only, to throw this into the air (about eighteen inches) and whilst in flight, pick up a jack from the ground before catching the thrown jack in flight. The pick-up was put down and the other three jacks treated in the same way. Next, the jack was thrown and two at a time picked up, then three and one and finally all four must be picked up together. When there were five jacks in hand, all were all thrown into the air and all five jacks must be caught on the back of the hand. If successful, the player continues with another round. In order to collect the jacks on the ground into a reasonable group for picking up, the player was allowed three turns of throwing the jack and whilst in the air, he could the brush jacks into a group. The flying jack must never fall to the ground or the turn was passed to someone else.

Games around water

The closest rapid stream ran from three artesian-like springs in the upper fields of Street's Lane past our house and continued onto the lower meadows to marshland and the Wardles pool. A century earlier, it was an open stream (according to early Ordnance Survey maps) running along the west side of the lane, but by the early twentieth century as miner's houses were erected and the lane re-constructed, the stream was culverted in a nine inch (250mm) underground pipe along east side in front of the more modern properties. At full flow, water thundered out of the pipe into the gulley on the railway property opposite our front gate. We frequently paddled and played in this stream which was clean and uncontaminated. As in most rapidly flowing water, water cress grew in abundance and I picked it for consumption at home, in salads. It had very peppery taste and, several sprigs sprinkled with salt between two slices of bread, created a very agreeable sandwich.

The stream passed into a culvert under Landywood Lane which was just about large enough to crawl through but it was so long that none of us had the guts to crawl its entire length! We used it for playing 'boats' (A A Milne referred to 'Pooh sticks'), the first stick through obviously the winner. It was quite an energetic game since we placed our boat in the stream at the entrance of the culvert and then climbed quickly up a high batter (embankment), across the lane and down the opposite batter to reach the exit where our boat would appear.

'Boats' was a lot of fun but God surely created streams to be dammed! There was something magnetic about running water that attracted us to this activity. On several occasions, we even damned the piddle flowing in the gutter along the lane after a delivery horse had relieved itself! We regularly dammed our main stream where it crossed the lower meadow, using anything we could find in the near vicinity to obstruct the flow; sods of earth, large stones, mud from the stream walls and tree branches. The finished dam might be fifteen or more inches (40cm) high, holding back a reservoir of water six to eight feet wide. It was quite a skill to build a dam when the stream was in full flow after heavy rain but, with a group of us working together, it was possible as we proved on many occasions. The art was to narrow the width of the three feet (metre) cutting by building in from each side thus narrowing the width until the remaining gap was of a size which could be blocked by dropping in a carefully selected large rock or clod of earth. It was not easy because, as the cutting narrowed, the flow accelerated. Once we had dropped our rock in place, we worked at super-human speed to build up the centre section of the dam. As the water level rose we frantically raised the walls higher and higher, paddling in the water now up to our thighs, until we reached the maximum achievable. Having reached our goal, there was then the excitement of creating a small hole below the waterline which quickly increased in size breaching the dam. It soon released an enormous bore of water downstream which dislodged and carried large stones like a mighty river in flood. The project could take a whole morning or afternoon, but there was a great sense of triumph when we were successful.

At the bottom of the meadow, the stream fed an area of marshland which was a haunt for three or four pairs of snipe who, in most years, set up nests in the reeds. They were quite safe from egg pilfering because the bog was difficult to enter without long Wellington boots, not easy to acquire during the war years. Adjacent to the marsh was a triangular pool set within a 'V' shaped pair of embankments which had carried railway tracks during an earlier industrial period. The sleeper imprints were still present and were large enough to suggest that it may have related to construction of the main line in the 1850s and 60s, at the time when the track ended at Landywood Halt. On the other hand they could have been earlier mineral line tracks between here and Watery Lane (Hilton Lane). A fairly large triangular pool of water was entrapped within these two embankments and the main line track and was always referred to as 'the Valley'.

We played around four ponds quite close to home, the Tenscore, the Valley, the Wardles and a small round pond in Snape's field in our lane. All were full of life though the latter two might dry up in a hot summer and did not usually contain fish. Frogs and toads abounded and in Spring all were brimming with spawn. Frogspawn was so plentiful that it frequently appeared as large jelly mounds rising about three or four inches (10cm) above the water level. We usually collected some in a jam jar which we kept on a window sill at school in order to watch the tadpoles hatch and grow. After a few weeks, dozens of small frogs left the pools and they could be picked up by the handful.

The Valley pool was about two feet (60cm) deep and held a larger selection of water creatures since it contained water all year round. In summer, great crested and common newts were easily disturbed from their shelter within the pond vegetation. Well-camouflaged caddis fly larvae abounded. Pairs of frog's eyes popped up between floating weed, taking note of flying insects. Bright blue lacewings flitted over the pond surface and dragon flies zoomed around the bushes on the embankments. When I studied biology, in my teens, these ponds became my source of organisms and simple algae for analysis under the microscope.

The Tenscore pool was the largest and deepest pool, with bulrushes and irises growing around the perimeter, but since it was fed by a rapidly flowing stream, there was little pond weed and it was sometimes possible to see the bottom. The stream originated from a spring in the high fields behind Fisher's farm, crossing beneath Landywood Lane and across the meadow towards the pool. Coots and moorhens nested within the bulrushes around the Tenscore and there were three or four types of fish in the pool, the commonest being gudgeon. There were also pike because we frequently found young pike in the stream below. It was not, however, a pool in which we could paddle since the perimeters at that time were the bases of the slag heaps and therefore very steep. The water was around four or five feet (1.5 metres) deep and the level never changed, even during the summer, since the pool had a weir at the exit. It had obviously been created by the mine owners, presumably to provide water for the large boilers which were adjacent to it.

We never knew why the pool had been given its unusual name and dad and granddad could not help. 'Ten score' was certainly a term used for a pig weighing two hundred pounds (100kg), a score being twenty pounds. Dad frequently told the story as we cycled past the marl hole on the hill in Saredon Road, of several pigs drowning in the pool on their drove to market. Since those days it had been referred to as the 'bacon pit'. Was there an analogy? Had something similar happened to a ten score pig or pigs at the site of the Tenscore pool?

We frequently tried fishing the large shoals of gudgeon with a bent pin and bread or worms as bait, but were never successful. We could see the fish nibbling the bread through the crystal clear water, but they seemed to have the wisdom of Solomon and avoided jumping on the hook. I was never aware of any significant catches from the pool, even by the professional fishermen, whom I regularly passed when journeying to Cheslyn Hay. The overflow at the weir ran into a long brick-lined culvert running beneath the railway sidings and main rail track, probably 50 yards (50 metres) long. It emerged as a brisk stream running across the Wardles meadow, and known as Wyrley Brook. It was yet another stream near to home which contained minnows, sticklebacks and, as stated, an occasional baby pike. Unfortunately it also contained steam-oil residue from steam condensate from the many steam engines at the pit, but more of this later. Due to this, there were rust coloured deposits tingeing the green algae and water cress but otherwise the stream ran fast and very clear and we spent many happy times trying to disturb fish from the patches of reed, catmint and forget-me-not flowering along the banks. At the other end of the meadow there was some two acres of marshland which in Spring became a field of pale lilac as the ladysmocks came into bloom. Along the hedgerows, in the shade, carpets of bright yellow celandines abounded with their highly polished green leaves.

Further away, along Coppice Lane in Cheslyn Hay, was Hatherton reservoir, used for topping up the adjacent canal which ran towards Wedges Mills. This was much larger than anything near to home, but similar to Norton pool. It was too far from home to be a regular playground but I often cycled past it and, if I had time on my hands, stopped to look at the water birds. During the warm summer months it was frequently used by swimmers. Unfortunately, in my youth, it did claim a life when a teenager presumably suffered cramp whilst swimming in the cold water, but dad had previously warned me that there had been others over the years, and I should not get into the water. When the wind was in the right direction, there was usually a diabolical smell from the 'monkey muck' works (Cannock Agricultural) nearby, where they created glue and fertilizer by rendering down animal remains. Whenever I had been shopping in Bridgetown or Cannock, I usually pedalled furiously past the works holding my breath as much as possible, sometimes 'taking off' on the hump-backed canal bridge!

We fished and played for hours in the streams, marshes and pools around us and in addition, during the summer, we used the year's fresh crop of reeds for weaving. A group of us sat in a meadow by a pool and, after collecting our medium, industriously created whips, baskets or parasols. For a whip, some thirty of the longest reeds were very carefully pulled from a tussock, ensuring that they were whole, of equal length and not too brittle. A bundle of eighteen were tightly bound with individual reeds, starting at the root end of the bundle, in order to craft the stock of a whip. It was important that this binding process was completed very neatly, since the final appearance of the stock reflected the skill of the maker. About ten consecutive reeds were wrapped around the bundle, creating a stock some ten inches (25cm) long. The protruding tops of the reed bundle were now separated into three groups of six and neatly and tightly plaited to create the thong. The completed whips were judged on final length and overall appearance. It was a skill which had been passed down and mom had taught me how to make the objects on some of our country walks, binding and plaiting as we walked long. A parasol was a similar technique with a longer handle and the protruding reeds bent over and fashioned to create a basket-like woven canopy. This activity, like so many other things we did, kept us occupied and was something we worked at whilst chatting among ourselves, much like a group of women knitting together. When really on our uppers for something to do, we could at least look for four leaf clovers and hope for good luck. It was rare to find one but I did find two or three during my early lifetime!

The smaller of the local ponds was that in Snape's field. It was at the lowest point of two or three adjacent fields and simply collected field drainage after rain. It usually dried up during most summers. The adjacent stream from the three active springs in the next field was not connected to the pool. The meadow was grazed and the grass kept short by Jack Snape's cows and it was relatively flat over about half an acre, making an ideal sports ground. We learned for the most part to avoid cowpats, but occasionally we needed a wash down in the pool! At least twice a week, during the summer months, we played football, cricket or rounders on this pitch. It also provided some mid-winter sport since, being the shallowest pool, it was usually first to freeze in a cold spell. It had the advantage that, if we went through the ice, there was no more than nine inches (23cm) of water beneath.

At this point it is appropriate to refer to our winter games. A freeze-up or snowfall certainly brought plenty of entertainment. After a good fall, particularly after the snow was compacted in the lane, the older boys created slides. The surface of these was often glassy and extremely slippery. After only a short run up, we could slide on our shoes for some thirty or forty feet (10 to 12 metres), and by taking a longer run up, the older boys were able to extend the slide further and further to seventy or eighty feet (25 metres) or more. One slide started by Eric Gibb's house and ended just short of our front gate, about one hundred and fifty feet (50 metres)! It was a very exhilarating winter sport and we all had a very healthy glow. It was a sad day when the thaw eventually came and the slide was no more.

Snowballing between gangs was commonplace following a fresh fall of snow. We threw the snowballs with some force and at close range and therefore any ice in the composition was severely frowned upon since it could cause injury. Nevertheless, the occasional ice-ball did get through and, if it landed on an exposed part of our body, it hurt considerably and sometimes resulted in a bruise for the next few days. An apology was always forthcoming and when I look back, I am reminded how caring we were towards each other, rarely doing anything with malice. We were not quite so friendly if we were attacking the 'Wyrley bonk' (Cheslyn Hay) gang with snowballs!

With any snowfall, someone in the gang would appear with a sledge, usually home made from spare timber their father had to hand. They were amateurish vehicles but usually did the job which was to allow us to sled down the railway batter by Shant's bridge. It was very steep and we rocketed down at quite high speeds. A well built sledge with rounded runners allowed a run off into the field at the bottom, but a poorly constructed one frequently dug in and we shot out off the seat, finishing the run on our backsides. On one occasion, with wet, icy cold, bruised buttocks after doing the first run, I sat on the railway fence and laughed at the others as they suffered the same fate. We played until our woollen gloves were soaking wet and hands so frozen that we could barely use them. This was the signal to go indoors and get warmed up again. Mom inevitably went mad and yelled at me for getting my clothes so wet. She demanded that I take them off before I caught 'double pneumonia'. Then came the 'hot-aches' as we referred to them. As my hands warmed by the fire, the pain in my fingers became intense, so much so that I vowed never to repeat the experience, but always did!

During one snowfall, someone pointed out a broken window pane in Liza Clift's bedroom window, patched by a piece of cardboard. It was a small pane, about six inches by four inches (15cm by 10cm), and ideal as a snowball target. We threw snowballs from the lane cheering anyone who had a near miss. Something like one hundred snowballs peppered the wall and sash window before one of us had a direct hit, so much so that it carried the cardboard with it as it flew into the bedroom. Our vision of a snowball slowly melting on Liza's bed meant that we quickly scarpered down the lane to pastures new.

During a very hard winter, a pond might freeze to a thickness of over an inch (25mm) allowing us to cross in safety. However, thickness was not easy to estimate and many were the times that I reached about five feet from the bank and a disturbing loud crack heralded a ducking as the ice gave way. The worst incident happened in the middle of the Valley when the ice cracked the length of the pool, gave way and created a 'V' shaped pocket in which I sat immersed nearly up to my neck. I was alone at the time and it was extremely frightening. Due to the slippery ice walls, I found myself unable to get out and had visions of freezing to death or drowning. My heart pounded like a machine gun in my chest. After a great deal of ineffective clawing, I did gain purchase on some weeds and managed to scramble out, my clothing saturated, but I learned a lesson about ice that I never forgot. When temperatures plummeted really low and ponds were well frozen we enjoyed hours of fun making slides from one side of a pool to the opposite bank. Before leaving for home, we would if possible break the ice to allow water to flow over the surface and create a new ice rink for play next day.

Games on a windy day

A fine windy day often inspired us to fly a kite and with this came the need to make one. Cousin Bob taught me how to construct a kite when I was eight or nine years old. We cut thin straight branches from hazel or willow bushes and stripped them of their bark to make two 'canes' or spars about an eighth of an inch (3mm) in thickness and twenty four inches (600mm) and fifteen inches (400mm) long. These we tied together to form a crucifixion cross and we then tied cotton from point to create the kite shape. During the war years, newspaper was used to cover the kite, wrapping the edges over the cotton surround and pasting with flour paste to form the completed kite. Thin strips of newspaper pasted over the spars tied the cover to spar and gave the finished kite rigidity. For the tail, a string with small faggots of newspaper at intervals was attached to the bottom and the length estimated and adjusted after its first flight. A ball of string costing a few pence was purchased for the line and connected to a loop of string attached towards the top and bottom of the main spar. The kite was now ready and we usually flew it in one of the meadows, running to get it into flight. The problem was that, whilst inspired by a windy day to build a kite, by the time it was built and the paste dry, the wind had subsided! Nevertheless, it was a day of fun and more often than not we had kites flying. The final flight was usually a nosedive into the ground, smashing a day's work!

One day, walking down the Cop from school, I was subject to the full force of a gale, something I had never before experienced. I was about seven or eight and not very big and found it virtually impossible to make progress. I had to lean at about thirty degrees into the wind in order to stay upright. At one point, a squall lifted me twelve inches (300mm) or thereabouts above the pavement and I was terrified that I would be swept away. I clung to the wall, holding on for dear life for about two or three minutes until it felt safe to let go. It was a unique and unforgettable experience and memories of it flooded back when, a year later, I watched Dorothy's experience in the Wizard of Oz!

A further widget we hurled into the sky during the war years was the streamer. This was simply a cloth pouch about three inches (75mm) by two inches (50mm) which was filled with sand to give it weight. A rope was attached to allow it to be swung over and over at high speed and then released into the sky as high as humanly possible. To this we attached coloured paper streamers about three feet (1 metre) long which fluttered as it fell to earth. I suppose it replaced rockets and other fireworks not available at that time. Red, white and blue streamers were commonplace as the war seemed to go our way.

Games around the railway

We frequently played on the railway track, albeit that it was illegal, but we were careful not to get caught! One of our first actions was to put an ear to the track to see if a train was coming. A train even a mile or more away could easily be heard. We often placed coins or nails on the track, so that they were flattened by the locomotives, to see what sort of artistic creation we could achieve. When not on the track, we spent hours sitting on the wooden fence along the embankments, either chatting, driving a pretend lorry or aeroplane (the controls stuck in the fence post) or watching the men adjusting the fish plates between the rails or knocking back the wooden retaining keys which train vibrations had eased out of their cradles. It was a great day if a complete rail needed replacing, when some twenty track layers came to the site and carried the long rail with special long handled forceps, ten men on each side. This more major work, which always appealed to me, was usually done on Sundays when there was no traffic which annoyed me because I was obliged to go to Sunday School and missed some of the fun.

Sometimes a passing train would oblige us by spewing out a cinder, which in the summer frequently set fire to the tinder-like grass on the embankment. Rather than extinguish the flames, we preferred to fan them and extend the fire until it burnt out at a natural fire-break. Even then it was not uncommon to urge the fire to cross the barrier if this was possible. Considering the many times that trains ignited the embankment, only on a handful of occasions was it necessary to alert the fire brigade because the tar-impregnated fence posts had caught fire. On the occasions that we were around, we were sensible enough to beat out the fire if there was a chance of a fence post catching fire, sometimes using our 'anatomical hosepipes' to quench the flames. We considered it important to save the fence or where would we sit to watch the world go by! In this way we saved the fire service from many call-outs.

Entertainment

In our homes in the 1930s, most had a wireless (radio) but, like many others, we did not have any other source of music, even though record players, pianos and harmoniums had been around for many years. Aunt Ruby had acquired the family gramophone, which had belonged to granddad. It was a square box, in dark oak, with a lid which opened to display a picture of a dog and the caption 'His Master's Voice'. At the side, a handle wound the spring which turned a circular table, when the brake was released. After putting a record on the turntable, a swing-arm with a protruding needle was gently placed on the revolving record and music was produced as if by magic. It was yet another thing that I did not understand and pondered on how the music was being produced. It was obvious to me that a new needle created a better sound than a worn needle, but why?

On many occasions, I pestered aunt Ruby to allow me to play her gramophone. My favourite record was a track of Sandy Powell, the comedian, playing the part of a somewhat tired and exasperated policeman. I played the record so many times that I narrated the script word for word as it was playing. Other records of the time included songs such as 'The laughing policeman', 'The beau gendarmes', 'O for the wings of a dove', 'In a monastery garden' and 'Abide with me'. I played them over and over again and sang to them. Uncle Joe was a bit sensitive about 'Abide with me' since it had been played at his mother's funeral. When aunt Ruby had been driven to distraction by the incessant repetitions, she ushered me out on the pretext that Pat needed her sleep.

There was very little entertainment in the home using pictures apart from books but I have an early recollection, at the age of three or four, of mom and dad taking me to a cinema in Cheslyn Hay. Obviously memories are vague, but I am fairly sure it was in Rosemary Road. Mom paid at the door and we went inside and found three seats where we could sit together. I can clearly recall it was a poorly lit, cold and uninviting building. I felt quite frightened by the place, the walls were drab and if I had not been sitting safely between mom and dad I would almost certainly have started howling. A piano was being played but almost inaudible because of the hubbub of conversation and coughing due to cigarette smoke. After about ten minutes, the lights went out throwing us into total darkness. I clutched at mom who put her arm around me and hugged me tightly to her. In an instant, the wall in front of me lit up and pictures appeared. I was awestruck but also a little frightened by the moving images. Then, looking at mom's face lit by the flashing reflected light, I could see that she was happy and I soon settled and got to like it. I have no recall of the actual films at the time except there were a lot of men in uniforms running around and I presume it was the Keystone Cops. Mom and dad and the audience laughed out loud, and so did I. It is the only time I recall going to this cinema and it presumably closed shortly afterwards.

A year or so later I was taken by mom to the larger commercial cinemas in Cannock, Bloxwich and Walsall, some of very high quality, but others poorly furnished and referred to by dad as 'flea pits'. I visited most of them during my childhood. A memorable early visit was with mom to see 'The wizard of Oz' at the Danilo cinema in Cannock which started in black and white and spectacularly changed to colour when Dorothy crashed into the land of Oz. It was the beginning of regular visits to cinemas with mom, usually on Saturday afternoon. Dad rarely came with us on the pretext that he had too much to do in the garden. To be fair, he had also worked at Gilpin's for several hours in the morning.

If we were going to see a film at the 'Picture House' or 'Danilo' in Cannock, we always had tea at Stanton's Restaurant in Wolverhampton Road before returning home. An alternative was the Gaumont cinema, on the Bridge in Walsall, where they had their own very posh restaurant between floors. Mom ordered a pot of tea for two and two slices of rich gateaux, about one shilling and sixpence (7.5p). In later years, rationing and shortages led to restrictions at home and it was a special luxury to eat out at these restaurants.

The modern cinemas like the Danilo and Gaumont were more classy than some of the others, like the Forum and Picture House in Cannock. We always arrived before the lights went down and sat on the front row of the balcony. We were entertained with a visual display, rather ostentatious satin drapes dramatically changing colour to the rhythm of the music. At the Danilo, the first picture always appearing on the screen as the drapes rose was a Stanton's advertisement, extolling that their bread provided a balanced diet. This unchanged message, week in week out, was so boring that it put me off Stantons! Get out of the way, I thought, and lets get on with the real films. Having said this, I also found some of the main films extremely boring and I was persistently warned about shuffling and fidgeting in my seat, disturbing other film-goers. Some, such as the Dracula stories and Peter Lorre in 'Maltese Falcon' frightened me terribly, whilst others like 'Brief Encounter' had mom crying, and I never understood why. I always preferred comedy films, in particular those starring George Formby, Will Hay, Laurel and Hardy, Abbott and Costello and the Marx brothers, or cowboy films starring Roy Rogers and Trigger, his wonder horse. The 'Gaumont British News', shown between the main films, was important to us, keeping us informed in moving pictures of events happening both on the war front and at home. It brought to life stories we were listening to on the radio and either worried us more or lifted our hearts. Most children attended 'Chum's Club' on Saturday morning, but more of this later.

It was quite common, particularly during the war years, for amateur film shows to be held in church annexes, using the old favourites of cowboys and funny men. All films in the early years were silent and it was the 1950s before a sound projector was used. The hut at Jacob's Hall Lane Primitive Methodist Church and Great Wyrley Institute were common venues and later Great Wyrley Wesley Church. Although the shows were amateurish, with breaks to change the film, they were very enjoyable evenings, particularly during the dark winter months. Cowboy chases always brought out a high level of excitement and screams of delight when the sheriff's posse came to the rescue of the good guy who was singly holding at bay about ten bad guys. 'Cowboys and Indians' films usually stimulated a game for next day, when we made bows and arrows from hazel canes and Indian headdresses from chicken feathers.

Walking home from the film in the dark, we invariably yelled at each other at the top of our voices as we recounted the film, and 'pshew! pshew!' as we shot at one another. Shouting aloud somehow seemed to take away the fear of darkness on moonless nights, particularly during the blackout of the war years. The fact that it was impossible to see who you were shooting was immaterial! When walking home alone, I was always conscious of accelerating through the darkest parts of a lane, eyes scanning rapidly from side to side, in case someone hostile was lurking in the hedgerows. I felt particularly vulnerable whenever I spotted a dark silhouette approaching, even though it was more than likely someone I would know. I tiptoed in the hope they would not hear me, and thereby not see me, as I took a wide berth around them. When I had passed, my pace quickened to create distance between us! On a moonlit night it was so much more comfortable because the lanes were almost as bright as if there were street lamps. In the 1930s, there was never more than one street lamp (about 75 watts) at a junction of the lanes which only illuminated a few yards in each direction.

Mobile and delivery services around home and other reminiscences

A fish and chip van visited the village on Fridays for many years, but ceased service in the mid 1930s. Mom frequently related the anecdote of my cousin Jack Baker, auntie Hilda's son, who on Friday evenings ran along Benton's Lane and Watery Lane (Hilton Lane) shouting "Chippo!" which was the signature call of the mobile fish and chip vendor when alerting his customers. On hearing Jack's call, many women ran out with a large plate or bowl to be first in the queue. Jack, hiding behind the hedge, was highly amused both by the response and by the bewildered look on the women's faces when there was no van in the lane. They reassuringly convinced each other that they had heard the call, before ambling back into their houses. It was obviously a comical situation from which Jack got immediate pleasure, and further enjoyment when he recounted the story to mom and dad. To some it was not considered funny and on a later occasion it was the menfolk who came out of the houses to see only a back view of Jack as he sensibly took flight down the lane!

Summertime brought out the ice cream vendors. A mobile service was provided by Rosa's, I believe of Italian origin, who worked from Cannock. The van was small and distinctively painted in pillar box red. At the rear, a shiny ice-cream coloured dome adorned a turret from which the vendor served his customers. His vehicle was easily recognisable, so that we could see him coming up to half a mile away, giving us time to run into the house, hoping to get thrupence for a wafer or a cornet. The ice cream was kept chilled in a box of ice of ice. The wafer tool, a rectangular box on a handle, allowed the salesman to sell half inch wafers at thrupence or one inch at sixpence (1.2p or 2.5p). He laid a wafer biscuit in the bottom of the tool, spread in ice cream with a paddle and laid a biscuit on top. A button in the handle allowed him to pop out the completed ice cream, which he served to us on a small square of grease-proof paper. Whether a wafer or a cornet, they were a delight to eat. Pressing the wafer biscuits squeezed out the ice cream around the edges which could be licked off, and the process continued until the ice cream had gone, leaving the crunchy biscuits to devour as the final pleasure. If eating a cornet, the norm was to bite off the tip and suck the ice cream down into the cone.

A variant on the ice cream van was Wall's tricycle vendor. He had a large box between two cycle wheels with hand rail for steering and a single wheel behind. The box was painted deep blue and showed logos for Wall's ice cream. On the front of the box, visible to all as he approached, was the slogan, 'Stop me and buy one'. He invariably shouted this as he approached and we did stop him if mom was with me with money. In fact prices were as low as one penny (0.4p). The box, which spilled out a frosty mist when he opened up, held packaged ice cream, essentially frozen fruit-flavoured sticks in a cardboard outer. My favourite was always the penny lime bar, a five inch long stick which was triangular in cross section and green and tangy inside, which I adored. The ice cream was much harder and therefore lasted longer than the loose ice cream sold by Rosa's.

Milk in the 1930s was delivered to our house by Sally Glover who kept a farm across the fields between Hilton Lane and Walsall Road. She carried the milk churns in a one horse float which had obviously seen better days. The dilapidated leather tackle was such that the shafts were somewhere above the horses head rather than alongside its body, cantilevered by the weight of the full churns placed rearwards of the axle. She was a florid-faced elderly lady who wore a shabby old brown coat, which was even worse than granddad's clothing, and a pair of fingerless woollen gloves. Mom had to take a jug to the gate to get the milk which was drawn from the churn with various brass measures, according to the customer's requirement. The measures, a gill, a half pint, pint and quart, had long handles and were housed inside the churn, hanging from the rim. The milk was very fresh and often still warm. Many children at the time, including myself, were infected with bowel tuberculosis from this untreated milk but, for most of us, it was only a mild infection with occasional belly ache. There was some advantage to this in that it gave us immunity to tuberculosis in later life.

When war broke out, mom changed her milkman to Ernie Smith who had a bungalow and small holding at the bottom of Spion Cop (Gorsey Lane). He did not keep cows himself and I think collected his milk from Hobble End farm at Newtown. He kept a lot of chickens and sold their eggs to customers on his milk round. He would also take orders for chickens for the table. He sold live chickens in various stages of growth to families who wanted to rear a few in their garden for eggs. He was a kindly man, tall, slim and another with long neck and prominent Adam's apple. His wife Lizzie (nee Dunn) was a very pleasant lady whom I was to meet in later life when we sang together in the choir. I have to confess that I hated Ernie's method of slaughtering chickens, which was to grab the chicken by the neck and wrench it to break the neck. It was very quick and effective but reminded me very much of the times I had had my neck stretched which I shall describe later. I felt for the poor chicken!

Our weekly grocery order was delivered to our home from William Perks, grocer, opposite the cenotaph in Cheslyn Hay. His driver was in his twenties and tended to throw the delivery van around the lanes like a waltzer car at a Pat Collin's fair ground. I am fairly sure it was a Morris van of about 1920 or so and was far from healthy. During school holidays, if idling my time, I hung around at the top of the lane at the due time and begged him to allow me to lend a hand with his deliveries. He was never one to refuse a pair of hands and welcomed me on board. The first point to observe about the cab was that it had no door on the driver's side. This had long since fallen off or had been removed for his convenience, allowing rapid exit whilst still on the move, a practice he used a lot. Gravity or friction brought the van to a standstill whilst he ran alongside offloading a box of groceries. The seats in the cab had exposed coil springs protruding through the worn leather covers which were tentatively covered with a tattered cushion. On the passenger side, the floor of the cab sported a large hole which allowed full examination of the road surface beneath. When he accelerated, I was mesmerised and disorientated by the road surface flowing rapidly backwards, so much so that I felt I might fall through the floor if I did not hang on to the dashboard. The accelerator itself was a piece of automotive art, a length of string, tied at one end to a lever on the carburettor and the other to the steering column. He transported us between houses by pulling the string with his right hand and steering with his left hand. A heavy foot on the brake pedal caused an alarming scraping sound as bare steel rubbed against bare steel. It was a van that in recent years had not been loved, only beaten into submission, nobly bearing the scars of hard labour. So many vehicles in the late 1930s and early 1940s were in a similar state of repair and only if there was a major catastrophe, not uncommonly a half shaft breaking (whatever that was!), would they be taken to a garage for professional attention. Anyway, Perks' van was the only vehicle in which I had ridden, apart from buses, and I thoroughly enjoyed the experience and did my bit in delivering the boxes of groceries to customers in the lane.

A later home delivery service provided dad with his 'neck oil', as beer was frequently called in grandma's vocabulary. The slogan, "Beer at home means Davenports", on hoardings and at the cinema heralded home deliveries of beer from Davenport's, a Birmingham brewery. Mom ordered two cases of six bottles of beer per fortnight, a dozen bottles to last dad for the period. Thereafter the lorry called every Friday, collecting the empty bottles in their orange wooden crates and delivering two more. Several families in the lane had similar standing orders. It was not uncommon whilst pedaling to school after lunch to see the Davenport's driver parked in the gateway of Snape's field for his lunch break and enjoying his own fare to wash down his sandwiches. I assume it was a perk of the job.

The local shops I visited

Let me go on to the village shops that I regularly visited when running errands. For the most part, purchases for daily living were made at a handful of local shops which I refer to in other places, William Perks, the grocer; George Keeling, the butcher; Mr. Eccleshall, the greengrocer; Mrs. Challinor and Florrie Moore, the 'corner shops'; Liza Sambrook, groceries, bread and milk; Owen's, the fish and chip shop and so on. Most days, mom would send me on an errand to one or other for something she needed.

'Corner shops' stocked a variety of items used in everyday life. Mrs Challinor ran the shop in Landywood at the end of Benton's Lane and I shall describe hers as an example of the several around. It was possibly the shop opened in Landywood by my great great grandmother, Betsy Ann Bird. I have only recently uncovered her history and certainly the houses around the shop were owned by granddad in my early years. During my first few years it had gas lighting, which always held my attention, since she pulled a chain and lit the mantle with a match. I didn't understand why there was no switch involved as at home. The front of her shop had a large window with advertisements for Fry's chocolate set in the glass and a door with a bell which clanged and brought her into the shop from her living room at the back. The window, separated from the shop by a low net curtain, was not generally well displayed, but used more for storage of items which had not made shelf space within the shop. Exhibited on the shelves along the walls of the shop were closely packed seven pound sweet jars, tinned goods and boxes of all manner of goods which she had to ferret through if you asked for something unusual. The out-house in the backyard was a storage area with barrels for vinegar, lamp oil (paraffin) and turpentine, along with cartons of other goods. No doubt the rest of the house in which she and her family lived was also put to similar use. People used the shop to top up on items which would more usually be purchased from the grocer or other specialist shops but being 'round the corner' did not require a longer journey. As children, the local shop was also somewhere that we could spend a penny or two (1p) pocket money. The following items are representative of what could be purchased in her shop.

Loose items:
Vinegar by the pint (760 ml), lamp oil (paraffin) by the pint or quart (1.5 litres), turpentine by the pint, for all of these we needed to take empty 'pop' bottles. Balls of whitening (egg shaped and weighing about one pound (500g) which were mixed with hot water to make whitewash to paint walls), blocks of salt (about four pounds, 2kg) for preserving and curing, sugar for jams and preserving, loose sweets (confectionary) weighed out from large seven pound jars, usually one to four ounces (30g to 125g), dried peas (for soaking overnight) by the pound (450g).

Tins and jars:
Jams, tinned fruits, tinned vegetables, cocoa, Bourn-vita, Brasso, Zebo, Mansion polish, boot polish, Gibb's dentifrice.

Packeted goods:
Soap powders, chocolate (various), tea, porridge, corn flakes, shredded wheat.

For the smoker:
Cigarettes (Player's, Woodbine's, Capstan and others), loose and packet tobacco (shag cut by the inch (5 to 10 cm)), matches, one penny (0.5p) clay pipes and cheap briar pipes.

For the seamstress and clothing:
Cottons of various colours, small skeins of wool for repairing socks etc., dyes of several colours, various tapes, buttons (usually packs of six on cards) and other fastenings, zips, curtain hooks and rings and needles for sewing and knitting. Socks, stockings, safety pins, hair grips and hair nets.

Medicines:
Cough mixture, Aspro (aspirin), Beecham's powders (for flu), castor and olive oil, senna pods and Syrup of figs (for regular bowels), Victory V lozenges and fisherman's friend (for the throat), Vaseline, Germoline (for grazes) and other patent medicines.

Other products:

Small toys such as dolls, playing cards, spinning tops, skipping ropes, gas mantles, pencils, pens, ink, writing pads, envelopes, post cards and paper balls and streamers (Christmas decorations).

I am sure there were many other items since she seemed to sell 'everything' but the list is reasonably representative of shops such as hers, Florrie Moore's and Liza Sambrook's. In addition, Florrie sold greengrocery and Liza sold grocery items and bread. However, there were other shops in the village which I visited less frequently but are worth a mention. Come with me as I cycle around the village to the shops I visited, starting on Walsall Road in Great Wyrley.

The Walsall Co-operative Wholesale Society stood at the end of Hilton Lane opposite Dr. Middleton's surgery and 'The Star' pub on Walsall Road. It was the largest grocery and hardware store in the area and used regularly by mom, if only to get the 'divie' (dividend). We might buy a broom, bucket or washing bowl or the occasional grocery item. For every purchase, we gave our number '52108' and received a small ticket, not unlike a raffle ticket, which was a receipt for the purchase. Every quarter mom received notification by post informing her that she had earned a dividend and when and where this would be paid out. On pay day, I was obliged to stand in a very long queue at the store to collect one pound, three shillings and four pence (£1.16) or thereabouts in cash. People who used the Co-op for their weekly groceries picked up significantly more, ours seemed little more than pocket money in comparison.

Cycling down Walsall Road towards Cannock, on the right, is Great Wyrley Post Office run by Annie Garratt. It was here that Miss Liddle, my favourite teacher, lived. I occasionally used it for postage stamps or a postal order but could use any of three Post Offices in the neighbourhood, depending on other shops I had to visit. There was Annie Garratt's, Parsons' Landywood Post Office opposite Jacob's Hall Lane and Wootton's Post Office in Low Street, Cheslyn Hay. I used the latter most frequently and it was from here that Mrs. Holloway delivered our mail, since our home postal address was Street's Lane, Cheslyn Hay.

Just below and opposite Annie Garratt's Post Office is Ghent's Furniture store, standing back from the road opposite the dirt track which is called 'Love Lane'. Although Ghent's sell furniture they are more frequently used by villagers for furniture removal. Their three ton dark olive green van was often seen outside a property in the village being loaded with household contents. Mom did not really purchase from Ghent's, but preferred a shop in North Street, Bridgetown for our home furniture. When they were setting up home I was wheeled monthly to Bridgetown in my wheelchair to pay the installments for their furniture.

We next pass Wigley's clothing and haberdashery shop, a double fronted premises, where mom purchased much of our clothing, particularly underwear. Generally she used shops in Walsall for our top clothing such as coats, dresses and suits, though as a child mom purchased the occasional suit for me from Wigley's shop. A small grocery shop further down Walsall Road beyond the school belonged to Mrs Belcher but I never visited it since the Co-op was nearer home.

Frank Cowern, wholesale grocer, owns the premises on the corner of Norton Lane, opposite Great Wyrley Institute. It was from here that I obtained much of the timber used for various jobs at home, particularly for staging and shelving for the greenhouse. I spent many a Saturday morning waiting for the warehouse men to empty a bacon box which measured about thirty by twenty four by nine inches (800mm x 600mm x 200mm) and was an excellent source of three quarter inch (20mm) timber planks, difficult to get during the war years. The boxes cost five shillings (25p) but were worth it. Other people knew of this source of timber, but I made it my business to arrive early so that I was first in the queue and rarely left Cowern's without a box. It could be a three hour wait but, as I struggled to walk the large box home across handlebars and saddle, I was more than happy with my acquisition. By the time dad had returned from work, I had disassembled it, always saving the nails, and we could now get on with the construction job planned.

Dakin's Garage stands on the corner of Station Street and has doors opening onto this and onto Walsall Road. I often peered in when they had a car in parts and tried to understand what they were doing. One day I watched them draw out a broken rod of steel, the half shaft, from the rear axle of a coal lorry. As I have previously alluded to, many vehicles seemed to come to a standstill because of a so-called 'broken half shaft' and I hadn't understood. Now, as I looked at the oily broken steel rod on the garage floor, it became clear. Such revelations as this gave me a real uplift and I pedaled away smiling at my new knowledge. Dakin's also sold petrol from pumps on the roadside. In the 1930s the pump had a winding handle to draw up the petrol into a glass reservoir with markings to measure the required volume which was then emptied into the car's petrol tank.

I would now usually cycle home along Station Street and, either up the dirt track to Wyrley Hall and across the meadow to the main-line railway crossing, or alternatively up the siding beneath the railway station to the same crossing, thence through the Plant pit to home. On this occasion we must back track to the Co-op store and this time cycle up Walsall Road (towards Walsall).

About a hundred yards along on the right is Cowern and Hartshorne, our local chemist. Most of our patent medicines, Cod liver oil and malt, Scott's emulsion, Milk of Magnesia, Fynnon salts, Andrew's liver salts and so on, were purchased here. Our prescribed medicines were dispensed by Dr Middleton himself at the back of his surgery and were free since we were on his panel. However, medicines were also dispensed and could be purchased in the shop, when we simply asked, say, for our cough mixture of choice and he would dispense Ipecacuanha and morphine mixture, from a brown quart (1.5 litre) bottle on his shelves, bearing the label 'Mist. Ipecac. et Morph.' On rare occasions, when on errands to Cheslyn Hay, I might use Fereday's Chemist, opposite Cross Street.

Burke's newspaper shop is immediately opposite the Great Wyrley chemist and here, every Saturday evening, we queued for the pink 'Sporting Star' for the commentaries on local football matches. The paper arrived at about quarter to six so that reports and football scores were as at half-time, with a few final scores and comments in the Stop Press. At about six o'clock, a line of men could be seen ambling along Walsall Road with heads deeply immersed in the paper. By this time dad was already listing the final scores from the radio, using a blank template in the Daily Express.

Every week, during the football season, he had a bet on a football coupon which he brought from work, a line of predictions costing a minimum of sixpence (2.5p), and with fixed odds. As he listened to the announcer and logged the scores there was usually a "got that!" or "damn!", more frequently the latter. He preferred to get three draws correct since it paid the best odds but more frequently bet with four away match wins or eight home wins. On the whole, he just about broke even and never had large wins. Just after the war, greater odds became available with the appearance of 'Littlewood's of Liverpool' pools. There was then a chance of winning £75,000 on their 'Treble Chance' lines and almost everyone thereafter posted their coupons to Liverpool. Dad only ever had small wins. Uncle Joe always professed to being far more successful than dad but this was because he only extolled his winnings. The money for the bets had already been spent and did not seem to come into Uncle Joe's balance sheet!

Cycling further along the main road, the first butcher's shop on the right belongs to Fred Lawson, who's somewhat rotund stature suggested that he may have consumed a fair amount of his wares. There was a slaughterhouse behind the shop. Fred Perry and Bert Baker, a cousin of my mom, were butchers in the shop and were in later years contracted to slaughter our pigs at home. I am not sure why these were not chosen as our suppliers of wartime rations, but I suspect it was possibly a distant family rift which took mom to Mr Keeling in Cheslyn Hay.

The next shop is Albert Price's grocery shop which at the time seemed a fairly new and very compact single storey building. Albert was a very nice man and always very obliging for the few items I purchased there. His home, a bungalow, was in Gorsey Lane next to Ernie Smith's smallholding.

At the top of Shaw's Lane opposite Great Wyrley Wesley Church is the coal business of Wilf Sambrook. He was a short man with a moustache, much like that worn by Hitler. He was pleasant and very welcoming but always looked grimy, no doubt due to helping his driver in his large barn full of coal. Cooking and heating in our bungalow was by coal and every three to six months I accompanied mom to place an order. A knock on the door usually brought Mrs Sambrook to attend to us. She was obviously the book keeper in the family. She ushered us through to the lounge which was rather dark and had a thick sprinkling of coal dust everywhere. She did not seem to have the drive for tidiness and cleanliness, which was frequently the norm in some older people's homes of the time. She pulled a scrap of paper from a large old bureau and wrote down mom's order. The coal would be delivered in two or three days.

Wilf's driver delivered the coal in a tatty old brown lorry, the sides of which were buckling outwards due to years of assault by hefty lumps of coal. Some days the lorry was seen carrying loose coal by the ton (or half ton) and on other days it would be loaded with about forty hundred-weight (50kg) sacks of coal. These were filled on scales in Wilf's coal barn, using two fifty six pound (25kg) iron weights. The deliverymen humped the heavy sacks on and off the lorry and on his back up people's drives or entries, a significant distance. The sacks were emptied into the customer's coal bunker or in a heap at the back of the house. It was a very demanding occupation and the driver and his mate were relatively slight men, certainly not of body-builder stature. The coal was delivered to our house as a half ton (500kg) of loose coal which was tipped at the front gate. Dad and I transported it up the drive in the wheel barrow, building a retaining wall at the front of the coalhouse with the larger lumps. The smaller pieces were then thrown in behind the wall. Half a ton of coal packed the coalhouse to about three quarters full.

Continuing along Walsall Road, on the right is Liza Sambrook's shop, which I visited two or three times a week to get a Stanton's two pound tin loaf, mom's favourite bread. The bread shelves are stacked with bread from almost every bakery around. It is also a general store and provides grocery provisions for the local residents. It is one of the most popular shops in the village, possibly because of Liza's delightfully pleasant and kind personality, and she always has time for a chat. She never minded carrying 'a slate' which helped many of the poorer housewives feed their family between wage packets. I am proud to say that it was her granddaughter, Janet, whom I subsequently wooed and married in the years following this chronicle.

Steadman's (in 1946 it became Livesey's and in 1949, Evans') fish and chip shop was on the corner of Bentons Lane opposite the Memorial Gates. Before the war we bought our fish and chips from Mrs Pretty on Mount Pleasant in Cheslyn Hay but moved our custom to the new Owen's shop which opened next to Ernie Smith's bungalow and was a little nearer. It was a new shop and sported a brand new chip fryer in white enamel and with gleaming chrome fittings. They supplied high class fish and very crisp chips. Mr. Owen knew the importance of maintaining the fat at the correct temperature and incessantly fussed with the coal fire, sweating and working like a beaver. Mrs Owen served the customers in a very efficient way whilst he also worked flat out on the chipping machine, saying very little to anyone, just pulling the lever to produce bucket after bucket of freshly cut chips. He threw half a bucket into the hot fat which exploded with foam and he lovingly tended them to produce the crispy dreams everyone loved. The women in their respective shops, Mrs Owen and Mrs Pretty, always worked with bare arms and it was not uncommon to see blisters due to hot fat sputters, which were I suppose a mark of the trade. Even batter bits, removed from the fryer after cooking fish, were not thrown away. There was a special container for these each side of the range. A halfpenny (0.2p) worth of Owen's batter bits, a large bag, made a delicious snack and were purchased by many children particularly during the war years when potato crisps were in short supply. With the development of Owen's new shop, I only occasionally shopped at Steadman's because it was further away and the fish and chips would go cold. Livesey's fish and chips were considered far too greasy by mom and I rarely shopped there, unless Owen's was closed. I, on the other hand, always enjoyed fish and chips no matter where they were from, and would have cycled anywhere to get my fix.

Beyond Benton's Lane is Wilf Mears butcher's shop, again with a slaughterhouse behind his house. We never really purchased here but it was aunt Sarah's favourite meat shop. I loved Mears' pork pies, since they are so peppery and succulent, particularly when freshly baked. During the war years, mom was so unhappy with the meat provided by George Keeling in Station Street, that she obviously made a significant *faux pas* in not using either Wilfred Mears or Fred Lawson. Perhaps as a past shop assistant in Cheslyn Hay, she felt she should support trade there. Who knows?

Though not a shop but worth a mention since he knew us boys quite well, Bobby Morris lived in the row of houses beyond the butcher, set back from the road and next door to John Thomas, who was in my class at school. As we cycle a further few yards, we come to George Hall's cycle and spare parts shop opposite the Wheat Sheaf pub, with a repair shop behind. He also supplied petrol from a single pump outside the shop. During the 1930s, many houses still used lead acid accumulators in their primitive wireless sets, which George supplied and recharged. The accumulator heated the valve filaments

CHAT 'N' CHAR DATES 2016 17

Held in the Main Hall at the Salem Church second Thursday in the month.

13th October 2016
10th November 2016
8th December 2016
12th January 2017
9th February 2017
9th March 2017
13th April 2017

EVENTS CALENDAR

Held in the Main Hall at the Salem Church last Thursday in the month at 7.30 pm

27th OCTOBER 2016	" THE FINISHING TOUCH OF THE BUTTON" TONY KELLY
24th NOVEMBER 2016	"100 YEARS OF MOTOR BUSES" MARTIN FISHER
26th JANUARY 2017	" THE MEDIEVAL EXECUTIONER" JOHN S. WHITE
23rd FEBRUARY 2017	"YOU CANT ABDICATE AND EAT IT" MARY BODFISH
30th MARCH 2017	"SIR JOHN BETJEMAN" RICHARD FIELD
27th APRIL 2017	7.00PM- ANNUAL GENERAL MEETING- 7.30 PM-P. CADMAN

CHAT 'N' CHAR DATES 2016 17

Held in the Main Hall at the Salem Church second
Thursday in the month.

13th October 2016
10th November 2016
8th December 2016
12th January 2017
9th February 2017
9th March 2017
13th April 2017

EVENTS CALENDAR

Held in the Main Hall at the Salem Church last Thursday in
the month at 7.30 pm

27th OCTOBER 2016	" THE FINISHING TOUCH OF THE BUTTON" TONY KELLY
24th NOVEMBER 2016	"100 YEARS OF MOTOR BUSES" MARTIN FISHER
26th JANUARY 2017	" THE MEDIEVAL EXECUTIONER" JOHN S. WHITE
23rd FEBRUARY 2017	"YOU CANT ABDICATE AND EAT IT" MARY BODFISH
30th MARCH 2017	"SIR JOHN BETJEMAN" RICHARD FIELD
27th APRIL 2017	7.00PM- ANNUAL GENERAL MEETING - 7.30 PM - P. CADMAN

and, depending on the number of valves in the set, it started to go flat after a week to ten days, the quality of reception falling as a result. When I made a purchase either at George's shop or Hassall's shop at the top of High Street in Cheslyn Hay, some six to twelve accumulators were usually charging behind the counter, the many connecting wires looking not unlike a busy railway junction. This regular exercise cost the owner a penny or two (1p), and it was commonplace to pass the lady of the house carrying an accumulator in one hand and shopping in the other as she walked home. I generally called on George Hall to purchase a part for one of our bicycles, perhaps a repair kit or new inner tube. George's daughter Grace was older than me and in my teens we regularly worked together at the Wesley Church.

Further along Walsall Road beyond Wharwell Lane we come to Matthews, the cobbler and, opposite Jacob's Hall Lane, Landywood post office which I frequently used and refer to elsewhere.

With regard to the shops in Cheslyn Hay, come with me through the Plant pit and across the Coalpit fields, lifting our bicycles over the stiles. Straight ahead is the dirt track which is Mount Pleasant but we will turn down the dirt track to our right (New Horse Lane), a narrower track with overgrown hedgerows. On the gable wall of the house at the end is a Bisto hoarding which is periodically changed but always the same message, a smell of food wafting into the boy's nose as he proclaims 'Ah! Bisto!' Here, if we turn right into Station Street, the first shop on the right is Billy Brough's hairdressing salon and a little further along George Keeling's, the butcher, referred to elsewhere. On the same side further along Station Street beyond the rec' was the woodwork shop of Mr Hudson. He was often seen making a coffin for someone recently deceased and as always, when a specialist was at work, I had a nose in the doorway to watch him.

Turning to the left, up Station Street, and first on the left is William Perks, the grocer. This is a double fronted shop opposite the cenotaph. Every week I called in to take an order for our groceries which were then delivered to our door. On occasions, I was given a penny to buy broken biscuits from a tin by the counter, much cheaper and more variety than the undamaged biscuits, but tasted the same! Biscuits came in large tins about twelve inches (30cm) cube, and a stack of tins, all different, were built up like a wall at the back of the shop. Butter, tea, sugar, flour, dried fruit, etc., were usually loose and weighed out according to the customer's need. A whole truckle of Cheddar cheese was cut into wedges on a board with cutting wire. Butter was scooped out of a barrel and patted into shape before wrapping in grease proof paper. Tea came in plywood tea chests lined with metal foil, and a quarter of a pound (125g) was weighed and poured into cones of red paper bearing the 'Perks' logo. Sugar and flour was weighed from large canvas sacks. William and his assistants had a knack of wrapping loose ingredients quickly and efficiently and though they were not sealed with adhesive, they never fell apart.

Cycling up High street, on the right is the police station with prison cell behind and then Hackett's, another butcher, in a small stand-alone cottage type building. Further along on the bend is the Bricklayer's Arms and, shortly, on the left the other entrance to Mount Pleasant where Mrs. Pretty's fish and chip shop is located. On the corner of Landywood Lane (top of Jeff's knob), is a double fronted shop, looking a little neglected, but Mr Thacker sold animal food stuffs there. He later moved onto Mount Pleasant where he already had a barn for storage. On the opposite side of High Street is the off-license that I called in many evenings for a bottle for dad and granddad, just before the

Salem Methodist Church. Opposite the church and standing back from the road is the Glenthorne greengrocery and florist shop. Continuing up the High Street, on the left, opposite Cross Street is Fereday's, the Chemist, with steep steps and next door, I think, a ladies' hairdresser. Higher up High Street, on the right opposite aunt Nance's home, is the second Perk's grocery shop, I think brother to William. It was a much older building, probably nineteenth century, and not as salubrious as the lower shop. Next door is Stanton's cake shop (where my story began!). At the top of the street outside the Red Lion, the green bus (Harper's) stands awaiting departure to Cannock and opposite is Hassall's general store. There are several shops higher up just before Pinfold Lane which I pass when visiting Uncle Ray, but rarely use on my errands

To make our way to the Post Office and newsagent (our paper shop) run by Mr Wootton, we turn right downhill into Cross Street, passing Hart's butcher's shop on the left with the chapel lower down and the large house (I think Hawkins) on the right, and turn right at the bottom into Low Street. Half way along on the bend is the Post Office. Several of us sometimes used the area of waste ground next to it as a dirt track for cycle racing. At the end is Rosemary Road and opposite was the building which I remember as being a cinema, referred to earlier. I occasionally used the extension of Rosemary Road as a route to Bridgetown. Further along this dirt track, running for a distance alongside it were the remains of another old railway track, similar to the those on Coalpit fields referred to later.

In all, I suppose I visited nearly twenty shops in the three villages. A shop not mentioned on my tour is Eccleshall's greengrocery in Landywood at the bottom of the Cop. It was attached to Owen's chip shop and built in about 1939. Both Mr and Mrs Eccleshall served in the shop. He had a horse and cart (and later a lorry) which was used for home delivery from 1940 onwards. Mom often purchased greengrocery from his cart when he appeared in the lane. His horse frequently tickled us when it displayed the length of its maleness which nearly touched the road and occasionally produced a river of urine which invariably flowed many yards down the lane.

[Foot note:
In closing this chapter, I would like to make reference to the journey along Walsall Road described so ably by my old pal Bob Cooper in the Great Wyrley Millenium Souvenir and whose clever idea I have latched onto in visiting and describing shops of the villages. I would like to thank him for kindly allowing me to draw on his inspiration to make the subject more readable.]

High Street, Cheslyn Hay where mom and dad met. Stanton's shop was adjacent to the first telegraph pole on the right and dad's home opposite, by the car.

Harold Carpenter (dad, born 1905) and Ida Baker (mom, born 1907) pictured here around 1929

The cottage in Benton's Lane where I was born. Mom is standing at the gate in 1932. It is the house where, in my teens, I cut my teeth in learning the art of running repairs to property.

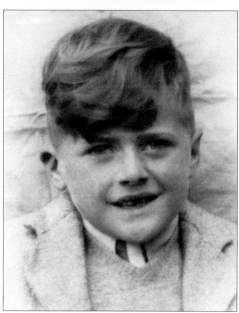

My first school photograph at 5 years of age, taken in the summer of 1938

Grandma and granddad, Bob and Liz Baker, photographed around 1910.

*Photographed in granddad's garden with cousin Ron in 1937. I appear concerned about something.
'Hurry up dad, I need to go!'*

Our bungalow in Street's Lane, here pictured in c.1955.

Granddad, grandma, mom and cousin Ron picking irises for sale six years after the garden was elevated by tipping refuse. The junction of Street's Lane and Landywood Lane (Shant's Bridge) is over the hedge behind them. Taken with my first camera, a 127 Coronet.

On holiday in Bournemouth in 1945 just after WWII ended.

CHAPTER 8

'Arrival of evacuees - c. 1940 - 41'

Back to my chronicle, in June 1940, mom and dad were asked if we could house a child or children who had to be evacuated from homes in towns in danger of invasion or bombing by the Germans. They gladly agreed to the request, as did many residents in the lane. Since we only had two bedrooms, it was recommended that they should find a boy of about my age, so that we could sleep together.

One evening, at about seven o'clock, we saw two ladies walking down Shant's bridge wearing uniforms of the Voluntary Service and leading eight boys, who were walking two by two like a small squad of soldiers. They wore labels with their names pinned to their lapels, gas masks were slung round their neck and they carried small cases or parcels with their belongings. We made our way to the front gate where one of the ladies offered mom a boy from the troupe. Uncle Bob and aunt Sarah took another boy and the residual troop moved on along the lane.

Mom led an apprehensive-looking Peter Hollett up the drive into the house. Dad and I were always very shy and followed behind. Peter was asked if he had eaten and he confirmed that he had. It was almost my bed time and I had mixed feelings when, a little later, we went to bed together. Mom tucked us both in, but there was stony silence, neither of us breaking the ice that night. Peter must have felt terribly lonely and homesick and I was somewhat apprehensive at the thought of this change in my life. It was next day before we really said 'hello', until now having done no more than eye one another up. Mom on the other hand was very good when she met strange people and was soon chatting to Peter about his home and family in Margate. Because of shyness, I needed more time.

As the days passed, I became acclimatized to my new 'brother' and we began to share each other's experiences. From my point of view, Peter had all the things that I didn't. His play ground was the seaside which I had only seen once for a brief encounter. Many nights, as we lay awake chatting, Peter enlarged on life in Margate. He had a brother David, younger than himself whom he obviously missed. He described in detail the very large amusement ground near his home called 'Dreamland' which had thrilling rides and sideshows. I boasted that I had been to Pat Collin's amusements in Sutton Park and the Wakes Week in Bloxwich, but in reality had to accept that this was a far cry from having an amusement ground almost next door and all the year round. I had a small Meccano construction set, 'Set 1A', but Peter was, at home, using the large angled rods only found in the much larger Meccano sets. I was overwhelmed by the thought of a later series

Meccano set and he agreed to write and ask his mom to send them to him. He also had a cycle with large wheels and again would ask his mom to send it to him. The differences in our life styles were the subject of pillow talk for many nights, and slowly we melded and he settled into his new life with us.

We obviously had differences, some to my advantage. Peter seemed to like things that I hated, particularly strong tastes. Mom was always feeding me patent medicines of one type or another and Peter was also expected to take his medicine. Every other day we were fed cod liver oil and malt which I found totally repulsive but Peter loved it. If I could I would always offer him my spoonful when mom was out of the room. The sickening thing was that he really seemed to enjoy it. Ugh! Every Friday evening we had a dose of syrup of figs or failing this, senna pod tea. The slightest sniffle or tummy ache and out came the Scott's emulsion.

There were probably around thirty evacuees in the village. At school, regardless of age, all were put into one class in order to help them settle and feel less home sick. It was felt unwise to separate them into their correct classes for a while. As it happened, the classroom used was ours. Mrs Mountford had by now taken over her husband's class and we continued with Miss Liddle in the classroom next door.

There were four or five evacuees in our lane so that my immediate group of playmates rose from four to eight. However, it was to be short lived since two of the boys returned to their families within a week or two, one was aunt Sarah's evacuee. Their families had purposely moved house into the country so that their children could live with them. Within weeks, Peter and Georgie Wright, who was living with the Farrington family, were the only two remaining in the lane.

Signs of change started to appear around us. Looking in the direction of Bloxwich and Walsall we could see many barrage balloons in the sky. We were told by David's dad that cables were strung between them to bring down enemy planes flying into them. We cycled closer to them for a 'nose' and found they were extremely large and constructed of silver fabric. As we neared it was possible to see the various cables connected to them.

The first air raid siren sounded at about eleven o'clock at night. Mom woke Peter and I and dad led us all to granddad's air raid shelter. We made our way in total darkness, since torches were not allowed. The buried poultry shed, illuminated by two candles, looked very snug inside and, because of the freshly white-washed walls, there was plenty of light. Peter, cousin Ron and I were put in small bunks and grandma, mom and aunt Ruby lay in three others. Dad and granddad went out onto Shant's bridge where they had a good view in all directions. It was far too exciting to go to sleep and we lay awake waiting for planes to come and drop bombs on us. We occasionally heard planes go overhead some said by dad and granddad to be German planes because of the droning sound they made, though they were more than likely RAF planes. It was an hour or two before the 'All clear' when we could return to our own beds, which by now were stone cold. It became commonplace to get up at night and go to the shelter. As the war progressed, granddad or dad came down from their viewpoint to report large fires on the horizon in the direction of Walsall. Sometimes, when the siren sounded in the early evening, we were allowed to go onto the bridge to see the search lights sweeping across the sky and we could hear the persistent banging of anti-aircraft fire. From this vantage point we occasionally saw fires burning on Cannock Chase. These were apparently decoy fires to attract enemy bombs to that area, where damage would be minimal. For young boys it was an exciting time but we were never to witness bombs exploding which would have been the icing on the cake!

Following a night of air raid warnings with heavy anti-aircraft barrages, it was not uncommon to go out of the house in the morning and find pieces of shell shrapnel and pieces of shattered roof tiles on the back yard. Two scars on the roof of the bungalow were visible for many years thereafter. Some pieces of steel might weigh eight ounces (250gm) or more and were extremely jagged. They would certainly have caused a severe injury or more likely death had they struck anyone. We kept the largest of them on the mantle-piece for many years, as a souvenir of the war years.

Life during daytime hours went on as usual. On Saturday, mom sent us both shopping. I went to Keeling's, our butcher, to get our meat ration. We were allowed one shilling and two pence (6p) per person. She always told me which cut of meat she would like and to remember the corned beef (which was not rationed at that time). I duly asked the butcher as mom had instructed me, but I would never know whether the joint given to me was good or bad. I simply handed over the money, about three or four shillings (15 - 20p) for our week's ration, and conveyed the meat home. Obviously we would get smaller portions of the better cuts of meat and I presume the butcher tried to balance quantity against quality since it had to last for a week. The corned beef made a cottage pie for one day's meal. When mom saw the small piece of gristly meat I had brought home, there was uproar,

"Where the bloody hell has he got this from, the knacker's yard! Did you tell him what I told you? I'd a good mind to take it up there and wrap it round his bloody neck! What am I supposed to do with it? I expect he's kept a good piece of sirloin for himself!" she yelled.

Her hysterical screaming could have been heard down the lane. I nervously re-affirmed that I had asked for the cut she wanted, but with impassioned anger she slammed the meat down on the table. I am surprised that she did not blow a fuse. Mom saw the Sunday roast as the most important meal of the week and it was an injustice of wartime that she was prevented from serving it to the family. As the weeks passed, she was going to find that many foods would become inferior in quality and, in many cases, not available.

Whilst I was collecting the meat, Peter was expected to get our place in Stanton's queue in the High Street to await the delivery of cakes. He arrived at around nine o'clock and stood outside the door, a queue of people slowly building behind him. I joined him there after taking the meat home. It was frequently two hours before Stanton's van arrived from the bakery with about four trays freshly baked family sized cakes and several other trays of small cakes and bread. We were allowed one large cake or a box of small cakes only and mom usually wanted a large Madeira cake. She could bake a Victoria sponge sandwich or small cakes herself, but large home-baked cakes went stale very quickly, she used to say, whereas a Stanton's Madeira cake would last most of the week. A favourite of mine was a bread and butter sandwich with a slice of Madeira cake as filling and the thought of this relieved the hours of boredom and constant nattering of women whilst waiting in the queue.

We not only queued in Cheslyn Hay, during school holidays we were also sent to queue at Taylor's cake shop in Bloxwich. We caught the Wyrley Whizzer from Shants bridge and within fifteen minutes we were in Bloxwich, standing in a queue for another Madeira cake!

A regular passenger on the Wyrley Whizzer was Mrs 'Pretty' (Harriet Hawkins) and every day at eleven o'clock she could be seen sitting at the front of the bus, travelling to Digbeth, Walsall for her fish. She was so named by locals because she was blessed with a very unattractive face and, in view of this, was the butt of many a joke. She was in reality an extremely nice lady who ran her fish and chip business from her shop on Mount Pleasant. Her produce was of the highest quality, very fresh fish with thin crisp batter and freshly cooked chips. Either Peter or I made the journey to her shop every week, after dad had returned from work, to collect fish and chips for one evening meal.

"Tell yer mam this is a bootiful piece of fresh cod an' I know her'll enjye it", she pronounced with authority, her voice distorted by a totally blocked nose, as she carefully wrapped the crisp fish in grease proof paper and then two pages of the Express and Star,

"That'll be one an' thrupence, thluv" she said, giving me change.

On many occasions in later years, I was to witness Mrs 'Pretty' at Phillips fresh fish shop in Digbeth in Walsall. She was turning over large cod and haddock fillets in boxes of ice, making sure she had the pick of the market to cook later that day. Her laden shopping bags were always so heavy that she physically struggled to get them back to the trolley bus to make her way home, her face highly flushed with the strain. She always promoted fresh fish in her shop and fresh it certainly was.

Every third Saturday morning without fail was hair-cut day. Peter and I set out very early, usually before Billy Brough, the hairdresser arrived at his salon on Station Street. Our early arrival was in the hope that he would cut our hair before the men began arriving. Billy was a part time hairdresser, who cut hair most evenings and Saturday morning and worked elsewhere during working days. The salon was the front room of a normal residence. Hot water for shaving was provided from a silver samovar heated by gas. We always had to wait for the ritual filling and lighting of the samovar before he would start cutting hair. There was no running water and he obtained refills by knocking the inter-communicating door between him and the back property. We sat there silently, mentally urging him to get a move on since we knew that at any moment a man might walk in. We were taught that children should always give way to adults but on many occasions we did successfully have our trim before nine o'clock. On other occasions we might have to wait until nearly noon as one man after another came in. We sat patiently reading either John Bull or Picture Post, an excellent magazine with outstanding black and white photographs of topical subjects. I think I read virtually every Picture Post printed from cover to cover during that period. I also liked John Bull's competition called 'Bullets', a competition to produce a witty comment in few words on a given topic. I avidly turned to this page first where the results of the previous competition inevitably drew a smile. Two famous ones were, on a wedding theme, *'Aisle, altar, hymn'!* and on man's effort, *'On and on he plodded; anon applauded'*. Trying to think of a good entry for this week's theme at least passed the time. Billy Brough could cut a man's hair in about ten minutes and a boy's hair in five minutes, afterwards spraying the hair with a perfumed atomiser before combing. We heard all the chit-chat about Cheslyn Hay in his salon and on my return home I usually recounted them to mom, after her invariable first remark to me,

"I see he has cut bloody great steps in your hair again, I could have cut it better with the garden shears!"

She then set about combing and refashioning it into the waves that she preferred to see. Peter had straight mousy hair which she was unable to get into waves, hard as she tried, and frequently told him that he should have hair like mine. Would anyone want his hair to look and behave like mine, I thought, since it was forever falling into my eyes! Mr Bickford frequently embarrassed me in front of the class by telling me that he was going to find a girl's ribbon or hair grip to keep it out of my eyes.

Sometimes the outcome of an errand was not as mom had anticipated. Peter and I were sent one day during the Easter holidays to get a cake from Taylors in Bloxwich. As we alighted from the Wyrley Whizzer, I caught sight of a boy walking out of a shop on the corner of Samuel Street, eating a toffee bar. Such items were becoming quite rare in shops and the sight certainly made the old saliva flow. We went into a huddle and felt that mom would be far happier with sweets than she would a cake which we could get at any time. Our plan was to go into the shop individually and ask for two penny toffee bars, the limit per customer. The four toffee bars made a rare sight in the bottom of our shopping basket. Since we were both wearing grey balaclavas knitted by mom, a fashion at the time, we thought the wizened old lady was unlikely to notice if we took them off and did a second run. This we duly did. She served me but challenged Peter.

"Haven't I just served you?" she queried, giving him the evil eye.

He was briefly taken aback by the question but quickly gathered his wits and explained that his twin brother had told him that she had sweets! We were now the proud owners of eight toffee bars and were itching to get home to tell mom how well we had done. She was appalled by our stupidity, blamed Peter because he was older than me, yelled a few expletives at us and stressed that under no circumstances would we be allowed any of our acquisitions. Over the next few days, she repeated the story to anyone who would listen, sharing a good laugh with them. In the end she did relent, as she invariably did, and we consumed the toffees.

Dad usually undertook most of our shoe repairs, though our best shoes were taken to the professional. We used Matthew's shop, in reality a wooden shed at the back of his house in Providence buildings on Walsall Road, opposite the gully to Jacob's Hall Lane. It was fascinating to stand at the door of the shed and watch him trim off and polish leather on his various machines. Unfortunately he was not always reliable in his expected date of completion. Frequently promised next week, but I usually had to make several trips to his workshop before the shoes were ready. For this reason, I was glad that dad had a shoe last. It was possible to buy a piece of leather and sprigs to make a repair from Woolworth's. At other times he used the leather from ruptured transmission belts from Gilpin's which was extremely tough and cutting it to shape with his knife was extremely hard work. His finish did not look quite as professional as Matthew's though he tried very hard. He had to cut and sand off the edges of the heels and soles by hand before melting on black or brown wax to seal them, and on the whole it was a job well done. He also stitched shoes by hand when the stitching was coming apart. Grandma and granddad always brought their shoes and boots to him.

"Harold, purra few stayel studs in these ta mek um last a bit lunga, theers a good chap" was the norm from granddad, and when dad handed them back,

"That's a bostin job, that is, Harold, a rayel bostin job!"

Even when dad pointed out that the sole was actually coming away from the upper and was beyond stitching, the repair had cost him nothing and granddad was happy,

"Dunna thee werrit, ode son, them'll still last me a gud year a' tue".

A few months after Peter arrived, near the end of the summer holiday, we had our second brush with the law. We were both out picking blackberries so that mom could make jam. I was aware of the best bramble patches around us for large juicy fruit and I led him to one of the better ones which was a hillock in Jack Snape's field just before Upper Landywood. In fact we always called it 'the blackberry patch'. To carry our blackberries, we had taken a wicker shopping basket lined with paper, which we would try to fill before returning home. Although we were doing well, after clearing the patch, there was still an inch or two in the basket and we wandered on across the fields picking from the hedgerows, meeting David and Eric on the way. We had walked the perimeter of several fields, some of which were hitherto unknown territory, when Eric remarked that we were approaching Whalley's farm (Fisher's farm) on Upper Landywood Lane. We had never approached it from this direction before and went to have a look. We came across an enclosed garden and using an adjacent tree, David looked over the wall to see trees laden with ripe apples. This was manna from heaven and he, Eric and I climbed over to help ourselves whilst Peter stayed outside to look after the blackberry basket. We had not really got as far as picking apples, though David was already up a tree, when Mr. Whalley came up behind us, twelve-bore shotgun broken over his arm. He yelled at David.

"Come down, you!"

I was terrified since I had seen him use the gun to dispatch a wayward dog and I did not fancy a load of buckshot. We were all three ashen.

"You three can come with me", and we followed meekly as he directed us out of the farmyard. I looked apprehensively at the gun. I am sure Mr Whalley had not loaded it but I was scared stiff at the sight of it. I thought he was going to take us home to bawl at mom but he directed us left up Jeff's knob towards Cheslyn Hay, and ushered us towards the police station by the cenotaph where he knocked the door. There was no reply.

"You three wait here", he said, "the sergeant will be in the cells round the back!"

He left the three of us standing there and disappeared round the corner. We looked at each other, shrugged and raced as fast as our legs would carry us past the cenotaph, up the cart track (New Horse Road) and across the fields towards the Plant pit. We looked back frequently, knowing the range of a shot gun, but we were free. Mr. Whalley did know us by sight because we regularly watched him working his fields, but did he know where we lived? We were terrified.

Next day, mom asked me if we had been scrumping at the farm. My intense blush was a sufficient answer and I was given a rollicking. We later challenged Peter with telling mom but he insisted that he had done no such thing. As he handed over the blackberries, he had simply told her that I had stayed out playing with David and Eric. Yet again, it was bobby Morris who had called on mom to inform her of our antics. I dared not enlighten her that we had been frog-marched to the police station or she would have had apoplexy. I seems that Mr Whalley had known that I lived in the bungalows!

Peter became very much part of family life and was game with many chores which had not been part of his earlier life, such as collecting manure for the garden. We set out with a two wheel wagon made from a large box with long handles and a pair of pram wheels. I knew the best meadows to harvest manure. We jumped over five bar gates into fields of cows along Upper Landywood Lane, many belonging to Mr Whalley, looking for dried cow-pats. These we lifted with bare hands like stiff pancakes, disturbing hosts of working insects beneath. We made stacks of them, about ten high like a stack of plates, which we then humped back to the truck and made journey after journey into the field, until the wagon was full. Back home, the cowpats were intermixed with garden compost and dug into the garden. During the early gardening season, we made this trip at least once or twice a week. Similarly with horse manure, although I took a shovel, it was far quicker to use bare hands even for fresh manure! It was not uncommon to push the wagon home with muck-stained hands, unless we passed a stream on the way.

All our carts and wagons were constructed from scrap timber and wheels from dumped prams and pushchairs. These had usually been put out by families who no longer needed them and after rusting in the garden, they were thrown out. Sometimes we collected them from the Council tip in Holly Lane. We mostly constructed four-wheeled wagons using a wide wooden plank and the front two wheels made to steer using a cross plank which swivelled on a single nut and bolt. We sat on a seat over the rear axle and used ropes, much like horse reins and our feet to steer. Having the railway bridge and hills in the lane, we could 'cart' at quite high speeds along the lane and since there were few vehicles on the road, it was quite safe. We set up elaborate levers for braking but they were inevitably unreliable and we usually dragged our feet on the road, or steered the wagon onto a grassy embankment.

From about seven years of age, mom insisted that I attend Upper Landywood Sunday school and Peter was expected to attend with me. The Sunday school was held in the tiny Methodist Primitive Chapel by Philip West. He asked that we call him Philip, rather than Mr West, which was unusual at the time since he was a mature man. His hips and legs had been severely crippled since childhood and he walked with a very disabled gait, using leg irons and two sticks for stability. On occasions we arrived to find the Sunday School not yet open and wandered round to his house in Upper Landywood Lane and walked slowly back to church with him. Sometimes he was very late and we were invited to wait in the house by his relative (a sister, I think). It was quite distressing to watch him struggle to get his leg irons adjusted in order to stand up, which he was only able to do with difficulty, but would not allow anyone to help him. He was a lovely kind man. I found later that, surprisingly, he had been raised in a Church of England, not a Methodist church, and yet here he was leading Methodist services. Every week, we attended Sunday school at 10.00 a.m. and 2.00 p.m. going home between services for Sunday lunch.

Annually during April or May all Methodist churches held a Sunday School Anniversary. Chosen hymns and anthems were sung by about ten adults and fifteen children at Upper Landywood Church. We were trained two or three evenings a week for about six weeks by Tom Morgan and on the Anniversary day performed at three services. On the day, we were obliged to wear white shirts, a blue and white horizontally striped tie and matching blue and white belt with a silver hook buckle. For the 1941 event, mom was obliged to purchase two of these uniforms for both Peter and myself. This may be the last time since clothes rationing followed about a month later.

I had a pleasant soprano voice and was frequently asked to sing a solo verse in one of the hymns. It was a moment of utter terror on one occasion, the first service of the day, when I had forgotten my words and Tom Morgan played on without my verse. Thereafter, I was advised to have a folded hymn sheet in my hand by my side, just in case it happened again. With this reassurance, it never did. A year later we experienced a conductor for the first time. This was Howard Benton, who was brother-in-law to several members of the church. He used far more authority than Tom ever had and in some ways was a little frightening. I frequently think back to these days since we must have been the first Anniversary choir conducted by Howard who later became famous for his choral skills, first conducting the Cannock Chase male voice choir and, during the second half of the century, the Cannock Chase Orpheus Choir.

I enjoyed Sunday School, particularly visits about every two months from Joe Nicholls and Jim Fletcher, staunch Methodists from New Invention Church. They usually attended on special days, such as Prize Day. This was an annual event, a book prize was given to each scholar, the size and quality based on their level of attendance. Inside the front cover, a rather elaborate gold-leafed sticker showed the name of recipient and teacher. Everyone received a book and it was a day when every scholar attended. Joe Nicholls could hold us spellbound with his stories and had a few kind words to everyone as he handed them their prize.

In the lane, our gang had become larger since the arrival of both the evacuees and others who had come to live in the lane. With more people, games became more fun. The war stimulated us to play war games and we each made our own rifle from wood using either knives or, in my case, a spoke shave from dad's tool box. Bayonets were always made by laying a six inch nail on the railway track, which a passing locomotive would then flatten to create the blade. We divided ourselves into two armies and attacked each other across the fields, using camouflage and crawling on our bellies like real soldiers. There were always arguments about whether one or other of us had been shot and usually the one who shouted loudest won. It was during a vociferous battle with a gang of boys from Cheslyn Hay that evacuee Georgie Wright was pushed down the embankment of the Tenscore pool, rolling into the steam exhaust ditch at the bottom which contained around three inches (8cm) of steam oil. Earlier in the day, he had been out with Mrs Farrington and had joined our game still wearing his pale blue worsted suit. When he lifted himself from the ditch, though not hurt, his suit was caked in thick brown oil residue. We were horrified and lost for words. The Cheslyn Hay gang cheered aloud at their victory and disappeared homewards over the hills. Georgie was given a rollicking and gated for a few days by Mrs Farrington. We had a great deal of fun during this period and our battle field embraced a very large area, including the deep railway cutting alongside the lane.

Four new youngsters had moved into Plant's buildings, the terraced houses adjacent to David Loach. Tony and Ann Marshall were near to our age and became regular playmates. They had, I think, moved to Landywood from Blakenhall. Mr. Marshall, a miner, was a stickler for discipline and backed up by Mrs Marshall. He was one of three father's in the street who were not averse to removing their belt and using it as they followed one or other of their off-spring into the house.

In the next house but one, Barry Dorricot moved in with his father. His mother never appeared on the scene and we were loathe to ask questions in case she had recently died. He was about two years younger than we were, but played many games with us.

Next door to him lived the Clift family and, throughout much of my early childhood, old Mrs Clift lived there with Joe Plant as a lodger as I have already said. She died during the early war years and her son and his daughter moved into her house, again without the mother. My mom always referred to him as 'Dr. Clift' because he continually extolled his knowledge about anything from brain tumours to calluses when conversing with her and was happy to give anyone medical advice. He was a member of the St. John's Ambulance brigade and no doubt extremely skilled in first aid but had obviously read more widely, albeit no more than the average Family Doctor book found in most households at the time. His daughter, Diane, was two or three years younger than we were, and rather shy. She did not play with us a great deal, though played with cousin Pat. Boys and girls generally played in same sex groups.

In all, by the mid to late war years, there were about twenty children of varying ages living in the lane, about ten of whom were within a year or so of my age, though of course the evacuees were only temporary.

Peter (Hollett) was two years older and in top class where he was taught by Mr Shipman. In this class he was able to sit for the scholarship examination which could allow him to gain a place at a grammar school. The subsequent news was that Peter had been successful and by mid summer of 1941, we heard that he had been offered a place in September at Stafford Grammar School. This meant he would be leaving us for another family nearer to the new school. It was a sad thought because I had enjoyed having a 'brother' for just over a year. When the day of Peter's departure came, I sadly watched and waved as he rode his cycle up and over Shant's bridge into a new life. I must admit, I did enjoy the new spaciousness in bed at night.

During that summer, school gave us all a new task. The government had asked that everyone pick rose hips, from which rose hip syrup would be manufactured. It was a good source of Vitamin C and would replace orange juice which was no longer available. The hedgerows during the Spring had been a mass of dog roses and the fruiting was excellent. We took baskets or buckets and, after filling them, took them to school where a very large heap was created on a tarpaulin in the playground ready for collection by lorry. Not a single rose hip remained on the hedgerows around us during that or subsequent summers. A fruit that we had hitherto used as itching powder, tipping the fluffy seeds into the neck of someone's shirt or blouse for fun, was now going to help with the war effort.

Men in the village, who were too old or had been spared army call-up to work in industry, became members of local Home Guard platoons. Dad joined the Gilpin's platoon. He was eventually provided with a khaki uniform and a standard army Lee Enfield .303 rifle. This he was obliged to keep clean and oiled using a pull-through, an oily rag tied to a length of string with a weight. After a month or so, I was allowed to do this for him, but he impressed on me the instructions given to him. After introducing the pull-through, I must carefully pull the string down the middle of the bore and not allow it to rub against the sides. To do so may make the bore uneven and the rifle less efficient when fired. Once a week dad attended formal parades where they were taught army skills such as drill, guard duties and assault tactics. About every two weeks he was put on the roster for overnight guard duty at Gilpin's factory. Mom always felt vulnerable when left alone at night and, as we sat on the settee listening to the radio, we clung to each other for comfort and I then slept in her bed.

The Home Guard frequently played inter-platoon war games, and Gilpin's were often up against the Cheslyn Hay platoon. The battlefield was usually derelict properties and waste ground, such as the Coalpit fields and around the Nook Colliery. They were obviously not provided with rounds of ammunition and the 'bangs' to imitate rifle shots were made by pulling a cracker, a larger version of the ones used in Christmas crackers.

A bundle of five crackers was tied to the barrel stock of the rifle, each with a string which extended to the trigger guard, and 'fired' when the enemy was in sight. Hand grenades were smoke bombs. The battles between platoons could be very realistic with a great deal of noise and smoke. We were allowed to watch so long as we stayed on the perimeter of the battlefield.

Dundalk Lane was an ideal area and commonly used for their army games. There were abandoned cottages about half way along and plenty of scrub land, shale heaps and high hedge rows along the lane. We could hear plenty of shouting and cracks of gunfire. The men camouflaged themselves extremely well and, whilst watching one battle, I totally lost sight of dad. Even when the men were called to parade outside the cottages to listen to the officer's debriefing, I was unable to recognise him. I was a little apprehensive, but thought perhaps that he had gone home, or could he have been left for dead on the battle field? In fact, he was in the front line some six feet away from me, face painted black with coal sludge and twiglets of oak pushed into his cap and tunic which slightly covered his face. I was amazed how effective camouflage could be and, from then on, we used it in our own army games.

Dad's Lee Enfield rifle sat in the corner of our sitting room for about three years and I became quite an expert at stripping it down and re-assembling it. I regularly held the rifle to my shoulder, setting the distance on the rear sight, sighting a target and pulling the trigger, clicking the firing pin. I was not to know that both practices would prove useful experience for target shooting when I joined the School Cadet Force in later years.

CHAPTER 9

'The signs of war around us - c. 1941 - 42'

The news on the radio and in the newspapers was quite depressing at times particularly when we were informed of increasing aircraft losses and the tons of merchant shipping lost in the North Atlantic. At school we created a wall chart on which we recorded the losses as they were published. Every Sunday, the totals appeared in the News of the World and I always looked at the table of aircraft losses before anything else, even before perusing the football tables to check the position of the Wolves. At times we became quite downcast as we added information to our chart, particularly when our losses exceeded those of the enemy. A loss of a major warship led to even deeper despondency as happened when HMS Hood was sunk by the German battleship Bismarck. Fortunately the latter was sunk by our navy about week later which brought a fleeting uplift to our increasing despair. The number of merchant ships sunk by German U-boats in the North Atlantic was grave and it seemed that we were losing the war. There were rumours that we might even starve. I suppose we were not really aware of the amount of our food which was imported until it was explained by Miss Liddle. After this, our attitude in class was that we would do our utmost to grow more food at home! I went home and gave this message to mom and dad. We closely watched the trends on our chart and on the rare occasions when newspapers showed German losses to exceed ours, we cheered and danced with joy as we entered the figures. All to often, by next day, they had reversed again. How we hated Hitler and the Germans!

Whilst this news was appalling, the air raid warnings at home were actually becoming fewer and we now rarely used the air raid shelter. There was certainly nothing like the activity of a few months earlier. As we stood on Shant's bridge during a cloudless evening, we sometimes saw flights of dozens of our own aircraft flying over Churchbridge towards Norton Canes, no doubt on their way to Germany. There were still air raids on London and the industrial Midlands, the Germans presumably picking off factories producing armaments but none were really near to us. During the hours of darkness, we still occasionally saw searchlights in the Walsall direction scouring for aircraft, sometimes followed by a clatter of distant anti-aircraft guns.

We were never aware of bombs falling locally or of any audible explosions, but we had a surprise one morning when cycling to school. Some one hundred yards (100m) short of school the lane was being controlled by ARP wardens. The road surface near the junction of Holly Lane and Gorsey Lane was covered with great clods of earth, large stones and sandy soil. When we reached the site there was a large conical bomb crater on the roadside about twelve feet (4 metres) in diameter and six feet (2 metres) deep. It must have made a fair noise but no-one admitted to hearing it. Though very near to school it had not caused any damage. The only house nearby, immediately next door to the school and occupied by Jack Snape and his family, was unharmed, not even a shattered window pane. Over the next year or two, the crater was a source of clay for house martins which built about a dozen nests under the eaves of the school building.

Curiously, a few months later, another bomb exploded in fields at the end of Love Lane, not all that far from Great Wyrley Junior School. We cycled to see it and the crater was of a similar size. Had the German bombers aimed for our schools, we thought? Most unlikely, but what a coincidence, and how near we were to everlasting school holidays!

Whilst these bombs had caused no real damage, it was a very different picture when making a journey on the Midland Red from Walsall bus station to Birmingham. The ravages of the bombers were clear for all to see. Buildings en route had been blown apart and in the centre of Birmingham whole sections of the city were wiped out leaving large open spaces, precariously unsupported walls of buildings and charred heaps of rubble. There were signs of recovery in that commerce was plodding on in and around the ruins and temporary bus stops were created to get shoppers there. During the worst of the bombing we never knew from one visit to the next where in the city the Walsall bus would put us down and reload. Bus inspectors frantically helped bemused passengers find their bus home, frequently just pulling a numbered bus into the side of the road, and ushering us on board. Whereas the normal bus stop for Midland Red 118, our bus, was in New Street by the ABC cinema, during this period it moved to the Gaumont cinema about 400 yards away, since traffic was not allowed in the centre.

It was around this time that we heard that America was going to join us in fighting the Germans and, stimulated by this, Mr Bickford decided we would paint the American flag in our Thursday afternoon art class. We had already expressed our patriotism a week or two earlier when we painted the Union Jack. For the 'stars and stripes', we started in the same way by drawing a half inch selvedge line around the sheet of drawing paper (roughly a modern A3 size). We marked out the left upper corner box of the American flag and divided it into forty eight three quarter inch squares for the stars followed by horizontal lines for the red and white stripes. Using the blackboard, Mr Bickford explained how we could accurately draw a five pointed star on a small three quarter inch square of paper which we then carefully cut out. This was our star template around which we drew in each of the forty eight boxes, before erasing the pencilled grid. Painting the blue background for the stars was quite difficult as we tried to create an even background. Mr Bickford walked around the class, looking over our shoulders, frequently displaying anger if anyone dared paint over a line. Since I knew the selvedge was later to be cut off, I carelessly allowed paint to wander over this line. He was extremely angry even though the areas which mattered had been painted with great care. I don't think I ever understood Mr Bickford's tantrums. It was a thing I was not used to from dad. Had he been a woman, I would understand since mom was equally unpredictable. A week or two later, we painted the Russian hammer and sickle and it proved impossible to prevent the 'acres' of red background looking patchy.

Reminders that we were at war were all around us on posters displayed on buses, in public buildings and on the streets. Slogans reminded us of the part we must play both to defeat the enemy and to survive and are worth a mention.

"Careless talk costs lives", were cartoon posters which changed frequently so that the message stayed fresh, reminding us to be guarded in our comments in case German ears were listening to our conversations. The posters had the style and appeal of seaside postcards, so much so that I looked forward to the next poster in the series. A new poster on the buses depicted a potential spy listening to our chat and we surreptitiously looked around and identified someone on our bus who we were convinced was a spy. In a huddle, we considered our plan and decided that, when he alighted, we would follow and capture him and take him to the police station!

"Keep digging for victory", and other food related posters asked everyone to contribute to the war effort by growing more of their own food. Dad dug up all our lawns to grow more potatoes. Leaflets, newspaper and magazine articles and Margaret Patton on cinema advertisements gave advice on creating appetising meals from our meagre wartime rations.

"Make do and mend" posters pressed everyone to repair rather than discard worn clothing, in order to reduce the demand for raw materials. It was very common to see working class people walking around with holes in the elbows of jerseys and cardigans or in the heels and toes of socks. Such holes were repaired by darning at least once during the life of a garment in order to get more wear from it. Middle class people such as our school teachers frequently had leather patches sewn onto the elbows of jackets and around the worn cuffs to reinforce them. The poster was simply extrapolating what was the norm for working class people. Mom and grandma were frequently seen neatly darning, using a wooden 'mushroom' to give shape to the heels of socks as they carefully constructed a woven darn. Woollen garments which were beyond repair were unravelled and mom used the reclaimed wool to knit another garment. She could use wools in different colour combinations to create a completely new design, sometimes dyeing reclaimed wool with a dye costing sixpence (2.5p) from Mrs Challinor's shop.

Later in the war, the *'Squander bug'*, a devil-like rat in cartoon form with swastikas all over its body, appeared in newspapers, on posters and as cards that we could collect for a few pennies as a set. They were similar to cigarette cards, but the difference was the quality of card. Cigarette cards were printed on glossy card and the squander bug on dull wartime quality card which was far from appealing. I think there were twenty cards in a set, and we regularly did swaps, but I was never able to complete my set. He advised everyone to be careful not to squander or waste money and to put it away safely in the National Saving scheme. He was often shown whispering in a shopper's ear, asking whether their intended purchase was really necessary.

At school, in addition to the chart of Britain's gains and losses, we created a newspaper poster which was also displayed at the front of the class. Every morning, Miss Liddle cut off a thirty inch (750mm) length of an unwanted roll of wallpaper on which two or three newspaper headlines were emblazoned with coloured blackboard chalks, much like a billboard outside a newsagents shop. This kept us daily abreast of the national and world news and particularly progress of the war. It was a joyous moment when we started to record the successes of Monty and the eighth army in North Africa.

The problem was that the successes did not help on the rationing scene and in early summer things were even worse. We were mortified when sweets and biscuits, of all things, were rationed. This initially had more affect on us than other forms of rationing since it was comfort food. Hitherto mom could go to a local shop and ask for a quarter (125g) of sweets, which were weighed out from one of the large jars behind the counter. Now we were going to be allocated one or two coupons in our ration book to last for a month, each being worth about an ounce (30g) of sweets. Both mom and I had a sweet tooth and we were not impressed by the news. Dad was not very bothered since he had quite carious teeth. As far as I was concerned, I missed the freedom to buy sweets when I fancied them. However we quickly found alternatives. It was not uncommon to find pieces of tar pitch after electrical engineers had been at work repairing or joining underground street cables, and it made quite a palatable chewing gum. It tasted a little like tar but it was something to chew and it was common practice among kids. We bought cough and throat sweets (such as Zubes or Chlorodyne lozenges), Horlicks tablets or anything else available 'off ration' that we could suck. However, many other people had the same idea and these items frequently became under-the-counter products, only supplied to regular customers. Aunt Ruby usually had superfluous sugar and tried to make toffee but, more often than not, her skill for overcooking things meant that it turned out black and bitter and essentially inedible. We became acclimatised to its strong flavour, probably no worse than pitch, and usually consumed most of it but would certainly have binned it in peacetime. Spanish root or liquorice stick, a yellowish dried piece of wooden stick, began to appear in Chemist's shops. After I started at Moss Close school (in a year or so), the Chemist shop at the top of Lichfield Street by Mellish Road always had a large basket of Spanish root outside, each stick priced according to weight, and they did a roaring trade with pupils. By the time we reached the Number One bus for home, our mouths were bright yellow! It had the same flavour as the liquorice pipes and the liquorice ribbons we had hitherto eaten. Palatable as these various items were, there was nothing like a real sweet and I was always waiting for next month when our ration coupons came into date again.

Bread changed colour from white to a dirty grey colour. It was proclaimed on Ministry of Food posters as being very nutritious, because of vitamin and mineral additives. Granddad decreed that it was grey because it contained the husks and millstone dust swept from the mill floor, which would normally have been discarded. It was palatable and did not deter him from cutting a thick slice and loading it with chunks of fatty bacon for his supper. If eaten with homemade jam, egg or loads of lard or dripping with salt, it was certainly not as bad as made out by the adults. Sometimes instead of toast for breakfast, we had porridge but it was never a great favourite of mine.

At least we had plenty of garden produce and eggs from granddad's chickens, and mom was able to provide one or two proper meals a day, but rationing was miserable and obviously much worse for any family relying entirely on rations. Most people had a garden if only small in some cases, but not everyone seemed to have the desire or the skill to use them. Queues outside shops were becoming commonplace, particularly if there was a fresh delivery of something in short supply. The jungle tom-toms would sound and women came out of the woodwork and formed a queue.

The war helped in one important way in that it led to a new interest which subsequently changed my life. It came about because during the summer holiday we were able to attend school and teachers would care for us. In my case it was not strictly necessary but it was a help to children of mothers who worked in factories producing war-related products. It was not compulsory, but about a dozen children did attend Landywood school on most days. Miss Liddle frequently seemed to draw the short straw and came to school to look after us. As one project, we developed a small vegetable garden at the top of the school playground and built a small garden pond.

On nice days Miss Liddle took us on trips into the countryside and it was these country walks with her which led to my new interest, the study of wild life around the greater community of Great Wyrley and Cheslyn Hay. She took us along footpaths I had never known, such as 'Darky lane' off Jacob's Hall Lane, a dirt track used by coalminers travelling between their homes in Little Bloxwich and the Sinkin'. On our walk she pointed out wild flowers, trees and the wildlife in the rapidly flowing streams, meadows and hedgerows. I avidly picked wild flowers and leaves from trees and bushes and asked her to name them. Some we took back to school and she taught us how to dry press and name them. For me it was a period when I began to understand the things that I had seen in abundance and had daily passed by without giving them a second thought. I knew the names of commoner wild flowers such as buttercup, daisy, chickweed, groundsel and so on but there were so many others that I was now observing and naming. I asked her many things on these outings and she seemed to be a fount of knowledge. One day, I felt the urge to put a question that I really needed an answer to. Where had I come from? For several months I had, like most children I guess, asked mom and dad where babies came from and got no further than the gooseberry bush, a stork or a gift from Jesus. Nothing I had seen so far in life had given me any real inkling to where babies came from and the need to know was becoming more intense. I had seen hen chicks hatch from eggs, but even though I had spent my life in the country, I had never witnessed the birth of animals. I recall in my earliest years looking very closely at the gooseberry bushes in granddad's garden. They were extremely prickly and seemed to be the last place on earth that a baby would be left! I never plucked up the courage to ask Miss Liddle and I am not sure what her answer might have been had I done so. I would like to think it would have been the truth.

Following that summer with her I was to spend many happy years in the countryside and developed hobbies which would be frowned upon in years to come, such as collecting bird's eggs and later butterflies. Everything was in great abundance in the fields, streams and hedgerows and collecting became a three-dimensional diary of what I had done and seen.

I couldn't wait to get out into the great beyond but I had reached an age where during the school holidays mom expected me to do more around the house. Every day before going out to holiday school or play, I was expected to help clean the house. Firstly she would carefully empty the twenty four hour collection of ash from the fireplace, picking it through for morsels of unburnt coal which could be used to start the next fire. This was followed by lifting rugs and mats and taking them outside to shake them. Lino floors were dusted and periodically polished with Mansion polish and all quarry floors were scrubbed with soap and water. Once every week the cast-iron cooking range in the sitting room was blacked and polished with 'black lead' (Zebo) until it shone like a mirror. During the week the fire bars in particular began to show base metal after glowing red hot on occasions and needed to be re-blacked. It was in front of these bars that we toasted. A slice of bread, pikelet (crumpet) or a bun was put on a fork, with an eighteen inch (450mm) handle, and held in front of the glowing embers until toasted, turning over for the other side. Somehow the toast cooked in this way was better charred and had a greater depth of flavour than that produced by later electric toasters, but it was not uncommon to get a cinder of coal in your mouth. I frequently made a slice of toast as a snack between meals, coating it with jam, lard or beef dripping sprinkled with plenty of salt. It was something which I could carry outside and eat whilst chatting or playing.

By the time the grate had been buffed up, it shone brightly. I next had to polish the metal ornaments around the fireplace with Brasso, such as the copper kettle which sat on the range and the brass fender, until they gleamed. After replacing the shaken rugs in each room, I was expected to remove ornaments from the various surfaces, dust and polish them with a dry cloth, and wipe off the surfaces before replacing them. These chores usually took a good hour and a half to complete if the two of us were working and I couldn't wait to reach the last room so that I could get out to wander.

Monday was wash day and always a hard grind. Early in the morning dad filled the boiler in the brew'us and lit the boiler fire, so that by about 8.30a.m. the water would be bubbling like a cauldron. Clothes-washing was done in a tub which in our case was a large beer barrel cut off at about two thirds height. Clothes had to be separated into whites, coloureds, woollens and dirty working clothes. To the tub was added about twelve inches (300mm) of piping hot water, soap flakes (usually Lux Flakes) and a lick or two of a Reckitts blue bag until the water was coloured. The first batch of whites were then dollied vigorously for about three or four minutes. The dolly was made from a six-inch (150mm) diameter block of tree trunk which was castellated on the bottom to create four prongs and attached to a robust 'T' handle which could be held in both hands. It was a heavy device and dollying was quite hard work but not nearly as hard as mangling the clothes after the wash to remove surplus water. Our first mangle was attached to the rim of the tub by two clamps. It was fine for light work but, when a thick blanket was put through, it inevitably worked loose resulting in a heap of hot blanket and mangle dangling over the back of the tub. Mom would let out a few choice expletives and not uncommonly blame yours truly for not tightening the clamps sufficiently. The pressure springs on the mangle had to be released, the mangle reclamped and the process started again. No matter how much the clamps were tightened the mangle worked loose. It may have been a design problem or mom's high expectations of it, but it regularly marred washday. Eventually we acquired the free standing Victorian style cast iron mangle which grandma no longer used and mom's recurring washing day utterances, 'damn and blast it', 'this bloody thing', 'oh, bugger, bugger, bugger' and others, became a thing of the past.

The mangled clothes were collected in a wicker clothes basket at the rear of the tub, and then carried to the washing line which was almost the full length of the garden path, some twenty yards (20 metres). The clothes were pegged out using pegs made of hazel and sold at the door by gipsy ladies who were camped in Jones' Lane. A sale was always accompanied by, "You will have a lot of luck this year, my dear". No sale might result in a spell on the family, or so mom thought, and hence she usually managed to spend a little with them. The Monday wash usually took the whole morning without a break after which the tub and the whole back yard was washed down with clean water to avoid soapy stains when it dried out.

Mom became extremely concerned when soap was rationed in early 1942. She was meticulously clean and her weekly clothes' washes were quite large. After a while it became clear that the soap ration did not meet her weekly needs and she became quite fretful about it. It had cut her normal soap usage in half and there is a point where, trying to use less to eke out the ration, does not produce a useful lather. Her distress was made worse by the fact that aunt Ruby with a family of four, not only had more soap ration, but never used what she had. She simply bought her full rations of whatever commodity and hoarded anything unused as though it was gold. She eventually half-filled an enormous wardrobe with packets of Oxydol soap powder and Lux soap flakes. She was happy to fling open the wardrobe doors and show mom her treasure but would never give or sell a packet to her. Mom became very irate with her Scrooge-like behaviour but to no avail. She even offered to pay double for soap powders but somehow they were a wartime treasure, and were not for sale. Even grandma tried to intervene, without success. Mom simply soldiered on, rationing what soap she had between washes. I was frequently sent to scour shops for sticks of shaving soap which was not rationed, though in short supply. I might have to cycle as far as Bloxwich or Cannock. A small stick cost sixpence (2.5p), significantly more than an equivalent weight of washing soap. Every time I returned successfully, a broad smile appeared on her face and she planted a large kiss on my forehead. To mom this was a small piece of gold and, brandishing the stick, she celebrated the fact that the wash could go ahead. Using a cheese grater, we quickly produced home made soap flakes and got on with the job.

After fulfilling my duties at home, I could now go and find my friends. We had our favourite places for a powwow, usually a place where several of us could gather in a group. Our favourite places for such a parliament were on the large granite rock in the top field, sitting on the wooden railway fence, or in one of several large oak trees.

The blue grey granite boulder stood in the top field. It was some five feet (1.5 metres) by four feet (1.3 metres) by three feet (900mm) high and shaped like a two-man tent with a pointed ridge. It is impossible to say where it had come from, but it was certainly not the type of rock generally found in Great Wyrley. Perhaps it was remains of the last ice age, but taking note of recent work on our forebears, was it a relic of early man? Its long axis was due east-west and it was also in line with the old stones which stood just inside the field on the east side of the Cop (Gorsey Lane) some 400 yards (370 metres) away. Having said this, the stones in Gorsey lane were at the edge of the field and may have been moved by early farmers. Our stone was much larger and heavier and as far as we were concerned, was simply a large stone on which we could sit astride and have a natter.

Of the oak trees near home, we used one tree more than any other. It stood at the bottom of the batter (the Shants bridge embankment) and had always been called 'the monkey tree'. It was an oak tree which had obviously been pushed over in its youth, possibly at the time the railway was laid down in 1858. It had then matured at an angle of about thirty degrees to the horizontal and the trunk, about fifteen inches (400mm) in diameter, could literally be walked up rather than climbed. The branches had spread horizontally, creating 'benches' some ten feet (3 metres) above the ground, on which we sat, feet dangling beneath the foliage. We could sit in a circle and face each other as we powwowed. If we climbed to the top of the tree we were able to monkey along the branches so that they bowed and we could drop the few feet to the ground, which is probably how it acquired its name. It was a climbing frame created by nature and was far more exciting than anything at the council recreation ground. Being on the railway boundary, it was ideal for looking into passing locomotives since we were at their level. Adjacent to this tree, about thirty feet (10 metres) away stood a very large upright oak, probably the same age. Using the two trees, the higher one as the crow's nest, with its panoramic view, and the monkey tree as our control cockpit, we could communicate with two cans attached by a long taut string as our telephone. This was made by punching a small hole in the centre of the base of two tin cans and threading a length of string, knotting the ends. It was ideal for communicating when playing war related games. We could speak to each other relatively quietly and report the deployment of our 'enemy'.

I suppose there were about two dozen mature oak trees within a short distance of home and many ash and elm trees which were not so good for climbing. We were very adept at climbing trees and, rather than climb down, we frequently crawled out on a branch to bend it downwards and drop to the ground. On occasion, we landed more quickly than we were expecting as the branch snapped, which was far more common with the ash trees. Rope swings sometimes ended the same way! One might have expected a few broken limbs, but at no time did anyone seriously injure themselves whilst climbing or playing in trees.

My experience in tree climbing proved very useful when I later started to collect bird's eggs. Tits used holes in trees and the large birds, such as rooks, crows and magpies, built nests near to the tree canopy. On one excursion I had quite an interesting experience when scrambling towards a crow's nest in the spinney at the end of Darky Lane. As I neared my target I was alarmed to be attacked by a female kestrel hawk which had obviously chosen to use the old nest for egg laying and was now insistent that I was not going to reach her clutch of eggs. Her talons struck blood and I bore the scars of the escapade for quite a while. Nevertheless, I did manage to collect an egg for my collection. Passing the spot two or three weeks later, I was able to witness the parents feeding nestlings and smiled to myself at how their mother had fought for their survival. I pointed my arm in their direction to remind the parents that they were responsible for the scars!

From mid to late 1942, air raid sirens, as I have said, were becoming less frequent, which was as well because granddad's air raid shelter was beginning to smell distinctly mouldy and was growing cotton wool and toadstools on the walls. A timber shed underground, with no damp-proof membrane, was an ideal culture medium for fungi. As time passed, wet and dry rot really took hold, and the walls began to develop black cracks and buckle, until the whole shelter caved in resembling a bomb crater. Uncle Bob's brick built underground bunker fared little better. It was now an underground reservoir for some two or three hundred gallons of water seeping through the walls from the high fields at the back of the house. In fact, it had never been used beyond the first month or so of its creation. This again had not been given a damp proof membrane.

Even though air raid warnings were now almost non-existent I had an immense fright one day whilst cycling home from Upper Landywood. The relative silence of a country lane gave way to a deafening roar approaching from behind and a Messerschmidt flew immediately over my head at tree top level, its swastikas and pilot clearly visible. I leapt from my bike into the ditch alongside the lane. Within five seconds I was deafened by a second plane hot on its tail, but this time a Spitfire. It was obviously a dog fight and I was shaking. I hid in the bracken for several minutes before I felt safe enough to make my way home. I pondered how different things might have been had they been firing their machine guns at the time. I parted the bracken and looked in all directions in the sky before climbing out. It was my one and only experience of fear during the war. I was sure my number had been called. Sometime later I learned that a German plane had crashed near Wedges Mills but I am not sure whether it related to this incident, since most crashes were kept hush-hush. I mused for some time on the fact that a German fighter plane had been less than a hundred yards (100 metres) away from me; a real and living nightmare!

Another wacky situation arose whilst out cycling with pals along the 'cut' (canal) towpath. It was a trip we frequently made, joining the canal via Moon's Lane dirt track by Spring Cottage farmstead. The track rose almost vertically up the canal embankment as it joined the canal at the pedestrian and elegant white swing bridges across the canal. We usually tarried here for a while, daring each other to jump the canal at this point, where it was narrow. No-one had the guts to do so, but it passed the time of day! We cycled on along the towpath towards Strawberry Lane bridge and became aware of a cacophony on the opposite bank. It was a group of fishermen who were obviously very irate about something. They were milling around the edge of the large triangular turning basin, opposite Gilpin's basin. The old shale heaps around the basin were a thicket of brambles, bracken and elder bushes with one or two oak trees. No-one in their right mind would try to approach the waterline at that point since there were walls around the basin some three feet high, but these men were on a mission. It became apparent that they were trying to land a large pike which had for some time decimated their fishing ground. Someone had hooked the monster and a considerable amount of time had been spent trying to land it, without success. Try as he may, the angler simply could not get it out of the water because of the walls. About five of them were shouting at each other, pontificating on the best way to land the enormous thrashing fish. Under no circumstances was the lineman going to lose his catch and was playing the fish as best he could. In the fields behind the shale hills someone could be heard shooting rabbits and one bright spark had the idea to engage him and ran for help. The others, still bawling obscenities, worked together to get the fishing line over the branch of an overhanging oak tree. We stood open mouthed watching the performance not entirely sure what was going on. The rabbit hunter was now at the canal-side talking to the men. Then with a tug on the line the pikes head was raised above water and – 'Bang!' The thirty pound fish thrashed no more. We stood there not really believing what we had witnessed. Shooting rabbits, yes, but we were amazed by this method of dispatching a fish. When they pulled it up from of the water, a good length of pike dangled beneath the tree branch, blood trickling down its body. It had taken six men and a gun to bring the king of the canal to heel, and their war cries and celebrating must have been heard in Cheslyn Hay, a mile away.

During May 1942 I was obliged to take a break from everyday life in order to enter hospital for an operation. I simply mention this in real time in my chronicle, but this episode will be the subject of the next chapter.

Our garden flourished as ever during the summer months, and crops were abundant. Meals invariably followed the seasons and were based on what was cropping at the time. The first meal of a crop was something we looked forward to year by year, such as the first crop of peas and broad beans which were served with new potatoes, grilled bacon and the liquor (bacon fat) from the pan poured over the vegetables. I particularly looked forward to the first meal of runner beans served with new potatoes, lamb chops and fresh mint sauce. We consumed plenty of very fresh vegetables even though the meat ration at the time left something to be desired.

Whenever the butcher produced a reasonable joint of meat, we had a roast on Sunday. It was frequently fairly tough to eat and sirloin always had a great deal of fat covering the joint. Monday's meal was invariably a stew made from the remains of the joint with fresh garden vegetables and herbs. Flavourings from the garden commonly used in dishes were sage, thyme, mint, parsley, onions and leeks and the condiments, salt, pepper and mustard. Mom would often make a sauce, either parsley, onion or white sauce, which helped to improve the flavour of a meal. As an alternative, leftover meat was minced and made into a cottage pie or perhaps used to stuff a marrow which dad grew on the compost heap. I always found marrow an unpleasant mushy vegetable but usually scoffed the seasoned meat stuffing. One or two meats such as offal and ox-tail were not rationed but, because of this, were in short supply. About once a fortnight mom did her shop to Walsall for our fix of sausage and black pudding from Marsh and Baxters. These were not yet rationed, but the shop limited each customer to about a half pound (125g) of sausage. When available I also enjoyed liver and onions. Two composite meats were imported, corned beef and 'Spam', which were available to some extent and made reasonable sandwiches. Mom also used corned beef with vegetables to make a cottage pie. Spam she occasionally fried as fritters which were a pleasant change. Some of her ideas for expanding meat products came from cookery tips in newspapers, which usually had vegetables as meal expanders, something we had plenty of.

When the salad crops came into season, we ate sliced leftovers of the joint, corned beef or Spam with garden salad. I was not a great salad fan but found it reasonably pleasant to eat with vinegar as a dressing. I adored cucumber in a sandwich, thinly sliced in vinegar, seasoned with plenty of pepper. Vinegar was a commodity which we bought by the pint from Mrs Challinor's shop. I had to take an empty 'R White' pop bottle which she filled from a barrel. It was cheap but did not last long. When mom could see 'mothers', fluffy growths of yeast, at the bottom of the bottle, it was discarded. I am sure it could have been filtered to last longer, but the sight of it turned mom's stomach and that was that! A fresh supply was indicated and I was duly dispatched to get a fresh supply.

During the warm summer months, most food stuffs only lasted a brief time. Milk quickly turned sour, butter rancid and cheese sweaty. Meat and fish only stayed edible for a day or so and, for this reason, daily deliveries and daily shopping was a must. Fresh fish was adorable, stale fish stank to high heaven and was appalling to eat.

We ate very well from the garden but there was always plenty of surplus stock to sell to passers-by who called in to see what seasonal produce was available. If we did not have what they wanted, someone else in the bungalows usually did. We often had excess of spring cabbage, tomatoes, cucumbers, lettuce, radish, spring onions, peas, broad and runner beans, carrots, parsnips and later main crop onions, all of which were welcomed by callers. They were sold at the going rate and the takings swelled out the garden fund for next year.

Whenever I felt the need for a snack between meals, I could go into the garden and pull a fresh carrot and wipe it on the lawn to remove the soil, before eating it. Such delicacies were never washed under a running tap, a peppering of garden soil simply added to the experience. Raw peas made a very pleasant snack, firstly opening the pod and eating the young tender peas and then carefully peeling the fibrous membrane lining the pea-shell before eating the fleshy pod. There was always a large crop of rhubarb in granddad's garden growing very robustly in the moist ground by the drainage culvert. Thick stems of the plant grew here with leaves some eighteen inches (45cm) across and because it grew rapidly, it was very crisp to chew. A stick of raw rhubarb with a paper cone containing a small amount of our sugar ration was a delight. Dipping the stick in the sugar took the edge off the tartness, without destroying the intense acid taste which astringed my mouth. Gooseberries were likewise eaten green, six at a time, the acidity virtually stripping the flesh from my tongue and the inside of my mouth! If I craved sweetness, nothing was better than a handful of very large loganberries growing in abundance on sticks up the south wall of the old cowshed. Granddad and aunt Ruby had apple trees and I would stuff several of the windfalls into each trouser pocket to eat with friends in our camp. My stomach's cravings always seemed to be easily satisfied by raw garden produce. If we were out playing, we might nick an occasional swede from the edge of the farmers field, peel it and cut it into wedges with a pen-knife. I suppose we used considerable energy running around but we easily satiated our bellies from produce growing around us. However these between-meal delights only supplemented the very good meals cooked by mom.

She was a very good pastry cook and, although we bought cakes from Stanton's and Taylor's shops, she tried to cook at least once a week, making a sandwich, a dozen small cakes and individual jam and lemon curd tarts. She sometimes made a large jam tart which covered a dinner plate and we had wedges with custard as a pudding. Home baking of pastry always created a slightly burnt crust around the edges of a tart which gave it a most enjoyable flavour.

For us fresh eggs were in good supply but if a family did not keep chickens, a substitute came in waxed boxes in the form of egg powder, equivalent to about a dozen eggs. Mom did use the powder for cooking purposes to supplement fresh eggs, a measure of egg powder being equivalent to one fresh egg. It was a poor substitute when compared with cakes made from fresh eggs but still made a reasonable snack. Aunt Ruby was, as I have already said, an appalling cook and cousin Ron's internal clock always registered mom's cooking days. When the smell from the cooking wafted into his nostrils, like the 'Bisto' boy, Ron followed the odour trail to source.

"Aunty Ida, can I have a kairk?", he would plaintively ask.

"Yoe can 'ave just one and tek it outside t'ate it, and doe drop yer crumbs on my flure!", would be mom's stern reply.

Ron would happily go away relishing the still-warm cake as he turned the corner home. Next time mom returned to the plate it was apparent that twelve minus one was ten, Ron unable to resist the temptation had helped himself to another. Next cookery day, she allowed Ron his cake as usual and waited. In less than a minute, a hand came round the doorframe and stealthily lifted another cake. For the next few years, Ron came for his fix of aunty Ida's cakes. Sometimes he would creep into the house and make straight for the pantry before saying 'hello'. This fore-armed him with the knowledge that there was a plate of cakes and the question soon followed,

"Gorra a kairk, aunty Ida?"

113

If he had had his allowance, the answer was usually 'No!'. Ron slunk from the house calling mom a miserable sod or bugger and inevitably, some minute or two later, we could hear thuds and clatters as Ron, now in his own garden, threw large clods of earth or anything to hand at our back door. The mess outside was unbelievable and looked as though a wheelbarrow of garden rubbish had been overturned on mom's generally prim backyard. Mom thought it was funny and somehow loved to taunt Ron into having a paddy just to see what his reaction would be. He knew and she knew that as he was on the other side of the garden hedge, there was little hope of catching him. She would run to the hedge and threaten him with the broom, but no more. It occurred frequently, but still next week Ron would present himself at baking time. Mom had a soft spot for him and he could get away with murder, actions I would have been walloped for.

Away from home, the crowd of us spent a lot of time in the lower meadows, either fishing, paddling or building dams. It was also a good area to look for bird's eggs since there was plenty of gorse and bramble around the Valley pool which attracted pipits, finches and yellow hammers. On one occasion Bert Badger's ducks had obviously escaped his farm yard and were having a great time swimming and foraging in the pool. It had never happened before. Bert and Margaret Badger lived at Lower Landywood Farm which was at the end of the village. It was really a smallholding with a few adjacent fields. From our point of view the Badgers were best known because of their enormous pear tree. Come September we were able to buy a large paper carrier bag full of pears for sixpence (2.5p), or could purchase smaller amounts for a penny or two. We called them 'tets', small pears which were quite sweet and something the gang of us could munch on whilst sitting in the monkey tree. But, to get back to the ducks, we determined to drive them back from the Valley pool towards the farm. They became defiant and made it quite clear that they did not want to leave their newly found wading area, making an almighty uproar and flapping and quacking as they flew to and fro treading the water. We on the other hand were intent on getting them home and surrounded them like sheep dogs, eventually getting them herded and on the move. Obviously Bert or his wife had heard the commotion and duly informed PC Morris. In no time mom had yet another knock on the door and was told that I had chased the ducks and it would affect their laying and it was not to happen again, or there would be a summons. Why do adults never believe the true facts? We were trying to get them home! It was the first time that the ducks had been in the lower meadows, even though it was the Badger's field, and we were only trying to be helpful. Poor mom, she aged a little more after the bobby's visit. She so easily became uptight about things.

She became even more uptight when she remembered it was chimney-sweeping time. It happened about every two years and we knew exactly how she would react to the biennial soot bath. The problem with coal fires was that over time the chimney became thickly caked with soot, which had to be cleared if the fire was to continue drawing well. It also reduced the likelihood of a chimney fire which could theoretically lead to a house fire. Although the thought of a chimney fire terrified mom, she regularly used a newspaper to draw a freshly laid fire! Smouldering coal very quickly re-ignited when drawn in this way and flames roared up the chimney. More often than not the newspaper caught fire and the flaming pages were hastily pushed into the fire hole. From here the blazing mass accelerated up the chimney at high speed and dense smoke and flaming newspaper fragments emanated from chimney pot, covering local gardens.

Everyone ran outside to witness the fiery display and mom also watched, terrified lest she had caused a house fire!

When it came to chimney sweeping, sensible people would have employed a professional, but not granddad. They cost money and he could sweep the chimneys himself, or he did until dad came on the scene. Thereafter he expected dad to climb on the roof. Whilst a chimney sweep would use proper brushes and also bring furniture covers and a seal for the fireplace, granddad's method was to find a good bush and pull this through with a rope. A search was made in the hedgerows for a nice globular bush about two feet (60cm) in diameter, usually holly because it was hard. This was tied to the end of a long rope and a house brick or weight attached to the other end. Dad, carrying bush and pull through, climbed onto the roof using granddad's ladder, now fairly rotten and with virtually every other rung missing. Granddad at least had the grace to steady the bottom. The brick was now lowered down the chimney, carrying the rope with it.

In the living room below, grandma and mom had prepared the room, moving furniture and covering what they could. An old sheet was draped from the mantle-piece, held in place with bricks, and each side pressed against the wall to make a seal. Granddad, chimney sweep extraordinaire, came in and reached under the drape for the rope. Tugging hard on the rope, he pulled the bush down the chimney. Soot could be heard falling like an avalanche behind the drape.

"Stop pullin', Bob!" screeched grandma, "your meckin' a rate puther, the damn soot's comin' out this side! Ida, let gue a bit, gimme mower of the sheet over 'ere". Her face was now looking decidedly sooty, the whites of her eyes gleaming through, and the look she gave granddad was sufficient to kill.

Finally, there was a whoosh as the bush fell into the fireplace and the drape shook and bulged well into the room, pulling the retaining bricks off the mantle-piece. Mom was yelling at anyone who would listen about 'this bloody mess'. When the shower of dust finally settled, the pull-through had to be removed and about three buckets of soot carefully shovelled out of the ash-pit. This was a job for grandma. There was no way she would trust granddad to do it since he would leave a trail across the floor and fill the room with even more soot. This fiasco was repeated in the other houses and always seemed to turn an otherwise peaceful life into another war front, the faces of the participants resembling miners just emerging from a shift at the coalface. For someone who was as inherently spick and span, it was obviously a torture mom had to endure. And the soot? This was always saved and used on the garden to prevent pests.

At about this time, mom responded to an advertisement for a railway trip to Sutton Park and bought tickets from the railway station. The train stopped outside the main town gate and hundreds of people descended on the park to join the crowds already there. Many families were gathered along the banks of the stream just inside the gate picnicking and paddling, whilst others made their way to Pat Collins' fairground which was a permanent fixture in the park. I was immediately taken by the steam railway which was about ten inch (25cm) gauge and was running perfect replicas of express locomotives hauling about six carriages. It was a thrilling ride though woodland scenery, the locomotive chuffing and whistling in full voice as it pulled coaches laden with laughing and excited children. In the centre of the fairground was the dragon ride, where fiery dragons cars coasted up and down at high speed, carrying about ten people in each car. Along the park fence, a roller coaster constructed of timber and about thirty

115

feet at its highest point, was full of adults and children screaming as it accelerated into the dips. Around the perimeter were wooden buildings which housed the 'Ghost Train' and weird shows such as the big fat lady and various unusual dwarfs. An arcade of slot machines entertained and provided prizes for skill. I changed sixpence into pennies and tried the machines, hoping that I could manoeuvre a crane to pick up a model car. Try as I may, I had no luck, the jaw always opened before reaching the receptacle and I was convinced that all the machines giving prizes were fixed. My first experience of the ghost train was quite memorable, a skeleton which came to life, a demon laughing raucously, another train (it seemed) heading straight for us on collision course and the creepy feeling of going through a large cob web stretched across our path. It was a wonderful fairground and, over the years, I spent many happy half days there.

One evening towards the end of the school holiday, I met Colin Parsons making his way to wolf cubs, decked out in his uniform. Perhaps it was the sight of the uniform or maybe I needed something to do, I cannot remember, but I was easily persuaded to go along with him and I eventually joined the wolf cubs at Great Wyrley Wesley Church. The pack's Akela was Donald Shorter, a senior scout, who lived on Mount Pleasant in Cheslyn Hay. In view of clothes rationing, we were not expected to wear a uniform, but we were able to buy the necessary green and yellow neckerchief and a leather waddle for one shilling and sixpence (7.5p) from Akela. Mom managed to get some wool which she dyed dark green and knitted a pullover for the purpose. Our headquarters, for small meetings and equipment storage, was the men's choir vestry but we played games in the Primary Sunday School room. We were supposed to work for badges for skills such as tying knots, first aid, fire lighting and various crafts, but Don Shorter was not the most stimulating person in this respect. A few weeks later, we attended a jamboree in Walsall along with several wolf cub packs from around the area, where our skills were tested in competitive games. We did not win. In one game members of the team had to run, in turn, to a table at the end of the room and tie a specific knot requested by a referee. I was given a reef knot which I had tied so many times, but with nervous fumbling fingers, I handed over a perfect granny knot! On another occasion we made a trip to Beaudesert where we set up camp and had a sing song around a campfire. I stayed with the Wesley cubs until I reached scouting age, about eighteen months, but never had the urge to join the Boy Scouts. I think by then, having started grammar school, I was required to do homework which took priority.

At the beginning of the new school term, I entered 'top class Miss Jones' class at school. She was a fairly fiery lady who we found it best not to cross. We always knew who was in charge and acted to her command. She was much shorter than Miss Liddle, slim and had auburn hair with an occasional grey streak. She was school pianist and had a piano in her class used for singing lessons, which she controlled with a rod of iron rather than a baton. She was well educated and ideal for a top class in school. I enjoyed her teaching, but many found her a hard taskmaster, particularly after the gentleness of Miss Liddle. She had a sharp temper and frequently raised her voice or used a cutting remark to get over her message, which usually sufficed to settle the class down. I am not sure that anyone really felt comfortable in her class and it is the school year about which I have least recollection. I do recall that we were now using pen and ink which I think we had started a year previously. It was a messy procedure and blots on work were commonplace and not liked by teachers. Desk tops were camouflaged by irregular patches of ink spilled and dried on over many years of use. Teachers kept a supply of new pen nibs which came in boxes of ten or more and our inkwells were refilled from a pint bottle of blue-black ink kept in the classroom cupboard. I was quite a fast writer with pencil, but pen and ink slowed me down considerably and I was never happy with it as a medium. However it was to be and we had to put up with it.

With the approach of autumn, farmers were active in the fields, Mr. Whalley in the fields behind our house and Mr. Snape higher up the lane. The wheat, barley or oats were ready to reap and machinery which had over-wintered in the barn was brought into action. Mr. Snape of Landywood farm always had reasonable equipment which seemed fit for purpose but Mr. Whalley inevitably seemed to have problems. His was a horse-drawn reaper-binder but the pair of horses seemed to spend almost as much time stationary as they did pulling the harvester. He was frequently seen remonstrating with the motionless machine, whipping it with his cloth cap and shouting expletives at it. The problem was usually brought about when a stone entered the cutting blades, jamming the motion. This caused the drive chain between wheels and cutter mechanism to snap and the broken chain inevitably fell beneath the reaper and had to be retrieved. Since he never seemed to carry decent tools with him, I stood and watched incredulously as he repaired the break using string from the binder. The result was inevitable, a few more yards of reaping, the weak string joint snapped and the binder once more ground to a halt. He might try this first aid a time or two but eventually his exasperation was plain to see and he turned the horses for home, I am sure blaming the war for his predicament. Spares were almost certainly difficult to come by, but why did Mr Snape not seem to have the same problems? A year or two earlier there had been a blacksmith's forge on Upper Landywood Lane, just yards from Mr Whalley's farm gate, which would no doubt have done such repairs, but it had now closed down.

The reaper-binders in the 1930s were horse drawn machines, using two shire horses. They had a fairly large beater somewhat like a windmill which rotated, deflecting the cereal stems over the three feet (1 metre) 'scissor' blade, which cut them at ground level. The deflected cut stems fell onto a canvass conveyor belt which carried them upwards into the binder where a nine inch (22cm) bundle of cereal stems collected before being bound with string. A fork then rotated and knocked the tied cereal sheaf to the ground, resulting in parallel lines of sheaves along the field behind the reaper. The farmer sat on a seat at the back of the machine, guiding the horses on a long rein. I was fascinated by this machine and spent a great deal of time trying to figure out how it tied the knot in the string. Unfortunately it was never stationary long enough to study it closely and farmers were very busy people. At the beginning of the war, Mr. Snape bought a Ferguson tractor to use for his farming jobs, but Mr Whalley continued with horses both during the wartime years and after the war.

Towards the end of the war, whilst watching Mr Snape's farmhands reaping with his tractor and reaper-binder, the driver shouted that there was a fox in the middle of the field. One of the hands was dispatched to collect the twelve-bores from the farm house. Four hands were directed to the corners of the field, each with a gun, waiting for the fox to break out. The tractor continued working spirally towards the centre and when it reached a point where there was now only some thirty feet (10 metres) of uncut cereal, the frightened animal was driven to make the break across open ground.

Guns blazed!

For a moment it sounded like a battlefield, eight shots were fired but all four men missed the target and the fox lived to harass the chickens a little longer!

The cereal sheaves were collected in pairs by helpers who created stooks of six or eight standing sheaves which were reminiscent of lines of scout's tents across the field. The cereal was allowed to dry for a few days before being loaded by pitchfork onto hay wagons and carried to the barn area of the farmyard where ricks were created about ten feet by twelve feet and eight feet high (about 3 by 4 by 2 metres). Here the cereal would stand until the thresher arrived.

Threshing machines were not owned by farmers, but hired from a peripatetic company. Over a few weeks, the machine visited each farm and it was a fun time of the year for us. The threshing machine was a large non-descript wooden box about the size of a gipsy caravan with steel wheels. In my early years it was towed by a steam traction engine though, by the start of the war, this changed to a Ferguson tractor. The steam tractor, smaller than those at Pat Collins' fairground, chuffed and hissed as it passed us by, occasionally giving a musical toot of its whistle to warn folks around a bend in the lane. Behind it was towing the thresher box, a living van for the men and then a straw bailer, the retinue looking like an archaic railway train.

Once on site the machinery had to be aligned, the thresher box directly alongside a cereal rick. There was a lot of huffing and puffing from the steam tractor, cutting deep ridges into the ground, as it was manoeuvred to face the thresher box. A very heavy belt, some thirty feet (10 metres) in circumference and about four inches (10cm) wide was looped between the large flywheel of the traction engine a smaller pulley on the side of the thresher box. A slimmer belt was stretched between the latter and the straw bailer parked in line behind.

"Everyone stand clear of the belts" shouted the driver, as the flywheel of the traction engine slowly turned.

The inert wooden box suddenly came to life, rumbling and chattering as its innards did the things that threshers do. Behind, the feed arm of the bailer moved backwards and forwards like a piston rod on a steam engine, waiting for its first feed of straw from the thresher. The belts seemed very loose and oscillated up and down as they travelled at fairly high speed and I wondered why they never came off the flangeless pulleys, but they never did. In later years, when the Ferguson tractor replaced the steam tractor, it had a small pulley to the side of the engine to drive the threshing machinery.

Two farm hands now climbed on top of the box and began feeding in wheat sheathes, passed down from the top of the rick by two others with pitchforks. One man cut the string with a sharp knife before pushing the cereal stems into the machine. Husks were blown out of a chimney at the side of the box and resembled yellow snow as it was caught by the wind and settled over the adjacent ground. Straw, exuded in a stream from the back of the thresher and into the bailer where it was compacted into long rectangular bales which were tied with two loops of wire before being ejected at the rear. It usually took a whole day to thresh the farmers annual crop of cereal. At the rear of the machine, a man placed a hessian sack on four hooks before turning a wheel to open the hopper and fill the sack with grain. The sacks were carried into the barn and stored until sent to a flour mill. When the rick reached the final layer of sheaves, rats raced in all directions. They had created nests at the base of the rick and were now running for their lives, literally. Those that were not so lucky were skewered as the farmhand thrust in his pitchfork and terrible squeals emanated from the base of the rick.

Farming was indeed a hazardous business and, during later years, friends were injured, one fatally. Alan Jones fell off the back of a tractor in the field at the back of his home in Shaw's Lane, badly injuring himself. A teenage boy whom I had known at school and whose name eludes me, though I think possibly McIntosh, was killed when lightning struck his pitchfork in one of Mr Brassington's fields. At our age though, playing around the farm was always great fun and I suppose we were fortunate in avoiding serious injury.

As the weeks passed after harvest time, the fields were turned over ready for sowing next year's crops, renewing the annual farming cycle. Farmers had mixed farms and many fields were grazed by milking herds of Freesian cattle and were the source of the cowpats we collected for garden manure.

Every year, as the cooler autumn weather set in, fire cans became the norm, made from any type of tin can, be it a large fruit can or a larger paint tin. We usually found them in a dust bin or on a refuse tip and, using a six inch nail, we punched several holes around the sides and bottom of the can. A long wire handle, sufficient in length to protect our hands from the flames, was attached to the rim. A small fire was started in the bottom and by swinging the can in a circular motion, over and over, the tinder very quickly caught alight. We could then add thicker wood or coal from the mining slag heaps and we soon had a small personal brazier. Tending to these, keeping a steady fire, ensured that we were kept occupied for some time. Occasionally we might try to roast a potato on top of the can but the result was inevitably a potato with black seriously charred and sooty skin with a raw interior. These homemade braziers were an important part of camp life and after setting up camp were used for warmth and for cooking.

The mining ruins around us contained all kinds of materials which we used to build a camp, be it sheets of corrugated steel or even derelict coal tubs. For camouflage purposes we often set up camp inside a large briar patch on Holloway's tip or in the top fields. These large domes of blackberry briars, some twenty feet (6 metres) in diameter, were hollowed out by climbing underneath and, using gloves, pushing branches aside to make a cavity several feet (2 metres) across. Sheets of corrugated steel were tied into the 'roof' to keep out rain and a brazier set up either within or just outside the door. Here we would powwow for hours, sometimes cooking on the fire. Ingredients were not easy to acquire during the war years but one or other managed to get a little flour so that we could make flour and water biscuits or even a potato pasty. In reality, the 'food' was quite revolting but we still ate our creation and convinced each other that we were enjoying it. If it rained, we had limited shelter from the lining sheets and before long the signs of a badly leaking roof appeared, either the brazier hissed and started damping out or rainwater started dripping down our necks. At this point, it was no longer fun and feeling very cold and wet we were forced to make our way home.

In our camp we copied things our parents did, smoking being a good example, and our camps made ideal smoking dens, away from prying eyes. Smoke was already emanating from our braziers and cigarette smoke did not therefore attract attention. A fag (cigarette) was surreptitiously acquired from the cigarette case of someone's father and lit from a fire can. It was then passed around the group, each taking a drag. I never particularly enjoyed smoking but felt it was necessary as I grew up, since it was something all men did. Occasionally we might buy a penny clay pipe from Mrs Challinor's shop and pack it with dried dock seeds before lighting it. If this was not available, we could create a pipe reservoir from a large scooped-out acorn and insert a straw as a stem, to suck on. I look back in horror when I think of the number of times we searched the roadside and filled our pipe with the tobacco from fresh fag ends discarded by the miners making their way to and from work. Yet we never thought twice about such practices and fortunately, it seems, never suffered any adverse affect.

With the approach of Christmas, at home it was time to make the Christmas cakes, mincemeat and Christmas puddings. The washing-up bowl was thoroughly cleaned and this would be the mixing bowl. Dried fruit, suet and spices were common to the latter two. Dried fruit was not easy to come by but I think mom did find dried currants and added carrot and apple to make up quantities. Various mixing fluids such as beer were the binding agents. Once mom had started to mix, we all took turns in stirring the mixture, wishing for something as we mixed. In the case of the Christmas pudding, a small silver Joey (thruppence, 1.2p) was added to the mixture which would bring luck to the finder, or bad luck if they broke a tooth! The pudding mixture was put into a basin, covered in grease proof paper, and then a cloth cover. It was steamed for about six to eight hours and would again be steamed on Christmas day. The Christmas cake was iced about a week before Christmas and then I decorated it from about nine years of age with a small piping bag made with greaseproof paper

Christmas came that year and, as always on Christmas Eve after going to bed, mom crept into the bedroom to see if I was sleeping. I never was, but she quietly placed a pillow case of goodies at the foot of my bed, apples, a packet of sweets and chocolates, a boxed game such as draughts, one or two books and a trapeze monkey. The latter was made from plywood from a tea chest by someone who worked with dad. It was articulated and threaded on a twisted string loop between two vertical rods which, when squeezed, caused the monkey to somersault. It had been painted with silver, red and blue enamel paints and was a wonderful little toy which gave hours of amusement. Wooden toys were the norm during the war years whereas before the war metal toys had been a more common present, such as boxes of six lead soldiers. These were usually painted to represent famous regiments such as the Grenadier Guards. Cousin Bobby had a wooden fort and we frequently played together with our soldiers. My pillow case before the war had contained more sweets such as sugar mice (a mouse made of granulated sugar with painted eyes and whiskers), oranges, nuts, tin plate toys (a bluebird racing car, a train set, a motorcyclist with side car and a drumming bear, all wind-up action toys), hard backed nursery rhyme and fairy tale books, a cowboy's six shooter with explosive caps, a large spinning top, boxed games and a small Meccano set. During the war, metal was not available for such goodies. Mom and dad did everything possible to keep up the spirit of Christmas but it was certainly much sparser than before the war.

Their efforts were apparent when Christmas day arrived and I was to learn why dad had been padlocking the cowshed at the top of our garden to keep me out. I had assumed it was because he and mom had been tentatively talking about keeping a pig in there, but in reality he had been working away on a large wooden crane as a Christmas present. It was complete with jib and pulley and a crank to wind in the rope and it swivelled through a complete circle on its wheeled chassis. He had painted it bright red and over Christmas, I think I hooked everything possible, such as cups, bundles of cutlery and parcels, lifting them from floor to dining table and vice versa. It did not have the finesse of the detailed models constructed by Eric's father, but it was a delightful present which made a very happy Christmas day.

For lunch we were able to have roast chicken from granddad's flock, stuffed with sage and onion stuffing. This was always a luxury meal and it was the only time of year that we had a roast chicken. At other times in the year it was always casseroled chicken and vegetables, using a chicken considered to have reached the end of her useful life as an egg layer. Granddad's dictum was to kill the bird, however sick, before it took its last breath and fell to the floor. If it hit the floor we couldn't eat it! Occasionally a bird did have tumours and other things that did not look normal when grandma extracted the innards but, what the hell, it was going to be cooked! The Christmas roast chicken was so different and the crispy brown skin was to die for. Along with the presents, it was the highlight of Christmas day. Christmas pudding was in reality a kind of carrot cake with spice but, with lashings of custard, it was just as delicious as the real thing.

During Christmas afternoon we were allowed to use the front parlour. Dad had lit a good fire and the room was warm and everything smelled new. This was a rare experience for if I dared to enter this inner sanctum at any other time, except to clean it, mom would turf me out. There were apples and pears in a fruit bowl and a selection of chocolates and sweets. It was all very cozy and I imagine like spending Christmas away from home. My toys were there, but we also played board games, such as ludo, and tiddlywinks which always caused great delight. Somehow spending the day in the parlour brought an extra dimension to Christmas.

CHAPTER 10

'A children's hospital and other medical things - c. 1942'

Shortly after starting the new school year in August 1941, we had to undergo a medical examination, which was the norm about every two years. Our mothers were asked to attend to be with us during the doctor's examination. After listening to my chest with a stethoscope and prodding my belly, he examined my back and found that I had a problem which, to date, had passed unnoticed. He explained that my head was tilted to the left side and I was developing a twist in my spine. A twisted spine (scoliosis, he called it) must he said be treated early to prevent it getting worse and he would refer me to see a specialist. An appointment duly arrived two or three weeks later for me to attend a clinic in Walsall and the following month mom dressed me to the nines for our trip there.

67, Bradford Street, Walsall was an old double fronted Victorian building in a part of the town beyond Halfords' cycle shop and the Bradford arcade that I had not visited before. We were directed to the waiting room which was poorly lit and full of school children of all ages, some sitting pensively and looking worried, others unperturbed and noisy and could have been at a fairground. I had walked into the unknown and was afraid and very close to filling my trousers! We had to wait some time before being called through to see the doctor. His name was Mr. Allen, an orthopaedic surgeon from Birmingham Children's hospital.

Mr Allen examined me and confirmed the school doctor's findings, afterwards explaining that my problem was due to a condition called torticollis. He questioned mom about my birth which she described as prolonged and difficult and, at this, he said he believed the big muscle down the left side of my neck had been stretched so much during my delivery that it had been badly torn. This, he explained was why I had been badly bruised after birth (black and blue as mom described it). He could feel that 'the muscle' was now tight scar tissue, not normal muscle, and as I was growing taller the left side of my neck was not increasing in length due to the tether. My head was being pulled down and my collar bone up, and my left shoulder was now higher than the right side. He explained to mom that I may need an operation but, in the first instance, he would refer me to the masseuse (physiotherapist) to see if she could stretch the muscle. He called her into the room, a heavily built lady with a stern face, and demonstrated what he would like done.

I had an appointment to attend the masseuse department every week on Tuesday afternoon. It meant that I would have a half day from school with a trip into town but I was quickly to learn that school was the happier choice. I had to strip to the waist and climb onto a leather topped couch. The masseuse fastened a belt around my body, she said to prevent me falling off but it soon became apparent that it may have been to stop me escaping! She gripped my head firmly between her two hands and stretched my neck upwards, then towards my right shoulder and finally twisted my head so that I was now looking at the floor over my right shoulder. It was excruciatingly painful. She was using a considerable amount of force and I was at the point of screaming out with pain when she returned my head to its natural position. This she did three or four times, each time hurting more than the last and then I was released from the couch. I returned in stunned silence to the waiting room and mom. She handed my card to the receptionist to make an appointment for next week. I told mom that she had almost twisted my head off and that it hurt like hell, but her comment was brief, that if I did not have it done I would have to go into hospital. The thought that this may happen caused *her* a great deal of anguish and I therefore suffered many weeks of hell which equated, I am sure, to that meted out in medieval torture chambers. It never became easier to take and it hurt immensely every time. I simply learned to suffer in silence, for to scream out would be 'cissy '.

After some three months, I saw Mr Allen again and we were told that stretching had made no difference and, as I grew older, I would without doubt develop a severely twisted spine. He was now certain that I needed surgery to cut the muscle from the bone, releasing the tether to that side of my neck. I would be sent for in due course and he explained that it would be a country hospital since they were not admitting patients to the Children's hospital in view of the heavy bombing raids over Birmingham. Mom left the clinic mortified, her face ashen. It was the one thing she had not wanted to hear.

In May 1942 the postman delivered the letter that mom was dreading. I had to go into Standon Hall hospital, near Stone. It was a hospital she, dad and friends had never heard of, but they eventually found that it was near Stoke, about twenty miles away. From mom's point of view it was too far away and she not could understand why I could not go into Walsall hospital, since it was not really being bombed. Unfortunately there was no choice.

The first thing that caught mom's eye was the list of items I had to take into hospital, pyjamas, outdoor clothes, towels, soap, toothbrush and so on. All items had to be labelled with my name. This caused some consternation and signalled a trip to town to buy new items. I certainly could not take into hospital my every day wear, whatever would the hospital staff think! So started the countdown to hospital admission. My name was written in black Indian ink on small lengths of tape which were sewn into all of my clothes and then all were neatly pressed.

The night before setting out I must have a good bath so that hospital staff would note that I was well cared for. Though we had a large enamelled bath in the bathroom, it was rarely used since there was no hot water on tap. Any hot water needed had to be boiled in the brew'us boiler and carried through. Usually we bathed in a galvanised bath on the hearth in front of a warm fire, using hot water from kettles boiled on the hob. At the time, it helped with the wartime water regulation, which limited us to using no more than five inches of water for bathing. Mom toyed with the idea of using the bathroom for this special occasion but relented when I objected to getting out of the bath in the unheated room. So I bathed on the hearth with mom watching over to ensure that I thoroughly washed every inch of my body. After drying off, she made sure that my hair was set into waves. I was now nearly ten years of age and hated this babyish attention but, as always, she insisted that everything was to her liking.

Next morning we set out. Aunt Ruby tagged along to hold mom's hand. We caught the bus from Benton's Lane to Cannock and then a Midland Red bus to Stafford. We then had a similar journey on a green bus towards Stone. The bus dropped us off outside the gates of Standon Hall and we walked down a very long drive, probably a quarter of a mile.

The hall was set in acres of ground with very large nicely trimmed lawns and surrounding woodland. I had never seen anything quite like it before, it was awesome. We entered a dimly lit entrance lobby panelled in dark wood with an enormous staircase at the far end and large corridors to the left and right. A lady came to meet us and mom handed her the admission letter. A matron, wearing a dark dress and distinctive white hat, came down the stairs and greeted us, telling mom which ward I was to be admitted to. I would be under the care of orthopaedic surgeon, Mr. Wainwright, and would probably have an operation in about two days time. At this point mom burst out crying, grabbed hold of me and, pressing me to her, blubbed that I could not stay. She insisted that she was going to take me home. I started to cry because she was crying. Matron tried to console me but mom clung to me even more tightly, repeating that I could not stay. A lady doctor was called, a very kind lady in a white coat, who explained to mom the long term consequences of not having the operation. She told her that all mothers reacted in a similar way when they had to leave their children and eventually, supported by aunt Ruby, mom was consoled. She kissed me good-bye, tears welling from her eyes, and I was conducted up the large stately flight of stairs to my ward. A staff nurse took me to the window to wave good-bye. I could see mom and aunt Ruby turning the bend at the top of the long drive. I waved to them but they were too far away and I wept silently as I finally watched them pass from sight. The nurse comforted me and introduced me to other boys on the ward who would be my new friends over the next week or two. For the first time in my life, I was away from home alone. In a brief moment, I knew I had to be brave and felt solace in the arms of the nurse and my tears dried. I was a little troubled when I had to undress and get into my pyjamas with so many strange people around but this embarrassment soon passed and it became the norm.

Next morning, I found that I must still attend school and followed a line of boys from the ward. It was a separate building, probably a converted stable, in the large courtyard. The teacher provided sufficient work for the whole morning. Some of the reading books were those I was using at Landywood school and arithmetic was very similar. During the afternoon we were usually given an art project such as painting or modelling from clay. We also went on nature rambles into the surrounding fields and woodland. I thoroughly enjoyed finding and painting fir cones. By using different oil colours inside and outside the scales, we created ornaments or Christmas tree decorations.

Hospital care continued around the schooling and teacher released us immediately when a request was made for us to go back to the ward. The first day I was called to have an x-ray. I did not know this at the time, I was simply taken into a sparsely furnished room with a very hard table on which I was asked to lie. A lady (radiographer) straightened me up and dangled a piece of string over me from the end of a trumpet-like device. She measured with a ruler and went over to a control bench. There was a brief humming noise followed by a thud after which the nurse told me I could go back to school. Later that morning, I was sent for to see Mr Wainwright who it seems drew a purple line down my back to teach a young doctor about twisted spines. I was unaware of this artwork until later when nurse asked who had drawn on my back. She was finding it very difficult to remove, and apologised for rubbing so hard.

Next day we had to stay on the ward because it was the doctor's ward round. I heard him tell sister that I was to be prepared for theatre next day and then he moved on to Goronwy Evans in the next bed who had curiously twisted ankles. Staff nurse Rosser whispered to me that I could go to school and off I trotted.

That evening I was not allowed to eat anything and was taken to a side room at the bottom of the ward where nurse asked me to remove my clothes and put on a white gown. I was told to climb onto the table and lie on my side. The next thing I knew was that nurse was putting a large tube into my bottom, the like of which I had never before experienced. Before long I felt some curious sensations in my belly and the urgent need to go to the toilet which got worse and worse and I shouted to nurse to let me go to the toilet.

"Please, nurse, PLEASE, I can't hold it, I need the lavatory, PLEASE, NURSE!", I begged her, but she continued.

After what seemed like eternity, she told me to sit up and sat me on a bed pan, another new experience, though I had used a washing-up bowl at home when I was confined to my bedroom. I splattered the pan with the worst diarrhoea I had ever experienced, something like a tap at full force. The pan won't hold it all, I thought. I was terrified that I was messing the bed but nurse comforted me and showed me the rubber sheet beneath the bedpan. It was only later when I returned to my bed that Goronwy, who was about three years older than me, told me that I had been given an enema and explained that nurse had filled my bottom with soapy water to clean out my bowel ready for theatre. He had had an enema before his operation and staff nurse had explained what she was doing.

Next morning, I was still not allowed anything to eat or drink. Halfway through the morning, a nurse came and removed my pyjamas and told me to lie flat on a green towel she had put on the bed. She then painted my chin, neck and body with bright yellow iodine, similar to that used by Nurse Radcliffe at Landywood school. I had to turn onto my belly and she painted my back in the same way before wrapping me in a green linen sheet. I had no idea what was happening to me and lay there expectantly but without any great fear. Within an hour, a porter came to collect me on a trolley.

He pushed me into a small room with a very distinct smell. A very nice lady looked down on me and explained that she was going to put a piece of cotton wool on my face and that I should try to blow it away. This I did several times and suddenly inhaled an intense vapour smelling similar to that I experienced on entering the room. The lady told me to blow the smell away, which I did frantically. Within seconds I had the sensation that I was whirling at high speed through a tunnel that was getting narrower and narrower and felt very frightened. It was as though I was leaving this world and entering some Alice in Wonderland setting, then nothing!

It was some time later that I became aware of someone calling my name. Through a haze I recognised Nurse Rosser. The first thing I did was to turn sideways and vomit but she had a bowl ready. I retched into it repeatedly over the next hour or two. My neck felt as though someone was trying to strangle me, but I had no pain. My hand searched my neck and found a wide collar of sticking plaster which extended onto my chest. I found it difficult to stay awake and at times dozed into sleep.

Later in the day I was awakened by meals being served and a nurse, who I had not seen before, came to me with a meal and started to feed me. I was still feeling very sick and didn't want food, but she insisted. It was soon evident that the vegetable I hated most of all was on the plate, beetroot! I took the forkful she offered me but quickly gave it back to her in a projectile vomit. I felt weak and plaintively whispered that I did not like beetroot. Fortunately she took it away, only to come back later and try again to persuade me that it was good for me. I tried hard to eat it for her, but it was a horrendous experience, certainly my worst day in hospital.

Next day I sat on the side of my bed with the help of a lady in a white coat and then she held me as I took a step or two. I felt woozy and weak. When I looked down I had a large purple black bruise covering most of the front of my body down to my groins. Goronwy and Joe Harris came and chatted after they returned from school and convinced me that I would be better in two or three days. Their forecast was true and I did get stronger quite quickly.

Mom and Dad came to visit me the following Sunday. Since there was no morning bus service from Cannock to Stafford on Sunday, they had walked the ten miles to Stafford. She just had to see me and waiting for the afternoon bus might have meant she would be too late for visiting, which was unthinkable! They brought me fruit and sweets, for which I was thankful because I now had something to share with Goronwy, Joe and the other boys. They also brought fresh eggs and nurse told me to write my name on them so that they would be reserved for me. Mom was fussing over me, very relieved that the operation was over, albeit that I had an enormous plaster on my neck. Her face changed dramatically when I opened my shirt and she saw my enormous bruise, now beginning to turn yellow. They were informed that I would be in hospital for about two weeks. Good-bye still brought tears to mom's eyes, but on this occasion I was less affected. In fact, I felt more grown up living away from home and was happy to continue the experience for two more weeks.

It was some four or five days after the operation that I was dressed in day clothes and allowed to walk around the ward. There were children with all kinds of illness, some with plaster casts from their ankle to the middle of their chest, some with a large frame over their bed with ropes, pulleys and weights. Other children, with tuberculosis of the spine, lay on their stomachs in a padded plaster cradle, shaped to their bodies. For washing, a top cast was applied and the whole 'coffin' turned over so that they were now lying in a cradle on their back. The original was removed to reveal the front of their body for washing purposes.

Goronwy Evans had one leg in plaster. The other ankle was very badly twisted and would, he said, be dealt with when the other came out of plaster. It had been straightened in an operation two weeks before I came to hospital. The twisting he explained was due to rickets (vitamin D deficiency). Joe Harris had a bone infection in his foot and had a plaster of Paris with a window allowing access to the heel so that nurses could change dressings. Like Goronwy, he was going to be in hospital for some time. Many children were tethered in some way to their bed and would be so for many weeks. It seemed I had very little to worry about and, before long, found myself raring to go and was able again to attend the school classroom for lessons.

I had noticed Goronwy and Joe sending each other messages in secret code which intrigued me and I asked if I could join in. This was not possible, they said, they were not allowed to share the secret code. However, they explained about the Ovaltiney's club and since Goronwy had a form to introduce new members, we completed it together and posted it. My membership card, my badge and 'The official rule book of the League of Ovaltineys' came shortly after I arrived home. The rule book detailed the secret code used by members with strict instructions that it must not be divulged to any other persons. We continued to write to each other after leaving hospital, always including an encoded message for deciphering.

During my stay, talk among the boys on the ward, ten to twelve years of age, had inevitably turned to girl-friends and I declared Mavis Whitehouse, a girl in my class at Landywood School whose home was in Long lane. Mavis had sent me a Valentine card, my first ever, about three months before entering hospital. After discharge, this information led to every letter from Goronwy or Joe asking me to expand on our relationship. Had Mavis and I been out together and more importantly, had we kissed? Goronwy always passed on numerous kisses from Nurse Rosser, my hospital heart-throb, who he insisted sent her love. I really hoped so since I had loved her so much whilst in her care.

Whilst in hospital, Miss Liddle also excelled. A few days before I was to be discharged I received a bulky letter. It contained a letter from Miss Liddle enquiring about my well-being and sixteen individual letters from children in my class and news about others who could not write. The letters were from Mary Round, Gordon Challinor, Harriet Jones, Glenys Rigby, Kathleen Sadler, Margaret Rowley, Dorothy Turner, Ann Lomas, Basil Layton, Derrick Cadman, Kathleen Butler, Colin Parsons, Cynthia Snape, Mavis Whitehouse, Jacqueline Deakin and Lilian Wiggin. Peter Doody was apparently very ill, Alan Holdcroft had hurt his eye and Eric Gibbs was on holiday. Others who had not been able to write but were in my class were Dennis Hitch, Brenda Holloway, Betty Harper, Freddie Hughes, Rex Wiggin and Ernest Evans. Receiving so many letters from my school pals left me feeling very important, something like a hero must feel when returning from a victorious war. The letters told me that Eric Gibbs had gone on holiday to Evesham and that Colin Parsons was feeling very lonely without us. He had therefore been given the job of ringing the school bell between lessons, a job which gave us all a sense of importance when selected. I read the letters over and over again. I even marked them as if I was the teacher marking their work in class and I couldn't wait to see them all again.

The dressing was removed from my neck and I was checked over by the doctor. I was very surprised to find that there was no large wound under the plaster as had been the case with Goronwy and other boys. They had gone into the gory details about how many stitches I would have in the wound under the dressing which I would have to have removed. In reality, there was a tiny wound about a quarter of an inch long and yet I had an enormous bruise down to both groins, which was now bright yellow. In a way I was disappointed since I would have no wound to show my friends when I returned home. From the doctor's point of view, all was well and I was to be discharged home.

Since the day of discharge was a weekday, dad was unable to collect me and mom came accompanied by aunt Ruby and cousin Ron. The operation had been a success and mom was re-assured that it would prevent any deterioration in the spinal twist. There was a broad grin on her face and we left the hospital after I had hugged Nurse Rosser and said my good-byes to my friends.

The bus service from Stone to Stafford, was not very frequent and the next one would be at least two hours. Mom decided we should not hang around and should walk to Stafford, about six miles away. It was not long before Ron, who was six years old, was getting niggled about walking so far. He had already walked up the long drive of Standon Hall and back again and was getting very tired. After about half an hour aunt Ruby decided she was going to thumb passing vehicles, to hitch a lift. Eventually, a large lorry stopped and the driver agreed to drop us in the centre of Stafford. It was with some relief that the four of us scrambled into the cab and we just managed to squeeze into the relatively small space designed for one passenger. Aunt Ruby gestured to Ron to sit on the engine cover which was within the cab. With a few adjustments, we managed to close the door and the driver moved off.

After a mile or so, Ron's face was noticeably becoming redder and he was grimacing. He had been periodically lifting his bottom off the engine cover until, unable to take any more, he explosively yelled that it was too hot. Mom put her hand on the cover and couldn't believe that Ron had been sitting on it. Poor chap, he had been slowly cooking and had an angry red bottom with a blister for several days. I felt immense joy when I walked into the house after being away for so long and looked forward to recounting my adventure to my family and friends. I still had residues of my large bruise to display as my war wounds.

Not long after leaving hospital mom got into trouble with her teeth. She had complained of toothache on and off for many months and it was now incessant. On cold days she walked about doing her housework with a scarf round her mouth and had now reached the point where she could no longer stand the pain. She already bore a deep cavern-like scar on her left jaw, the result of a severe dental abscess in her youth. Rather than the abscess being dealt with properly, nature had been allowed to take its course, presumably because of the cost. As a child, I frequently asked her whether it was a bullet hole since I knew from films that bullets caused holes. Mom had always been 'sweet-toothed' and usually had at least two teaspoons of sugar in her tea, even during wartime restrictions. It had resulted in carnage to her teeth and, when she visited the dentist with her toothache, he told her all were seriously decayed and advised extraction. He would know that most working class people would not pay the cost of fillings or corrections. In any case, fillings, I knew from school, required the tooth to be drilled with a treadle machine which unpleasantly vibrated the tooth and whole skull. It was not an experience most people chose to repeat.

Next week, she made her way to Mr Guthrie, the dentist, who was fairly new to the village and worked from his bungalow on Churchbridge knob, just below Leacroft Lane. She was given gas by Dr Middleton and all her teeth were extracted. She arrived home looking ashen, badly shaken and mopping her mouth with a blood soaked man-size handkerchief. She spent the rest of the day spitting blood into a basin which grandma frequently washed. As the days past, her gums recovered, but her voice had changed and I remember finding it funny and laughing about this new persona. However, there was no more of the incessant toothache and she was a much happier person.

Some months later she attended Mr Guthrie for a mould of her mouth so that dentures could be made. She came home and told us that Mr Guthrie had put an enormous gob of clay in her mouth which had made her retch.

"It was wuss than 'avin yer damn tayth out. I was 'eavin' and 'eavin' and he was yellin' at me not to open me damn mouth! I could 'ave bloody kicked 'im!" she confessed.

We all laughed until tears streamed from our eyes. It didn't take much to make mom retch, a hair on her food was guaranteed to. She was later fitted with false teeth and suddenly looked younger again, but never stopped cursing her new false teeth which she was adamant had been made for someone else.

Dad also had a very poor set of teeth. Most were missing and the remaining teeth were stained yellow due to smoking and showed black patches of decay. He was not unique. This display of oral art was about the norm for the working class of the day and if a particular tooth played up, it meant a trip to the dentist. Granddad was, among his many other skills, the dentist to his grandchildren. Any of us suffering toothache were told to open our mouth for assessment and he would prescribe accordingly.

"Thee'st got a big 'ole in yer tooth, ode son, tha' shouldst fill it with wearter and sit on th'ob 'til it biles!", he would utter as he walked away chuckling.

Granddad had been my dentist during the shedding of most of my milk teeth. I would suffer a loose tooth until it hurt like hell when attempting to eat. Every time I yelled, mom urged me to visit granddad and had little sympathy when I chose to give it a miss. Usually grandma had passed on the message and granddad would appear on the scene.

"What's up, ode son, let's 'ave look. I con see it. Are, its this un as is movin' …", he muttered and gave a lightning flick with his finger.

The tooth flew across the room clattering against the door. Recovering from the sudden shock, followed by a feeling of elation, I retrieved the tooth and tonight would swap it for sixpence when the tooth fairy arrives! I then ate like I had never eaten before, having starved to some extent because of the pain. On one such occasion whilst feeling ravenous, aunt Sarah came back from shopping at Mears, the butcher on Walsall Road, and gave me a small pork pie that had literally just come from the oven. Over seventy years on, memory still recalls that delicious fare, so juicy, so peppery, so unforgettable!

Mom was terrified of doctors and, whenever she sought their help, invariably found difficulty understanding what the doctor had said. She had her fair share of acute illness, thankfully none of it of a serious nature. One visit to Dr. Middleton with a sore tongue resulted in her coming home and enlightening all that she had 'inflamed blood tasters'. I suppose it explained the soreness and she was happy with the diagnosis and even more uplifted when told it was not cancer, her eternal dread. It was many years later, when studying the tongue, I learned about the taste buds and, in a flash, mom's problem all those years ago, came to mind. She had been advised that she had inflamed taste buds!

Another misunderstanding followed an episode of severe loin pain which required an emergency admission to hospital. I was extremely frightened by her reaction to the acute pain and stood at the front gate, ashen faced and fighting back a tear as the ambulance whisked her away. She was investigated in hospital and returned home a few days later to paint the picture of her admission with some relief. She said that she had to go to the operating theatre where she had a paragram operation. Her audience of family and friends listened inquisitively. No-one had heard of the operation and it was not in *The Home Doctor* or dictionary and even Mr. Clift, the 'street doctor', did not know. I discovered years later, whilst studying the kidney, that the operation was a special x-ray for stones which is performed in the operating theatre and called a pyelogram, which no doubt would have been in *The Home Doctor*. Her fear of doctor's was not helped by an unnecessary remark from Mr. Hamilton, an Ear, Nose and Throat surgeon at Walsall General Hospital. She had problems with her ear and was sent to see him. As a result, she had to undergo quite extensive surgery to remove a pearly tumour in her ear. She recovered reasonably well but suffered with post-operative headaches. At a follow-up visit to the Out-patient's department she tried to explain to him about her headaches but the 'almighty' boomed at her,

"You have come here with your bloody ear, not your bloody head. Go and see your own doctor!"

Mom was mortified and desperately hurt and when she suffered a headache always reviled him, "That bloody detestable man, if he'd done his bloody job right I would not now have this problem".

CHAPTER 11

'Starting Grammar School - c. 1943'

By 1943 sausage and other uncontrolled meat products, which had helped ease meat rationing, now also became subject to rationing. I suppose it was this that led to mom and dad discussing whether we should keep a pig and our own poultry to make provision should rationing become even tighter. We were self-sufficient with potatoes and vegetables but were reliant on George Keeling, our butcher, for meat and on many occasions his provision left a lot to be desired. If rationing did tighten further, mom didn't feel she could provide the quality meals that a working man and growing schoolboy needed. The idea of keeping a pig was probably something discussed with others in the village who had had similar thoughts. There may even have been a government pamphlet on the subject since there were dozens of leaflets on all manner of topics!

Dad thought it was eminently possible since, when granddad carved up the land between the four bungalows, our garden was left with the old cowshed, a brick built edifice measuring about fifteen feet by twelve feet (5 metres by 4 metres) with a window in the end wall. The door in the opposite wall was split like a stable door allowing the upper half to remain open. It already had a built-in slurry gully to carry away cow excreta and would make an ideal home for a pig. He set about constructing a sty in one corner of the shed using timber sufficiently strong to hold a pig. Mom, in the meantime, completed and posted a buff application form to Staffordshire County Council Offices for permission to keep a pig. In the response we were told we would be allowed to keep one pig and would receive ration coupons for our allowance of pig cereal every month.

And so it was. At the beginning of April, mom and granddad purchased a pig from Penkridge market. The plan was that it would be slaughtered about three weeks before Christmas to provide quality meat for that season and cured ham and bacon for the following year.

Sharpes' pig cereal and bales of straw were ordered from Sid Snape's farm shop, in Upper Landywood, who agreed to deliver the order to our house every month. Sid's shop was a large wooden hut standing on a brick base set back from the lane and next to the chapel and old cottages. A counter in the front half allowed him to sell cereal, pulses and other loose produce by weight and at the rear was the storage for sacks of cereal, bales of hay, straw and other items needed in a smallholding.

The boiler in our brew'us became a large saucepan for boiling pig food. Undersized potatoes along with household scraps such as vegetable peelings were boiled, a pound of cereal added, and this recipe created a large bucket of sloppy food which the pig relished and very quickly put on weight. The smell in the house during this process was appalling, but it was something we learned to tolerate. It was the same in other homes. Whenever I called on John Bird, a school friend who lived in New Street, the house was usually perfumed by boiling pig swill, and his mother frequently had her arm up to the elbow in the bucket of slops, breaking up the vegetables, to ensure the pig did not choke whilst scoffing its food.

Dad also constructed a chicken coup and enclosure from bacon boxes from Cowern wholesalers. A dozen Rhode Island Red chickens from granddad would provide both brown eggs with rich yolks and chickens for slaughter. The chicken run was surrounded by wire netting which was five feet high. The hens happily scratched away at the soil searching for the food and gravel which had been thrown in. During dry weather they excavated quite deep holes in which they could crouch and throw loose soil over themselves to clear their feathers of mites. Dad's hitherto tidy garden had become a smallholding but there was still sufficient space for his gardening requirement. In fact, he was now even producing his own manure! Straw cleaned out weekly and loaded with pig urine and 'pooh' was laid out in a new composting area behind the shed and with months of inherent steaming and rotting would be most useful for growing potatoes. Whatever Hitler did to our country, it seemed, we would at least have sufficient food. In reality my friends, whose parents had not relished the stink of pigs or didn't have space for a pigsty, survived equally well on government rations with plenty of vegetables to maintain their body health.

Keeping a pig and chickens meant, of course, that one day they would have to be slaughtered. I referred earlier to Ernie Smith wringing the chicken's neck when he killed one for his customers and that I was unhappy with this method. Granddad used a different technique which was to stun them by quickly pushing a sharp knife into the auricular to cut through the brain and then bleed them by cutting their throat with the knife. I am sure there was momentary pain but the bird instantaneously became unconscious. Even so their wings did flap fiercely for a few seconds until the muscles became deprived of oxygen and the carcase finally became lifeless. Animal slaughter around the home place at the time was not uncommon and I was never upset by the scene since meat has been the natural food of humans for thousands of years. Mom and grandma always gave the exercise a miss. Animal slaughter was something most of my school friends had not experienced and some were keen to ask what it was about but, as might be expected, others pariculary girls did not want to know.

After slaughter a bird had to be plucked of its feathers. The bird's legs were tied and it was hung, breast forward, from a washing line post to facilitate plucking. It was a job I hated, but mom usually insisted. On a windy day, feathers blew everywhere. The breast feathers came away easily by gently pulling downwards, but the long quill feathers on the wings and tail were so tough that they cut into my fingers, hurting like hell. Once the carcase was cleared of feathers, mom rolled up a newspaper to make a large spill which she set alight in the fireplace. Like an Olympic runner, she ran into the garden with her torch, charred paper blowing everywhere, and played the flames over the chicken carcase to remove residual hairs. This she did meticulously knowing well she would retch uncontrollably if she found a hair when eating the cooked bird.

The chicken now had to be 'drawn' (its innards removed) and mom would never do this job because she was likely to vomit on the spot. I certainly would not do it at that time because it really did reek, which meant grandma, as always, drew the short straw. Whilst in service, she had probably plucked and dressed poultry and geese many times. The kitchen knife was well sharpened on the doorstep and the chicken's head removed. She then cut a circle around the chicken's anus to break into the inner cavity. She thrust her hand inside the bird as far as it would go and with a sweep of her hand and a gentle pull, the innards came out in one horrible bloody mess. The liver and neck was retained and the rest wrapped in newspaper and dumped. The cavity was well washed inside and the bird hung somewhere cool until required. Rarely was a chicken young enough to be roasted. It was more likely to have provided eggs for a year or two prior to slaughter and was destined for a recipe requiring casseroling with fresh vegetables. It was still a rare meal and therefore thoroughly enjoyed. With an eye on Christmas, a cock chicken was grown on during the summer months and slaughtered for the Christmas roast.

During this time the government set up its 'Wings for Victory' campaign to persuade everyone to buy National Savings stamps to fund the war effort. We were advised at school that it would allow us to build more planes and ships. Hitherto, we had collected funds with such events as a mile of pennies which were laid out up and down the school playground and, if achieved would raise over £200. We did not achieve a mile but we collected just less than half of this amount. During the launch of the campaign, large red, white and blue banners stretched across the metal fence either side the memorial gates on Walsall Road displaying "WINGS FOR VICTORY" and directing us to the recreation ground where a genuine Spitfire was on display. A queue of children lined up to sit in the cockpit and handle the controls. It was the first time I had witnessed an aircraft on the ground. Frequently we had set up make-believe cockpits on the railway fence at home. Sitting astride the wooden fence like a jockey we attached levers to the wooden posts and thrust our joysticks forward making the sounds of diving aircraft as we held make-believe dog fights. Now, sitting in a real cockpit and pushing forward a real joystick was not only a wonderful experience but allowed us to create better-informed cockpits in our games, setting up rudder control pedals to turn.

Staff in a marquee set up on the site extolled the need for more Spitfires and gave out stamp collecting cards on which we could affix thirty sixpenny (2.5p) savings stamps and thereby gain a fifteen shilling (75p) single unit Savings Certificate. After the war we would be paid back one pound and sixpence (£1.025) for every certificate we held. The stamps were on sale in our classrooms at school and, every week, mom gave me sixpence or a shilling (5p) to buy stamps. Sometimes I was able to buy a special stamp for a half a crown (12.5p) and felt very important as I handed the money to Miss Jones. There was a National Savings thermometer chart in each class and a larger one outside school which showed how much each school was contributing to the war effort.

Come the end of August, I entered top class and Miss Jones was taking over the class from Mr Shipman, a teacher at the school for many years, who had just retired. In the past four years, therefore, I had had only two teachers. We had reached a much higher level of arithmetic with decimals and complex fractions. More complex written problems replaced the mental arithmetic that we had been used to and we were given papers with several questions which we were expected to answer. We were taught how to construct interesting essays and then asked to write an essay on any subject given to us by Miss Jones. I was not aware at the time, but this was leading to an examination which some of us would be sitting in early spring, the Scholarship examination used by Staffordshire Education Authority to choose pupils for its allocated grammar school places. A few years later, this became the eleven plus (11+) examination. Miss Jones spent some three or four months carefully coaching us for the Scholarship examination and we now had a good idea of the format that it would take.

In Spring, about a third of the class would be taking the examination. On the day, we entered our classroom to find half of the desks had been piled along the side wall and the other half spaced apart in the middle. We sat one to a desk and, after instructions from Miss Jones, a question paper was handed to each of us for the arithmetic examination. The questions were exactly of the form that we had been taught and, being my strongest subject, I found it quite easy. In fact, I had answered all questions well before time was called, including the thorough check Miss Jones had stressed we should carry out before handing in the paper.

In the next examination we were asked to write an essay. We were given a choice of subjects and I chose to describe 'A journey from tree to chair'. My imagination ran riot and I described a large knurled oak tree (probably one of the many I knew well) which had grown undisturbed for a hundred years. It became painfully aware of very sharp axes cutting into its trunk, every blow making it quiver, shaking off its acorns. It creaked and toppled, crashing to earth where its arms were removed. The tree trunk was rolled and floated on the river where lumberjacks guided it towards the sawmill, something I had learned from Miss Liddle years earlier when teaching us about forestry in Canada. My tree trunk was caught in a huge log jam but was eventually freed by lumberjacks jumping from log to log in their spiked boots. From here on, being mechanically minded and having observed the steam driven saws at the Plant pit, I was able to describe the sawing of my tree and the work of the carpenter in making a chair. I think I could have written forever. Unfortunately I did not have time to read it through and I handed in a several page essay.

I had enjoyed the examination but I am not sure that I yet understood the implications of taking it. I had never met nor was aware of any boys who went to the grammar school. It was certainly not something we ever spoke about in the lane. Hitherto, it had not really been the expected direction taken by working class lads. I had frequently witnessed uniformed schoolboys hanging out of the windows of the 8.30am train to Walsall which passed our house every school day. It had not really registered that they were on their way to grammar schools and I may be joining them if I passed the examination.

A week or two after the examinations, we witnessed quite an unusual behavioural problem in class. One of the boys, who had throughout school been of excellent conduct, became uncontrollable. *Robert* (I shall call him) had decided to argue with some vehemence with Miss Jones over the answer he had given to a question she had asked the class. She was not enamoured by the objectionable way he had spoken to her and yelled at him, ordering him to go and stand in the corner, immediately! He did not move, and she repeated her command two or three times. She tried to lead him there, but *Robert* remained stubborn and Miss Jones left the class to see the headmaster. Mr Bickford came in and ordered Robert out of the class. He refused to leave. Mr Bickford took hold of him to pull him towards the door, but he slumped to the ground, refusing to go. The headmaster slapped his thigh and *Robert* responded by screaming and kicking landing Mr Bickford one in the crotch, visibly hurting him. Eventually he was dragged along the floor out of the class. We all witnessed the event and could not believe what had happened, nor could we understand why it had happened. *Robert* was always a quiet well-behaved boy, a friend to everyone, who had never before been in trouble. Somehow a simple argument with Miss Jones had led to him snapping and with every reaction he dug a deeper hole for himself. He was totally out of control, but a while later he had quietened down, returned to the class and was no further problem. It was the only time we had ever witnessed such a reaction to a teacher. Normally we did exactly as told and if we refused, which was extremely rare, it may result in the cane. We knew this and accepted the punishment.

The charts on the classroom wall now frequently showed that losses of German planes and ships were exceeding our own losses. We cheered as the up-dated figures were added, just as we had done a few weeks earlier at the news that General Montgomery's Eighth army had pushed back the Germans, who were in full retreat. Church bells were ringing for the first time since war had been declared. Life was great! We were on the winning side, or so it seemed. We abhorred the monster Hitler and could frequently be heard singing about him and his cronies, to the 'Colonel Bogey' tune,

> *We are the night shite shifters,*
> *We shift shite by night singing-*
> *Hitler has only got one ball,*
> *Goering has two but very small,*
> *Himmler has something sim'lar*
> *But poor old Goebbel's has no balls at all!*

We gave no thought to the vulgarity, everything was allowed where these beasts were concerned. Above all, the tune and words were very funny and sounded so triumphal that we repeated it over and over again. On a dark night it was not uncommon to hear a rendition somewhere in the distance. If not this song, the distant voices were singing a current jingle or song from the radio and if not singing, were telling gags about the Germans, which were commonplace from comedians on the radio and invariably led to a throaty laugh.

There was quite a lot of comedy on the radio. I particularly enjoyed the 'Happidrome' on Sunday evening with comedians 'Ramsbottom and Enoch and me', where 'me' was the theatre boss. Their signature tune, frequently tripped off my tongue without thinking,

> *"We three in the Happidrome,*
> *We're working for the BBC,*
> *Ramsbottom and Enoch and me"*

On Saturday evenings, "In town tonight" started with inspiring opening music recalling the busy streets of London and the sound of traffic. Over this the announcer like a paper boy called

"In town tonight! – IN TOWN TONIGHT!"

He would suddenly shout "Stop!" and with this, the cacophony of traffic and music stopped. It was time for London and everyone in the country to sit down and listen to the show, an excellent variety programme with top singers, instrumentalists and comedy acts.

A similar variety programme was 'Monday night at eight' with its opening theme with which we always joined in,

It's Monday Night at eight o'clock,
Oh can't you hear the chimes
They're telling us to take an easy chair.
So settle by the fireside, take out the Radio Times
For 'Monday night at eight' is on the air!

Probably the most popular comedy programme of the week was ITMA (It's that man again) with Tommy Handley, Mrs Mop ("Can I do you now, Sir!"), drunken Colonel Chinstrap ("I don't mind if I do!"), Fumph (a German spy) and many other participants whose catchphrases were everyday parlance to us. We habitually used the catchphrases as we chatted amongst ourselves.

On Friday night I was invariably frightened out of my wits by 'The Man in Black''. It was a series of horror stories, after the watershed at 9.00pm. It opened with the haunting voice of Valentine Dyall,

"This is your storyteller, the Man in Black! Tonight our story begins when……"

He might then describe some haunting setting in darkest Africa accompanied by sounds, such as a green mamba slithering along the keyboard of a piano, tinkling along the ivories as it neared its unsuspecting victim sitting reading in an armchair. In another tale, a victim already highly charged by a frightening story about a killer snake, looked under his bed to see two eyes peering at him, like cat's eyes reflecting his candle flame. He immediately died of shock! It was not a snake but reflecting 'eyes' set-up by his killer. I was terrified by the series of stories and frequently hid my head in a cushion whilst the story was unfolding. For many nights, before getting into bed, I looked beneath it with my heart pounding in case there were reflecting eyes.

The songs of the time reflected the life of soldiers missing home and were frequently played on the radio and we sang to them at the top of our voices. Mom, in particular, had a very attractive voice and could be heard joining in from any room in the bungalow.

'Ma, I miss your apple pie,
Ma, I miss you too!

and

'Kiss me goodnight, sergeant major
Bring me up a nice hot cup of tea!'

Many songs during the war were spirit-boosters. Music was played every morning and afternoon in radio programmes such as 'Worker's playtime', keeping workers in ammunition and plane-building factories singing and working to the beat. Songs by Vera Lynn (which later became famous), were sung by everyone, 'We'll meet again' and not forgetting the bluebirds over the 'White Cliffs of Dover'. As a bird observer I never understood this song but perhaps bluetits over the white cliffs didn't fit the lyric.

During early summer whilst waiting for a bus at Benton's Lane, it was becoming commonplace to be passed by long convoys of American army vehicles which were very different in appearance to our own armed forces' lorries. Until then, the commonest war vehicle passing us had been those of RAF with sixty feet long trailers, carrying wings and fuselages of aircraft to assembly plants. Two similar lorries had brought the Spitfire assembled in the 'rec' on Wings for Victory day.

American personnel were now regularly observed on street corners and in shops. They had presumably arrived to help with the war in Europe but nothing official was ever said. Over the next few months the numbers increased considerably. As time passed, we might also see an occasional Yank with an arm around a girl in the village. Local girls were eager to get her hands on a pair of nylon stockings and groups could be seen chatting to the Americans. Until now they had been using dyes such as gravy browning on their legs to mimic stockings, getting a friend to draw a black line at the back of their leg for the seam. We asked if they had any gum or chocolate, usually a jaunty 'Got any gum, chum?' which we had been led to believe did the trick. It didn't! They were obviously generous with gum and chocolate, but used them as merchandise to buy goods or favours, usually the latter.

In May, it was announced at school that Eric Gibbs and I had passed the Scholarship examination and would be going to Queen Mary's grammar school at the beginning of next school term. For a while there was a degree of coldness between our gang of four, perhaps due to a little jealousy. Boys who went to grammar school we were told were cissies and we would have to wear a school uniform. It lasted a day or two and then we were all mates again.

Within a week or so, I was taken by mom to Queen Mary's Grammar School in Walsall to be interviewed by the headmaster, H M Butler Esq. M.A. Cantab. We were directed to a seat in the rather dark dingy entrance hall of the headmaster's house where another mother was waiting for her son to come out. It was something I had never experienced before and for which I had not been counselled. Neither mom nor dad had experienced an interview and were of little help. I found the ordeal somewhat frightening and had no idea what to expect. After a few minutes a thin pale boy emerged, wheezing and gasping for breath. The headmaster, followed him out and spoke to his mother.

"I presume Paul is allergic to cats", he remarked to his mother, who nodded rather cautiously.

The headmaster called me into an equally dim study, where a shabby black cat lay by a smouldering almost extinguished fire. He was rather stern as he asked questions about what I had done at school and what my hobbies were, always referring to me as 'Carpenter' rather than my Christian name. The approach was nothing at all like I had experienced at Landywood school. It is unlikely that Mr Bickford was aware of the interview otherwise he would without doubt have prepared us for the ordeal. As we returned home on the bus, mom told me that Paul Baker suffered from severe asthma and was allergic to cats, his mother had said. She was extremely worried that the illness may have lost him a place in the school. It didn't and I spent seven happy years with Paul as one of my friends, an extremely intelligent boy.

A few days later mom and dad received a letter to say that I was offered a place at Queen Mary's Grammar School, along with details about the school uniform and requirements of the school. They were so proud that they had to tell everyone. Fortunately Eric had also been offered a place so we could make the daily journey on the bus together.

In no time, mom was dragging me to Walsall to buy a school uniform from Buxton and Bonnets in the Bradford arcade. They knew everything about Queen Mary's uniform and provided the red, green and yellow ringed cap, matching tie, navy blue blazer, grey short trousers and the badge for the top pocket. The badge, a replica of the school shield, was one of the most expensive items, since mom had decided to purchase the heavily embossed version with polished gold braid. Mom was so proud and over the moon that she was happy to pay any price to see me in the Queen Mary's School uniform! I have to say that the embossed school badge of the day did give a higher level of elegance to the school blazer and I felt very proud when I wore it. Not so the school cap which was the butt of jokes by non-QMS friends and frequently it had to be rescued from the gutter where a side swipe across the head had sent it flying like a frisbie. I never really liked wearing a hat of any kind and was only too glad in future years when we were out of sight of school prefects or masters so that the offending article could be relegated to a pocket. The final purchase was a leather satchel to carry my books which was purchased from Walsall Leather behind the Savoy cinema and, as always, mom chose the best that they had, raiding the gardening 'nest egg' for the necessary funding.

At this time, Eric and I had started train-spotting more seriously. We had, of course been interested in locomotives for a long time but now began collecting the locomotive numbers (engine numbers we called them) including the shed number from whence it came, displayed on the smoke box at the front of the locomotive. The local engine sheds were 3A, 3B and 3C which represented the locomotive sheds at Bescot, Bushbury and Walsall respectively. The main number was on the side of the locomotive cab and, if together, Eric and I would agree to read and record one number each. The problem in collecting the numbers came with the much faster express trains, frequently pulled by a named locomotive such as 'Duchess of Malone' which appeared on a nameplate over the central wheel arch. It was extremely difficult to read and memorise the name, particularly when it was a historic name we had never heard. One of our favourite spots to collect numbers was the railway bridge over the Wolverhampton to Stafford main line, on the Watling Street (A5) at Gailey, about five miles from home. We cycled there whenever we felt the urge. Here, in particular, it was impossible to read the name-plate of a train travelling through a deep cutting at eighty miles an hour, before it plunged under the bridge beneath us. We had a split second before we were enveloped in smoke and steam! In later years, we could check the name in Ian Allen's book of locomotive numbers, but this did not appear until the end of the war. When it did appear, we learned that our attempts at reading the nameplates of many of the locomotives at Gailey had not been entirely correct!

When together, Eric, Colin, David and I quite often played war games during the long vacation. Pairs of us went in different directions into the countryside and then set about finding and tracking each other until we could eventually set an ambush and trap our opponents. It was great fun and meant a great deal of crawling on our bellies behind and through hedgerows and in the long grass. We were frequently covered by nature's own camouflage, goose grass and its 'bobby buttons', fallen leaves or hay clinging to our clothing like limpets or sometimes, like the Home Guard, we might cover ourselves in bracken and branches. It was amazing how close we could get to our opponents without being seen, but a broken twig or a bird panicking and taking flight was usually a giveaway. At times we may cheat and ask other friends out playing such as the Evans',

Sylvia, Margaret or Tommy, if they had seen our opponents. Once within range, the fight could begin!

Our army weapons were homemade rifles shaped from wood and perhaps a bayonet pressed from a six inch (15cm) nail by placing it on the railway track. However, by mid-summer cow parsley was fully grown and we could cut the long hollow stems for pea shooters, using the developing hawthorn berries as ammunition. These were quite effective if we could find a stem of cow parsley with a reasonably close fitting bore. Being hit on the side of the face by a berry was quite painful. Using a real projectile in this way at least enlightened our opponent that they had been 'shot'. When using our make-believe wooden rifles it was easy to claim that the 'shot' had missed and an argument would ensue, invariably with no agreement.

We had several home-made weapons at our disposal. Before the war we could purchase a cowboy's pistol with caps which made a real bang. The explosive caps were not available during the war. We therefore carried a homemade pistol created with rubber bands which we pushed in our waistband. It fired rubber bands and was quite useful at close range. The gun was very easily constructed from two pieces of wood. The hand grip was a piece of wood half inch square (12mmx12mm) and about 5 inches (12cm) long (we sometimes used a clothes peg). The other piece of wood for the barrel was the size and shape of a ten pack of cigarettes. Four evenly spaced rubber bands held the pair together in the form of a pistol. A nail knocked into the underneath of the 'barrel' formed the trigger. Squeezing the trigger now opened a gap between the handgrip and barrel and a missile (another rubber band) was inserted about a quarter of an inch (5mm) and the trigger released to grip the rubber band. The protruding rubber band could then be stretched over the nose of the barrel. It was then simply a case of take aim and fire! The missiles were very effective and stung up to about 7 feet (2 metres). Our supply of rubber bands during the war years came from cutting one eighth inch (3mm) sections across old bicycle inner tubes. Although the latter may have been repaired several times during its life there were always segments of unworn tube from which rubber bands could be cut.

We also created catapults made with strips of rubber and a patch for the ammunition again cut from a tyre inner tube. A 'Y' shaped forked branch could be cut from the hedgerow. During army games we fired lightweight berries such as unripe blackberries as ammunition. We may at times fire pebbles at a target of tin cans to see who could achieve the highest score but never at each other for obvious reasons. Some older boys and young men from Upper Landywood, who shall remain nameless, were frequently seen firing catapults at birds, though thankfully not very successfully. One did however have an air pistol which was more successful. It might have been understandable if he had been shooting for food but it was not the case, the dead birds were simply left to rot or await scavengers. Of course, any Robin Hood story or film would inspire us to make bows and arrows, usually from hazel, but obviously not a tool we would use in modern warfare!

One day whilst in the middle of a war game, there was a bit of drama relating to our eagerness for train spotting. We knew that a 'namer' (as we called named locomotives) came down our own line towards Stafford every week-day at 11.20 a.m. Eric and I were tracking Colin and David in the allotment alongside Tom Farrington's tall dahlias. Eric heard the whistle of the express train and we frantically broke cover and raced across the lane, up George Gretton's drive, through his back gate, across his garden and over the railway fence, in order to get the locomotive's details. We were soon aware of bellowing and turned to see George Gretton running along his garden path shaking his fist, followed closely by Millie, his wife.

"Come here, you two!" he bawled.

Without a second thought we raced along the railway embankment with George following and then down the embankment into a shallow cavity used as a hideout on previous occasions. It was quite small but we huddled closely together, our limbs scratched by jagged pieces of clinker which lined the hole. Peering through the tall grass and bracken we could see George about twelve feet above us, hand shading his eyes, as he scanned the track and across the other side. He marched up and down for about five minutes, no doubt pondering how we had disappeared from sight, and then gave up the chase. We were rather annoyed with him because we had missed the details of the locomotive! A little later we walked down the lane to find Colin and David who had seen us race out of the allotment yelling "The namer!" but had been oblivious to what followed. For a few days, we gave George a wide berth, unsure whether he knew which scallywags had run across his vegetable patch. Since Eric was the only boy in the lane with bright ginger hair it is more than likely that he knew at least one of the culprits. Though we passed him many times afterwards, he never referred to the incident.

Having grown somewhat over the four years since my first bicycle, the time had come to upgrade from twelve to sixteen inch wheels. It was not easy to get bicycles during the war years since most steel was used for creating the instruments of war. We managed to find one at Halford's in Walsall, a black New Hudson bicycle, but very utility looking. So much so that, apart from the shine, it looked old even before it was taken from the shop. There was a problem at the outset in that even with the saddle at its lowest position, I was unable to reach the pedals correctly. Dad sorted this by making wooden blocks for the pedals to raise them about an inch (25mm). It worked and I was able to use it though cycling was very clumsy and my feet frequently slipped off the pedals. It managed, but within a few months rust appeared and the chrome began to peel off the handlebars and wheels.

We cycled everywhere except into Walsall town centre, and gave our cycles plenty of wear. Laden shopping bags would be hung from the handle bars, usually one each side to balance. Empty shopping bags were much more of a hazard than full ones since they easily became trapped between wheel and forks and the rider may then become a projectile over the handlebars! I suppose it happened about once a year but the most serious was when racing downhill from Sid Snape's shop in Upper Landywood. The bag became trapped, the bike bucked and I was thrown off and gamboled once or twice ahead of the front wheel resulting in grazes to my face, arms and legs. Fortunately no bones were broken, just my pride. I had many falls as a small boy but luckily never suffered a broken bone. Panniers for carrying bags were not easy to get and, in any case, I would have felt like Nurse Evans rather than a tough guy. I did have a large saddle bag for a few items of shopping.

The degree of wear and tear on our bicycles was usually severe because of the amount of use they had. Tyres lasted about two years and during that period I would have at least two punctures which had to be repaired. Occasionally a side wall of the tyre gave way and a balloon of inner tube protruded. When an inner tube was beyond repair it was replaced with a new purchase from Mr Hall on Walsall Road. I became quite adept at removing the tyre and repairing or replacing the inner tube at a very young age. Since there were no gears on war time cycles, the chain stretched due to the pressure exerted and frequently came off, usually at most inappropriate moments. The rear spindle was simply slackened with a spanner from the saddle bag and pulled backwards to tighten the chain. When it was no longer possible to take up the slack, I removed a link to shorten the chain since a new chain was fairly expensive. Brake pads needed to be replaced at least once a year since rapid breaking was merciless on the rubber and the time would come when metal was heard scraping against metal. About every three years, pedals needed changing, usually because the ball bearings had fallen out due to lack of lubrication. I certainly did not lubricate as frequently as I should and gave my bicycles a really hard time. Even though the quality of this new bike was poor, it kept going for some years and the level of exercise provided kept me very well toned.

Come September, I started school at Queen Mary's Grammar School. We would spend the first school year at Moss Close, a large converted house on the corner of Mellish and Buchanan Road. This would mean two bus journeys to get there, the number one and number six. In view of the fact that I would be travelling every day on Walsall Corporation buses, I needed to get a weekly bus pass. The single fare from Benton's Lane to Walsall was tuppence ha'penny (1p) or a half a crown (12.5p) per week. Walsall bus station to Mellish Road was a penny (0.4p), another ten pence (5p). A weekly pass would cost two and a penny (10.5p) and this could be purchased from the ticket office in Walsall bus station. I dutifully joined the queue of schoolboys at the office and obtained my first pass, and thereafter had to do so every Friday afternoon.

One of the first duties at school was to get our textbooks from a bookseller who attended school on the first two days. The introductory letter had provided us with the list of the books I needed and informed me that Mr Hudson (Hudson's book shop, Ablewell Street) would be present on the first day. Many boys already had their books, some purchased, some from an older brother who had passed through the school. I had to purchase my books, 'Experimental Science' by Brown for four and sixpence (22.5p), 'First and Second Course in Arithmetic' by Borchard for three and sixpence (17.5p), 'The New National Song Book' by Stanford and Shaw for two and sixpence (12.5p) and books for five other subjects. In all they cost just over a pound.

Compared with those at Landywood School, the classrooms there were very small and teachers changed from lesson to lesson, something I had not been used to. We also had to stand when a teacher came into the class. Mrs Dennison, the French mistress, came in to take our first lesson,

"Bonjour!"

"Bonjour, madame!", one or two boys replied.

"Asseyez vous, tres doucement!", she said, gesturing with her hands to sit down.

I sat down. I did not have a clue what she was talking about. She asked questions in French and expected an answer. I was not very enamoured by a teaching method, whereby we were expected to quickly become fluent in the spoken language. She was also very hot on pronunciation and expected us to speak like a Frenchman. I became quite good in this respect, only because it was a language which sounded better if you could roll an 'R' with your tongue, and I appeared to be adept at this. I never really understood the spoken word without going through the arduous task of translating word by word, a very slow process which seemed to irritate her. I also had to come to terms with good old Oxford English before struggling with a foreign language.

When it came to English grammar, I found the teacher, Mr Symes ('Old Daddy'), to be quite unpleasant and I was constantly belittled by him, more so it seemed than others in the class. He was fairly tall, slim, gaunt-faced and with white hair and a white goatee beard, which I felt gave him a frightening demeanour. I had been brought up in a home and community where a broad black country accent and language was the norm and my natural childhood speech was now causing me serious problems.

The Great Wyrley accent was a combination of Black Country and earlier forms of speech, possibly gipsy or romany. Grandma and granddad, in particular, had grown up in an era when travel was limited and may not have had regular contact with people with other dialects. Grandma had been in service but it had not, it seems, affected her speech and it is possible that the house to which she was attached was fairly local, such as a farmer. They had also pre-dated radio which began to bring 'Oxford speak' into people's homes. Their speech, and particularly grandma's, had therefore retained components which might have been more at home a century earlier. Mom's and dad's speech was modern Black Country for want of a better term. An example of what they might say to me was;

"You can't do that!"

Grandma: "Thee cossna do that!"
Granddad: "Yoe conner do that!"
Mom: "Yer car do that!"
Dad: "Yoe cor do that!"

"You mustn't go there!"

Grandma: "Thee mustna gue theer!"
Granddad: "Yoe munner gue theer!"
Mom: "Yer car gue theer!"
Dad: "Yoe munner gue theer!"

For Grandma, 'Thee', 'Thou' and 'Thy' were pronouns in everyday usage in her conversations. The other occupants of Street's Lane were younger and though Black Country was the norm, some had originated outside the area and had inflections from elsewhere such as Eric's family with a Worcestershire accent. I therefore grew up with a mixture of local and 'foreign' inflections due to the closeness with my pals, most of whom had a Black Country accent as at home.

Now at Queen Mary's, whenever I lapsed into my black country mode in answering a question, old daddy Symes' face would grimace and he would stress my error aloud in class and, as might be expected, an audible titter rippled through the class. I found it a terrifying time because I could never relax and fell further and further behind since I was afraid to put up my hand to answer questions. Any written work also reflected the grammar of Great Wyrley, which apparently hadn't mattered at Landywood school but was now heavily underlined. My mum could not understand my first term report which was far from the glowing reports which had been the norm at Landywood primary school.

Another new adventure was Latin, which was not too bad and spoken roughly as written. The one or two Roman Catholic pupils in the class were in their element, since their church services were in Latin, and they streaked ahead of the rest of us. The Latin Master was a priest, Rev. Williams (I think) nick-named 'Holy Joe', who walked around the class with a steel edged ruler. It was a fairly simple language to understand once we had learned the declensions of the various nouns and verbs. In Latin, the norm is to put the verb at the end of a sentence – 'the cat the mat it sat on' – not too difficult to comprehend, though longer sentences could be a nightmare. If Holy Joe considered a translation of a sentence or answer to a question was foolish, he struck the offender across the back of the hand with the edge of his ruler, usually raising an enormous painful wheal which later became a bruise. His habit of standing behind you slapping the ruler in the palm of his hand, whilst you were trying to answer, never helped the thought process.

Punishment in school could be vicious and was most often three to six hard lashes across the buttocks with a thin cane usually by the headmaster of Moss Close, W E Terry, nick-named 'Wet'. The accused would be taken out of the classroom into the corridor or onto the landing upstairs outside his office, where the deed would be performed. The lashes would ring out along the corridors and into the classroom where we counted each stroke. When our classmate returned we sat in silence feeling for him. Some came in with a hardened 'I can take it' look, but most had a pained expression and tears running down their cheeks. During the next break we would see the large angry red streaks, some with blood, across the buttocks and thighs resulting from the assault. In comparison, my red thigh from a slapping by Mr Bickford, seemed very insignificant. Fortunately I was never subjected to these barbaric acts at Queen Mary's grammar school, but there were regulars who did not seem to learn as a result. I had seen the cat-o-nine-tails used in pirate films and to me the punishment meted out seemed little different. Although I had never been thrashed, I was still hurting psychologically but suffered in silence and never told mom and dad. For all I know, Eric may have told his parents but they never let on.

My strongest subject at primary school had always been mathematics and this continued to be the case at Queen Mary's. Then we started to move into areas which were new and rather more puzzling such as algebra and geometry, but I enjoyed the challenge. It took a while to get the hang of equations 'If $x + 4 = 9$, what is x?'. We were taught that we had to move the 4 to the other side of the equation and change its sign, now becoming minus 4 , so that the equation becomes '$x = 9 - 4$', and x was therefore 5. It was easy to do as instructed and I had no problem except I could not see the point of it all. Then one day it dawned on me that it was a mathematical language, the letters simply depicting an unknown quantity. In other words, if I was given a bag containing an unknown number of oranges and given four more, and told that I now had nine oranges, mental arithmetic would immediately tell me that there had originally been five in the bag. Algebra had simply put that analogy in an equation, $x + 4 = 9$. Once the penny dropped, the subject became easy and I had no further problems.

A subject I found particularly interesting, though entirely new to me, was Physics. Towards the end of the first year we had to walk down to the main school for our introduction to this scientific subject which was done by a very nice senior master, Mr W A Burn or 'WAB' (as in 'job'). We sat at benches in a laboratory and he taught us about levers, pulleys, density and specific gravity, demonstrating the theories he was explaining by appropriate experiments. I was particularly fascinated by the Eureka vessel, a small galvanised can with a downward pointing 'teapot' spout. He filled the can with water until it was running from the spout. When it had stopped running he placed a cube of metal of known weight into the water and collected the water displaced in a measure vessel below the spout. Since density is determined from mass divided by displaced volume, the density of the metal could be calculated. Using different cubes, we were shown that different metals had different densities. WAB's demonstration of this experiment was accompanied by the story of Archimedes who jumped out of his bath shouting 'Eureka' (I have found it!) when he twigged how he might calculate the density of a metal. By this method, Archimedes demonstrated to king Heiron of Syracuse that his crown was not pure gold, but a mix of gold and base metal. In this way, physics was brought alive and became a favourite subject. After months of misery, studying subjects which did not really enthuse me, I had found a subject which stimulated my imagination, and every week looked forward to the lesson. Mathematics and the science subjects soon became my favourites and it was also apparent to me that the masters teaching these subjects were more humane and did not rely on the cane.

Wednesday afternoon was games afternoon when we had to walk to the playing fields at Mayfield. Here we started to play rugby football which I never felt was much fun, compared with the football we played in the fields at home or watched at the Molineux ground. Dad didn't understand rugby football so that even he did not care whether I played it or not. During the war, sports clothing was not easy to come by and mom did not feel she wanted to lash out on it. Sports equipment was not at the time actually demanded by Queen Mary's in view of the difficulties. The result was that I turned out for games afternoon with a pair of old grey short trousers, an old white shirt and my football boots. My first few games were a bit of a kick about but then they became more alarming. There was a degree of heavy contact which as quite a small boy I found rather painful. The worst came when I was placed in the position of hooker in a scrum, surrounded by much bigger boys who, looking back, were probably junior members of Walsall Rugby Football Club and needed to impress WAB, who was games master, that they had the necessary aggression for the game. To put it mildly, I was crushed to the degree of severe pain and next found myself under 'half a ton' of writhing human beings, unable to get out. Not understanding the game, I thought 'damn that for an experience' and I made any excuse I could to do cross country running, which was an alternative option. I often prayed for a wet Wednesday afternoon so that sports would be cancelled and we could stay at school for the afternoon.

The cross country run was quite enjoyable. I was naturally a sprinter and therefore distance running was inevitably a mix of walking and running between bouts of severe stitch. We left Mayfield pavilion, running along Princes Avenue and into the arboretum extension which we crossed diagonally coming out on the bridleway leading to Mellish Road. Turning right, we ran the length of the Aldridge Road dual carriageway, over the canal bridge and right into Longwood Lane to its junction with Sutton Road. Then left, up Three Crowns Hill, and right at the top into Skip Lane. This hill was a killer after the long run and we invariably walked up. The final run back to Mayfield was always a gift, downhill along cart tracks across the canal bridge on Gillety fields, crossing Broadway at the Sutton Road junction and back to the pavilion. It was not uncommon for some boys to run along the canal towpath from the canal bridge at the end of the dual carriageway, getting off at the farm bridge on Gillety fields and joining the run at this point, cutting off nearly two miles. All too frequently, a prefect had been placed on Sutton Road canal bridge, and guilty parties suffered a detention!

By the end of the school year I was beginning to come to terms with the Oxford accent but my struggle due to my Black Country dialect had taken its toll. I seemed to be average in some subjects, but in most I was down in the lower half in class positions. What made it worse was that Eric was doing much better and his mom was all too happy to make this known, not to hurt me, just proudly extolling Eric's achievements. The problem was that friends asked mom how I was doing, and she had little good news. Eric was much more at home with the Oxford speak and he seemed to be able to relax and get on with his work. He was also more widely read than me which brought merit. Whilst he would jump to answer a question in class, I would freeze lest I should say something which might lead to ridicule in front of classmates. I listened intently to how the masters spoke and expressed themselves and after a few months I had, as I say, come to terms with the new language. In fact, I was now beginning to feel guilty about mom's and particularly dad's accents when school friends came to the house. I loved them too much to say anything which might hurt them, particularly my dad who had an extremely broad Black Country accent. It was a period in life where I felt very much alone and unhappy with my lot, but fortunately I had done enough to be elevated into a higher stream in the next year.

I finished my year at Moss Close in July and, come September, would be starting at Queen Mary's main school opposite the arboretum lodge in Lichfield Street. As I looked back, I had spent a year in a Dickensian old house which might have better suited a setting for a horror film than a school. The grounds were pleasant enough, a small playing field or lawn surrounded by large trees, some of which were fruiting walnuts which I had not realised grew in England. A fair number of the other trees were horse chestnut, but in Spring the flowers were pink as opposed to the commoner white flowers around home. On the right hand side of the entrance drive had been the dining room, a building totally out of character with the Victorian main building. It was a single storey concrete and brick utility structure with a concrete slab as a roof, much as one might find on an army camp. It was here that at lunch time every day, a queue of boys slowly made their way to a servery to collect food, eating at twelve-seat refectory style tables. Between the dining room and main building a track descended into a limestone quarry lined by large trees and adorned in Spring by rhododendrons. It was out of bounds to us, but in later years it became apparent that it was the shooting range for the cadet force.

In the lanes around home, a curious thing happened. The hedgerows suddenly resembled a Christmas tree, sprinkled with strips of silver paper about eight inches long and about half an inch wide (20cm by 1.5cm). We had no real idea where the 'decorations' had come from though they were so widespread across the fields that it seemed likely that they had fallen from the sky. We certainly did not witness planes doing so by day and the fresh crop in the mornings suggested that they were dropped at night only. We collected great bundles of it and wove the strips into table mats and boxes and used it for Christmas decorations. It happened on many occasions over several months, but it was only after the war that I learned they were aluminium strips, called 'window', dropped by planes to confuse German radar.

CHAPTER 12

'Around the Plant pit, local people and Gilpin's - all years'

Once more I shall pause my chronicle to look at further everyday issues, this time describing some of the major industry around the village.

During the early years of life, I suppose the most intriguing playground near to home was the Plant pit. There were several large mines in the area, but the Plant was a mere two hundred yards from home. I was always stimulated by things mechanical and here was quite a collection of machines using steam technology. Whenever I crossed the pit yard, whether on an errand or at play, I invariably stopped by open doors to peer in and watch the machines in action. Grandma and granddad knew the pit well since they had once been caretakers and lived in the cottage at the entrance to the pit yard. In her early teens, mom had helped grandma clean the administration offices for Mr Screen and often boasted how spotlessly clean and tidy they kept them. Granddad had been a miner and, before he retired, a certificated shot blaster and first aid man. The latter had obviously given him a great deal of satisfaction and as we sat passing the time of day on the embankment in his garden he would expound on his training in the subject. With an air of authority, he demonstrated to me how he would stop arterial bleeding if a man's foot was traumatically amputated. I had to lie on the grass and he found a round stone from the garden which he then placed behind my knee, bending the knee to trap the stone tightly. He explained there was a main artery behind the knee and the stone was pressing it firmly, staunching the blood flow. For higher level bleeding, he would use a tourniquet on an arm or leg, and set about demonstrating this. Taking off his rope trouser belt (he never wore a leather belt), he tied it round my thigh and twisted it with a length of hazel to tighten it. He would then look at me with a wise expression on his face, as much to say, it is easy if you know how. It seems he was never confronted with any significant medical emergency. Such an event would, I am sure, have led to life's fulfilment for a trained first aider, but it was not to be.

When walking into Cheslyn Hay, I usually took the short cut through the Plant pit yard and followed the footpath past the Tenscore pool and across the field (Coalpit field). Depending on whether my errand was to the upper or lower village I either walked along Mount Pleasant or down the old wagon track (New Horse Lane). The old pit field was an area of poorly fertile land consisting largely of low hills of shale from early mine workings. The vegetation on the hills was largely scrub; gorse, weakly looking blackberry patches, the occasional hawthorn bush and ground vegetation. Several pedestrian and cycle tracks ran across the field, used by miners travelling to and from the pit. The boundary of the field along the mainline railway sidings consisted of larger hills of shale about thirty feet high with valleys between where mineral lines had run in the past. All the boundaries of the patch were mixed fences of barbed wire and uncontrolled hedges with a smattering of oak and elm trees. It was an area which was ideal for children to play war games and for the Home Guard to practice and they often did, as shown by the smattering of discarded cracker strips used to mimic rifle fire. In season, the vegetation in the pit fields was a very good area for bird's nesting. One of my cuckoo eggs came from a meadow pipit's nest there.

When I was around nine years of age, the largest shale heap which had been used over the past fifteen to twenty years was over a hundred and fifty feet (50 metres) in height and now more like a small mountain, which we regularly climbed. We had not been allowed on it during my earlier years because the hawser was constantly in motion transporting tubs of waste for dumping at the summit. It did not stop us trying but we usually got a 'flea in the ear' and told to go back down, either by the workmen emptying the tubs or those greasing the hawser rollers along the track.

All pit machinery in the 1930s and 1940s was driven by the steam produced in the enormous boiler house where four large boilers sat side by side. Each was about twenty feet (six metres) long and about seven feet (two metres) in diameter, with two fire holes which were stoked at intervals by two black-faced and rather sweaty boiler house men. They were expected to keep up a head of steam and regularly threw shovels of coal onto the glowing furnace, spreading it around the firebox with rakes with handles about eight feet long. Similar tools were used to remove the glowing clinker of spent coal from beneath the grate, raking it into empty coal tubs which ran on a track in front of the fire doors. The fires were drawn and smoke extracted by two large chimneys, some sixty to eighty feet high, belching smoke over the adjacent countryside. Above the rear wall of the boiler house was a track for coal tubs from the coal face which kept four large bunkers charged with coal for the boilers. The tubs of spent clinker were pushed outside and hooked up to the hawser for disposal on a heap at the foot of the 'mountain', where lorries sometimes collected it for path building. The system was extremely efficient and the steam produced was fed around the yard in well lagged pipes, some above and some below ground. As I wandered around the pit yard, the hissing of steam came from all directions. The life blood of the pit machinery it seemed was dependent entirely on the relentless work of two men.

On most cold nights, the glow and warmth of the boiler house was an attraction to old Tumpter, the local tramp. He would doss down for a kip in the emptiest of the coal bunkers and was sometimes still there when we called in at breakfast time. During the night he was almost certainly aroused by an appetising smell wafting past his nostrils as the night shift cooked their bacon and eggs, opening the furnace door and using their shovels as frying pans. A little coal dust did not seem to detract from the flavours, if the pleasure on their face was a measure of their gourmet experience.

During the warmer summer months, we habitually came across old Tumpter fast asleep under bushes in the pit fields and usually gave him a wide berth in case we woke him. We sometimes passed him in the lanes, dirty looking, skin deeply tanned and wrinkled and wearing a tattered coat held together with a piece of string, his shaggy mongrel walking behind. His worldly goods were carried in an old shopping bag looped over his wrist. He was usually singing at the top of his voice and if there were several of us, he might triumphantly step out in front of us, blocking our path, with a flirtatious hand gesture and serenade. Although he sometimes seemed threatening, he never was, he just liked an audience. We usually side-stepped him, tittering as we moved on. I was about ten when dad came home from work and told mom that old Tumpter had been found dead by the boiler house. Tumpter was unkempt, but he grew on you and was one of the curios of life, like others we met on our way.

Harry Parbrook was another eccentric we normally witnessed when walking the footpaths of the lower meadow. These were shortcuts from Landywood village to the pit, used every day by the miners. They converged on one path which passed under the main line railway at the 'kissing bridge', a name presumably acquired from its use by courting couples. It was quite dark underneath, even during daylight hours! Parbrook often walked this way. He never said anything to us, just looked ahead as he passed us by. He often seemed to be conducting music with great fervour as though, in his mind, he was in front of some majestic choir or orchestra. His strange behaviour was such that we made fun of his actions, as any young boys would, though we were never unpleasant to him. We occasionally walked in line behind him, mimicking his arm actions as he conducted his imaginary orchestra, before peeling away and laughing among ourselves. Dad told me at some point that we should not do this to Harry Parbrook, even though he was happy to tell me he had gone 'soft in the head'. Mom told me that when younger, he was a really nice man who was a regular church attender and was a very good singer. "It's a shame he has gone the way he has", she would say. I have since wondered whether Harry Parbrook, like some great composer, was hearing original music, or was he simply conducting some great church oratorio which he had performed in his younger days, such as Mendelson's 'Elijah' or Handel's 'Messiah'. I would like to think that it was the former and that his mental illness deprived us of a spark of genius. Whatever the truth, he always seemed happy in his own world.

Another person whom we often came across and considered a curiosity was the 'deaf and dumb' lady. I never knew her name, but she lived in a solitary cottage on the corner of Landywood Lane where it turns right towards Jeff's Knob. Her house must have been very damp and inhospitable because it was surrounded by marshland. If walking to Cheslyn Hay we could use a footpath, which cut off that corner the lane. We crossed a stile by the fast running stream which fed the Tenscore reservoir and the footpath passed across her yard, immediately in front of her door. When very young, I ran past her door in case she came out. She could not speak but gesticulated assertively at us with her hands and made squeaking sounds. My fear was related to the fact that, according to some, she was probably a witch. For several years I passed her when shopping in Cheslyn Hay, always wearing a belted fawn mac' and brown beret and always alone. She is another person from my childhood whom we dismissed as a freak and it would be lovely if one day, probably in another life, the wrong could be righted with an apology. She was probably an extremely nice person if she could have communicated with us and I have no doubt that it riled her when we walked uninvited across her yard.

Throughout my childhood and into my later life, it was common place for mom or dad to refer to someone's eccentric or stupid action as 'doing a Jellyman'. Jellyman had lived in Cheslyn Hay during their childhood and Jellyman and his mother were renowned for being oddball. It is said that the very first day he was setting out for work at the pits, he complained to his mother that he couldn't get his bottle (of tea) in his pocket.

"Well empty some out then!" was her exasperated reply, which he did.

When dressing to go home from the pit one afternoon, he couldn't find his waistcoat.

"Has anyone sin me wescut?" he plaintively enquired.

"Doe be daft, Jellyman, yove gorrit on!" came the reply.

"Its a good job yoe tode me, son, or I'd a gone wum withart it!"

Dad frequently told the story of four young pigeon-racers and Jellyman moving a small pigeon loft from the allotment to someone's back yard. It was a bit of a struggle to get it on the cart but they managed. As the horse moved off, someone happened to notice there was a missing person,

"Where's bloody Jellyman", he puzzled, "I thought he'd come t'elp us?"

" 'Arm still 'ere", came a small voice, " 'arm inside carrying the perches!"

Looking back, stories abounded but were they truthful reflections of Jellyman or had they built up as they were passed on by word of mouth, people adding a little more colour at each stage? Mom and dad always believed the stories and one presumes therefore there was something behind them. The Black Country was famous for its Aynuk and Ali stories and the Jellyman stories were probably an extrapolation of that type of humour.

To return to the description of the Plant pit, the two largest buildings in the yard were the Winding House and the Ventilation House. These were very much no-admittance areas and were clearly marked so. Sometimes on a very hot day, the engineer opened the doors of the Ventilation House, allowing me to peer inside. The building housed an enormous steam engine with a flywheel about ten feet in diameter. The most amazing feature was the cleanliness, highly polished red quarry floors, tiled walls and brass and steel shining more brightly than mom's brasses at home. The engine, painted in red and green livery with gold lined embellishment, turned noiselessly and the engineer tended it with an oilcan as a horticulturist might lovingly tend his prize orchids. Glass oil cups sat on the main bearings and had to be replenished at regular intervals to ensure smooth running of his beloved but he was blindly attentive and oblivious to the fact that he had a spectator. At times I could stand there for some fifteen minutes, hoping to catch his eye, in anticipation that I might be allowed to stand on hallowed ground, but it never happened.

In the Winding House, the steam engine was similar but not so well loved in terms of cleanliness. The engineer sat on a high chair and at the sound of a bell, he set his machine in motion. A steel cable, about an inch in diameter, was feeding to and from a very large drum, pulling one mine cage up whilst letting the other down the mineshaft. An arrow on a large 'clock face' ahead of him slowly turned, moving from the start point to a mark at the other end of the scale, indicating to the engineer that he needed to decelerate and stop the engine. I had seen many steam engines, traction engines and large and small locomotives, but nothing compared with the sheer size, majesty and beauty of these two steam engines.

The smaller steam engines around the pit yard were not so well cared for and were in use as workhorses in several areas. There was an engineer's workshop with a lathe, drills and steam hammers and even a small steam engine next to the stables to chop hay for the nose bags of the Shetland ponies, which were hard at work at the coal face. These machines were caked with dirty lubricating oil and had probably never seen a cleaning cloth since they were installed. It seems that anyone using a steam engine was taught to give it plenty of oil. The floor of the hay cutting workshop was earthen and impregnated with sticky oil. The workmen in these areas never really objected even if two or three of us stood inside the door to watch them at work. In fact, they seemed to enjoy our presence, and joked with us, usually pulling our legs about girls. When we were about twelve, they often gave us a cigarette which we would light and have a drag each until it was about to burn a finger tip. 'Craven A' seemed to be one of the favourite cigarettes at the time. It was probably the reason for visiting the workshops when several of us were together!

The largest outdoor steam engine was used for shunting purposes. Between the pit and the LMS main railway line was a large shunting yard with four parallel tracks linked by sets of points. A steel cable with hook was attached to the tackle of a large shire horse and, after releasing the clutch of the winding drum, it plodded along the track dragging the steel rope some two hundred yards where it was coupled to a line of trucks delivered into the sidings from the main line. The steam engine could pull a line of perhaps twelve trucks to the top of the slight incline adjacent to the main offices, where the brakes of the trucks were applied. The shuntsman could now release individual trucks down the incline, controlling their brakes with his uncoupling pole. In this way, by simply using gravity, trucks were moved around the loading area. Once filled, trucks were run down the incline to be assembled for a main line pick-up. Hundreds of tons of coal left the Plant pit every week to be distributed to all parts of the country. Local lorries also pulled alongside the loading bays. Each had weighed in empty at the weighbridge by the main gate and would weigh again on the way out to get a ticket showing their net load of coal. Drivers also used the large scales provided on the loading bays to fill one hundredweight (100Kg) coal sacks for home deliveries. So busy were the bays that a stockpile of coal never really collected, even though tubs were leaving the pit cages every minute or two. No sooner, it seemed, had tubs emerged from the mine, than the coal was on its way to a customer, either locally or nationally.

In the mineshaft, two cages travelled along guide-cables, each bringing two tubs of coal to the surface. A coal tub had ten inch (250mm) wheels and was about 36 x 30 x 26 inches (900mm x 750mm x 650mm) and ran on 18 inch (450mm) gauge steel tracks. They probably held about a quarter to half a ton of coal and could be pushed on the level by one person. When a cage arrived at the surface, a man raised the gate and pulled the tubs out onto a rail track towards a turntable where they could be rotated to one of several tracks leading to the loading bays on the coal wharf. Cages appeared every few minutes and the pit top was a continuous hive of activity. Some coal tubs were emptied directly into railway trucks, which held twenty tons of coal, others emptied onto piles of coal along the loading bay for collection by coal lorries. An occasional tub would be rotated in the opposite direction and tipped into a boiler house hopper. Tubs of shale from the mine were collected on another track and several then attached to the hawser, delivering them to the top of the large slag heap. At the end of a shift, each cage delivered about ten miners to the surface, who then reported to the lamp house for a head count and refueling of lamps for their next shift. Over the years, I saw lamps change from the cylindrical brass Davy lamp to head lamps with batteries. At home, we knew the shift had finished when the pit sounded a loud steam whistle.

It was quite a frightening experience to stand at the top of the mine shaft and peer over the railings, so wide, so deep and it seemed bottomless. At week-ends it was extremely silent, no sounds emanating from the bottom, even though we knew that there were pit ponies and stable boys below. On the odd occasion we would toss in a tiny pebble to see if we could hear it land. In reality we were stupid, quite oblivious of the fact that it would have reached a speed of a bullet when it reached the bottom! We commonly did this in the several disused mines in various locations around us. These were not in-filled, but simply covered by a brick dome about ten feet (3 metres) in diameter. There were two such domes on the west side of Hilton Lane by the dogleg in the lane, sitting on a shale hillock about six feet (2 metres) above the level of the lane. Walking up Hilton Lane at sunset, the domes were silhouetted on the hillock like large cathedrals of past industry. Two similar domes also covered shafts on the shale heap to the west of Streets Lane, about a quarter of a mile from home and a further one opposite Gilpin's canal basin. A hole had been punched in some in earlier years and we were able to drop in a stone to hear it splash at the bottom.

All around the Plant pit and coalpit fields, there was evidence of earlier mineral lines from the Plant pit to Gilpin's Edge Tool factory and the canals at Churchbridge and Upper Landywood. Walking along paths around the fields on my many rambles in search of bird's eggs or butterflies, I was conscious that my stride was modified by the regular ruts along the walkway. In these had lain sleepers, now removed, used for mineral lines along which the coal tubs from various pits, had travelled to their destination. The width and spacing of the sleeper recesses, particularly the track from the Plant pit to Gilpin's basin on the canal at Upper Landywood, were very well preserved.

I often visited a similar mineral line down Jones' Lane which was still in use, between Harrison's No.3 pit (the Sinkin') in Slackey Lane (Hazel Lane) and the canal wharf at the Grove pit on the edge of Wyrley common, where the Sinkin' sent its coal for transport by canal. The track ran a very straight course under bridges on Wyrley Lane at Little Wyrley and Jones' Lane. Eight to ten steel tubs were drawn by a continuous steel hawser running over rollers which lay between the tracks. The tubs climbed steeply for the last hundred yards from Jones' Lane bridge on to Harrison's pit concourse. There I periodically passed the time of day with the linesman whose name eludes me, Tom I shall call him, an elderly man, who 'lived' in a small hut by the bridge. His job was relatively simple but obviously important to the functioning of the system. When he heard the tubs approaching he rose from the chair in his cozy hut and picked up a large spanner and a stick, which he scooped into a well battered bucket containing grease. The tubs, descending by gravity from Harrison's, had a tie bar at the rear anchoring them to the hawser to prevent them running away. At the bottom of the incline Tom's job was simply to tighten the hawser clamp at the front of the tubs and release that at the rear, at the same time giving a good dose of grease to the pivots. He did the reverse on the empty tubs making the return journey. Life was probably quite boring for him and he greeted me, and I am sure everyone else, like old buddies. He usually sat in solitude in his hut about five feet by four feet but it was dry and very warm due to the small fire grate in the corner which sported a gnarled sooty kettle for his cup of tea. Tom stoked up by simply pilfering a piece of coal from a passing tub. At certain times during the day, he walked the track with his stick and bucket of grease, lubricating the rollers over which the hawser tracked, hitching a lift back on a line of tubs going in his direction. Such a simple job, but without Tom's input the system would no doubt have overheated and ground to a halt.

The mineral lines around the Plant pit had preceded my dad and he was not aware of any in use when he was a child. Granddad talked about steam locomotives around Cheslyn Hay which were smaller than those on the main line, but did not recall the tracks that I had found. The Walsall to Rugeley railway reached Landywood in 1858 or just before, and Landywood Halt by Shant's bridge was used by trains transporting passengers to and from Walsall. The arrival of the main line at this time will have started the death knell for transport of coal from the Plant pit to the nearby canals. During the late 1930s, the only canals I saw transporting coal were the Wyrley and Essington canal, carrying coal from the Nook Colliery towards Bloxwich and the Pelsall canal, carrying coal from the Grove wharf. Both canals were heading towards the industrial Black Country. The barges were very few and far between and probably continuing to feed just a handful of Victorian factories.

With regard to the early mineral lines emanating from the Plant pit, I have no knowledge how the tubs were transported. Since there were bends in the track, a hawser was unlikely. It seems more likely that they were drawn by horses at the time the canal was built (around 1820) just as the barges were. The longest visible track from the Plant pit to Gilpin's basin was uphill for most of the journey but a large Shire horse could probably have pulled two full coal tubs up the incline. Two horses, one each side the track, would obviously pull twice the load. The width of the sleeper recesses was about three and a half feet (1.3m) and it was obviously a single track, but there was sufficient space for paths each side for horses.

Set adjacent to this track to Gilpin's basin, some twenty five yards below where it crossed Landywood Lane, was a disused red-brick building with pitched roof which we called 'the barn', about twenty feet by twelve feet (6m by 4m) in size. Its name, 'the barn', had probably arisen because barn owls used it as a roost and nesting place, certainly during the whole of my childhood. The building was not large enough to be an agricultural barn. The owls were sometimes seen towards the close of day and could only be described as most beautiful creatures. The building itself, from its position immediately adjacent to the track, may have played a role in the workings of the mineral line but could equally have been some other early industrial building.

I sometimes wondered whether at any time the tubs had been drawn by narrow gauge steam locomotive which would have much stronger pulling power. I had never seen any evidence of such, but fascinated with steam, I daydreamed of what might have been. I would sit on the shale hill at the end of the Tenscore pool, looking at the curved track beneath me running up towards the barn and daydream of a small steam locomotive being coupled to a train of tubs. Leaving the pit wharf, it then chuffed round the long curve, passing the dynamite magazine on its left, before rumbling over the steel and wood bridge by the side of me, which spanned the stream feeding the Tenscore pool. In my mind's eye, I watched it puffing furiously as it climbed the gentle gradient passing the 'the barn', giving a 'toot' as it approached the level crossing of Landywood lane. On it would proceed through the cutting between more old shale heaps before passing Fisher's farm and a small building adjacent to the track.

This small building, some twenty feet by twelve feet (6 metres by 4 metres) by the roadside on Upper Landywood lane was, in my early years, a blacksmith's forge and looked as though it had been for a long time. On many occasions, I stood in the doorway and watched as the smithy pumped his bellows to blow air into his coke to raise the temperature and then removed white hot metal from the furnace. This he hammered into shape on his anvil, frequently creating a horseshoe, and then plunged it into a bucket of water with a loud hiss of steam. It closed down around the beginning of the war, I am not sure why. It may have been lack of business, military call-up or even difficulty in obtaining metals. It never re-opened.

My imaginary locomotive now crosses Upper Landywood lane where the track begins to level and it can breathe steam more quietly as it traverses the half-mile long clinker embankment built to the level of the canal basin and standing six feet above the adjacent meadows. I walked this track on many occasions throughout childhood. At this time, it was the most preserved of the track bed and was now a long straight footpath with blackberry briars on either side. I hopped and skipped from hummock to hummock, between which wooden sleepers had lain in past years.

For the locomotive, it had been a journey of roughly a mile from the pit wharf. At the basin, barge hands emptied the coal tubs into a pair of waiting barges whilst the locomotive, now attached to empty tubs, free-wheels almost silently apart from the toots of its whistle, as it back-tracks downhill for reloading at the pit. Sadly this train journey is no more than a dream, but the many remnants of mineral tracks that I came across in the 1940s generated pictures of a busy mining area, which no doubt played a significant role in early industry. I hoped that the coal tubs had not all been horse or hawser-drawn and that there had at least been one small locomotive involved in the process. Sadly I have no evidence of this and can only continue to dream!

The dynamite magazine on the curve of the track contained explosive for shot blasting below ground. It was a domed brick structure, rendered and painted white and encroached upon and partly covered by the shale heap. It was furnished with a heavy steel door and secured by bolt and large padlock. Covering this structure were the earliest and the best blackberries in the area, obviously ripened by the sun reflecting from the white dome beneath. It was a secret I never divulged to my friends and year after year it was with trepidation that I gathered a large basket of luscious fruit from this bramble patch. I would never climb onto the building, even in my teens. I cautiously pulled back the briars overhanging the roof with a notched hazel stick before carefully picking the fruit. I always had concerns that any sudden vibration, such as falling on the roof, might send a shock wave through the magazine and "Boom!"

Another small gauge track appeared to run from the Plant pit towards Station Street. The track had largely been filled with clinker waste to make a path for the miner's to walk to homes in lower Cheslyn Hay, but there were sleeper recesses beside the footpath which petered out towards the railway station. Along this path, metal railings separated it from the railway property. In the middle of the fence, a swing gate allowed access to the railway crossing constructed of railway sleepers laid between the several main-line tracks. It allowed access to the other side about fifty yards beyond the signal box. I would then walk or cycle to Station Street down the side of the main-line siding which carried goods to and from Gilpin's and Hawkins' tileries. Above me to my left towered the wooden trestles which carried the main line and the station itself. At Station Street there was a gated railway crossing which was normally closed, but controlled by the engine fireman when trucks were being shunted along this track. From here the route of the track ran alongside the marsh and Gilpin's down to the wharf at Churchbridge. Half way along was a branch line to Hawkins' tileries but I do not recall this being used at the time. On the opposite side of the main line was a cycle track which we called 'new road' which ran between Station Street and the Watling Street (A5) at Churchbridge. If going to Bridgetown, I frequently took this route passing under the Hawkin's branch-line bridge. Towards the end of the track was the canal weir, where I think overflowing water maintained its level after the Churchbridge locks had been opened. The overflow ran into Wyrley brook which was already quite wide at this point.

At Churchbridge wharf, goods delivered by rail were loaded onto lorry trailers and hauled to destinations around the area by three-wheeled Scammel tractor units. These were bizarre looking vehicles in brown and cream livery with dome-shaped fronts and relatively small wheels. The trailer would be laden with all kinds of packages in transit, coils of lead pipe, bundles of steel rod and so on, destined for various businesses.

Churchbridge must at one time have been a significant canal route, presumably taking coal and goods from the Coppice mine, Rosemary tileries and the Plant pit to markets elsewhere in the Midlands. I cycled and played alongside a flight of about five locks which lifted the canal quite steeply over a very short distance, usually pushing my bike up to the old lock-keeper's hut and freewheeling back down at high speed, a great switchback ride! I never saw narrow boats on this canal, but the water in the locks had a beautiful clarity in which fish were clearly visible swimming in and out of the pondweed. The leaky lock gates allowed sheets of water to cascade into the lagoons below, no doubt well-oxygenating the water in them.

From the main-line railway crossing by the signal box, I could also walk down the grazing meadow and past the farm onto Station Street nearer to Churchbridge knob on Walsall Road. Granddad often related the story that these meadows had been the setting for some of the Great Wyrley maimings, about thirty years earlier. Several horses had been slashed with a knife and Edalji, the vicar's son, had been found guilty and sent to prison for the offences. On some occasions when I walked along this footpath, the church sat dark and hidden among the trees and brought the story of these sinister happenings to mind. I suppose I had Dracula films to thank for this

To the west of the Plant pit was the shale 'mountain' mentioned earlier, waste which had been laboriously extracted to allow miners to reach the coal seams. It was blue grey clay and shale which seemed totally infertile to anything but coldsfoot and ragwort and clung terribly to shoes and clothes when we climbed it. Like all other mounds around the pit, it had been carefully placed not to interfere with the mineral lines or the cutting of the brook which formed the Tenscore pool. The mountain was a blot on the landscape when walking along Landywood Lane but nevertheless a monument to all the miners who by toil and sweat had mined it from the bowels of the earth.

Mines like the Plant pit were cutting through the very deep seams of coal, but there were still local workings mining the shallow seam. It was this latter seam which had been mined in abundance for over two hundred years, to which the piles of shale in the many fields around bore testimony. Most of these were quite ancient and now covered with relatively normal vegetation. Some interested me because they were no longer shale and appeared have metamorphosed into clinker, presumably due to heat within the pile. I had seen the conical heap at the Sinkin' smoking and occasionally flaring on more than one occasion. One such pile, largely of ash, was in the meadow on the left along Landywood Lane just before Chetter's cottage. It was now a very large rabbit warren, covered by a half inch (1cm) layer of rabbit pellets. A man, I did not know him but saw him several times, collected his dinner by shooting a rabbit from the ditch or grass verge on Landywood Lane. After waiting a while to see if his shot had attracted anyone's attention, he surreptitiously crept through the gorse to collect his 'bag' and then cycled away, his 12-bore strapped to his cross bar. He had obviously not noticed that on occasions I was sitting at the top of the big shale heap, watching him.

Opposite our house, across the railway track was a large meadow, in the far corner of which sat Caddick farm, a white two-storey cottage with outside buildings. This had once belonged to granddad and grandma who would often tell the story of the pigs that became drunk. A barrel of home brewed beer sat outside on a wooden trestle constructed by granddad (in his inimitable way I suppose!) which collapsed and the earthenware barrel smashed. The yard was flooded with the contents and the free range pigs quickly moved in. After a while they wandered aimlessly around the field, sometimes on three legs, sometimes on four, sometimes standing, sometimes rolling over, apparently a sight to behold and causing raucous laughter. It is a story I have since heard relating to other parts of the country and may therefore be apocryphal, but it was always told with great conviction to anyone listening. I had the impression mom had witnessed the event as a child and it may therefore have been true. In later years George Cooper purchased Caddick farm and was resident for most of my childhood. When I was in my late teens, he dropped a shaft into the coal seam beneath the meadow with a simple hand winch to raise the coal bucket. He worked it alone, using a ladder to get to the bottom of the shaft, and was producing small quantities of coal. Sadly one day in the late 1940s a lining brick dislodged and plummeted down the shaft, hitting him on the head, causing brain injury. He died in hospital within hours.

Another shaft mining shallow coal was on Whitehouse's land in Upper Landywood and accessed from Street's Lane. It also had a windlass to lift the buckets and had been used over many years. Shallow heaps of shale were strewn over about two acres, some of which had metamorphosed to ash and now used to create the access road for lorries. One day several of us, including Donald Gretton, were trying to release the windlass to allow the bucket to be lowered down the shaft. We managed to free the safety catch and the windlass started turning, accelerating as the bucket careered down the shaft. The rotating winding handle struck Donald on the head causing an extremely nasty gash which could have proved more serious or even killed him. Blood streamed from the gaping wound on his head, pouring down his face onto his shirt, and he was obviously dazed by the impact. Two of us had to help him home and his mother, as might be expected, was none too pleased. We were extremely frightened by the incident and could never bring ourselves to play there again. The wound needed hospital attention, but fortunately did not prove to be too serious and he was soon his normal self.

It did not stop further silly pranks, however, and a year or so later when playing in the shunting yard at the Plant pit, we pulled the retaining pegs, releasing the brakes on three full twenty-ton railway trucks. They slowly rolled down the incline towards the gates to the main-line track and were beginning to gather speed. When we realised the enormity of what we had done, three of us pulled down hard on the brake handle of one truck and the three of us miraculously found sufficient strength to apply the brake, stopping the trucks before the end of the shunting yard. Many times we had watched the shuntsman at work, noting how he released the brakes, how he uncoupled the trucks and how he stopped them. He of course had the advantage of a long pole with small uncoupling hook which he could use as a lever to apply the brakes. We had no such tool and, like

155

young hooligans, we released the trucks which could have smashed through the gates onto the main railway line. Risk taking was part of our development and the excitement of meddling with something grown-up, creating an adrenaline rush, seemed to override common sense. On this occasion, had we not stopped the trucks, we may well have ended up in the cells for endangering the main line. I look back on that day with horror.

The other big industrial unit in the area was Gilpin's factory at Churchbridge, situated where Walsall Road (A34) crossed Watling Street (A5). My dad, as had his family before him, worked there. He polished edge-tools of all descriptions; axes, adzes, shears, knives, scythes, hammers and many others. He was paid for piece-work, so that he always worked extremely hard. By the time I started at Queen Mary's school I was considered to have conquered the mathematics necessary to complete the calculations for his weekly work sheet and I enjoyed the challenge. He simply brought home his grimy cash book in which he had entered the quantities of the different tools he had polished. I totalled these and, given the price paid per dozen, worked out his wage for the week. Some items may only pay three pence (1p) per dozen and he might work on two gross of these. Others, usually samples for sales purposes, may pay four shillings (20p) a dozen. I searched through the many entries for these items first since his income for the week built more quickly and I could reassure him that he had had a good week. A week's work at the time was paying just over four pounds.

During school holidays, I occasionally cycled down to the factory to see dad just before he finished his shift. I stopped at the gatehouse and politely asked if I could go to the polishing shop where dad worked. I was never refused and made my way up the hill to his workplace. His colleagues knew me and usually shouted some remark through the almost deafening noise,

"Hallo, Perce, that wheel's free and there's a bucket of 'ommers across theer for yer to gerron with!", someone would gesticulate.

There were about eight polishing wheels in the shop which seemed not to have changed since the beginning of the industrial revolution. They were constructed of solid wood, probably oak, about thirty inches (750mm) in diameter and four or five inches (120mm) wide. The rim was coated with carborundum and was spinning at high speed, driven by large belts from a pulley shaft at the rear which ran the length of the shop. This ancient device and was now driven by a large electric motor but had, without doubt, been driven by steam until the early years of the century. As I reached him, dad was usually finishing polishing the last bucket of castings which he would apply to the wheel until the face or blade was highly polished and smearless. With a look of satisfaction, he tossed it into a waiting receptacle.

The last bucket was not the end of work, the wheel now had to be dressed and made ready for his shift next day. The main switch was thrown and the wheels slowly, it seemed like forever, reduced speed until they could be braked using a piece of scrap steel pressed against the wheel. Dad then collected a pot of hot animal glue from the stove in the workshop where it had been heating through. The glue came in thin slabs about nine inches by three inches (25cm by 8cm) from the 'monkey muck' works and was dissolved in a type of bain-marie. As he painted it on the surface of the wheel, it stank to high heaven, a smell I knew from the factory a quarter of a mile away. The rather heavy wheel had then to be lifted from its bearings, with the glue still tacky, and rolled in a tray containing carborundum powder, coating the whole circumference evenly. It was restored to its bearings to dry overnight and, after dad had washed his hands in an indescribably dirty sink, we could go home.

Occasionally if he finished early, he showed me around the factory, the pressings shop where an enormous power press shaped white hot steel ingots into hammers, twist drills, axe heads and so on and then through the shop where wooden handles were formed on lathes prior to being married up with hammer, axe, adze or pick heads. Trips around the factory always fascinated me and I felt very important on such tours. I was being shown areas which were primarily for adults and certainly not for children. I watched open-mouthed as spectacular showers of sparks were created when the enormous steam press hit the white-hot ingots of steel or when a long train of sparks cascaded behind the grinding wheels as the steel was applied to them. I had never before seen anything quite so awesome.

This industry resulted in health problems for dad and throughout his life, he suffered problems with white fingers due to vibration, though at the time no-one was aware of the cause. Unfinished tools were stocked outside in containers and dad thought that icy temperatures were causing his problem, so he carried as many as he could into his workshop to warm up overnight. When affected, his fingers looked totally bloodless and he would spend time in front of the fire trying to get the circulation to return and as a result suffering chilblains. In cold weather they were frequently too stiff to move and he was obliged to passively work them to bring them to life. This problem reduced sensation in his hands and he was very prone to serious injury without realising the extent of the injury. Some injuries were appalling but he rarely complained and soldiered on. The first-aid man at the factory would apply a dressing and dad coated it with animal glue to keep out the dirt and make it last longer. The noise in the factory also led him to suffer profound deafness in later years.

At Christmas, Gilpins arranged parties for worker's children which included a meal, a visit from Santa Claus and a show. Upwards of sixty children attended, tucking into the spread, which during the wartime years was a special treat. On one occasion early in the war, my present from Santa, who was usually drawn into the canteen on a sleigh, was quite an expensive 'Jack-in-the-box, which I played with for a long time. Without doubt, the best part of the party was the entertainment at the end of the day. The canteen housed a stage with curtains and, since I had never been to the theatre, this was my first experience of a live show. There were jugglers and magicians doing tricks which held us spellbound. Vocalists sang the songs we knew and we joined in. Best of all was an act using marionettes to tell and act out fairy stories, all in brightly coloured attire and with glamorous lighting. It was enthralling. I was generally quite shy but I made as much noise as anyone else when the situation called for it. The level of noise in the hall was deafening. Later I had the joy of repeating details of the party and theatre in minute detail to mom and left her under no illusion how great it had been.

Dad was a life-long crown green bowler and played for the Gilpin's team. At the works, alongside the railway yard was an immaculate crown bowling green, the surface of which was as fine and as regular as velvet. Dad was an excellent player and when he played near home I was always in attendance. He kept his set of woods in a leather case and, at an early age, he explained to me the rudiments of the game, such as how the bias worked, demonstrating on our lawn. I practised getting the bowl as close as possible to a stone he placed on the lawn to represent the jack. Sometimes he explained on the

Gilpin's green how the six inch crown on the green affected the bias, depending on whether you bowled over or round the crown. Dad was excellent and usually could be relied on to win any end which he was drawn to play.

In a critical match between Gilpin's and a Cannock Chase team, I was scoring for him and getting more and more thrilled as he pulled ahead, 18-10. I ran to him excitedly to show him the score card. Foolishly I thrust the card in front of his eyes just as his opponent bowled the jack, without realising how critical it was for him to observe his opponent's action. This led to him losing the next six points and I felt terrible as the match seemed to slowly fall from his grasp. I sat perfectly motionless, not daring to move in case I did the wrong thing as the score reached 18-18, and then the old spark came back and he won the remaining points. He came to me and gave me a ticking off, one of the only times he ever did so. He went into the bar as he always did to enjoy a pint with his pals, no doubt having a laugh about my gaff! I sat outside on a bench, feeling a little hurt, but as always someone brought me a Vimto to keep me going, and spent a few moments chatting to me.

CHAPTER 13

'The middle of the war - c. 1943'

Continuing with my chronicle, by 1944 things on the front line appeared to be improving as the Germans were being pushed back and, a few days before Shrove Tuesday (pancake-day), there was good news on the home front. Lemons had arrived in the country and were on sale in the greengrocery shops for the first time for years and every family was to be allowed one fresh lemon. I ran to Eccleshall's shop in Landywood and joined the small queue that had by now collected. Mr Eccleshall put a cross with indelible pencil in a column on the back of the ration book. When he handed me the lemon, the sight of the small yellow fruit brought so much joy and I lovingly caressed it as if it was pure gold. After the horrendous losses of merchant shipping that we had charted in class a year or two before, this was a sign that some overseas produce was now getting through and it was exciting.

Mom made pancakes on Shrove Tuesday as she did every year. I always enjoyed them with a good sprinkling of sugar but this year we were going to have them with a squirt of lemon juice, as cheerfully recommended by the newspaper. I was quite looking forward to the new experience but, after the exultant build-up to the occasion, it proved a flop. In reality it spoilt my pancake, adding a disappointing sourness which was not for me. I had obviously not remembered how tart and astringent lemons were, even though they were no worse than the green rhubarb and gooseberries that I avidly ate in season. Over the past few years I had eaten and enjoyed my pancakes with sugar and now felt very let down by my first lemon. What, I thought, was all the fuss about?

Regardless of this small indication of better things on the horizon, there were still significant signs of war. We were witnessing ever increasing numbers of American army lorries travelling along Walsall Road towards Walsall. Some were enormous in comparison with our own army lorries and had high wheel suspensions. At first we looked on with awe at the American monstrosities, but when their convoys were taking ten minutes or more to pass, it became quite exasperating, particularly when waiting for a bus. No longer could we rely on punctual buses. No-one knew why there were so many fighting vehicles but we assumed they had come to help defend the country if Hitler tried to invade. On June 6 things became clearer. We heard on the radio and later read the large banner headlines about D-day and the massive invasion of the Normandy beaches by our armed forces along with the Americans. Almost as quickly as the strange army lorries had appeared, they were gone, the Walsall Road was back to normal and life could continue.

I spent the Spring adding to my bird's egg collection which I had started a year or so earlier and I was now becoming quite proficient at finding nests. To date I had about a dozen different eggs, all carefully cradled in cotton wool and stored in a segmented display box which I had 'knocked up'. I searched for bird's nests alone and only one egg was removed from a nest, which did not seem to disturb the nesting pair. Those of commoner birds were very easy to find and in great abundance such as blackbird, song thrush, yellow hammer, chaffinch, greenfinch, house and hedge sparrow, magpie, peewit, robin and wren and I had a specimen of each in my collection. Interestingly, the robin's egg came from a nest in the ditch used by the poacher as a hide to shoot his rabbits (referred to earlier). After he had cycled away with his 'bag' I went to collect the spent cartridges from the ditch, as trophies. The robin was startled and flew off her nest and, gently parting the grass, I exposed five pale cream eggs with brownish blotches. I was delighted with the find and carefully removed an egg and blew it for my collection.

Blowing eggs was important in order to remove the contents for preservation purposes. This I did using a hawthorn spine to prick a small hole in the narrow end and a slightly larger hole in the rounded end. Gentle blowing through the small hole resulted in the white and yolk being evacuated through the larger hole, not too difficult with a robin's egg, but very difficult when dealing with a tiny wren's or tit's egg! The eggs would then keep forever, subject to storage against breakage.

Searching for the rarer bird's eggs was quite time consuming. When I saw a wanted species of bird, I spent considerable time surreptitiously tracking it to get a possible location for the nest. One bird, the skylark, was not going to make it easy. I watched them for hours rise into the sky singing with gusto. I hid under hedgerows awaiting their sudden drop onto the meadow and, after a short while, I stealthily moved to the environs of where they had landed, hoping that I might disturb them on the nest. It never happened. They were brilliant in the art of camouflage and deception and, even though there were several pairs in the meadows in the lane, they always outwitted me. From their vantage point on high, they obviously knew I was there and ran rings around my efforts. I criss-crossed many fields but their camouflage was astounding and I never came across a nest nor did I know anyone with a skylark's egg

Egg collecting had usually finished by May or June but I developed a further collecting hobby which covered the rest of the summer and equally took me on long journeys into the countryside. This developed as a result of meeting a new friend at Moss Close. Donald Provost had just immigrated from Canada and joined Queen Mary's part way through term. We were having lunch one day and chatting about collecting when he mentioned his dad's butterfly collection. Next day, he brought to school a case of expertly mounted North American butterflies and explained in some detail how his father had prepared them for display. The butterfly had been put to sleep using ethyl acetate, prior to laying it out on a board to straighten and spread its wings. It was then mounted in the glass case using a pin through the thorax and very impressive it was. I was enthralled and, in view of the large number of butterflies around home, I quickly caught the bug and began to create my own collection. Unfortunately I had no access to ethyl acetate and would not have a clue where to obtain it and so I experimented in the garden with cabbage white butterflies. They were the bane of dad's life since their caterpillars could ruin a crop of cabbage in a few days. I found that by rapidly squeezing the thorax of the butterfly between my fingers, the insect was not only instantly killed but also obligingly opened its wings flat, in the presentation position. I did not need ethyl acetate nor the lengthy laying out between sheets of paper. I was able to put a pin through the thorax and display it on a backing board. It was not as perfect as the Provost collection, but allowed me to display my catch. Eventually I built a glass covered wooden case in which I could keep and display my collection. In all, I collected fifteen different species of butterfly from the meadows within a few hundred yards of home which are listed in a later chapter. Some such as marbled white, painted lady, small blue, orange tip, gatekeeper and brimstone were rarer than most and took longer to collect.

When I spotted a butterfly needed for my collection, I followed it across fields, climbing over or crawling under hedges from field to field until it settled in front of me. I did not have a butterfly net but used an article of clothing such as a light weight shirt which I threw over it. By peeling the garment slowly back, I usually found the trapped butterfly uninjured. In this way, I caught sufficient butterflies to make a display of the fifteen species and, for the commoner varieties, showing the underneath and full colour display of male and female of the species. My collections of bird's eggs and butterflies took two to three years to put together, using most of my spare time, and many exhibits were the result of miles of walking, running, climbing and stalking. By the summer of 1947 I had collected specimens of all I thought possible around the village and I gave them to Miss Liddle for her classroom nature cupboard.

Cousin Ron was now eight years of age and sometimes came with me on my jaunts into the countryside, just for the walk. His behaviour was a little unpredictable and therefore not ideal for tracking birds. I simply observed as we walked along, pointing out some things to him, but keeping others to myself and I would go back to check these another day. I showed him how to use a blade of grass stretched between the thumbs as a gazooka and we used the tall plantain flowers (ribwort plantain) to make guns which we fired at each other. We had a lot of fun and chatted incessantly, laughing a lot and simply became heady on the country air.

I had for a while been going to the Chum's Club at the Danilo cinema in Cannock on Saturday mornings and Ron now joined me. We were hooked on the cartoons and serials such as 'Flash Gordon' and no way were we going to miss a single episode. During the serial, we gasped, bit our fists and along with hundreds of others, shouted and screamed throughout. The end of an episode always left burning questions, boomed out by the announcer as Flash Gordon's rocket plunged headlong and out of control into the mouth of a fiery volcano-

"Can Flash Gordon restart the rocket engine?"
"Will he and his crew escape inevitable death?"

Of course they did, but we had to be sure and Ron and I would eagerly be back next week! In general it was a Saturday morning of great enjoyment, but on one occasion it proved to be sheer hell. The Flash Gordon serial was always shown at the end of the programme and, whether the shorts had not arrived or the manager had suffered some form of apoplexy, I do not know, but we had to sit through Noel Coward's *Blithe Spirit* which was showing that week. We were so bored and the auditorium became like a playground with missiles flying in all directions. It was impossible to hear the dialogue, even if we had wanted to. The usherettes, with torches scanning seats like searchlights, tried to hush children and get them back to their seats, to no avail. For about an hour, it was bedlam! Fortunately, they did eventually show Flash Gordon otherwise they would have had a real riot on their hands!

Cousin Ron was always a bit of a comedian and could very quickly hold family or friends rapt with his antics. I have mentioned some of them before and as I have said mom loved him to bits and couldn't wait for her next laugh. His remarks more often than not followed a misunderstanding but the more we laughed the happier he was with the fun that he had unwittingly created. Walking along Shaw's Lane one day, on the way to the bus stop, he noticed and commented on the privet peacock in the front garden of one of the bungalows. It was a piece of topiary designed and always kept neatly trimmed by Howard Benton, later a well known local choirmaster. Ron's eye caught the small oval cast iron sign on his picket gate, *'Please shut the gate'*.

"Look!" he implored, his voice now in descant, "Please shoot the cat!"

I buckled, as much by the quizzical expression on his face of 'what have I said?' as by his misreading of the sign! I didn't stop laughing until we reached the bus stop.

It was nice to have Ron tag along for company though some days, when we had warm summer sunshine, I chose to walk alone, wearing only shorts. My exposed skin bronzed very quickly during the summer months. When I felt like a respite, I would settle down in the tall grass of a hay meadow, lying among the tall buttercups, scabious, cat's ear, ox-eye daisies and other wild flowers whilst around me a constant hum of working insects and the incessant rasping of grasshoppers filled the air. The brook nearby tinkled as water gently flowed over stones, but not a human voice or vehicle to be heard. It was heaven, my Elysian field! I lay there for about half an hour, lapping up the sun, usually day-dreaming of things I might make or do in dad's shed. I will, I thought, build my own railway locomotive from the pieces of metal I have collected and put aside for the purpose. I am not too aware of the intricacies of steam traction, but I am sure I shall cope if I work hard, and so I did. In the end it was not too difficult and what a pleasure it was to drive my creation along the main line, hand on the regulator, a toot on the whistle and a wave to my friends as I steam past them. I smiled with satisfaction and, with a start, I awoke from my dream and frantically brushed away a large grasshopper which was using my face as a launch pad! Damned insect!

I used my cycle to visit more distant pastures such as Darky lane, just below Jacob's Hall, a favourite haunt of mine. It was a well trodden footpath, used by the army of miners making their way to and from work, between Little Bloxwich and the 'Sinkin'. If I turned left at the T junction, the path ended at a five bar gate. I leapt over it into the meadow where there was a brook and a small copse of conifer trees. It was in the latter that I managed to get my kestrel egg. The brook at this point was about three feet (a metre) wide, very shallow and the water babbled downhill over a bed of stones. I sometimes lay by this stream for a break, looking over the meadows and fields towards the Grove and Little Wyrley.

The other direction at the T junction took me towards Little Bloxwich. The hedgerows each side the path were a hive of natural activity, birds, insects and the occasional small animal scurrying through the undergrowth. When I spotted something, I stopped and explored the vegetation and ditch for things of interest. On one outing, I left my cycle at a stile and wandered along the footpath and lane towards Saddler's farm at Hobble End, the home of Kathleen Sadler, a classmate at Landywood school.

As I approached the farm, I noticed about a dozen prisoners-of-war in the open barn, I think Italian, wearing grey 'uniforms' and preparing lunch. On a simple brazier outside the barn, bubbling away furiously was an industrial-sized paint can full of unpeeled potatoes. It was the unusual technique for cooking potatoes that caught my eye. They were boiled whole and only after cooking were the skins peeled away. It was a method of cooking not used by us, but the finished potatoes did look very fluffy and appetising. We didn't communicate apart from a smile and a gesticulation or two, but they seemed happy for me to stand and watch. I think they were amused by the way I was gawking at the cooking methods. They were occasionally speaking to me, perhaps even inviting me to lunch, but my Italian was not too hot! When I finally left them, they waved a cheery farewell. I made my way back to my bike puzzling over the fact that I had spent about twenty minutes with the enemy and had never once felt afraid. They had looked so happy and were freely joking amongst themselves, yet I had spent two or three years hating them, deriding them and cheering when their countrymen had been slaughtered. They seemed normal people like us, doing the things we do, albeit differently. I cycled away, pleasantly confused by the experience.

Other strangers came to Landywood, namely those who had been displaced by invasion from their homelands. Nissen huts were erected in Holly Lane opposite my *alma mater*. The residents were mainly from Poland, a country that had suffered very badly at the hands of Hitler and the Russians during the war. Since I no longer attended the school I did not see much of them though I did occasionally see strangers, some in uniform, in local shops. As might be expected, there were liaisons in the village and Mr Bickford had given strict instructions that girls at school should not associate with them! Later residents were I think members of the Polish Resettlement Corps, an organisation which was created in 1946 to prepare Polish ex-servicemen for life in Britain. I later learned that during the war years, many Poles had reluctantly left their homeland, escaping across the border into southern Europe before making their way westwards towards France. Those who managed to make their way to ports around western Europe were rescued by ships of the Royal Navy and brought to Britain. The Holly Lane camp was one of many similar camps around the United Kingdom.

On most sunny days I was predictably out in the country but on wet days I usually busied myself constructing things either in the greenhouse or the cowshed, now shared by 'Grunty', the pig. I had watched dad over the years and had acquired his ability to put my hand to many jobs. We had a number of good edge-tools, from the Gilpin's reject bin, but we had a poor selection of saws and my attempts at normal woodwork were not therefore particularly good. I was much better with model making which only needed a modeller's knife. We could purchase balsa wood modelling kits for aeroplanes from a shop in Walsall bus station for about three shillings (15p). It entailed cutting out the spars and frames for the model (which were printed on sheets of balsa) using the knife. Very thin strips of the same material purchased in lengths were then glued to these cut-out forms to construct the three-dimensional aircraft fuselage, tail plane and wings. I liked doing my balsa wood modelling in the greenhouse when it was empty since I could spread out the plans and materials along the staging. Here, I could relax and the balsa cement could dry without disturbance. I knew if I had spread them over the dining table, mom would inevitably swish them away at meal times, to lay the table.

When completed, the aircraft frame and wings were covered with tissue paper which was doped with varnish to make it taut and give added strength to the whole structure. The struts used in construction could be seen through the translucent skin and this, along with the red, white and blue roundels and tail-plane identifications which came in the form of transfers, gave the plane a stunning appeal. The propeller was rotated by a rubber band. About a hundred turns were applied before letting go to set the propeller spinning. I constructed a Hawker Hurricane fighter, Beaufort bomber and a Wellington bomber but none flew, although 'FLYING MODEL' was emblazoned on the carton. In fact, I never saw a balsa wood model of a wartime aircraft fly. The only planes which seemed to fly were gliders with large wing spans but these never had quite the same appeal for me as did the warplanes.

From an early age, I was captivated by any new experience and, as I have intimated, was particularly fascinated by tools and machinery. It was on one of my many visits to Gilpin's factory that I caught sight of the wood lathes used to create the handles for chisels. Employees using cutting tools were turning the handles with ease from square timber and very fast to boot. When I needed rounded material, I used dad's spoke shave and sand paper to finish and it was neither easy nor did it create a great result. On the way home, the cogs in my brain started whirring and very soon another project was born. It should not be too difficult to construct a lathe, I felt, particularly if I could find a power unit to rotate the timber. This was, in fact, the stumbling block since nothing at home included an electric motor and it was not the sort of thing I was likely find on the refuse tip, my first stopping place for such oddities.

Sometime later, I walked into aunt Ruby's house when she was dressmaking using the Singer sewing machine. She was treadling away and the fly wheel was racing like mad. My eyes lit up, there was the answer! I looked carefully at the construction and raced off to dad's shed, it stank somewhat because of the pig, but my lathe had to be constructed there since it had a strong work bench. I needed a large wheel to act as my flywheel from which a belt would transfer motion to the smaller wheel at the lathe head. I was able to find an unused front bicycle wheel and disassembled the ball-races so that I could insert a cranked spindle. After hammering a length of metal rod to create the crank, I jammed it in the wheel axle slot. The crank would now be turned by the connecting rod from a wooden treadle. I had to construct a wooden frame beneath the work bench to support the components, but soon had the flywheel spinning at high speed when treadling. I couldn't believe how easy it had been to construct and surely it was all downhill from here!

I now had to construct a lathe stock above the bench which would hold the material to be turned on my lathe. Having no metal skills, other than plumbing, and no metal drill, I knocked it up from a block of hardwood using a wood brace and bit to make the hole for the spindle. This would be rotated by a small pushchair wheel connected by a rope belt to the flywheel. Treadling certainly resulted in the lathe stock spinning at high speed but there was very little power due to belt slippage. Very gentle hand pressure was sufficient to stop the stock turning. I was never going to turn substantial items on my improvised lathe but I did turn small wooden items such as small parts for wooden model planes, gun barrels for model tanks and spindles for chair legs, doll's house sized chairs that is!

I have to admit that my efforts were extremely amateurish and I could only look on in envy when I watched Eric Gibbs' father create his very professional looking models of army vehicles. The tanks even had realistic tracks made from metal. The difference was, I suppose, that he had very good modelling tools such as a pedestal drill and fret saws, always locked away when he was not in the shed. Dad was not really into modelling and therefore any skills I might acquire had to come from closely watching Jack Gibbs. Unfortunately he preferred to work alone and when Eric and I entered his holy of holies he usually locked away his tools and went into the house. He did not seem to teach the skills as dad had done. From what I gleaned, I needed proper modelling tools if I was to achieve anything and my hopes were raised when I saw an advertisement in the *Birmingham Gazette*, now our daily newspaper, extolling 'Hobbies' the modeller's shop in Birmingham. This company was selling fret saws and fret saw machines which might allow me to emulate some of the skills of Eric's dad, I thought.

On our next Saturday visit to Birmingham we found Hobbies store in the Bull Ring and I was staggered by the number of people in the shop and also queuing outside to get in. It was obviously a very popular place. No way was mom going to wait in the queue and neither was I going to get a fret saw machine when she saw the price in the shop window. I tried to reason with her to at least buy a simple fret saw now we were here, but her mind was made up and I was still trying to persuade her as we sauntered up the steep steps into the market hall, now roofless following earlier bombing raids. Inside, I was drawn to a large five hundred pound bomb which had dropped on the city but had not exploded. The case was now empty and used as a giant money box for the war effort. I could not believe that bombs were so big!

We browsed the line of small wooden shacks which were temporary shops and dad's eye caught a second hand wrist watch for three pounds which he liked and mom persuaded him to buy it from the gardening profits, a sort of present to himself for his hard work. Although I felt that the money would have bought me a basic fret saw, I would never begrudge dad anything, and was glad when he bought his watch. It proved to be a bad buy. It stopped and started repetitively for about three months and he took it back next time we went to Birmingham. The guy shook it and put it to his ear and declared that it had been over-wound. The shaking he gave it was such that it must have dislocated half the cogs from their bearings! It was dad's fault and beyond repair, was his declared diagnosis, and he would neither replace it nor make a refund. Dad, a shy somewhat meek man would never argue with such pomposity and he had to accept the ruling.

With the tools available to me, including my newly constructed lathe, I was very much limited to wood as a medium but it did not stop my continued dream of using metal to build a steam locomotive, even though I hadn't a clue where to start. I was now becoming so assured that I could make anything that the true requirements for such projects never crossed my mind. Who needs metal turning lathes and steel drills when others might help in this respect?

My first attempt at metal work by default followed a session playing with cousin Bob next door. When his dad was at work we sometimes played with the steam engine, given to him one Christmas just before the war. It had a simple brass boiler with a steam pipe to a piston and cylinder which drove a flywheel at enormous speed when at full steam pressure. It was a toy that had been around for many years and sometimes used to provide power to Meccano constructions. The boiler was heated by a methylated spirit burner. It was a great toy and it inspired me to try to build one. I took a few dimensions from the engine and thought it best to start with the piston and cylinder. I asked dad if the metal drilling could be done in one of the workshops at Gilpins, and gave him a drawing of what I needed.

"Of course, son, a workmate of mine will knock it up in no time!"– I was assured.

He felt it would take about a week and I was itching to get my hands on this first component. After reminding him on numerous occasions over several weeks, the parts did eventually appear. The cylinder bore had been drilled on a pedestal drill and had been shaped along with the piston on dad's carborundum wheel. The reader should take my word for it, this was *not* the way to engineer such items. In their defence neither dad nor his friends were aware of this, since they were not trained in this skill. The piston and cylinder were a reasonable fit but by no means air tight. They were never going to work with steam. I was rather deflated! If dad's mates could not create it on the engineering tools available at Gilpins, what chance did I have.

The idea that I could engineer a steam engine or locomotive was I suppose preposterous, but I regularly had such daydreams and believed in my ability to construct things. I assume it has been a primitive instinct of man since the dawn of time. Common sense should have told me that bashing a lump of cold metal with a hammer barely dented it and there was no way I was going to shape metal with the tools at home. The penny did eventually drop and the subject was put on a back burner until the necessary technology crossed my path many years later.

Returning to the basics of daily living, we had for some three years now lived with clothes rationing and an annual allocation of points to purchase items of clothing. A pair of socks required one point, a shirt would be perhaps three points and a three piece man's suit may cost as many as twenty four points, about a year's allocation. It was very restricting particularly for someone like mom who was fashion conscious. As a result, she regularly visited the markets in Cannock, Walsall and Birmingham looking for second hand clothes which did not require points and were also cheap. Somehow she needed the buzz which a 'new' dress or coat brought to her and she left the market stalls with a bag full of second hand clothes, like a child with a new toy. After a thorough wash, or several washes, and modifications to make them fit, mom ventured out in her new gear. Frequently, women she met thought they were new clothes and I must say, she looked quite good in some of the acquisitions.

Some of mom's purchases from rummage stalls or church bazaars cost only a penny or two, and were well beyond further use as garments. They were therefore used for rug making. White or pink under–slips, for instance, for a penny (0.5p), could be washed and dyed with a cheap fabric dye from Mrs Challinor's shop. They were cut into strips or small pieces to be used for 'bodging'. The rooms at home were covered with simple linoleum with one or two scattered cheap Belgian cotton mats which did not wear well and, in any case, were currently unavailable. Grandma and mum, who were very adept with most materials, were now making rugs to adorn the floors of our homes. Hessian sacks were used as the backing into which the scrap materials were inserted as rug pile. Two methods were used. In the first, small pieces of cloth, about two inches by one inch (50mm by 25mm), were pegged into the hessian in neat rows using a special tool called a bodger, which had a spike and a small sprung jaw to grip the piece of cloth in order to pull it through. The second method used a hollow 'needle' with pointed tip as a looping tool. It was some three eighths of an inch (10mm) in diameter. A long strip of three quarter inch (20mm) material was fed down the hollow centre and a stitching action used, from the reverse side, to create a looped pile. Even worn out stockings could be used for this purpose, again dyed and cut spirally from top to toe, making a long continuous ribbon. Everyone in the family took their turn bodging or needling a row of pile. Obviously, the more colourful the material scraps, the prettier and more appealing the finished rug which, when finished, had a thick one inch (25mm) pile. A large assortment of coloured clothing was on sale on the rummage stalls and mom ferreted around for specific colours to complete some intriguing pattern she had in mind. Often she started with an oval colourful central pattern and then used up the oddments around the perimeter. The rugs were extremely warm and very comfortable to lie on, particularly in front of a blazing fire. Unfortunately if a lump of coal exploded and fragments flew out of the fire, the smouldering wool in the rug stank appallingly. Most hearth rugs showed burn scars from exploding coal which was not an uncommon event.

Mom was also an avid knitter and the clickety-click of knitting needles was a part of daily life. She never purchased woollen clothing, all items were created by her own fair hand. Over the past year or so there had been a dearth of wool and that available was usually in drab colours, but signs were improving and coloured wools again started to appear in the shops. The knitting needles were brought back into service in a big way. During the shortage, she had been limited to dark grey balaclavas, pullovers, gloves and socks, but now she could create brighter garments. One of the first was a grey pullover for school incorporating Queen Mary's red, green and yellow stripes. She was able to complete a pullover in a day and a sleeved cardigan in two days. I always felt like running when I saw her empty out her wool purchases onto the table, because I knew I would have to hold the skeins between my out-stretched hands in order that she could roll it into manageable balls. It was so boring and time consuming and I moaned perpetually as I stood there with tiring arms. I usually resorted to day-dreaming of better things and when the wool snagged, tightening the ball, I received a flea in my ear for not concentrating on the job in hand. Boring, so boring and at times I felt like screaming.

Most children at the time became quite adept at knitting since, at school, we had been asked to knit six inch squares using any old wool we could find at home. Some of the wool was left over when knitting another garment, whilst other wool might come from unravelling an old woollen garment which had worn and was now beyond repair. The squares when knitted were sewn into large patchwork blankets to provide warmth to servicemen or others in cold climates. Wool was also provided at school to knit socks for sailors. I was a square patch man and, though I regularly saw mom knit hollow tubes with three needles to create socks and gloves, I never had the urge to take it up. We did, however create hollow woollen tubes for fun, using the technique called 'corking'. All that was needed was a cotton reel, which at the time were wooden. We tapped four steel tacks into the top of the reel equally spaced around the hole. To begin, the wool was passed through the hole and wrapped twice round the tacks. Pulling the bottom loop over the top of each tack in sequence created a hollow tube which was pulled through the bottom and, loop by loop, increased in length. Using oddments of different coloured wools, we created segmental patterns, some several feet long and competed with one another as to who had produced the longest rope.

We also used wooden cotton reels to make 'tanks'. The rims of the reel were notched with a knife to create the track of the tank. A piece of candle (about half an inch, 1cm) was hollowed by removing the wick and acted as the lubricant. A rubber band, passed through reel and candle was tacked to the reel at one end and a pencil or stick passed through the loop at the candle end. After rotating the pencil about fifty times, when placed on a flat surface the 'tank' motored along for several yards (metres). We held competitions to see which was fastest or travelled furthest.

Many items constructed with wood, wool, cotton and other raw materials were controlled during the war. Factories were rationed in the quantity and type of materials available to them. Most manufactured goods bore a label, the 'Utility' mark, which identified them as using approved materials. It was displayed on most goods, two segments of a circle embracing the number 41, 'CC41' and was essentially government endorsement that the item was not shoddy, simply produced from materials in limited supply. The items of furniture and furnishings did look basic compared with their pre-war counterparts but were functional.

Some materials in short supply were applicable to mom's hobbies particularly the silks and linen which she used for embroidering cushion covers and so on. As always she had to make do with substitutes and in place of linen, she persuaded William Perks, our grocer, to sell her canvass sacks which were used in wholesaling flour and sugar. When washed, the canvas made an excellent base for heavy table cloths or bed spreads which she embroidered with whatever silks or wools she could lay her hands on, usually obtained from Richmonds in Walsall. If she could get iron-on transfers of patterns, she used them but, when not available, I drew an outline for her from a magazine picture which took her fancy. Using a pantograph I had been given for one Christmas, it was possible to enlarge the outlines to fit the material. The early designs were very simple because of the shortage of silk yarns, but as products began to return, the design improved considerably and mom was able to sell her creations to make a few shillings for more materials. She had developed granddad's trait for selling superfluous goods and soon we had regular visitors purchasing her creations. She might take an order for a pair of matching cushion covers or an antimacassar, tablecloth or bedspread. Quite often, someone calling for a pound of tomatoes also went away with a pair of embroidered cushion covers!

When at home from school and at week-ends, I was expected to play my part in the 'shop', perhaps picking a seven pound (3 Kg) basket of tomatoes and weighing them out into pound (450g) bags ready for callers. When I say bags, it was usually newspaper parcels since bags were not easy to come by. In later years we were able to buy paper bags by the gross (144) from Birmingham market. We were always busiest on Fridays and Saturdays after pay day when people had a little spare money. I was also expected to cut all the long-stemmed flowers with gypsophila so that mom could make up bunches for sixpence, a shilling or one shilling and sixpence. These were displayed around the backdoor in buckets of water and callers made their choice.

Whilst mom was selling our surplus to regular customers at the door, granddad sold his surplus on a wholesale basis to local shops such as that of Florrie Moore on the corner of New Street in Landywood. She made a reasonable profit selling his high class and very fresh produce. Since starting to dig for victory, almost an acre of garden around the bungalows provided Landywood residents with very fresh vegetables. Granddad would return from a negotiation with Florrie and beckon me,

"Teck this sacker banes (beans) to Florrie Mower's shop, ode son. Her 'as ter pay yer ten bob."

On the crossbar of my bicycle I transported a twenty pound sack of enormously long runner beans to Florrie's shop, returning to granddad with a ten shilling note (50p). Next day I saw the beans in front of the shop, selling like hot cakes at nine pence a pound, a fifty per cent mark up. When I next saw granddad I jokingly told him that he could have made fifteen bob (75p) for his beans.

"That's 'ow yoe do business, ode son, er's 'appy an' arm 'appy. I grow um and 'er sells um. Yo'll see, er'll want another lot next wick", he explained.

I think I understood, but still wondered why he didn't sell them himself and make more money. As he said, he was happy and she was happy and I made several more trips as he had predicted. At the end of the day, I think he had the best deal. He had only to pick the beans, there was no hassle of bunching, weighing, finding change and so on.

Growing vegetable crops did not always proceed smoothly. I have already alluded to the cabbage white butterfly which could decimate spring cabbage in a day or so if not dealt with. There was nothing quite so dispiriting as seeing good crops of peas, cabbage, carrots or onions, and then see them ruined by pests. There were no adequate pesticides and sometimes nothing could be done. The Ministry of Food played a significant role at this time in advising on growing crops and avoiding pests. When dad saw an advertisement in the *Cannock Advertiser* for a local Ministry of Food event, he was intent on paying a visit. The advisers were set up in the Drill Hall in Market Street, Cannock, just beyond the Forum cinema. At this meeting we learned about rotation of crops and specific remedies for the commoner pests. Dad certainly hated carrot root fly because a row of very healthy looking carrots, when pulled, were found to be ruined by a rusty canker-like appearance of the root. He was keen to try anything which might rid him of this problem. When infected, the carrots were no use either for showing in horticultural shows or for selling, though the lower half could usually be used for home cooking. Cabbage club root was a little more obliging in that it showed by the wilting of the plants very early in life, allowing a new crop to planted elsewhere in the garden. The only gardener's tip he had used to date was to sprinkle soot on the surface after seed sowing in order to keep the infecting insects at bay. At the Drill Hall, a selection of leaflets were available and posters and films were shown, dealing with all manner of gardening subjects and pests and dad was in his element. We collected a dozen or more leaflets which we studied at home.

Although the main garden and lawns were largely turned over to digging for victory to provide vegetables for consumption, dad grew flowers including dahlias around the perimeter of the plots which mom sold in bunches at the door, but the glut in mid-summer could not always be disposed of in this way. The excess were picked from the three gardens, aunt Ruby's, granddad's and our garden and could amount to some three dozen bunches of flowers. These were put into a large clothes basket with two handles and hawked around the village, in the early years by Peter Hollett and me, but in later years I was joined by cousin Ron. Our reward was a percentage of our sales. We sold mixed bunches for sixpence (2.5p) or one shilling (5p). Some gluts of less popular flowers were bunched and sold cheaply at thru'pence (1.3p) and sixpence (2.5p) because they were not as popular as mixed flowers with gypsophila. This was always the case when granddad's massive plot of flags (irises) came into flower or when dahlias were at their most prolific. Granddad had for about three years planted flags on the tip he had used to raise the garden in order to develop the soil. In later years it grew very good vegetables.

We invariably returned home from our hawking with an empty basket, having visited every house in a quarter of mile radius. My pocketful of money was duly shared out pro rata between those who had contributed flowers and us, the hawkers. In time, our job became easier since we made our way directly to those we knew might purchase a bunch of flowers. Some customers frequently purchased two bunches of flowers, one for home and one for the graveyard.

As the flower season drew to a close, in late August, our attention turned to the start of the new football season and the main topic of discussion at school became the league games and teams. At the time it was not uncommon to see a league player going home on the bus after a day's training, which stimulated further debate. Previous seasons, I had cycled with dad to Molineux, Wolverhampton Wanderers ground, some six miles away. We went there via top Essington into Blackhalve Lane to join the Cannock Road at Wednesfield. From here it was a downhill run to Molyneux and we parked our cycle in the backyards of back-to-back houses around the ground for the princely sum of thruppence (1.3p). Dad bought the cheapest tickets, I think one and sixpence (7.5p) for him and one shilling for me (5p) and we stood on grass terraces, cheering our team. Bert Williams was usually in goal, forwards Jimmy Mullen, Johnny Hancock and Roy Swinbourne leading the strike, fed by Billy Wright, a great centre half. After shouting ourselves hoarse for ninety minutes, we returned to the backyard where some three dozen cycles had been stored in a heap about six feet (2 metres) deep, the owners clearly making most use of the available space. Like solving some giant puzzle, our bikes were finally disentangled from the mass and we could strike out for home. Although a Saturday, we rarely saw a motor vehicle all the way home. The first mile and a half up Cannock Road was a long uphill struggle which always seemed so much easier after a home win. I was always relieved at the site of the 'Y' junction into Blackhalve Lane since I knew the road was now mostly level or downhill all the way home.

The popularity of the professional game meant that we regularly played football in Jack Snape's field, usually with four people on each team. Both teams played into the same goal which was between two piles of our clothes. It meant that a team could be defending or striking at any time during the game. When I say 'team', I am not sure whether this was how we played our games. We were certainly not great team players and very much played our own game, a case of every man for himself. We may have been a gang of friends but during a football game we would certainly tackle our own team if it meant putting our name to the goal. I think this may have been the reason I never gelled with games at Queen Mary's, where the team spirit and play was everything.

We had so many arguments during our matches, revolving for the most part around whether a ball had hit the post or 'gone in'. Everyone became very vociferous and each had a different view on whether the ball had crossed the pile of clothes, which was not too surprising since everyone had seen it from a different angle. We were not particularly rational and those who shouted loudest and collected believers generally won the argument. Many arguments inevitably related to the 'off-side' rule. David Loach professed to know the rules and was quite adept at calling "off side" when the opposing team scored. When asked to explain, he was not quite so forthcoming. We were off-side because he said so, and he knew that we were! A goal lost in this way generally led to more aggression on the field, more fouls and the game descended into chaos. When we decided we had had enough, we settled on the grass to powwow about something topical. Even in earlier days, it appears, the game was not always clean as dad often pointed out to me. He had played as an amateur in his teens and explained to me the tricks that they had got up to. In a high speed break, he would run alongside an opponent and gently tap his knee against theirs so that the opponent tripped himself. I have to own up to trying this move, and there is no doubt that it worked. The player gets up and brushes himself down, not entirely understanding how he came to be on the floor!

We played cricket on this same pitch in Jack's field, using an oil drum with the wickets drawn on in chalk. We would argue vociferously, just as in a football match, about whether a ball had hit the wickets or not. On such occasions, the girls were less passionate than the boys and usually made more sense or did if we had listened to them! In fact, it is noteworthy how well the girls played cricket, they were good at catching the ball and they rarely tired of running after the ball. In a boys only match, we might on one or two occasions run for a ball that had been slogged into oblivion, but thereafter the fielders would revolt and tell the batsman he could fetch it himself. The pond in the field also seemed to catch more balls than we did but the unwritten rule was that the batsman retrieved such a ball. He could paddle for it or go and look for a tree branch to drag it ashore. Paddling was not the usual choice because the bottom of this pool was deep mud, well trampled and manured by the cows, and a wash in the stream or a bath was inevitably indicated. In fact, egging someone to retrieve a ball sometimes provided more fun than the game itself. Thereafter, bowling with the mud-sodden missile left plenty of spatters on the batsman's person or, if he chose to leap out of the way, exposed his wicket to a direct hit, a no-win situation!

In the lane, we also played a variation on normal cricket which, so far as I recall was called 'clock cricket'. The person with the cricket bat must stand still and use the bat to protect his or her legs as though they were a wicket. Other people playing, from one to several, toss the ball and try to hit the batsman's legs from where they are standing. If they do, or if someone catches ball, they take the bat. It was a game that could be played anywhere and did not need a pitch.

I have already mentioned that formal amateur cricket matches were played on the Harrison's ground in Jones' lane where two of the stalwarts for many years were Len and Lena Wootton. The former was captain of cricket and, I believe, groundsman and the latter the pavilion hostess, providing fresh afternoon teas for the players. I always knew when there was a home game since Lena called in home on Saturday morning for the salad items for the catering. I always found her ceaseless banter on most topics amusing, whilst mom was serving her. She left our house with heavy baskets and by the time she had visited Liza Sambrook's shop on Walsall Road for bread, she must have resembled a pack horse as she trudged down the lane to the ground.

It was very satisfying, particularly on a sunny afternoon, to sit and watch Len Wootton lead out his team to hopefully dispatch the opposing side for little over a hundred runs and then, after tea, take the crease and prove his team was the winning side. A village cricket match in Jones' Lane was a typical rural scene with a back drop of tall hedges and many people took a picnic with them to make a long afternoon of it.

In earlier years, if I found sitting for hours watching a cricket match too boring, I would wander into the 'rec to play on the apparatus. The slide and chocolate box were quite fun, but the most excitement came from the 'liver stretcher'. It was an eight feet (2.4metre) long thick plank of wood suspended from a tall frame by a rigid bar at each corner. Along the plank, on which we sat astride, were handles which allowed us to hold on. When set in motion, usually by older boys or girls standing at each end and pumping it strongly like a swing, hanging on for dear life became important! Their idea was to get the plank as near to the top of the frame as possible, by which time, everyone was usually screaming and pleading for the drivers to stop. It was free and yet as exciting as anything at a fairground. Rarely did anyone fall off but when in full flight, had we let go of the hand holds, injuries could have been severe.

It was late summer and the annual crop of soft fruits was ready for picking from gardens and hedgerows. During July and August, we ate our way through many blackberries, but there were also wild raspberries, not in sufficient quantities to collect for jam but delicious to eat, as were the alpine strawberries which grew in plenty on the railway embankments. On one occasion, whilst picking blackberries on the Blackberry Patch near Upper Landywood, I noticed two or three bumble bees entering and emerging from a hole beneath the bramble. I assumed it must be a nest though I had never before seen one.

A few days later when the four of us were wondering how to pass the time, I recalled the bee's nest and we decided we would investigate further. We found the nest but were a bit wary since they were fully grown bumble bees and quite large. David had brought a spade with him and took his life in his hands as he plunged the spade alongside the entrance hole, turning the spit. It was the wrong thing to do! Dazed bees started to emerge from the hole and then more and yet more. Soon forty or fifty angry bees resembled a dog-fight as they zoomed aimlessly around the bramble and very soon around us. We took to our heels and raced towards the lane, fifty yards away. We turned to see the black seething swarm descending upon us at a rate of knots. Our feet never touched the ground as we ran at full throttle down the lane! A glance back confirmed that we had outrun them and we slumped on the grass in the upper meadow, gasping for air and laughing hysterically with relief at our escape. We convinced ourselves that we had luckily been spared death by bee sting. I made sure I gave the Blackberry Patch a miss for the rest of that season, just in case bees had memories!

In the hedgerows, sloes and crab apples were ripening in abundance but only one crab apple tree produced edible fruit, though still tart, and the others we used as missiles in our war games or sometimes as cricket balls. Apples and pears overhanging someone's boundary fence were always fair game, though the owner did not see it this way and, if caught, we were given a dressing down. We were rarely caught and by September, most branches overhanging the lanes were stripped of fruit.

An unusual nibble we looked for at this time was the pignut, a delightful snack. We knew the areas in the various meadows where they grew and after locating the foliage in the grass, which looked like short asparagus fern, we could start our dig using a hazel stick shaped as a dibber. After carefully removing the soil from around the roots of the plant, we hoped to unearth a sizeable pignut, about the size of a cob nut. We sometimes competed to see who could assemble the largest heap before sitting in a circle to peel and devour them, often coated with a little soil. They were more succulent than hazel nuts and it was so easy to see why free range pigs did so much routing with their snouts.

CHAPTER 14

'The last years of the war - c. 1944 - 45'

With the end of the long summer holiday in September 1944 I would now be entering Queen Mary's main school and a new set of masters. I would for the first time have prefects breathing down my neck and simply being seen outside school without a cap would lead to detention. What a thought!

At home, it was the time of year when various items were preserved, for consumption during the winter months. A major problem with preserving soft fruits in wartime was the shortage of jam jars, particularly the two pound size which were the optimal choice for the purpose. What jars we had were thoroughly washed, stored and used year in, year out. But, since tinned fruit was in short supply or non-existent, more had to be preserved, which meant more jars were needed. Occasionally mom heard that some shop or other was selling Kilner preserving jars, which always resulted in an urgent trip, more often than not to Walsall Co-op, before stocks ran out. At a time of shortage, everyone kept their ear to the ground for any whisper regarding stocks of items in short supply. Aunt Sarah always seemed to be the one in the know. I have no idea how she came by the information, since she rarely made use of it, but probably because she spent so much time sitting in the 'gossip' chair in local shops. She certainly seemed to understand the village tom-toms better than we did.

Mom preserved all kinds of fruit, tomatoes, blackberries, plums, damsons, loganberries, pears, rhubarb and anything which might make a meal or a pudding. Large baskets of damsons and plums were purchased from a friend of a friend who had trees in their garden. In later years, dad planted damson and plum trees so that we would have our own supply. The pantry shelves, by the end of summer, were heaving with preserves and jams for later consumption. Jam was not so easy to make because equal quantities of sugar and fruit were necessary, and sugar rationing meant limited supplies. We all had a sweet tooth, using over a spoonful in our beverages and little, if any, was left at the end of the week. The government did not provide extra rations for preserves, but mom was aware of a potential source. I have already mentioned how aunt Ruby hoarded rationed commodities. With four in the family and, therefore, a larger weekly allocation she was able to store about two pounds (1Kg) of sugar every month. Like the soap powders, this built up in her wardrobe as a very large stock, and mom was aware of it, but prizing any of the holding from her, even at a high price, was going to be like getting blood out of a stone. However, on one occasion she did relent and gave mom four pounds (2Kg) on the understanding that, in return, she was given four pounds of finished jam. It was a pyrrhic victory for mom since she netted four pounds of jam she would not otherwise have had.

Apples after picking were wrapped in newspaper and laid as a single layer in unused drawers or in a stack of tomato trays. Rooms other than the sitting room were not heated and therefore cool and the fruit lasted for many weeks. Every year we paid a visit to Albert Belcher, a colleague of dad's from Gilpin's factory who lived in Wedges Mills. In his orchard, mom selected about three different varieties of apple, purchasing a shopping bag full of each. During the cold part of winter, I loved nothing better than an Egremont Russet from his orchard which, when icy cold, was like eating an ice cream lolly. We had our own Bramley Seedling tree and these fruit always kept well until Spring. We also grew Worcester Pearmain, not so good for keeping, but were pleasant for early eating.

As well as garden produce, we had a glut of eggs from our first chickens which were preserved in Isinglass (or water glass), a fairly new product. The contents of the carton were put in a two gallon (10 litre) bucket and a gallon (5 litre) of water added. Eggs were washed to remove any detritus and immersed in the bucket. They could now be kept for about two months in the cool front room. Although mom was not keen on using them for boiling, poaching or frying, they were regularly used for cakes and other cooking and were certainly better than the dried egg powder available as a substitute.

The garden was at the end of its season, most vegetable beds now empty. Carrots, parsnips and leeks could be left in the ground and pulled as required. Brussel sprouts and cabbages would remain in the ground since they could stand the winter frosts. Onions had been pulled and had now ripened on the staging in the greenhouse. We plaited them into bunches and hung them from the roof of the shed. The residual runner beans were prepared and sliced ready for use and preserved in common salt, purchased in large blocks from Mrs Challinor. Alternate layers of beans and salt were built up in old jam jars and sealed.

Potatoes were hogged, which entailed harvesting the late crop and piling about four hundredweight in a heap on a thick layer of straw in a sheltered part of the garden. This was covered by a six inch thick layer of straw, followed by an equal thickness of soil. Potatoes would keep in this way over the winter months and when required were accessed by a small tunnel, reminiscent of the entrance to an igloo, removing about four pounds of potatoes at a time before resealing. If the winter had extreme cold spells, an occasional potato on the surface of the heap might get frosted and go black but the bulk of the store survived.

With the garden now fallow, the chickens could be let out of their run to roam the garden during the winter months, since there was nothing to damage and it could only improve the egg quality. The problem was that the whole garden became the territory of the large Rhode Island Red rooster and every time I came home from school he was waiting for me in the front garden. He obviously saw me as a threat and attacked, flying up onto the back of my neck and, what with sharp claws and pecking, it was quite a painful experience. I usually had to make a run for it but then had the bright idea of putting mom's washing line prop on the front garden hedge. When I arrived home, I used it as a jousting stick in an attempt to keep the monster at bay but in the end it needed a blow across his back to stop his fixation on me. I suppose it taught him that the front garden was my territory.

By mid autumn, I went out early most mornings to scour the two large meadows of

Caddick farm, at this time of the year covered with early dew. It was mushroom time! They were not particularly to my taste but mom was very partial to them and was always over the moon when she saw me returning with several large freshly-opened field mushrooms. She fried them with a small knob of butter and pepper, or in the liquor (fat) from the bacon rashers and clearly savoured them. Seeing her delight left me smiling with contentment, basking in the happiness I had brought her. I was able to pick about fifty or sixty large mushrooms over a period of two or three weeks and then it was over, until next year.

Though I was now attending Queen Mary's main school opposite the arboretum lodge, we were still obliged to visit Moss Close for lunch and it was quite a long walk, directly up Lichfield Street into Mellish Road. The return journey could be taken more leisurely, either via Buchanan Road down into the arboretum and out through the lodge gate or a walk along the Butts into Upper Forster Street. The walk back, particularly in good weather, made up for the quality of school food which was only really edible about two days in five. It was wartime and produce was not of the best. Mashed potato was usually reconstituted powder and by no means as palatable as that which appeared in later years. It had a most peculiar taste, certainly not of the potatoes we grew at home, and as I stood in the long queue at the servery, I could only hope that today there would be recognisable potatoes. Frequently, even real potatoes showed black 'bruises' which, I knew from my gardening experience, had been frosted. I would have died for a few chips, but the kitchen did not have this facility. Meat dishes could be quite gristly unless we had corned beef cottage pie. Cabbage, the most common second vegetable which I had always detested, had a reputation among pupils for being served on the left side of the plate and by the time you sat at the table, it had moved to the right side. On one occasion we actually witnessed a cabbage pile heaving on a plate. The spiel around the table from older colleagues was that the *al dente* cooking used to preserve vitamin C had not dealt a lethal blow to something living! Or was it all a caper, by these rogues? We never found out. In contrast to the main course, the sweets were always edible, jam or treacle sponges, spotted dick or jam roly-poly cooked in long steamers served with some semblance of custard. We made this daily trip to Moss Close, but more for the walk than the meal. In the summer months it was not uncommon to miss lunch and hire a rowing boat for thirty minutes on the arboretum lake or to go to town for a browse.

Whilst at Moss Close, I had to catch the bus down into Walsall bus station, but since the main school was reasonably close to town, I now walked from school to the No 1 bus stop, which left from outside the Savoy cinema. The journey there was none too pleasant. On the corner of Hatherton Street and Littleton Street was a leather tanning factory and it stank, and I mean STANK! The view through the open steel lattice windows was quite a dreary sight, animal skins, now a dirty grey colour, were slopping around in long rotating drums. The workmen wore rubber aprons down to the ground and wellies to protect them from tanning solution, which formed large puddles on the shop floor. Any stop to peer inside was brief because of the smell, but it was a factory essential to one of the main trades in the town. Then there were the lorries on the way to the tanneries which passed us by carrying a heap of fresh skins from the abattoirs, wobbling like jelly and dripping grease and blood onto the road. Likewise when sitting in the classroom at school, it was always obvious when a tannery lorry passed by an open window, the smell was disgusting! It soon became the norm to walk to the bus via

Lower Forster Street, by-passing the tannery. Walsall as a whole was very industrialised, several foundries making steel castings, tubes and heavy chains. The sulphurous smoke from these created a significant problem in foggy weather, a choking smog (smoke and fog), but more of this later.

The subjects we were studying at school began to change. English literature introduced classical Greek themes such as Homer's 'Iliad' and John Bunyan's 'A Pilgrim's progress'. One of the first homework exercises, in Greek mythology, was to put the first story we had studied into the form of a poem of about twelve lines. We were to become a modern Homer. My effort was not too bad and was accepted by Mr Kingston, the English master –

In the fields of Enna,
Where Persephone played so gay, (at that time – 'playful or merry')
The earth opened , and up came Hades
And took Persephone away.
Demeter sorrowed greatly
And looked for her daughter, all day.
Hades said, "In this gloomy land
You will forever stay.
My wife you are to be.
And never again will play!"

I found it very difficult to get interested in the classical subjects that I studied over the next year or two and became very bored. But, even Homer proved more interesting than Chaucer's Canterbury Tales which followed a year or so later. It was gobbledy-gook and I could never make sense of it.

"Whan that Aprill, with his shoures soote
The droghte of March hath perced to the roote
And bathed every veyne in swich licour
Of which vertu engendered is the flour."

In essence, when the April showers penetrate March's drought to the root and every vein is suffused with water, a flower is produced. Ugh!

Mr Kingston would read a section and ask for a translation. I was surprised by how many hands shot up, but then they were mostly boys destined for the classics. I simply did not have a clue and drearily spent the lesson listening to swots who seemingly enjoyed it. I just about tolerated the languages, French (taught by 'Froggy' Taylor) and Latin, and managed to hold my own. However I knew that in the science-based lessons, my hand would frequently shoot up with answers. The problem was that I would have to take languages and classic and literary subjects later for School Certificate! Oh hell! When it came to homework, mom and dad were not really able to help and the quality was frequently below the masters' expectation. At times I simply could not do the homework and became deeply disillusioned but kept my head down and plodded on.

Even in the science-based subjects there were surprises. In mathematics, trigonometry was added to the syllabus, a subject I had not heard of before, but I relished the challenge.

Logarithms were initially difficult to get a hold on and some of algebra and geometry was difficult but at least they were interesting. Physics and Chemistry I thoroughly enjoyed and they became very much favourite subjects. In general the masters at Queen Mary's knew their subject and taught very well.

For an hour and a half every week we made our way to the woodwork class in the new block. A very pleasant master, Mr Phillips, taught us the rights and wrongs in the use of carpentry tools. Although dad was happy to have a go at any do-it-yourself job, his woodwork skills were not particularly good. From the lessons I was now having, I was able to tell him that his tools were not up to scratch. Chisels and planes were incorrectly sharpened and I set about trying to improve the tools at home. When it came to using tools in class, the innate poor skills I had picked up at home usually showed through, and joints such as tenon joints were often not acceptable. The cross-arm tenon joint of my toothbrush stand was certainly not a push fit, more a case of the arm entering a yawning chasm, because I had crossed the pencil line when using the tenon saw. I did improve as time passed, because I had to, but I always struggled with saws and the large wooden jack planes which were about six times larger than anything at home. Even though no better than average at the time, the lessons stayed with me and became very useful in later years as did the choices of good timber and the best cuts for particular jobs that Mr. Phillips taught.

As 11.00 a.m. approached, the end of the second lesson, most people in class noticeably began to get tetchy, and the master taking the lesson knew it. Then, at the sound of the bell, there was a stampede as we raced to the cloisters to join the queue outside the washroom where Parky (Mr. Parkes, the caretaker) ran the tuck shop and sold trays of cakes from Hollins' bakery. The cakes were a penny (0.5p) or tuppence (1p) and three or four large trays would be emptied over the next few minutes. Sugar-coated fresh doughnuts were most popular and were always snatched first, hence the rush to be first. I was usually starving by 11.00 a.m. since I had breakfast at home at 7.15 a.m. in order to catch the 8.10 a. m. bus.

One morning, as we arrived at Benton's Lane bus stop, Eric Gibbs picked up a packet from the floor of the bus shelter and gestured to me,

"Hey, Pussy (my nickname), look at this!"

I looked at the mauve coloured packet in his hand, bearing the maker's name 'Durex'. I must have looked puzzled about his enthusiasm after all it was hardly a ten bob note. Looking inside he withdrew a smaller envelope and told me it was a French letter. I hadn't a clue what this meant. Eric explained that he had learned about them from his older cousin in Bromsgrove, where the family had spent their summer break. He told me that it was a rubber glove which a man put over his dick to allow him to fuck a girl without her becoming pregnant. I was a little bemused and did not really understand, though I gave a knowing smile. Fucking a girl and thereby getting her pregnant were not terms I was really *au fait* with. Eric carefully put the package back in its envelope and pocketed it just as the bus arrived. On the journey to school, he was behaving like a cat that had been given the cream.

When we arrived in our school classroom, Eric displayed his find to others and several were obviously better enlightened than me. He made play with them about my naivety at the bus stop (which was true) and I became the butt of several uncomfortable remarks. During the day, the Durex pack containing one French letter was put up for auction and by the end of the day, Eric had made a half crown (12.5p) for his find, bid by a rather weedy looking boy who shall remain nameless. I was amazed at the value put on the object and enviously considered what I might have done with a half crown. Thereafter, I made tracks for the bus stop first in case another was to be found but there were no more lucky finds and the subject was never broached again.

In class, commonplace banter revolved around last night's radio, football scores or collecting locomotive numbers. In this respect, we had a new location for obtaining the numbers, Ryecroft locomotive sheds (shed number 3C). These were at the bottom of the Butts in Ryecroft and we were frequently able to return this way to the main school after lunch. Several locomotives were normally being attended to in front of the sheds and it was both a source of more numbers and an education in the care and attention given to them.

During this year, an Air Training Corps (ATC) unit was set up at school by Flying Officer Barnsley. We were expected to join one of the Training Corps (army or air) or the scouts and I chose the ATC. They were held on Friday afternoons and sometimes ran into the early evening. About a year after the corps commenced, we were issued with blue serge RAF uniforms of battle dress type and once a month were expected to parade in our uniform which must be properly pressed, and with well polished shoes. We were inspected on the parade ground (school playground) by Mr Barnsley, the commanding officer. Occasionally we marched up Lichfield Road to the quarry at Moss Close for shooting practice and on the occasions we were in uniform, we proudly demonstrated to the public that our marching could outdo the Guards anytime. In class, we were taught aircraft recognition using silhouette cards and had to become proficient in identifying planes by outline only. We studied two scientific subjects which I found extremely interesting; astronomy in which we were taught the major constellations in the night sky with the names of their major stars, and the science of flight. As a child, I had often wondered why aircraft did not fall out of the sky. I had built models and knew the shape of their aerofoils in some detail but the science of flight had not yet been explained. Now I knew!

We were trained message transmission by Morse Code which was used a great deal during the war. Messages in both plain text and encrypted form were sent by wire (or broadcast by radio) between the armed forces. The code was based on a series of dots and dashes for each letter and number, transmitted as short (dot) and long (dash) tones. As air cadets, we were obliged to learn the code so that we knew it fluently and we undertook regular tests and training to send, receive and decode messages at speeds up to twenty words a minute in order to pass a proficiency test. In the year following the war it was very easy to acquire ex-armed forces Morse keys and buzzers for a shilling or two (5p –10p), which meant I could practice at home. In this way I became very proficient and able to send at thirty words a minute. It was a little pointless since none of us could really receive beyond twenty words a minute!

At break time at school, it became quite common to hear talk of fucking and some boys boasted that they had done so. I was very inquisitive but I still had no real inkling what it meant. Their knowledge and possibly their maturity seemed in advance of mine. From some of the casual remarks I gleaned that a boy's dick became hard and was put inside a girl. These conversations were frequently accompanied by a guttural laugh and I laughed with them though, in reality, I was extremely puzzled. I was still pre-pubertal or on the cusp and had no real comprehension.

The subject arose again in the lane when *William* (names in *italics* hereafter are pseudonyms) was walking with some of us in the top field. He somewhat superciliously informed us that he knew where babies came from and in particular how we were made. I was all ears, as this was something I had wanted to know for some time. We ambled towards the large tent-shaped granite boulder where we regularly held powwows. As we sat astride the stone, *William* told us quite explicitly that babies were made after the father had fucked his wife, his dad had told him so. The man put his dick inside his wife, moving it in and out until 'spunk', white milk, spurted out and it was this that grew to make a baby inside his wife's belly. Some of us laughed and berated him and called him a liar. He was unyielding, insisting that it was definitely how babies were made, his dad would not lie to him. I had difficulty grasping the mechanics of his story, I suppose mainly because I did not know where the father put his dick to plant the seed. I pondered a lot about the belly button. One thing was certain, there were parallels to what I had heard in the school playground and it was eventually accepted by all of us. As I walked home alone, I pondered deeply on what *William* had said. I could not bring myself to tell mom and dad what I had heard, but it was not too long before I asked again where I had come from, more in the hope that I would get the response that *William* had had from his father. The answer was predictable and I never asked again.

With Christmas rapidly approaching, at home the time had come to slaughter the pig which had now fattened to about twenty score (400 pounds, 200kg). Mom had religiously cared for it for about eight months and it would now provide meat for the festive season and cured hams and bacon flitches for the year to come. It was a big day which needed adequate planning and preparation. The butcher had advised that we would need a bench to lay the dead carcass on, along with lashings of hot water for scraping its hairy skin. Dad had already constructed the heavy timber bench and had also rigged up a hook in the beams of the cow shed for hanging the carcass for dressing. On slaughter day he stoked up the brew'us boiler and all was ready.

The butchers, George Perry and Bert Baker (mom's cousin) from Lawson's butchers on Walsall Road, arrived on cue and were welcomed with a cup of tea. The pig was allowed to 'escape' through the open pigsty door to the garden and, very adeptly, George put a stun-gun to its head and fired, causing the pig to fall to the ground unconscious. Almost instantaneously he grabbed his knife and cut the pig's throat releasing an enormous gush of blood. The pig involuntarily kicked a few times and was dead in a matter of seconds. It was the first large animal slaughter I had seen and was not really frightening or terrible to witness. It was certainly less gory than granddad's method of sticking a sharp knife into the neck of a fowl whilst it was still conscious. George Perry dispatched the pig kindly and all was over before the animal could have known or feared what was to happen. Mom hid herself in the greenhouse until the deed was done. She had after all spent nearly a year scratching the pigs back and talking to it.

After slaughter the pig was dragged onto the low bench and buckets of hot water thrown over the carcase to soften the hair which was scraped off with an adze-like tool. Opposite the scraping blade was a hook which was used to pull off the pig's cuplike toenails. It needed several pairs of hands to turn the pig over so that the opposite side could be scraped. Then, like pall-bearers, six people carried the bench into the cow shed for hanging. A special rod, a gambrel, was threaded behind the tendons of the hind trotters, which George had now exposed. By hooking a rope and pulley to the gambrel, the beast could now be pulled up and slung from the hook prepared by dad. Removal of the bench left the carcase gently swaying and all breathing a sigh of relief that the exercise had gone so well.

After another cup of well-earned tea George returned to the carcase, cutting the torso from top to bottom, releasing the bowel which flopped into a large bowl. The liver, heart and lights (lungs) were put in another bowel along with the kidneys. The caul, a lace-like membrane of fat, used locally in making faggots, was laid on top. The pig's bladder was given to me and I was told that I could inflate it to use as a football. This I later did with the help of dad with his cycle pump and we played with it in the lane, though it was a bit greasy and unpleasant. The carcase would now hang overnight to cool and rest, prior to butchering next day.

Twenty four hours later, and the carcase now stone cold, George Perry cut off the head and then sawed the spine from top to bottom, splitting the animal into two. When I tried to pick up the pig's head by its ears I was extremely surprised by its enormous weight. The eyes were closed but it appeared to have a smile on its face, just as I had remembered it in life, particularly when it saw a bucket of swill coming through the pigsty door. We had always been good to it, feeding it regularly with good quality swill and scratching it's back, which it adored, responding with short pleasurable grunts. Twice when he had been off colour, the vet had attended and given injections. As I looked at his face I hoped that, should there be a piggy heaven, he would be happy there.

Each side of pork was now split into a large flitch of bacon, a long line of pork chops and a ham. The two flitches of bacon and two hams would be laid down for curing on the concrete floor of the shed, which mom had recently scrubbed. The curing depended on a large amount of common salt (some twenty pounds (10Kg) or more), being rubbed in and covering each item. The salt was purchased from Mrs Challinor in blocks about twice the size of a house brick and weighing four pounds (2kg). George Perry also sent me on a special errand to buy eight ounces (250g) of saltpetre from Cowan and Hartshorne, the local chemist, needed for curing the ham bones. Apparently blow flies lay eggs around the bone ends and if this area is not properly protected with saltpetre, we might in a few days have the ham heaving with maggots. During the run up to Christmas, George Perry would slaughter about half a dozen pigs at various homes in the village.

For the next week, we and the extended family fed well on the fry from the pig. The only person who seemed to fancy the pig's brains was cousin Bobby next door. Aunt Sarah cooked them and Bobby sat and devoured the whole brain. I could only stand open mouthed as he scoffed at the lumpy grey porridge The rest of the dishes made from the fry were very much to my liking. Mom made a large batch of faggots using minced liver and lights (lungs) with onions, bread crumbs and herbs. Balls of mixture were carefully wrapped in a piece of caul, a mesh of fat, and lined up in a meat tin before cooking in the oven. The cooked faggots were eaten with a thick gravy and were delicious. Unfortunately aunt Sarah's efforts were not too good, possibly because she had been kept short of the important caul or may not have known that she needed it. Uncle Bob's response when he arrived home for dinner was rather curt,

"What the bloody hell is this ruck of dirt on my plate?"

"They're faggots Bob, made from Ida's pig", replied a plaintive aunt Sarah.

"Faggots eh! And couldn't we have had bloody straightforward liver and onions, it would certainly have looked more appetising than a ruck of bloody dirt!"

The liver was large enough for everyone to have liver and onions next day, which we did. It was fairly cool weather at that time of the year but, whilst the line of pork would hang and keep fresh until Christmas, the fry had to be eaten immediately. The other remaining item was the head of the pig and the trotters. The pig's bowel was cleaned out and went to someone in the lane who had a penchant for chitterlings. None of the family were interested in them. In all, nothing whatsoever was wasted.

Grandma's brawn could never be beaten. It was made from the head or chawl of the pig which had been cut in half by the butcher. First each was boiled with onions, carrots and herbs until tender. When cooled, the meat was picked from the skull bones and coarsely chopped before being well seasoned and packed into basins until full. Gelatine was dissolved in the stock and poured over the meat to fill the basins. A plate placed on top was pressed down by a heavy weight and the basins put aside for twenty four hours for the mixture to set. After the several years of third rate meat and corned beef, fresh pig brawn was a gourmet delight not to be missed. I could have eaten it until it came out of my ears. The same could be said about the long line of pork chops which was used for the Christmas meal. The butcher was given a piece of pork loin for his family and, for this, he kept a joint for mom in the cool room at his shop for a meal after Christmas.

The final task was the production of lard from the leaves of fat around the kidneys. These were cut into walnut sized pieces and rendered down in a saucepan. The hot fat was frequently poured off into a large bowl. The defatted lumps of leaf were allowed to cool and were real pork scratchings. With a little salt they were crisp, flavoursome delights which melted in the mouth and kept for several weeks in an airtight container. Once the bowl of melted fat had set in a cool place, we had probably twelve pounds (6kg) of best lard which lasted many weeks and was eaten as a spread on toast with salt, or in cooking and making pastry.

After four weeks had passed, the flitches of bacon and hams were considered cured. They were thoroughly washed to remove the salt and hung from a beam to the side of the fire place in the sitting room, where they stayed for about six months. Every week about four inches was cut from the bottom of a flitch and from this, rashers of bacon were be cut for breakfast every day. Granddad liked the fattest cuts and an end piece was sent round to him for his breakfasts. The ham was lighter to handle and would be taken down and rounds of ham cut for frying for evening meals when dad returned from work. An extra special meal was ham, new potatoes and fresh broad beans and peas, when these came into season in late May and lashings of the cooking liquor (fat) from the ham was poured over the vegetables. This was something I looked forward to, year in, year out. Somehow it introduced the new season of garden produce, when everything was at its best, and moved away from mashed potatoes, sprouts and stews which had been the norm during winter. After providing many meals, the last piece of the ham was boiled on the bone and served as cold boiled ham with salads or in sandwiches.

Whilst home life was very happy, at around this time at school, I had to suffer a degree of bullying, which I presume came about because I was very small for my age, had a crooked nose from my cycle accident earlier in life and was not yet worldly wise, certainly not sexually. Eric Gibbs, my long time friend, and George Gibbs, who lived in Jacob's Hall Lane, frequently name-called as we walked home from school and made unpleasant insinuations about what mom and dad got up to in bed, which I found distressing. The pair were not related in any way but they certainly behaved like a pack of hounds towards me when they and one or two others were together. Yet when separated, I found them both great friends. I had played a lot with Eric over the years and still did and I frequently visited George's home and met his parents and sister. In fact, she worked in an office in Butt's Road, just below Moss Close school, and we sometimes visited her in the lunch hour on our way to Ryecroft sheds. But George and Eric together were just not to my liking and I tried to avoid them and catch a different bus home. Their bullying was habitually orientated around sex and since I was still very much on a learning curve, not fully understanding their innuendos, it hurt a great deal and, at times, I felt violated. However, I was a boy and boys showed grit and for a year or two I just had to accept what was thrown at me. The bullying stopped when Eric and I were involved in a play fight. I think a group of us were in the top field and decided to wrestle each other rather than play any other game. They proposed that Eric and I fight and I won hands down, pinning my opponent to the ground so that he could not move. At last I was growing and had become stronger and in the pack, this counted.

Annually at Queen Mary's grammar school, Speech Day was a very formal event. We were expected to dress well, meaning that uniforms had to be clean and neat. At about 11am, the whole school filled the pavements of Lower Forster Street and Darwall Street as we made our way to St Paul's Church in the bus station where a service of celebration was held. The organ, a majestic instrument, which always brought a tingle to my spine, was played by Mr Boothroyd, a classics master. As we filed in, a printed order of service was handed to everyone, bearing the school crest and motto *'Quas dederis solas semper habebis opes'* and always contained the same three school hymns. The first was,

Father supreme, who rulest all, in grateful praise we sing to Thee
For benefactors who recall those distant days we soon forget.

and the verse so appropriate as the war drew to a close,

Nor let us in our peaceful years forget the names of those who died
On many a field, 'mid unknown fears, to right a wrong and troth to keep.

and then the School song,

Floreat Reginae Schola Mariae,
Shout the motto boldly, for her sons are we.
Nurtured (we usually sang 'tortured') in her classrooms in our early youth,
Where we learn to cherish chivalry and truth;
Learn to pull together, each one with the rest,
Playing up and striving just to do his best.
This shall be our watchword, 'Always play the game!'
Sound the old School's praises, trumpet forth her fame.
Though the seas divide us we will not forget
That we all are brothers with a common debt.
Let us pay by giving as we forge ahead
Service to our living, honour to our dead.

I make no excuse for including some of the words of these hymns since we sang them with great pride and the words have stayed with me throughout my life. I have often been known, in later life, to burst into song with these tunes and lyrics.

The whole service goaded us to strive for better things. The lesson (reading) was always taken from Ecclesiasticus, chapter 44.

Let us now praise famous men, and our fathers that begat us. The Lord hath wrought great glory by them through his power from the beginning. Such did bear rule in their Kingdoms.......... and so on.

The final hymn 'Lift up you hearts', sung to the tune 'Woodlands', also raised the church rafters, certainly as far as the organist was concerned, as he trumpeted out the descant theme. This hymn was written by Henry Montague Butler, intriguingly the name of the headmaster and one presumes a past relative. It was a hymn sung with increasing crescendo and by the final verse,

Then, as the trumpet call, in after years -
Lift up your hearts, rings pealing in our ears,
Still shall those hearts respond with full accord -
We lift them up, we lift them to the Lord!

We must have been heard throughout the whole of the town. The organ pipes were blasting out and rattling the whole edifice with sheer delight and we the vocalists smiled at each other as verse by verse we turned up the volume, finally letting rip in full voice. I know we all had great joy in our hearts as we sang these hymns and it was a day on which we were proud to be Marians.

During the afternoon, the whole school made their way to the Central Hall in Ablewell Street for addresses from various dignitaries and the annual Prize Giving. The most important Prize of the year was 'The Queen's Prize for History' which was given by the modern Queen Mary (wife of the late George V). I knew it was a prize I was never going to win because I seriously disliked history, though I did win the biology prize in later years. This was the pattern of Speech Day throughout my years at the school, and was always accompanied by a feeling of deep pride and finally deep thanks for where the school had led me over my years there.

Inside Upper Landywood Chapel at Harvest Festival.

With children on a Sunday School outing to Trentham Gardens, Stone (cousin Pat is on the left of the picture).

An outside view of the church taken in later years.

Great Wyrley Wesley Church as it was in its earlier years c. 1930.

The original members of Great Wyrley Wesley Youth Group, photographed in 1949. From left to right, myself, Eric Till, Jean Gunn, Margaret Rowley, Grace Hall, Dorothy Turner, Wilfred Sambrook and Vernon Bullock.

Mom and dad in the garden in 1949, photographed and the film processed during my 'photographic phase'.

In the Sixth Form at Queen Mary's Grammar School wearing my dog-eared uniform!

With colleagues outside our tent during ATC camp at Hullavington in Wiltshire in 1949.

A pinic with the Rowley family in 1950, possibly on Cannock Chase. At the back, dad, mom and Lettie Rowley. Seated on the ground in front, Margaret Rowley, myself, Bert Rowley and Ruby Wood (Lettie's sister).

A Landywood country lane not disturbed by opencast mining!

CHAPTER 15

'The first post war year - c. 1945 - 46'

In early 1945, everything seemed to be going well on the war front and newspaper reports were showing that the allies were pushing back German forces as they moved forward across Europe. Then in May 1945 came the good news, the Germans had surrendered! We shouted for joy. We had won! There is no feeling of elation quite like that experienced by people who find themselves on the winning side, whether it be a football match or a war. As we walked home from school, everyone we passed was laughing and joking. We were shouting at one another at the top of our voices almost to confirm that we had heard correctly and it really was the end. As much as anything else, we thought rationing, particularly sweets, would soon be over. As we excitedly ran home past the tanneries, for once even they smelled sweet.

Over the next week or so, the whole country celebrated. There was an enormous bonfire in the recreation ground on Jones' lane where an effigy of Hitler in the form of a guy was burned. Flags were not easy to come by and I created a Union flag by painting an old white tablecloth with red and blue gloss paint. We stretched it across a bay window at the front of the house. Many streets were decorated with buntings and they held street parties by bringing out dining tables and chairs from their homes. We did not have a party in the lane, probably because there was no local association of neighbours, we were all individualists. Parents of some families regularly attended pubs and their children were provided with a celebration party outside the pub.

Celebrations were soon over and any expectations of withdrawal of rationing were soon dashed. In fact, it became obvious that, before long, things were going to get even tougher. Within weeks of the war ending, there was a general election and Jennie Lee, the labour candidate, was elected to represent our area as Member of Parliament for Cannock and district. In fact Winston Churchill, whom we had seen at the cinema in brilliant Technicolor with the King and Queen being cheered for leading us to victory, was deposed by Clement Atlee and a Labour government. I was not really of an age to understand politics, but I remember wondering how we could dump the nation's saviour for someone I had never heard of! I felt quite despondent when the result of the election was announced, having assumed everyone would vote for Winston Churchill.

At school it was the end of term and leaving at the end of the school year was always an upheaval. We had to empty our desks and take all our books and implements home. Even though I had taken some books home over the previous days, the final day still resulted in a satchel so heavy and overflowing that it really hurt my back and shoulders when carrying it. I had to rest every few yards between school and the bus stop, but somehow I managed to hump the books home. Unfortunately it did not do my satchel much good, some stitches had cut through the leather.

I looked forward to the long summer holiday away from school. A few families took a holiday away from home, even during the war years, but it was not something that was really talked about in the family. Granddad would certainly have considered it a waste of money and frowned on anyone who had money to burn in this way. For this reason, I suppose, I never craved holidays away from home, in spite of some pals enthusing about their week at the seaside or in the country. Even though I had stayed at home, I could always outshine them for a healthy looking tan because I rarely wore a shirt. On my return to school after one summer holiday at home, Mr Chadburn (Physics) asked where I had been to acquire such a deep tan and was quite nonplussed and raised his eyebrows when I replied, "Great Wyrley, sir!"

This year, however, seemed different. We were upbeat about the end of the war and somehow we were up for something different. Mom was itching to have a trip somewhere but dad was as always concerned about the greenhouse and garden. Her prayer was answered when a day or two later aunt Ruby rather excitedly ran into our house and informed her that a relative of uncle Joe, who lived in Bournemouth, was going away for a week and we could have the house for a seaside holiday. Our dad's could not get time off work for that particular week and so moms and children would go alone. Ron and I could not contain our enthusiasm since neither of us had previously had a seaside holiday, though I had at least visited Rhyl. There were five of us, with cousin Pat, and we travelled to Bournemouth by railway from Great Wyrley station which took a whole day.

The journey soon became boring being confined to a carriage compartment for so long but, since Ron and I were both train-spotters and collected locomotive numbers, we were reasonably occupied. We saw so many locomotives and I was elated when we saw the large ten-wheeled locomotive, which Eric Gibbs had spoken about so often, which pushed long express trains up the Lickey Incline near Bromsgrove. We also collected the engine shed numbers and as we travelled down the country we were amazed at the number of shed numbers that we had never before seen in the Midlands. The problem was that constantly putting my head out of the window resulted in me getting a fragment of coal dust in my eye which stung quite badly, but fortunately mom was able to fish it out.

We were greeted at Bournemouth station by a taxi, another friend of Uncle Joe's extended family, and taken to a three bedroom terraced house. Having only eaten a few home-made sandwiches on the way, we were dying for something to eat, but we were so exhausted that we settled for a cup of cocoa and bed. Mom and I had the double bed in one room and aunt ruby and her children in the other. It was difficult to sleep for the first time in a strange bed and mom and I were tossing and turning most of the night. Next door, aunt Ruby was also having a very disturbed night and obviously in and out of bed. Next morning she revealed that there were fleas in her bed from the dog of the house, which was away with its owner.

Mom felt like bacon and egg and went in search of the frying pan. She found it on the floor beneath the gas cooker, unfortunately unwashed. I am not sure whether she expected a palace for her free post-war holiday, but she immediately broke into a tirade about filth and how she could not eat anything cooked in that thing. In fact, the lady obviously used her pan over and over without washing either to maintain the flavours or make her fat ration go further, but mom immediately set about a thorough wash and scouring of every pan in sight along with the various kitchen surfaces. Aunt Ruby made a trip to a local shop and purchased tomatoes to go with our own home-reared bacon and eggs which we had brought with us. After mom was satisfied with the level of cleanliness in the kitchen, we had a delightful meal of bacon, eggs, tomatoes and fried bread. I am sure the owner's pan would have been fine and mom's reaction was hardly charitable towards a free and generous gift of a free holiday. Unfortunately she was always tickle-stomached and I understood that she could not have eaten food so cooked.

Unpleasant as mom was towards her benefactor, aunt Ruby was perhaps more heartless in that she went on and on about the fleas in the bed. She purchased Keating's powder at a local Chemist's shop and, after breakfast, made the bed giving a very generous dusting inside with the insecticide. If anything, over the next few nights, cousin Ron was worse than ever. He itched and scratched and created scores of bloody scratches over his body and limbs. The bed clothing was duly taken outside and given a thorough shaking, releasing clouds of white powder. Things did settle but it was hardly a restful holiday because of the constant bickering between mom and aunt Ruby.

Access to the beach was via a very long zig-zag pathway down the cliff side which we, the children, found quite fun but mom and her sister constantly moaned, particularly on the upward journey. There was a funicular, but this was deactivated during the war and was not yet restored. The weather was sunny and the sea and beach were wonderful but, just out to sea, there were metal girders and spikes put there during the war as anti-landing defences. Whilst they spoilt the view, they did act as barriers so that children could safely bathe in about twenty to thirty feet (6-10metres) of water close to the beach protecting us from the deeper water beyond.

We used the local bus services to visit Christchurch and Poole, which was interesting, but for us, it was the beach at Bournemouth which made the holiday and everyday our moms grudgingly suffered the trial of the zig-zag path. In all, I found it a delightful first holiday at the seaside, but it might have been better without adults!

During this first summer after the war, people were definitely more relaxed, and holidays were the 'in thing'. Even in the lane, a family of four arrived on Holloway's shale tip for a camping holiday. They came from Leicester and this was their summer holiday. I am not sure why they chose Landywood nor why they chose to camp on a shale heap. They certainly had no relatives in the area. They pitched a camouflaged army tent and had palliases on which they would sleep. Kettles were boiled and meals cooked on a paraffin stove. The boy and girl were about our age and we quickly made friends and spent a great deal of time showing them around our patch, including our camp in the blackberry briar, a few yards from their pitch. They lived in town and a country holiday was a change for them and they seemed to thoroughly enjoy their stay. They joined in our games including our evening street game, tin can nerky.

Every evening in good weather at around 7.00 p.m., almost everyone up to about seventeen years of age, collected at the bend in the lane, just beyond Plant's buildings, to play 'tin can nerky'. It was the only occasion that we really met our older colleagues. The game is a variant on hide and seek. A can was thrown as far as possible, usually by one of the older boys, and the person seeking, chosen by the toss of a coin, had to retrieve it.

It meant a run of around fifty yards, since the can was always flattened like a discus and travelled a fair distance. The person retrieving it ran backwards to the start point, and was not allowed to look round. Cheating by doing so, meant the can would be thrown again. The period of time taken to retrieve the can gave everyone time to hide. The retrieved can was placed in the middle of the road at its start point. The essence of the game was that players 'in hiding' must use stealth to work their way back towards the can, they were not allowed to find a distant hiding hole and stay there. By creeping back as close as possible to the can, using the cover of hedgerows or long grass, they could then break from cover, touch it and shout 'TIN CAN NERKY!' Conversely, if the seeker sees a player, he or she must also run to the can and, touching it, shout the name of person and where seen. That player was then out of the game and the first seen became seeker for the next game. The seeker inevitably had to move away from the can to look behind hedges and so on, giving hiders a chance to break cover and touch the can. It was a game that everyone seemed to enjoy and required a great deal of skill. Some games may have over a dozen players and last the whole evening until daylight faded.

After the war, a new radio series, 'Dick Barton – Special Agent' started at 6.45 p.m. and this controlled the time our street games would start since many stayed at home to listen. Another radio special later broke up the game early at 8.00pm, 'Paul Temple', a serial in six episodes written by Francis Durbridge. It was my all time favourite detective series. I adored it and ran home about five minutes before the start and curled up in the armchair, eagerly awaiting the lead-in music, 'Coronation Scot'. It was always one of the subjects in the school playground next day as we shared our analyses and theories of who we thought the culprit was. Francis Durbridge all too frequently outwitted us.

Just after my birthday, the war in Japan ended when the Americans used atomic bombs on cities in Japan. It was great news but sadly coloured with astonishment when we learned of the devastation caused. Even so the end of that war did not seem to have quite the same impact as the end of the European war and there was no celebration.

In September, I returned to school to begin my third year. We were joined on our bus by new pupils from homes in Shaw's Lane. Jean Gunn had gained a place at Queen Mary's High School for girls and Norman Seedhouse a place in our school. To date I had worn short trousers which was the norm at the time and started this new school year in long trousers. I was still quite small relative to my friends, who had by now put on a pubertal spurt. Shoes with one inch (25mm) soles had just come into fashion and these helped me gain a little height! A day or two into the new term we were checked by Mr Parkes (caretaker) against standards of height and weight for age and those larger than the norm were entitled to the extra clothing coupons. I of course fell well below the line and was not entitled. Mom was disappointed because she was now limited in what she could purchase to replace my rapidly wearing school uniform but, by purchasing second hand clothes for herself, she usually managed to kit me out.

The dress code was important at school and prefects were always prowling to catch boys incorrectly dressed. We were obliged to wear our caps and ties at all times outside school and I was regularly booked for not wearing my cap. Prefects seemed to appear from nowhere and pounce on delinquents like me! One day I was caught whilst browsing in Smith's bookshop in Park Street by a pompous prefect who shall remain nameless. The 'bookings' accrued and at the end of each month, as punishment, we were detained after school and had to fill four pages of lined foolscap paper (a little larger than A4 paper) with lines of prose or verse copied from a book. Nothing as demeaning as a hundred repetitive lines at Queen Mary's! Paul Baker had invented a four pen device which he eagerly demonstrated to me to allow him to write four lines at a time, if caught. When he was eventually put on detention, which was rare in his case, the punishment took him about ninety minutes to complete since, as one might expect, his invention was useless for continuous prose. I was on detention most months because of my cap and managed to get my punishment down to a fine art by using the longer speeches and monologues from Shakespeare which, over the years, we had been obliged to learn for English literature homework. I was always a very fast writer and could fill the four foolscap pages in twenty minutes. In fact it was a brilliant way to memorise the Shakesperean works. The detention's prefect found it difficult to believe that I was legitimately leaving so soon. It led me to continue pocketing my cap and take the risk. Unfortunately two masters from Queen Mary's, Harold 'Porky' Hawkins from Cheslyn Hay, a maths master, and E A 'Maggie' Mason, a chemistry master from Great Wyrley, usually travelled on our bus and we were obliged to behave and wear our caps whenever they chose to sit upstairs.

An advantage of being in the main school was that we could spend about an hour in Walsall town during lunch break. We occasionally went into the shops, but it was also somewhere to walk outside the restricting confines of the school playground. I spent a lot of time looking at things in shop windows that I knew I could not afford. Every time I passed by, I scoured the camera window in Bell and Webster's chemists in Lichfield street hoping there may be a camera at my price. Most were second hand Leica's at prices around a hundred pounds!

When in the town, a favourite trick was for a group of us to stop in Park Street and look up to the sky, pointing over the shop roofs. Inevitably a group of inquisitive shoppers would stop by us and look up. We would remark 'how amazing!' or 'I wonder where it's come from' and walk away. Some shoppers stayed glued to the spot for some time, frantically trying to spot the UFO!

On market day, I enjoyed nothing more than standing and observing the stallholders, who were selling all manner of goods. Most sold fruit and vegetables, clothing, dress-making materials and shoes, but the ones I found really fascinating, were selling patent medicines or new gadgets for the home. One gentleman sold a special skin cream made from a snake. He pulled a realistic-looking python from a snake charmer's basket and then prepared to tell his captive audience of his new acquisition just discovered in darkest Africa. Using an oriental-looking dagger he demonstrated how a small incision was made in the side of the snake, and the ingredients for the cream were carefully extracted.

"This cream," he went on with authority and holding up a cardboard pill box containing about a spoonful of green cream, "was carefully extracted from a special gland in the snake known only to African healers! I buy my ingredients directly from them. It is a genuine natural cream and you will not find it anywhere else in this country. Tomorrow, I move on to Nottingham and if you want it, you need to buy it today." The crowd were rapt and listened attentively as he explained that the amount covering his little finger nail would heal every illness known to man! Small containers were sixpence (2.5p) for about twenty treatments or a larger container containing three times the amount for a shilling (5p).

I was not particularly interested in healing potions, but a man demonstrating a glass cutter caught my attention. I liked the easy way he was cutting a circle from glass and recalled a broken clock face at home. He could cut innumerable shapes and it looked so easy that I was sure I could emulate him. I invested one and thrupence (6p) of my pocket money and could not wait to get home. I tried to cut a piece of unwanted greenhouse glass, according to his demonstration, but to no avail. I never was able to cut circles, but in later years realised there was a significant difference between greenhouse glass and the glass he had used.

On every market day there was quite a cacophony in Digbeth and the High Street as market traders shouted their wares, trying to outdo each other. The back chat between trader and shopper equated to vaudeville, loud and raucous and full of *double entendres,* but it did the job. It gave impetus to an already bustling market.

"After your old man has eaten this piece of steak, missus, you'll feel the benefit!" would be followed by cackles and back chat which caught the attention of passers-by and drew us towards his stall.

Shops in the town centre were generally high class but some shops on the perimeter of town left much to be desired. Sometimes I would go into Stubbs' greengrocery shop on Lichfield Street opposite school to buy an apple to eat whilst walking round town. The shop was dingy, with little light and had a smell of rotting vegetation due to decaying vegetables beyond their sell-by date, particularly cabbage. This was nothing out of the ordinary, fruit and vegetables were frequently in greengrocery shops for many days prior to sale and nature had by then started the composting process. A shop in Lower Rushall Street selling 'homemade' fruit drinks, which quenched my thirst on many occasions had a quarry floor which was ingrained with thick dirt and had probably never been cleaned since the builder had laid it. A shop in Lower Forster Street which made and sold homemade potato crisps was thickly smeared by the mist of cooking fat from the fryer and the crisps themselves were appallingly fatty. Smith's crisps were in short supply during the war years and we were obliged therefore to sample his wares, or go completely without lunch.

So many of the perimeter shops of Walsall were dirty and must have attracted a great deal of vermin. Hygiene was not yet a high priority and in any case income for the shopkeeper was probably very low, compared to the corner shops around home which were generally clean and well stocked. As a growing boy, the lunchtime snacks in the shops around school relieved hunger, and that was all that mattered, to hell with hygiene! Even on the way home from school, I made use of the mobile hot potato ovens around town. The ovens, built onto a two wheel handcart, were heated by a coal fire beneath and two shelves cooked and stored the baked potatoes. I could buy a potato or potatoes for three pence or sixpence (1.25 and 2.5p) in a newspaper cone seasoned with a spoonful of salt from a bowl on the cart. These I consumed on the bus on the way home.

Our dreams of an end to rationing after the surrenders came to naught and, as the weeks passed, it was plain that not only was rationing continuing, but it was going to get worse. Bread was rationed during the next few months and the quality returned to the grey bread of the early war years. I seem to remember that we were allowed a one pound (500g) loaf for the three of us each day and the butter ration was reduced. Even the cereal ration for the pig was reduced. Rationing was to continue for several years because there was a dip in world production of grain. In 1946, we did experience one blessing when bananas hit the shops again. We were rationed to about one pound during the first month. Everyone tried to cheat, because the greengrocer simply put a pencil cross in a square on the back of our ration book and we used bread or something gentle to erase the cross, so that we could get seconds. I am sure Mr Ecclestone was aware of what we had done, but he usually turned a blind eye if he had a supply since they went off fairly quickly.

People living on government allowances alone must have found times difficult. We were fortunate to have the garden, the chickens and the annual slaughter of a pig and it was only the bread and butter rations which affected us. The flitches of bacon and hams, hanging in the recess in the living room, meant that we were able to have regular meals. The disadvantage was that we had a perpetual smell of cured meat in the house like a butchers shop, but we learned to live with it. Mom also kept grandma and granddad supplied with bacon or ham. In return, granddad might kill one of his chickens for mom, usually an old hen looking worse for wear and no longer laying eggs. It was not uncommon when dressing the bird to find that it had some tumour or other, but it was going to be cooked well and with plenty of fresh vegetables would taste as sweet as a fit bird. A boiled or casseroled fowl made an extremely tasty dish, particularly cooked in or accompanied by white or onion sauce.

We slaughtered pigs for several years, but not all went well and one year it went disastrously wrong. As I have said, during slaughter, the butcher fires a pistol with captive bolt into the pig's head to stun it prior to 'sticking' it (cutting its throat). This particular pig had grown to an enormous size, about 460 pounds (230 Kg). George Perry led the pig from the sty and grabbing an ear, quickly put the stun gun to its forehead. Unfortunately, the pig had other ideas and snatched its head to the side, resulting in George firing the eight inch bolt through his own forearm. Instinctively, he picked up his knife from the scraping bench and slit the pig's throat. The still conscious pig made a break for the open garden. George gently eased the eight inch spike from his arm and turned to assistant Bert Baker, now standing open-mouthed and looking more stunned than the pig, screaming at him to take over. The pig made about ten yards before collapsing from blood loss. Somehow, George could still use his wrist and drove his van to Walsall General Hospital. It appears that the eight inch (20cm) spike had penetrated through his forearm without injuring any significant blood vessel, bone, tendon or major nerve and in less than a week he was out of his sling and back at work.

We now had a very heavy pig which had to be scraped and was some fifteen yards from the hook in the pigsty on which it would be hung to cool. It was all hands to the plough and six of us managed to drag the dead weight back to the normal slaughter area where it was put on the bench, doused in scalding hot water and scraped. George continued to slaughter pigs and was regularly reminded to 'Watch your arm, George!' when he applied the stun gun to the pig's head.

After a pig had been formally butchered, grandma, as I have said earlier, used any pork off-cuts and the head to make pies, brawn and so on, using her culinary skills learned whilst in service. I was particularly partial to pork pie and watched enthralled as she prepared and baked her pie. It was a level of expertise that mom never aspired to, even though a reasonable cook. Grandma first made hot water pastry which she used to raise a pie case around a two pound jam jar. The chopped pork with seasoning was added and a pastry lid applied before baking. After allowing it to cool a little, she fed in a gelatine solution through the steam hole in the pie lid. I could not wait for it to cool. I adored a slice of her home-made pie with HP brown sauce and, as I avidly tucked into the mouth-watering delight, my eyes, semi-glazed by sheer pleasure, focused for the umpteenth time on the message on the side of the sauce bottle, *'Cette sauce de haute qualité est un melange des fruits orientaux'* (this high quality sauce is a blend of oriental fruits). The very first time that I translated this homily, I had felt quite impressed with my skill and, though not too fond of French, I appreciated the advantage of being able to read another language. I was, however, conscious of the fact that if a Frenchman had spoken the phrase to me, I would not have had a clue what he was talking about. But, French apart, the freshly baked pork pie left my taste buds and even my mind blown away.

Whilst cured meats kept well, fresh food was more difficult to keep. I liked fresh fish, but it was a food which was frequently disgusting when cooked at home. Mom would buy cod fillet or hake steaks from Walsall market as a change from meat, but so often, the fish was not particularly fresh. It had been many days between netting the fish and delivering it to the market and as a result, its flavour had become unduly strong. We usually ate it served with vegetables and a white sauce but to me it did not compare in flavour with the fish from the chippy. The battered fish from Mrs Pretty's shop on Mount Pleasant was to die for, crisp, white and very fresh. However it was not only fish that suffered, many foodstuffs did so since refrigeration in the home was rare. As stated earlier, milk soured very quickly, butter became rancid and unpalatable, cheese would sweat badly and meat only stayed fresh for a day or two. Vinegar quickly developed 'mothers' (overgrowth of yeast deposits) and whilst still usable, did not look good. As a result, meals during summer often tasted tainted, particularly those containing dairy produce. Some meals, I could not bring myself to eat because of this.

Now fourteen years of age and having served three or four years apprenticeship with dad, I was being called upon more and more by the adults to help with some job or other. Granddad handed over the keys of the cottages in Landywood to mom. I remember he simply wrote on a scrap of paper from an exercise book that he was 'hereby handing over the properties to Ida Carpenter - signed Robert Baker'. It was to him a contract, much like a Romany handshake, and meant that the rents now belonged to mom. Unfortunately it also meant responsibility for all repairs which were commonplace in old properties. When Mrs. Perry, in one of the properties, found a problem that needed attention, I would be called upon to effect a repair and before long would be up on the roof of the back kitchen making it watertight where the lead flashing had perished.

Although granddad always used dad for expert problems such as plumbing, he had usually himself taken on any woodwork jobs in his housing stock. One day I was asked by mom to look at movement and creaking in the floor of the front room of Mrs. Perry's house in Benton's Lane (my birthplace), which had been raised at the last rent collection. Mom hated collecting rents from houses where there was a structural problem. Rolling back the linoleum I found a sight to behold. It was granddad's handiwork as I had always known it! He had repaired a patch of rotted floor with timber from a banana box still bearing the Fyffee logo. The wood had obviously been chopped to size with an axe, nails everywhere had split the timber and in some cases were bent over. In fact, I found two layers of wood since the wood from the box was only half the thickness of the original floor boards! When I returned home for lunch, I painted the scene for mom and dad and they nearly choked on their food. Granddad never bought anything new if he could find some cheap alternative, preferably free, and it he had obviously used an axe for the whole job including using the back of the axe to knock in the nails! Even the nails, I imagined, will have been collected from some old fruit box and straightened on a house brick with the back of his axe, as I had witnessed him do on many occasions. It was difficult to get timber during the war years, but I think granddad's repair job had pre-dated the war and the necessary tongue and groove boards would have cost him little. Later that week dad purchased a length of tongue and groove floor board from Linford's timber yard in Cannock. It cost one shilling and was an exact match and made a perfect job of the floor, so long as my joints were not perused too closely. I was absolutely hopeless when it came to sawing timber squarely, but it was certainly better than the repair that it had replaced.

Many of the jobs I undertook were around home and family. Grandma frequently asked if I would do a job for her, having long since given up on granddad. After a job was completed she usually came out with the same remarks,

"Eee, just look at that! Thee'st just lark thee dad. Thee const turn thee 'and t'anythin, thee const. Giz a big kiss", at which point she would slip a sixpence or shilling piece into my hand.

"Dunna tell 'im (granddad) what arve gin thee", she would add, clearly disgruntled by the thought of his miserliness.

I loved grandma very much and did not want the money from her but I knew she would get upset if I didn't take it. She seemed to have come straight from a Dicken's novel, whose works I was studying in school. Her world was her home and family and no-one else was allowed into her time-warp. I recall asking her a year or so earlier where we came from.

"Dunna thee werrit ode son, tha' shuds'na myther on things that dunna concern thee", was the austere reply and I never asked the question again.

Doing DIY jobs on my own led me to becoming quite arrogant and thinking that I could do anything, but I was soon to be brought down to earth. The bungalow was now about fifteen years old. The walls of every room had been decorated annually with a coat of gloss paint usually purchased from Shaw's paint shop in Marsh Street, Walsall. Mom always chose a colour as near as possible to the pale cream already on the living areas and the pale greens or blues for bedrooms, which dad duly applied. I did help a little but preferred to slink away to find my friends. Painting walls did not really appeal to me and painting woodwork even less so. The age of the bungalow was beginning to tell in that unsightly cracks were appearing in the ceilings and mom felt that only papering would hide them.

"I'll do it!" I said, delighted to try my hand at something new.

So long as the cracks were going to be covered mom was more than happy with my offer and after yet another visit to Shaw's, the materials were to hand, four rolls of Anaglypta paper. Mom set about mixing a bucket of paste made from self-raising flour. The living room table was duly cleared to make a pasting table and the job began. I promised mom that we would have the job finished by five thirty when dad returned from work. It was now one thirty.

It has to be said at the outset, that I knew nothing about wallpapering nor had I ever seen anyone paper a wall let alone a ceiling. With great authority I pasted the back of the first length of Anaglypta. When I tried to raise it to the ceiling, standing on a dining chair, it was very heavy, wet and limp and prone to tear very easily. What happened over the next hour would have brought laughs and tears to the eyes if enacted on a theatre stage, though in reality it was a tragedy!

How to control and apply a soggy twelve feet (4 metres) of Anaglypta to the ceiling became a night mare. With sweat pouring from me, I tried and tried to get the sodden mess to adhere to the ceiling. Mom had the bright idea that she could control one end by pressing it against the ceiling with a sweeping broom! Grandma then arrived and joined the kafuffle. Seeing the mess we were in, she ran and collected aunt Sarah's broom and applied pressure to another area of the paper. I tried my best to line the paper correctly whilst brushing it to the ceiling. After what seemed an eternity, the first length was applied, but no longer with a raised pattern. This had long since been brushed out whilst trying to get the paper to stick. Undaunted, I pasted the second length and my assistants held it just below ceiling level like a festooned curtain, whilst I tried to line it up and get it to adhere. This length went on much better, but no sooner was it applied than giant bubbles began to appear, I had not, it seems, allowed the paper to soak before applying it. Trying to brush the air bubbles out simply resulted in wrinkles and again loss of pattern. It then became apparent that the paper had a repeat pattern which I had failed to line up. Nearly two hours work and an appalling mess to show for it! I was tired, covered in paste, annoyed with myself, sweating profusely and knew there must be an easier way, which did not involve periodically having a length of soggy paper wrapped around you. In a fit of pique, I pulled the whole unsightly mess from the ceiling.

Dad arrived home from work and mom filled him in with what had happened. He felt that he could have done the job had he been home. In reality, he also had never before papered a ceiling and his effort was only a little better than mine, though he did manage it after a fashion. He knew the paper should be folded in a concertina pattern, which would certainly make for easier holding whilst applying it, though he was not exactly sure how. Unfortunately, even after his efforts, some areas of the paper retained a raised pattern whilst other areas were like mine, a flat as lining paper. Mom was happy that the cracks had disappeared but they never papered a ceiling again!

I was always held spellbound when I saw a professional plying his trade, usually very easily, and I knew I would have to have a go to prove that I could do it. It was this approach which meant that dad and I became adept at many do-it-yourself tasks. We learnt by trial and error, knowing our first attempts would be unacceptable, knowing above all that we would never have the skills of the professional, but would improve with each effort. Subsequently I did learn how to concertina wallpaper correctly and support it with a spare roll of paper, whilst applying it to a wall or ceiling.

Within a year or so, materials unavailable during the war years, such as cement, were becoming accessible. Smith's Concrete works, on the Watling Street (near to the A460 crossing) at Cannock, started to produce concrete products such as curbing and paving slabs. Two chores I really hated were weeding our very long clinker-ash drive and cutting some two hundred yards (190m) of hedgerow around the garden and I was very chuffed when mom and dad, on seeing the Smith's advertisement, decided to lay slabs from top to bottom of the garden and drive.

'O joy of joys, no more weeding, but what a shame they don't do concrete hedges!' I thought to myself.

One hundred three feet by two feet (900mm by 600mm) concrete slabs were ordered, along with a two tons of sand and several bags of cement. The slabs weighed in at about one hundred and thirty pounds (60kg) each. The delivery driver had lost an arm during the war and off-loaded everything by hand (or more correctly by one hand and the stump of an arm). He worked so hard on the enormous load and I remember feeling totally inadequate. I was just fourteen years of age and still fairly slim and could neither lift a concrete slab or a bag of cement!

Over the next couple of weeks, the drive was transformed and looked very neat. The slabs were then continued up the garden path at the back of the house. My new task changed from weeding to washing the paths and drive from the top of the garden to the front gate. An hour of this was a fair swap for a day's weeding and it did have its funny moments. Grandma came round the corner to collect the newspaper and mom came out of the house just at the moment I threw a bucket of water across the yard.

"Look what you are damn well doing!" screamed mom, "Just look at me, I am sodding-well drenched to the skin, and a clean dress this morning!"

Grandma only caught the splash and we both fell about laughing at the expression on mom's face.

"It ay damn-well funny, get on with your job!" she retorted and forcefully thrust the newspaper into grandma's hand. She then grabbed the brush from my hand and gave the area another good brushing to get rid of her angst.

During my early childhood, I referred to the motorcycle belonging to David Loach's dad on which we regularly played. Many men in their early twenties had ridden motorcycles and some of these bikes were still around. There had for many years been an old motorcycle leaning against the fence in uncle Bob's garden. It had perhaps been loved in its day but had been left to the elements and was now very badly rusted. It was a BSA machine, probably of the early 1920s and I suspect bought second hand at the time. When I visited grandma, I sometimes sat on it pretending to drive, apprehensively looking over my shoulder in case I was spotted by uncle Bob, whom I knew would give me a mouthful of abuse. However, the bike was so heavily rusted that it was totally immobile. Cousin Bob, now about nineteen years of age, was obviously yearning for 'wheels' and I passed him one day struggling to take the motorcycle apart. The tools he had were not ideal, but he did manage to remove the carburettor and the magneto, which he took into the house to strip down. He enthusiastically cleaned them up and re-assembled them, sure, he informed me, that this would bring the beast outside to life. It didn't! He was unable to get even a cough from the engine, after pumping away for an eternity on the kick starter. Some weeks later, he bought a second hand Francis Barnet autocycle and, like all young men, was very proud of his acquisition. It was quite a small engine, about 150cc but certainly had the power to get him about at a reasonable speed. Second hand was the norm at the time since new road vehicles were still very rare in showrooms. He used his autocycle every day to get to and from work, always looking as proud as if it were a TT special. Its petrol consumption in times of rationing ought to have been outstanding, but this proved not to be the case as will be revealed later.

CHAPTER 16

'My experimental years - c. 1947 - 48'

January and February 1947, saw very extreme weather. We were accustomed to some snow, perhaps three or four inches (7cm to 10cm) at some time during every winter but this year there was a great freeze accompanied by blizzards. Some two feet (60cm) of snow fell in about twenty four hours and brought paralysis to road and rail. Whilst the snow was two feet deep on the railway track, strong winds had created snowdrifts in the lanes which were to hedge height, over six feet (2 metres) deep. Miners from the Plant pit, unable to get to work, set about clearing Landywood Lane. From our sitting room window we watched the blades of many shovels appear above snow level, as they deposited the snow to the side of the lane, the miners themselves invisible within the deep crevasse they were creating. Dad and I had to clear about four feet of snow from the back door using dinner plates to allow us to get to the greenhouse both for spades and so that dad could look after his recently sown seeds. It took most of the day to clear the drive down to the gate to allow delivery men to reach the door and dad to get to work should the roads be cleared sufficiently. Next day, dozens of airmen from Hednesford RAF camp were clearing the railway track outside our house. It was several days before rail and road traffic was seen again. It also created problems in getting vegetables from the garden, since we could not reach the potato hog or the vegetables over-wintering in the garden. We were fortunate that the bacon had just cured and we consumed this and bottled preserves until we could access garden vegetables.

About four days later we were able reach the bus stop at Benton's Lane to get to school, the sun was now shining and the snow was beginning to melt. As we travelled through Newtown, just below Bloxwich Golf Club, it was obvious that during the storm the snow had drifted to well over six feet (2 metres) deep across the whole width of the A34. It was a breath-taking sight, the right side of the cutting through the drift glistened brightly in the morning sunshine like an Arctic glacier, a sight I had never before seen. Had we been closer, we could have touched the top surface through the upstairs window of our double decker bus.

Fortunately, severe winter weather in the Midlands was sporadic and rarely persisted for more than a few days. Snow only occasionally created problems in travelling to and from school but fog was another matter, it occurred more frequently and could be quite a pain. It usually developed in the early afternoon and we were likely to be stranded on the way home from school, with few or no buses. The dense fog was a mix of normal mist and acrid smoke pumped out of the many chimney stacks of Walsall's heavy industry which settled to ground level rather than get dispersed at high altitude. It was commonest between late autumn and late February and a few were so dense that traffic was paralysed. It was sometimes impossible to see a friend walking less than six feet ahead. As the visibility deteriorated, bus drivers called it a day and crept back to the bus depot in Leamore. Two or three times during any winter we had to walk home from school, a trip of over five miles for me, which was no fun with a satchel of books for homework. On occasions our No 1 bus made the trip as far as Bloxwich with the conductor walking ahead waving a white handkerchief. Here, we were given the good news that this was the terminus and we would have to walk the rest of the journey! For me it was about three miles but, for colleagues from Cannock, was another six miles. The pungent sulphur dioxide fumes from industry could be tasted in the mouth and, on reaching our lungs, gave us a hacking cough. This type of fog, later called smog, was never a pleasant experience and we hated it. With a fall in temperature towards the end of the day, the fog froze on hair and clothing, clinging so hard that it could not be brushed off. Every breath we exhaled seemed to freeze instantaneously and we often challenged each other to see who could project a breath cloud furthest, forcefully using every chest and abdominal muscles in the process.

We suffered a number of deep frosts most winters, some leading to the ground becoming solid to a depth of six inches or more when the garden fork bounced off the surface rather than penetrate the soil. Crops such as carrots, parsnips and leeks which over-wintered in the ground were not then available for a week or two. Fortunately, we were usually able to break into the base of the potato hog to obtain a supply, carefully refilling our track to prevent frosting of the remainder. Brussels sprouts tolerated the very low temperatures and at such times were our only second vegetable, horror of horrors! The one advantage that such temperatures brought for us youngsters was that the pools froze over.

Despite arctic temperatures in late January this year, the gardening cycle had to get underway again. As in previous years, seeds had already been ordered from Dobbies (Seedsmen) of Edinburgh and had arrived. Dad's homemade propagators were brought into use, by this time constructed from a plentiful supply of orange boxes from Mr Eccleshall. Each box was covered with panes of glass to contain the heat. In the bottom, a false floor sat on two house bricks and allowed him to place his patent heaters beneath the seed trays. They were made from empty Mansion or boot polish tins with a small hole punched in the lid for a string wick and fuelled by paraffin. I suppose it was a modern version of the ancient oil lamp and certainly provided sufficient heat to germinate the seeds. Dad's propagators also kept geraniums and other tender stock free of frost over winter. The cost of this form of heating during a winter would have been a gallon of paraffin, about one shilling and three pence (6p).

Seeds germinated in a few days and, after spending a further week or so in a 'growing-on' propagator, the seedlings were ready for transplanting. It was usually well into February before dad lit the main boiler of the greenhouse to grow on something like a hundred trays of seedlings. We again used tomato trays, collected from the greengrocer's rubbish tip at the back of his shop, paying a few pennies (1p) each. They were designed for stacking with a two inch (5cm) gap between, which proved an advantage when moving around the greenhouse, and each held five dozen (60) plants. The seedlings were transplanted by all three of us, though mom was very adept and did most of it. Many varieties were grown, alyssum, lobelia, antirrhinums, asters, stocks, nemesia, mesembryanthemum, tagetes, marigolds and salvias. By late March, the over-wintered geranium stocks had produced new shoots and cuttings of these were rooted in the propagators and then grown on into new plants. The two staple geraniums that dad grew were Paul Crampel (bright red) and Prince of Denmark (salmon pink) and, over several years, hundreds of new plants had been created from the original stock, probably first acquired around 1935. The last seeds to be sown were tomatoes, cucumbers and melons since they grew quite fast and were not needed until the greenhouse was empty of the bedding plants and staging. Most of the plants were matured and hardened off in the four large garden frames behind the greenhouse, ready to plant out around mid May. Sufficient bedding plants were retained for our own flower beds and the excess sold to customers. Once the bedding plants were out of the way, plenty of horse manure was dug into the ground in the greenhouse and the tomato plants planted. Eight cucumber plants were put in plenty of rotted compost in the frames. Mom and dad had regular customers who returned year in, year out, for all types of plants, many coming back during the summer months to see how dad's garden was progressing, and perhaps to pick up gardening tips. Later in the summer those who had not tried their hand growing the cropping plants would come to buy the produce, particularly tomatoes, cucumbers and other salad crops.

Dad grew most things in his garden but, without doubt, his favourite flower was the sweet pea. The best quality seeds were ordered from Dobbies every year in ten different varieties, chosen for colour and scent. The sweet pea year began in February with deep digging and manuring a patch of garden of sufficient area to take six dozen six foot (2 metre) canes. During the war years, we were driven to using long sticks from the hedgerows, but bamboo canes were by now appearing again in garden supply shops, such as Clarkes in Cannock. Wooden frames were constructed at each end of the patch from which wires were stretched across the garden. To these, canes were tied at nine inch (230mm) intervals in four rows. The ground could now rest until May when the developed and hardened off sweet pea plants were planted out.

One of my jobs during the winter months was to create about four hundred wire rings which would tether the growing sweet peas to the canes, a far easier method of tying up than using raffia. It was also far cheaper than buying a box of a hundred from the supplier. I made them by winding galvanised wire many times around a broom handle to create a coil. This could then be pulled off the handle and cut along its length with wire cutters, creating about fifty rings at a time.

In March, dad prepared the sweet pea seed for sowing. He taught me that the seed had a very hard coat and, to both speed up germination and improve success, the seeds needed chitting. This entailed cutting out a small fragment of the coat without damaging the 'kernel'. The seed could now be sown in very deep trays to allow plenty of room for the long roots. In early May, the tops of the seedlings were pinched out so that each developed a strong side shoot. In late May dad chose the strongest plants and set one beside each cane. As they grew during the summer one strong runner was attached to its cane with the wire rings. The whole idea of this elaborate approach was to create strong flowers with a long stem and at least four large florets per stem. The 'icing on the cake' for dad was when he produced a twelve inch (300mm) straight stem with six florets. This he proudly paraded to everyone. It was a little like finding a four-leaf clover! For me, a vase of dad's sweet peas on the dining table was something to behold and the perfume in the room was intense. When the sweet pea plant had reached the top of the six foot cane, rings were taken off and it was lowered down the cane so that it could grow up for a second time, producing a second crop of flowers.

At the time the sweet peas were planted out, dad also set out rows of late chrysanthemum plants, taken earlier as cuttings from his over-wintered root stocks. These spent the summer growing in the garden to budding stage and were moved back into the greenhouse in September where they flowered from November on to Christmas. Moving them indoors prevented damage by weather, particularly rain, so that they were ideal for chrysanthemum shows which many villages held in late autumn. Amateur gardeners in the village showed enormous incurve and reflex chrysanthemums, some over six inches (150mm) in diameter.

Now nearly two years since the end of the war, rationing was still an issue, particularly cereals. Since the pig was an important part of our meat diet and Sharp's cereal was now more tightly rationed, mom was concerned that she may not grow. As it happened all was well, with plenty of vegetable peelings, undersized potatoes and a healthy appetite, the pig did continue to put on weight. This particular year, she did suffer an attack of some virus disease, with a rash all over, and required an injection from the vet. It was but a hiccup and the pig went on to make its normal weight.

General food rationing was probably worse than during the war and a great deal of graffiti appeared on walls, particularly outside shops. This took the form of Chad, a man with a long nose looking over a wall with an accompanying "What no ...." caption, when there were shortages of an item. "What no black pudding?", "What no cream cakes?" and so on. It was a sign of the times and caught on everywhere.

Tight though sweet rationing was, it was usually possible to trade money for sweet coupons. Friend Paul Baker was always happy for me to pay and he would use his coupons so that we could share a small lunchtime 'snack'. Fortunately he was not a great lover of sweets, and was happy with our deal. Like mom, I had a sweet tooth and had to have my fix.

Then, a small glimpse of something brighter occurred in Shaw's Lane when Mr Cooper, a baker, moved into the large house next to the old cottages. He built a small bakery at the back of the house and started making delightful fancy cakes decorated with icing, cream and meringue. They were a cut above the average 'fancies' of the likes of Stanton's and Taylor's but were a little more expensive. I assume new small post-war businesses were allowed an allocation of flour and sugar for the purpose. When I walked into his shop, I was mesmerised by the trays of colourful delights and I was allowed to choose my own selection of cakes to make up the half dozen mom had agreed to buy. Iced cakes were to me as good as sweets in alleviating cravings for something sweet. His daughter, Gwen Cooper, of my age, emigrated a few years later to America with a Red Indian whom she married. He was a circus performer and about five years later they returned on a visit to Wyrley Wesley Church when he gave an exhibition of lassoing and whip cracking.

At Queen Mary's, I was now in the fourth form and our classroom was on the corner of the school adjacent to the Lichfield street traffic lights. We were able to sit at open windows and chat as we watched life pass by in the street below. Steam driven lorries were still commonplace, delivering barrels of beer to pubs around Walsall. On occasions, whilst stopped at the lights, the driver might get out of his cab and stoke the fire beneath. The stinking lorries carrying hides from abattoir to the tanneries, I have already mentioned, and we habitually closed the windows until they were given a green light!

This everyday hubbub just outside the window was a pleasant interlude to our studies and led to Billy Hayes and Ken Paddock having a bright idea. Billy was the son of the owner of William Hayes Transport, the light blue haulage lorries which were commonplace in and around Walsall at the time. He agreed to provide a lorry horn and Ken would bring in an accumulator. They wired the pair through a push button and hung the horn outside the classroom window awaiting the next lesson. Mr Jones, a new master to the school who was taking an English lesson, frequently found his words drowned by the noise of traffic horns outside. He had been an army officer during the war, and if he suspected tyranny he was not going to let on. The lesson was badly degraded by Ken's antics but the new man weathered it to the end, somewhat bemused, but with chin held high. When he left the room, we were able to release the pent up belly laughs which had accumulated during that forty five minutes. We shall never know what was taught during that lesson, or the effect the horn had on the traffic, suffice to say there were no audible crunches in the street below.

I suppose my best subject at school was Chemistry and I thoroughly enjoyed EA (Maggie) Mason's lessons. For an earlier Christmas, I had asked for a Chemistry set as a present which had contained various chemical experiments for amateurs. It was never possible to repeat the experiments set up at school because the necessary reagents were simply not provided. This was not surprising since some of his experiments used concentrated acids which would not have made the ideal toy in the average home! I then came across an advertisement for chemical apparatus and a long list of chemicals in The Champion, my weekly journal of boy's tales, and accordingly sent for the catalogue. From this company I could obtain small bottles of dilute sulphuric, hydrochloric and nitric acids for sixpence (2.5p). Still not concentrated acid but a step up from the vinegar (acetic acid) and lemon juice (citric acid) used in my kid's chemistry set. Over the next year or two I spent most of my pocket money with this supplier, eventually acquiring quite a large set of equipment and chemicals, sufficient for a small laboratory. Most of the rest of my pocket money at this time was spent on British Empire postage stamps which I collected as a hobby. Again, I tapped a source for 'Stamps on approval' from The Champion. A selection of stamps in a folder arrived every month and I could purchase a stamp and send the folder back with my payment. The most I ever spent on one stamp was £1 on a rare stamp from Sarawak (Indonesia), simply because my album page for Sarawak was empty! An interesting aside was that, a year or two later, I gave my quite good stamp collection to my sixth form chemistry master for auction for a charity. I shudder to think what it would have been worth today. I collected many things but, after a while, another stimulus meant that I tired of them and gave them away. As I have already said, my nature collections were given to Miss Liddle at Landywood Primary school for teaching purposes.

Using the outlet in The Champion, I acquired a large set of chemistry apparatus and chemicals and now yearned for a laboratory in which to install the equipment, since spilled acid was not kind to domestic surfaces. I convinced mom that a lab would get the 'damn tranklements', as she referred to the equipment, out of her way. Surprisingly, she found this an excellent idea and we settled for a garden shed which would be both my laboratory and a private den which she promised she would never clear up. She never accepted my bedroom as my personal area where I could do as I liked. It was cleaned daily and any 'rubbish' (her view) was thrown away!

Dad felt that he did not have the time to build a shed and suggested we get someone else. Jack Loach, father of friend David, was approached and agreed to build a seven by five feet (2.1m by 1.5m) good quality shed for £20. It was duly completed and erected at the bottom of the garden. A laboratory bench was constructed inside and shelves provided for the glassware and bottles of chemicals. I also incorporated my desk, which had been constructed by dad as a Christmas present a year or two earlier. I was now very happy in that, not only did I have a laboratory, I also had my own den where I could store my belongings.

I repeated school experiments but also tried many experiments by simply working on chemical equations and trying to get a result. I was hampered a little by the fact that we did not have a gas supply at home and therefore a Bunsen burner was out of the question. I had to make do with a spirit burner, but it sufficed. Like any boy, I liked creating something which made a bang, such as hydrogen and acetylene gases and exploding them with a naked flame. The bottles of acid and other reagents that I purchased were relatively small and it was never going to be possible to generate large volumes of hydrogen. There was only sufficient to make a large 'pop' rather than the bang I would have preferred! Acetylene was easily created by pouring water on calcium carbide and was the gas used in bicycle lamps when I was small boy. A larger volume of this gas could, therefore, be produced and was more explosive. I tried to make gunpowder according to the original Chinese recipe but it only ever fizzled, probably because the oxidant, potassium nitrate (saltpetre) was always slightly damp. I added magnesium powder and iron filings to make fountains and sparklers. In all, I did what curious boys did, thankfully without singed eyebrows. I also tried to create new products and rendered down anything I could find in nature, such as lichens, producing unusual waxes, but I did not have equipment to analyse the end product. The big advantage of having the laboratory was that I could leave chemical reactions simmering, knowing that mom would not sweep them away. I think I was the only pupil at school who had his own laboratory. I pushed experimentation at home as far as I could but the time inevitably came when, because of funding, I could go no further and it was put on the back burner. However, at school, my interest in chemistry never waned, but then it was a professional laboratory and I enjoyed every day I spent there.

During the summer months, we frequently returned from lunch at Moss Close to the main school through the arboretum. When passing the boathouse, if two or three of us were able to scrape together the nine pence (3.5p) for a half hour on a rowing boat, we would do so and row out to the island on the lake. Getting in and out of the boat at the island was far from easy. We never actually capsized the boat but were so near to it on many occasions, meriting a yell from the boathouse man. We were also careful to be at the extremity of the lake by the time he was due to shout, "Come in Number five!", and caught as many crabs as possible, anything to get an extra five minutes for our money.

It was on such a walk back to the main school that a new interest developed following a chit-chat with Paul Baker. Outside school, we invariably discussed our hobbies, never school subjects. Paul Baker was very much into amateur radio and his insight into the subject was fascinating. I recalled the number of times as a child that I had looked at the radio at home and the aerial in the garden and pondered how we were receiving radio programmes through the air. It was not a subject that we studied in any science lesson and I had no conception of how it happened, which stimulated me to ask Paul if he could explain. This he did with some degree of enthusiasm, I think he felt like a teacher with a pupil. It is a technical subject and for this reason may lose some but I do not apologise for recounting my enlightenment in full.

His first description was well over my head. In essence, broadcasters transmit radio carrier waves at a constant frequency which have been modulated with a sound track (music, news, etc.). Our radio, he said, is then tuned into their frequency and strips off the carrier wave leaving the sound track to be listened to through speaker or headphones.

"Help!" I mused. Paul laughed at my reaction, took a quick draw on his inhaler and set about explaining a little more slowly.

As I rode home on the bus I thought over his remarks and felt that I did not really understand the business of waves and frequencies. He had explained that the transmitted radio waves created a current of the same frequency in the aerial wire in our garden. At least this told me how the radio signal reached our radio set, but then what? Back in the classroom he had drawn for me a simple electronic circuit present in all radios, a tuning coil (a coil of wire) holding hands with a condenser (capacitor). A current in such a pair of components will always oscillate (or alternate) at a fixed frequency so long as they are not changed. By using a variable condenser, with a knob which changed its value, the frequency of the circuit will be changed and it could thereby 'tune in' to different radio frequencies, and therefore pick up different radio channels. I kept going over Paul's words in my head and by the time the bus reached Benton's Lane I felt I had seen the light!

Next day I put another question to Paul, "How is the content of the radio programme transmitted?"

"Modulation!" said Paul. Again I must have looked blank which always brought mirth to his face and he went on to explain. Sadly every time Paul laughed he needed another puff on his inhaler.

The sound waves of speech or music reaching microphones, he said, are converted into an electrical wave and this is added to the basic carrier wave before transmission. This process is called modulation of the carrier wave and in effect is two waves built into one. In our home wireless set, the tuning circuit (coil and variable condenser) selects the radio channel by its frequency and the radio must now separate the two waves again in order to listen to the sound track. An analogy might be a gramophone record carried in its folder. In order to play the record, we must remove it from it from its folder. This, he said, is where a crystal or radio valve comes in, by blocking the oscillating carrier wave, it allows only the sound track to pass into our headphones. I understood and was gob-smacked how simple radio transmission actually was.

Paul explained his own hobby, shared with his friends, which used short wave receivers and transmitters, used by various public bodies such as police and aircraft. All their equipment was built from second hand spares and he told me where they could be purchased. The group of friends in Streetly had already set up short wave communication between themselves, which he said was illegal, but fun. I would very much have liked to join their 'club' but knew I would never be able to afford the parts required to build a transmitter receiver. In any case I was still on the bottom rung and had not yet built anything electronic.

As a start, Paul drew me a circuit for a simple crystal set and suggested that I construct this. The mention of a crystal set brought back memories of dad's stories about the sets they had used in his earlier years to listen to the radio, before wireless sets (radios) with valves became commonplace. Dad had explained how, in order to tune into a radio station, they had to tickle a crystal with a cat's whisker (a thin wire) trying to find a spot which allowed them to tune into the station. At the time, I had not really understood dad's account but Paul had now verified the practice and, more importantly, explained the function of the cat's whisker and crystal which only allowed a current to pass in one direction, thereby blocking out any alternating current, such as the transmitted carrier wave. It would however allow the sound track through to the headphones. When next I walked up the garden path I looked at the aerial wire, appearing like an unused washing line, and thought to myself 'I now know what you are about'. It clearly meant that one more question in the 'mystery box' in my mind was resolved. I was chuffed! And now I could try a little practical work.

With the end of the hostilities the government began selling off the artefacts of war and even Woolworths for the first time sold these as second hand goods. It was quite common to see items such as silk parachutes either on sale or advertised in newspapers for about five pounds, which women purchased to make silk clothing, particularly wedding dresses. My search for parts for my crystal set did not prove too difficult. Woolworths were selling very sensitive moving-coil headphones which had been used for radio communications during the conflict. I eagerly purchased a set for the princely sum of sixpence (2.5p)!   They also sold the appropriate crystal unit, but no longer with a cat's whisker. I had so wanted to tickle a cat's whisker but it was not to be! This unit had two crystals, one attached to a moveable arm that allowed various faces of the two crystals to touch. It cost me a shilling (5p). I purchased a variable capacitor from a second-hand parts shop in Proffit Street, again for sixpence. In fact, most parts at the time seemed to be around sixpence which was well within my pocket money allowance of one shilling and sixpence (7.5p) a week.

I carefully assembled and screwed my components to a piece of board, aligning them as shown in Paul's diagram, attaching the terminals by cotton covered wire purchased in coils from the parts shops. I coiled the connecting wires like springs which somehow gave an important and tidy appearance to my efforts. All I had to do now was wind my tuning coil. I was becoming quite excited.

I touched the two crystals and set the variable capacitor to their mid points. The tuning coil would be wound from a four feet (1.3m) length of the cotton covered wire, the ends of which were attached to their points shown on the circuit. I donned the headphones and, using a six inch (15cm) piece of broom handle, began winding the wire to form a coil, carefully placing each turn side by side without overlap. Thirty turns, thirty five, forty, forty one, forty two and then I drew a sharp intake of breath as music (broadcast on the medium waveband) faintly reached my ears and increased in volume as I added two more turns. It was a moment I have never forgotten. I had my own radio for about three shillings (15p)!

Next day, I thanked Paul Baker for the circuit diagram and I am sure he registered my excitement. He suggested that I now attempt a one-valve radio set, a far more powerful radio, and he again drew a circuit for me. The valve concerned was called a triode, a glass envelope, like a sixty watt light bulb, encasing a filament and other parts, with four prongs at the base.

A big advantage of a crystal set was that, if the headphones were sensitive enough, one could listen to a radio station with no more energy than that induced in the aerial by the transmitted radio waves. For this reason, a crystal set cost nothing to run. A one-valve radio set would cost only slightly more to build, but it had major running costs. The triode valve, used instead of a crystal, not only needed a hot filament like a torch bulb but also an enormous one hundred and twenty volts across the valve to make it work. The filaments in wireless sets of the time required only a few volts. Accumulators were usually used for this purpose which the lady of the house took every fortnight to one of the village shops for recharging. The cost of providing the one hundred and twenty volts was very expensive, fifteen shillings (75p) to be exact. I had savings of about twelve shillings (60p) which meant a bit of a slog to make up the remainder for the batteries, the valve and its holder.

The thrill of building the one valve radio set was much the same as I had experienced when building the crystal set. On this occasion, I tried my hand at soldering the contacts, something I had never done before. My first experiments were with plumber's solder, used for lead water pipe repairs, since this was in the tool shed and free. I soon found that it was not designed for copper soldering and was obliged to spend yet more of my pocket money on tin solder. About two weeks later I was the proud owner of a one hundred and twenty volt battery, a monster some ten by eight by three inches (25 x 20 x 8cm) in size. As I cuddled my heavy parcel on the bus from Walsall, my thoughts raced ahead to the moment I would be applying one hundred and twenty volts across the anode of my triode valve. I would soon have access to the radio waves across the world! These thoughts were a pipe dream but when I did complete the circuit some thirty minutes later, the volume of sound in the headphones almost blew my head off. I had achieved what I had set out to do and now had my own radio set. I proudly told mom and dad that I would be setting it up in my bedroom so that I could listen to the radio in bed. They smiled at the wonder of it all. I built a box to hold the equipment and batteries and laid out an aerial wire using the spout retaining clips along the length of the bungalow and in through my bedroom window. I stood at the bedroom door admiring my creation and, for once, I could not wait to get to bed to experience a new life. I would have light entertainment in bed, including a few horror stories such as 'Appointment with fear'.

That first night, I lay back on my pillow, headphones closely applied to my ears, and listened to sound which was, I am convinced, far superior to that of the radio set in the living room. The whole experience proved so soporific that I was soon in a deep sleep, aware of nothing until I awoke next morning to the news on my radio. This happened on several occasions and I thought little of it. When I awoke one morning, probably a week later, it dawned on me that the headphones, still applied to my head, were silent. It was with profound horror that I discovered that the high tension battery was now all but flat. Fifteen shillings might just as well have been flushed down the toilet! I had successfully achieved the project of building a one valve radio set but at a cost which even mom and dad might have found hard to bear. I had nevertheless fully enjoyed my personal radio, albeit only for a week.

Simple mathematics would have enlightened me that using a one-valve set for an hour or so each evening would at best have allowed only a month of listening. Perhaps if I had done the calculation earlier I would have used my creation more sparingly or looked for a another solution. A battery powered set was obviously too expensive to run and I would have to resort to using mains power to drive a bedroom radio set. I had friends at school who had achieved this, but cash for the parts was going to take a few months to get together and as the weeks passed the urge faded. I did buy the magazine 'Wireless World' for a while and looked enviously at the advertisements and the second hand electronic components available, but they were beyond my means and I was compelled to drop the hobby. I continued my association with Paul Baker and we had many philosophical chats which were very stimulating. On many occasions as we walked, particularly up the hill to Mellish Road, we were obliged to slow down because of his asthma. He could quickly become desperately short of breath and go deep blue in colour and had to take a puff or two on his inhaler before we could proceed. I felt desperately sorry for him, such a powerful scientific brain, but very much hampered by his illness.

Paul was off school for a week or two with his chest and I found myself walking to and from lunch with a classmate, not a close friend, though we sat adjacent in class. He had sometimes told me of his interest in conjuring and that he was a member of the Magic Circle. Now, walking together, I was a captive audience and he enthused about his hobby. Being in the Magic circle, however, committed him to secrecy and it was obvious that he was not going to explain the workings of his conjuring tricks. This did not stop him being very effusive about his illusions and, rather than tire of the one-sided ceaseless chat, I listened with some intrigue. He was very forthcoming with his new ideas for tricks and explained that he was building special equipment for a new illusion which he would be practicing before demonstrating it at this coming month's Walsall Magic Circle. The problem for me was that our tête-à-tête was so one-sided and I felt cornered and driven to listening only. I hated the secrecy and felt the need to converse on equal terms but would need to know more about conjuring if I was going to contribute. I visited Walsall public library for books on the subject. One in particular was the story of the great Houdini which outlined and explained some of his tricks and these, of course, became the subject of our next chat. My classmate was a little upset that someone had dared spill the beans! Sacrilegious! He was loathe to discuss the subject further but the various books had now given me insight into basic tricks using everyday equipment for simple props which I could make myself. I felt enlightened. I suppose my bible became 'The fifty best conjuring tricks' a book published by Foulsham's which I purchased for two shillings (10p) from W H Smith. It again contained tricks which cost little to set up. I became adept at one or two simple ones which, in the first place, amused mom and dad. Within a few months I had developed about six favourite tricks which I used both at church events and in amateur stage shows. Even so, my classmeate still saw me as a rank amateur and was never going to let me into his secrets unless I signed up to the Magic Circle. This I could not afford. I was persistent, probably annoying, in trying to get him to spill the beans and was probing one day as I walked to the wicket on the cricket field at Mayfield. He had obviously had enough and when I took the crease, he spread-eagled my wickets with a rather fierce yorker, his first ball! I read this as "get lost" and it was the last time I raised the subject with him.

At home, it was a sunny afternoon when two of us from the lane ambled up into the top field to see if anyone was around. It was where we usually met up with friends. As we turned the end of the blackthorn coppice we came across *William* (pseudonym) pitching the large white family tent, watched over by *Mary*. They had decided to go camping together and he made it clear we were not wanted. We shrugged our shoulders and wandered over to the stream where we sat on the lip of the cutting, feet dangling over the water. As we talked, we casually plucked at the buttercups, eggs and bacon (bird's foot trefoil) and daisies which carpeted the meadow, throwing them into the stream to see which was first to the waterfall.

Looking back, *William* had erected the tent and was tying the flaps together. We smiled at each other and pointedly cupped our hands to our ears pretending to eavesdrop on what they were talking about, but very little was audible. After a few minutes a rue smile passed between us and it was obvious we had both had the same idea. We stealthily crawled on hands and knees towards them. After quietly removing pegs along the bottom of the tent, we lifted the wall an inch or two, intent on surprising them. The sight that confronted us left me frozen and speechless.

Mary was lying on her back. She was not wearing knickers. *William* lay face down on top of her, his short trousers around his thighs. His naked bottom was rhythmically rising and falling. My God! he is fucking her, I thought. The motions of fucking had been discussed and demonstrated in our powwows and this was surely it. I turned to *Raymond* who was smirking as he silently tittered into his free hand. As I watched the scene before me, *Mary* was looking at *William* without expression. She was in no way disturbed, it seemed, she was accepting the game play. *William* was looking at the tent wall away from us, lost one must presume in the role of a practising married man. The motion continued in total silence and, as I lay face down looking under the tent flap, I was conscious of sensations in my own trousers that I had never experienced before.

After a while *William* lifted himself from *Mary*. We were startled to see that he was covered with blood and so was *Mary*. When he looked down and saw it, he quickly pulled away and we saw the colour drain from his face and his expression change to one of fear. We rather hastily dropped the tent wall and scampered back to the stream. Moments later, *William* was opening the tent flaps and saying something to *Mary* as he ushered her out of the tent. They were now dressed and she ambled down the field towards home without speaking to us.

William still looked ashen and was shaking as he came to sit by us on the bank of the stream. He blurted out that he had asked *Mary* to go camping with him like his mom and dad did. They would play mom and dad and he had asked her if they could fuck like a real mom and dad to which she had agreed. He supposed he must have done it too hard because he had made her bleed badly, obviously unaware that we had already witnessed it. I was still shaking by what I had seen and very concerned about what would happen when *Mary's* mom discovered the blood. We impressed on *William* that it was very likely that her father would come and thrash him and may even tell the police. He was still very frightened as we helped him pack away his tent.

In fact, nothing ever came of the incident and, as far as I am aware, it never happened again. Like all boys, we talked about fucking. I had now witnessed it and somehow felt more grown up by the experience and knew what friends in huddles at school were talking about. As I thought over the incident in later years, *Mary* had possibly started her menstrual periods or her mother had thought so and had given her a motherly talk on the subject when she reached home.

Queen Mary's Air Training Corps was now well established and I was thoroughly enjoying the subjects we were taught. Astronomy was an important subject since stars were used for navigation purposes and I was now looking into the clear night sky with much more understanding. We had very little light pollution in the village and it was easy to identify stars and constellations, particularly on a moonless night. The Milky Way was a clearly visible band across the sky but it was some years before I realised it was an arm of our galaxy. I think it was astronomer Fred Hoyle who enlightened us in one of his radio programmes. As I walked home on a sharp frosty night, eyes glued to the heavens, I easily recognised old friends as they rotated round the sky, Cassiopeia, the Pleiades (seven sisters), the Plough pointing to the Pole star, Orion with his belt and sword (at the end of which was a nebula), the planets and the many stars whose names I was expected to know. Once my eyes were dark-adapted, I gazed and gazed, awe-struck by the majesty of it all, my heart deeply feeling the wonder of God's creation. But what I would have given to observe the spectacular Halley's comet or some similar event. My interest in astronomy as a science continued to increase when people like Fred Hoyle began writing fascinating articles and speaking on radio about the origins of the universe.

As part of our development as air cadets, we made many trips to RAF camps to get flying experience and to learn the wider aspects of flight and airfield management. We visited control towers, aircraft hangars and RAF classrooms for information and training in their protocols. As a result of these visits, I was fortunate enough to fly in a Wellington bomber (designed by Barnes Wallace) and several other aircraft; an Avro Anson, Avro York, Oxford and Dakota (DC3) which were general duty transportation planes during and after the war. In fact about 200 DC3s became the logistics workhorse to and from Berlin when it was blockaded by the Russians in 1948.

My first and most memorable flight took place at Fradley airfield just outside Lichfield. Our pilot had served in the Polish air force and had flown with the RAF during the latter part of the war. He was determined to show us what flying was all about. His aerobatic display in a rickety old Avro Anson included diving very steeply from about five thousand feet before pulling the stick at what seemed to be thirty feet above the ground and then flying horizontally between the aircraft hangers. During the screaming descent the wings of the plane flapped like a bird, a very alarming sight when you are not aware that aircraft wings flex. It seemed that at any moment they might part company from the fuselage. I was sitting close enough to the pilot to hear screaming in his headphones and he quickly brought the plane to an even keel and then landed. During that flight, I encountered an exhilarating adrenaline rush of elation mixed with fear. As boys would, we made light of the events and joked about it afterwards in the mess. Fortunately our flight preceded the repulsive meal which was served in the mess or the pilot might have been ordered to do the mopping up in his cockpit. None of the other flights had such an effect though were very enjoyable, but an extra-special flight in a Lancaster bomber, I shall refer to later.

Hednesford RAF training camp on Marquis Drive, Cannock Chase, Shawbury, Cosford and Fradley RAF stations were closest to us and we attended one or other for lectures, films, demonstrations of equipment and guided tours of specialist areas. Some of the films, we were told, such as those recounting Operation PLUTO (pipeline under the ocean), Operation Mulberry (floating pontoons for the D-Day landings), the principles of radar (including the latest H2S radar) and others, were still under wraps so soon after the war and we were expected to treat them as secret. It was during the lecture about radar that I first heard about 'Window', the many thousands of aluminium strips which had been dropped from a plane preceding air raids in order to confuse enemy radar. I have met you before, I thought, recalling memories of collecting the strips from hedgerows along our lane at the height of the war. The lectures were very enlightening and explained details about the war which were not yet on general release to the public.

Part of our training covered armaments and we had to understand, dismantle, clean and assemble various guns from the normal army Lee Enfield .303 rifle to Browning guns used in aircraft. In the case of the .303 rifle, we were taught to disassemble and assemble it blindfolded. This came easy to me, having done so for years at home using dad's Home Guard rifle. The other guns I now had to master.

Queen Mary's shooting range was in the limestone quarry at Moss Close and was roughly a twenty five yard (22m) range for .22 rifles. About once a month we attended for shooting practice, using five shots each for target scoring and five shots for grouping. An ideal score for the latter would be five shots through the same hole on the target. This was obviously almost impossible to achieve and most of mine were five shots covering about one square inch of the target, a good result. On one occasion, whilst grouping, I fired four shots which were near perfect and just as I sighted for the fifth, a cabbage white butterfly settled on a yellow charlock flower just below my eye-line. It was a sitting target. I simply could not resist and spattered it with my last shot! I knew that the bullet had missed the target, and was filling my pants at my recklessness! When he saw four closely grouped holes on the target, the scorer assumed that one of my shots had gone through an earlier hole. I was happy to accept his view, conscious that I would have been in trouble for deliberately firing a round off target!

The immense noise echoing around the walls of the small confined quarry as many shots were fired in unison was in some ways similar to a daily experience at home. Day in day out our peace was disturbed by a deafening noise coming from the direction of Cheslyn Hay. It was not emanating from anything military or industrial, it simply registered that uncle Bob on his way home from work! Shortly after the war, he had purchased a second hand Morris 8 coupé to get him to and from his job in Wolverhampton. His excuse was that it would work out more cheaply than using two buses but, in reality, owning a maroon coupé appeared to be more a virility thing, which was obvious as he strutted around it and mollycoddled it on the drive. I assume he had a driving licence but I doubt if he had had driving lessons since he appeared to be limited to using two gears only, forward and reverse. Wherever he went, he travelled at twenty five to thirty miles per hour, but the engine was racing at four to five thousand revs. He probably felt like some racing driver, perhaps Malcolm Campbell in Bluebird, delighting in the high pitched noise emanating from his rear end. The problem was that he was going nowhere fast! I had never come across any other car driven in this manner. We could hear the high revs as he was leaving Cheslyn Hay, some half mile or so away and as he neared home, there was a crescendo not unlike an aircraft diving. The noise pollution continued for the three or four years that he owned the car. When, in 1950, the new small Austin A30 saloon was produced, uncle Bob put his name on the waiting list for a new car. After taking delivery, the coupé was put up for sale. A gentleman came to view it and purchased it. Second hand cars were usually snapped up, commanding quite high prices since new cars were still in short supply. The purchaser drove the Morris away and we watched him drive it up the bridge. The engine purred and it sounded like a different vehicle as he drove towards Cheslyn Hay.

Fuel rationing at the time meant that everyone was taking great care to get the highest possible consumption from their petrol allowance. Cousin Bob became frantic therefore when his Francis Barnet auto-cycle was giving poorer performance than his dad's car. He knew when he purchased it that there was a fuel leak and was told that the fuel pipe simply needed replacing and was not expensive. It soon became obvious that the vendor wanted to be rid of it. On thorough inspection there was a crack in the weld between tank and fuel tap. Bob tried packing the split with various compounds, to no avail. He tried to solder the area with a soldering iron but could not get sufficient heat to melt the solder. He could see no other way to repair it than by using a blowlamp and he asked to borrow dad's for the purpose. After emptying the fuel and detaching the tank from the bike, he brought it to our house to repair. Dad was not convinced that Bob knew what he was doing, but left him to it, assuming he would ask for help if needed. He applied the heat and was ready to apply the solder when there was a loud whoosh as flames roared from the tank. His face was badly scorched and he ran home with his face in his hands. He was taken to the hospital and fortunately the burns were grade one and two and would not need grafts. He was given penicillin cream to regularly apply to his face. Discovered by Alexander Fleming, it was first used during the war to treat wound infections in the armed forces. Dr Middleton said that it was the first time he had used it in Great Wyrley. Bob's face healed very quickly and without scarring.

At school, I continued to put the world right with Paul Baker but, a few months later, an unpleasant thing happened to him. We heard that he was chatting to a girl called Josie and started to rib him about it. The upshot was that we made a solution of silver nitrate in the school laboratory and painted an arrowed heart with their names on Paul's abdomen. We knew that the image would turn black as the silver oxidized in the air and would also be indelible. Rather foolishly, at home, Paul scrubbed his abdomen to remove the 'tattoo' and produced the image in angry abrasions since the silver solution, being slightly caustic, had weakened the skin. His mother saw this and raised hell with the headmaster. Mr Butler saw us and we were all very worried about the outcome since we had created the solution in the school laboratory. There was a strong possibility of expulsion from school in school certificate year! I suggested that I tell porkies and say that I had created it in my home laboratory, to my colleagues relief. The headmaster accepted this but mom and dad received a very unpleasant letter from him about how near I was to expulsion from school and that I must never again bring chemicals into school! For some reason I did not get a thrashing.

In the lane, there were by now several boys and girls, many of us in our teens and from a boy's perspective, the hormones were really kicking in. We were all admitting experiencing erections and for some it was eagerly displayed as a sign of manhood. *Frank* (pseudonym) was endowed with the biggest member of all and when erect was enormous relative to others. He was forever playing with his toy in front of us. He appeared to get great enjoyment and, for a moment, his face contorted and he seemed to leave this world as milky fluid spurted into air. The first time I saw his ejaculation the penny began to drop and I became yet more enlightened on how babies were made. It certainly added support to the story that *William* had broken to us several months earlier. When I say more enlightened, this was hardly the case, I still had no idea how a baby developed inside a woman. My first thoughts revolved around whether the fluid set inside, much like a blanc-mange, shaping a baby in the process! I also still had the problem of how some seven pounds (3.5Kg) of baby got out of its mother's belly unless it was through the belly button. There was so much more I needed to know. Many times thereafter, when we were out at play, *Frank* was seen to lose himself in his own world whilst working his colossus to a climax. Afterwards, he lay back on the grass, breathing deeply and smiling with pride at his achievement. It seemed to be a controlling factor in his life and he could think of nothing else.

From 1947 photographic films began to appear again in the specialist shops but were usually rationed and kept under the counter in that they only had sufficient supply for regular customers. The nearest photographic shop to Queen Mary's was Bell and Webster's Chemist in Lichfield Street. Most days during lunch hour, I perused their window both to learn what cameras were available and above all to see whether there was a camera that I could afford. It was a time of life when I was easily attracted by new ventures and here was a fad (I hesitate to call it a hobby) that I had not yet tried and I was itching to do so.

Most cameras on display were second hand pre-war cameras such as Leica, Rolleiflex and Retinas and well outside my budget. After a year or so, new production cameras began to appear and one in particular was within my price range, the Coronet camera which cost about £5. It was little more than a box camera but looked slightly more pucka. It took pictures one and a half inches (40mm) square using a size 127 standard roll film. I purchased one along with a film and when I reached home, I took pictures of mom and dad. Most people would then take the film to the chemist, but this would cost money. I think I had a touch of granddad in my genes and opted for the cheapest route, do-it-yourself film processing. I obtained a book from the public library and it seemed to be something that I could achieve with the appropriate developer and fixer chemicals. These were available at Bell and Webster and cost roughly the same as if I had my film professionally developed and printed, but the amount of chemicals would process several films for this cost. I felt I was onto a good thing, I could develop and print about four films for the price of one!

Our pantry had a quarry worktop and was easy to black out since it had a very small window and air vent. According to the book, I needed a red darkroom light. The best I could find was my rear cycle lamp which created a reasonable red glow in the blacked out pantry. I mixed the developer and fixer solutions in pudding basins at a temperature that was warm to touch. Unfortunately I did not have a thermometer to check the actual temperature. I left strict instructions with mom that she must not enter or she would ruin the film and I started to unravel the film from the spool. I had never done it before and did not know what to expect. In fact after removing it from the spool it insisted on staying coiled and I had great difficulty persuading it to lie flat in the dish. I did manage to pass it through the warm developer a few times for four minutes, as suggested in the developer instructions and then swilled it in water before running it through the fixer bath. When I expectantly opened the pantry door to see my achievement in daylight, I had in my hand a very black film and no images! The few shillings for film and reagents had been totally wasted, something I could ill afford. Unfortunately, I had no-one to discuss the situation with since none of my pals had ever processed a film.

When I read more and did a de-brief of my attempt, I had done so many things wrong. My red light was far too bright and did not have a correct red filter which was essential to prevent fogging of the film. I had no thermometer to check the solution temperature which was critical to correct developing. Even though the pantry seemed dark, chinks of light could get under the door. It was not surprising, therefore, that my first film was totally fogged (black). It taught me that photography was a very expensive hobby unless I had proper equipment. For some time thereafter I abandoned processing films and had the film developed but not printed at the chemist. A month or two later, Bell and Webster's started to sell POP printing cards which proved to be very simple to use. The photographic negative was laid on a POP card in a simple photograph frame and exposed to sunlight for several minutes. The card did not require developing, it was simply fixed in a solution of hypo (sodium thiosulphate, the cheapest photographic chemical) for a minute or two and created a very nice photograph in sepia tone. It was many years before I purchased a developing tank for normal film processing.

But to get back to uncle Bob, he had a good garden which grew good quality crops but, unlike his siblings, he never sold his excess vegetables. The unused ones were allowed to bolt and became compost-heap fodder. Until now he had never tried his hand with a greenhouse and obviously after observing dad's successes, decided to give it a go. As winter approached, he dismantled his robust air-raid shelter brick by brick. It had been no use as a shelter, and was no use for storage, because of constant flooding. He obviously decided on a lean-to greenhouse against a seven feet (2.1 metre) brick wall which he now had professionally built, using the second hand bricks from the air raid shelter. Unfortunately, uncle Bob had an almost pathological complex about mom and dad nosing into his affairs, and he not infrequently told them so, though nothing was further from the truth. Well, I think you may have gathered by now that mom is likely to have had an occasional peep at her brother's creations, we will put it no stronger than that! His weird mindset as a result of this led to him building his lean-to on the wall away from us so that we could not possibly snoop as next year he filled it with an array of plants.

The greenhouse was constructed using reclaimed timbers and it was very well built as one might expect from uncle Bob but, as it was developing, dad remarked that the orientation was completely wrong. Whenever I walked past the edifice, on a visit to grandma and granddad, it did look very professional, outstanding carpentry, nicely glazed and painted well. However, as dad had predicted, it was doomed to failure. In being so concerned with keeping out prying eyes, he had built the greenhouse on the north wall and it never grew a thing! The first tomato plants the following year had few trusses of tomatoes, were badly drawn and not a single tomato ripened. A few pot plants such as geraniums suspended on hooks just beneath the roof glass did get sufficient light but his useless air-raid shelter had clearly been replaced by another white elephant. The silly part about it was that there was sufficient room to have built his greenhouse on the south wall and it would have been an outstanding success.

With the arrival of Spring and the new cycle of life, boys, like the birds and animals around, seemed to develop a surge in hormones. It was *Raymond* (pseudonym) who next experienced an urge. We were walking across the wheat fields behind home in the company of *Brenda*. I was ambling behind them. Even though I was no longer collecting bird's eggs, it was still second nature to look in the hedgerows for nests or any other interesting bit of nature. *Raymond* and *Brenda* were in conversation and unnoticed by me, he was obviously chatting to her about fucking and the upshot was that she had agreed. He turned to me,

"Pussy, we're going to have a fuck, will you keep watch for us?" It was as casual as that!

I simply said 'OK' and we walked to the small depression at the top of the field, which was surrounded by low hills. I placed myself on a grassy knoll so that I had a clear view in all directions. *Brenda* pulled down her knickers. It was as though she knew what to do. She lay on her back in the grass, legs apart and waited. In fact it was the first time that I had had a view of a girl's bits and I wasn't sure whether I should have looked and quickly averted my eyes. *Raymond* suddenly seemed more anxious than the initial bravado and struggled nervously with his trousers. He lay on top of her and, after some urgent fumbling, started thrusting his pelvis. *Brenda* simply lay motionless as he, red-faced, laboured hard and fast, obviously not hurting her. He was soon bright crimson and seemed on fire but then it was over. He jumped up and fastened his trousers looking at me wryly as though to say, 'that's how you do it'. *Brenda* put on her knickers and we walked down the fields together as though nothing had happened. When we parted, I noticed a wry smile between *Raymond* and *Brenda*, nothing more.

Those returning from serving in the war were also by now generating new families and the government was driven to increase housing provision to accommodate them. The need was met by constructing prefabricated houses which began to appear in many villages. A similar process had occurred after the first World War, as a result of which, a small estate referred to as 'the Huts', though more correctly 'the hutments', was created on Walsall Road opposite Shaw's Lane. Here, there were a dozen buildings constructed of wood and brick and surfaced with weatherboard planking which was painted black. For their time, the early 1920s, they were very modern and included indoor lavatories and bathrooms. Similar estates were now required after World War II and were beginning to appear.

Until this time, there had been an allotment between Wharwell Lane, Gorsey Lane and Benton's Lane amounting to around two acres of land which provided gardens for about twenty families and had also played its part in 'Dig for Victory'. This land was commandeered to house a dozen or more families in an estate of prefabricated houses. The 'prefabs' were factory built concrete structures and arrived on site in sections which were bolted together. Like their forerunners, they also had modern facilities and, though small, the families seemed very happy with their new detached residences. For many, outside lavatories and lack of hot water on tap had been the norm, but these services were now standard features in their new homes. A ride on any bus at the time might reveal a new estate in development, one week an empty field or garden allotment, next week a new estate of prefabricated houses. Although they were expected to be temporary accommodation, they lasted for very many years.

Towards the end of 1947, a transformation occurred in my life. For nearly ten years I had habitually attended Upper Landywood Sunday school but Philip West, a sickly man at the best of times, became ill and the school was closed for the foreseeable future. It was a great shame. I had been very fond of Philip and much respected the way he had continued against the odds since he had, without doubt, suffered great pain for many years. No doubt due to the latter, he always stood in front of his class, propped against the communion table for support, occasionally re-arranging his posture for more comfort. When we collected him from home, as we often did, he laboured with two sticks, and there were noticeable grimaces on his face due to the pain which he would continue suffering until he simply ground to a halt. He was a fairly small man and sometimes I felt like picking him up and carrying him to church just to relieve his suffering, but I know this would not be accepted. Philip was a real Christian and, in his final years, he had borne the real pain that Jesus Christ had endured on the cross, which was only finally relieved when he met his Lord in person. He, like Miss Liddle, had played an important role in shaping my life.

Mom insisted that I continue Sunday school, even though I was now well into my teens, and was very happy for me to go with my friends Eric Gibbs and Colin Parsons who did their Sunday chore, as they saw it, at Wyrley Wesley Sunday school on the Walsall Road. As a child, she had attended the earlier Wesley Sunday School in Benton's Lane. I quite liked the atmosphere of my new school and continued there even after Upper Landywood re-opened with a new teacher.

At the Wesley, there were two Sunday school classes, at ten o'clock and at two o'clock. The morning superintendent was Will Turner and in the afternoon WJ (Bill) Garratt. The classes were very different from those I had been used to at Upper Landywood. Philip West was an Anglican and his classes were in that style with the catechism at the heart of his teaching and repeated aloud at each class. This teaching proved very useful to me since the assemblies at Queen Mary's were in the same format. I was able to recite the catechism and sing responses to psalms from memory, something Methodists do not teach. The difference between the Anglican and Methodist services was easy to see on the occasions that Joe Nichols and Jim Fletcher visited Upper Landywood Sunday school which they did about every six weeks. Being New Invention Primitive Methodists of the old school, they were flamboyant with it. They exuded a love of Jesus, the son of God, which literally exploded from them. Joe, a kind generous man, always sprayed us with saliva as words burst from his mouth whilst painting his pictures of Jesus and how much he cared for us. Deep within myself, I felt a truth in his teaching and wanted to be a Methodist like him. I suppose he is best described as a Billy Graham of his day!

Will Turner at Wyrley Wesley was a little like Philip West in his delivery but our repetitions were taken from the Sunday School hymnal of the Methodist Church and seemed much lighter than the doctrine of the catechism taught by Philip. The church building was much larger than Upper Landywood and we invariably sat in the back pew which allowed us to play 'battleships' if we were bored. We were soon brought to order by the playing of the piano to indicate that a hymn had been announced. Will Turner either was unaware of the lack of attention by his class or did not care and simply proceeded like an automaton. The fact that I was with my friends and the atmosphere was so relaxed, I stayed at Wyrley Wesley Sunday school though I did return to Upper Landywood some years later, as will become clear.

The afternoon class was much different from that in the morning. Bill Garratt was one of the stalwarts of the Church. I knew him from taking our medical panel payments to him in the choir vestry every month. He was a trustee of the church and also church organist and choirmaster. The pipe organ at Wyrley Wesley is an outstanding instrument with brilliant Diapason pipes at the front giving a very rich sound. Bill Garratt always attacked the organ with verve and was only happy when the whole church vibrated in unison! On occasions, he arrived in the church for the main morning service, before we had left the building after Sunday school and I listened in awe as the organ filled the church with music, the like of which I had never heard before. I sometimes fantasized that I was sitting at the console and was filling the whole of Great Wyrley with the beautiful sound, but then I was very prone to daydreaming!

At school, there were now more serious matters ahead of me. 1948 was school certificate year and I found some of the subjects I was studying very difficult to comprehend and retain. In Latin we were studying Virgil's epic poem, 'Aeneid', and I found great difficulty in both translating the lines and comprehending. Similarly with French, although I could speak the language well with excellent accent, my comprehension of spoken French was quite poor. The first examination was the French oral in the headmaster's office. I sat down and the examiner immediately fired a question at me.

"Bonjour, Monsieur Carpenter, quel temps fait il?" (*Hello, Mr Carpenter, what is the weather like?*), she asked. I looked at the face of the arboretum clock through the headmaster's window, brightly lit in summer sunshine.

"Bonjour, mademoiselle, c'est quatre heurs moins quinze" (*good day, miss, it is quarter to four*), I enthusiastically replied. She frowned.

"Le temps, Monsieur Carpenter?"   Ouch, I thought, and it went downhill from there!

In English literature, I thoroughly detested Charles Dickens' works and 'Nicholas Nickleby' was our set book for the examination. I found it totally boring and could never sit down and enjoy it. I did feel more comfortable with the set Shakespeare which was 'Henry V' which was perhaps helped by the fact that we went as a class to see the Laurence Olivier film *Henry V* at the Odeon cinema in Bloxwich. I was motivated to accompany the actors in their speeches, which we had learned parrot-fashion for homework. Finally, our history course covered the mid nineteenth century, essentially the various Reform Acts, which I again found terribly boring.

With the exams over I could relax. I was more grown up and, in particular, my hormones were telling me in a big way that things had changed. Among other things, I was now getting regular sensations in the pit of my stomach and frequent erections when our discussions turned to girls and sex which were almost daily events at school and in the lane. On one occasion, I was in the lavatory at home when I suddenly developed an extreme erection. Boys around me often talked about masturbating and some inner stimulus drove me to follow *Frank's* demonstration of working his monster and I soon came to a point where I started to get a sensation that I had never before experienced. My face was flushing hotter and hotter and suddenly, without warning, I felt the most forceful uncontrollable cramp-like surges reaching a frightening crescendo as I ejaculated. My legs turned to jelly, my body was shaking out of control and I had difficulty getting my breath. I was very frightened for a few moments, but with a deep in-take of breath I quickly returned to normality. The several forceful cramps had been uncontrollable and had hurt like hell and I panicked in case I had done myself harm. Then some inner voice assured me that all was well and in some ways very pleasurable.

However, it remained private to me and I never became an exhibitionist like *Frank*.

Unfortunately my distaste for and lack of study in history, English literature and Latin led me to failing the school certificate. I needed six subjects to pass and only managed five. I was obliged, therefore, to re-sit the whole examination in a year's time. This revision year started as usual at the end of August and I joined the class with a few friends who had also bitten the dust and some new colleagues from the other fifth forms. Billy Hayes became a close friend during this year. Since he would be going into his father's business he did not really need to struggle too hard but his inveterate humour sometimes made it difficult for me to concentrate. Often it was a barely audible aside just as I was answering a question put to me by a master which usually resulted in me getting a flea in the ear for not taking the question seriously. It took away the tedium of redoing stuff I had already done. Fortunately I was allowed to replace history with geography which gave me a new lease of life. I was taught by an excellent new master to the school whose name eludes me, though Dickson comes to mind. I really enjoyed it, probably as much as I enjoyed the science subjects. Among other things, he taught us how to read and use an Ordnance Survey map which has proved most useful throughout life.

Our new classroom looked down on the school gym which was also used by the girl's school. On summer days, their gym mistress insisted on open windows and the long legs of the girls, who wore only vest and knickers, delighted us as we lined the windows between lessons. The girls were aware of their audience and enjoyed it as we learned later but they kept straight faces and concentrated on the commands of the gym mistress lest she became aware of the distraction. I was now also beginning to like what I was seeing of the opposite sex and the uncertainty and shyness of the previous year or so was settling down. However, it was during this time, I nearly went a step too far!

During one of the evening games sessions in the lane whilst playing Tin Can Nerky, *John, Brenda* (pseudonyms) and I were hiding in a hollow caused by mining subsidence at the top of the field. It was the third game of the evening and we had decided that we couldn't be bothered making our way back to the can, the seeker could come and find us. For a while we chatted about ordinary things but then we started to talk with gung-ho about having a fuck to pass the time. *Brenda* indicated that she was game. It caught me very much off guard and, as she pulled down her knickers, I suddenly felt very frightened, my pulse was bounding in my head and I started to shake. I followed *John* in releasing the belt and buttons of my trousers and, in that instant, seemed to have no control over the degree of urgency that was overtaking me. *John* was first to get ready and lay on top of her, his trousers pushed down around his knees, and his buttocks soon thrusting. I sat there out of control, my hormones fully in charge of my actions - waiting, still waiting, please hurry *John* - when the silence was shattered as a few of the players came over the lip of the hollow and disturbed our seclusion. The seeker had failed to find us and they had called off the game, but another player had seen us go into the hollow. There was raucous laughter and cutting remarks as they took in the scene before them and we blushed intensely. *John* and *Brenda* were frantically re-arranging their clothing and I quickly fumbled with my fly buttons. The surge of hormones had now switched off and I felt mixed emotions, certainly annoyed at being caught in the process but, in another way, relieved that I had not done anything with *Brenda*, which no-one, of course, believed. A few nights later, I had a nightmare about the situation in which my mom found out what I had done with *Brenda* and I awoke terrified and in a sweat.

As I look back, I am conscious that these encounters were experimentation, probably no more than that. Maturing boys have hormone surges which have been a feature of civilization for all time. They are built into our genes, as for all the animal kingdom. In the situations I had witnessed over the past year or so, the girls were on the cusp of puberty, about twelve or thirteen years of age. To the best of my knowledge, the escapades were uncommon and, in any case, as the girls reached puberty they did not want to know about such approaches from boys as no doubt the danger of pregnancy was explained to them by their mothers.

I never again saw any associations between boys and girls in the lane, but then something happened to jar the status quo. During a nature walk, I was walking the perimeter of a field and to my surprise I disturbed *Brenda* and *Elizabeth* (pseudonyms) who were naked below the waist. *Elizabeth* was lying on top of *Brenda* going through the motions that a boy might in this situation. On seeing me, *Elizabeth* blushed intensely and they quickly dressed and walked away. My heart was pounding and I was conscious of blushing profusely. I said nothing and went on my way, pretending to search the hedgerows, though in reality I was stunned and my eyes were not really focusing on anything. The episode threw up another conundrum for me. I now understood a boy and girl relationship, but two girls? I did not know the answer and I could not talk to my pals about it because I did not want to embarrass the girls. One of them had obviously been very distressed by my discovery and I knew that they would have been teased unmercifully if their secret had come out.

It was during the autumn of that year that cousin Ron was taken ill with ear pain. The family tried all manner of things to relieve it, but it simply got worse. After a day or two of excruciating pain, and in the middle of the night, he was taken to hospital by emergency ambulance. It turned out to be mastoiditis, an acute infection of the air cells behind the ear. Ron was taken to theatre immediately for an emergency operation. Although his head next day was wrapped like an Egyptian mummy, the relief on his face was clear to see. For a while, the experience took away Ron's comic antics, mainly because he had to undergo regular dressing changes which he seriously disliked. I still clearly recall the strong fishy smell of the black treacle-like paste which the nurse spread on the dressings.

Within a week or two he was back to his old self and, as always, teasing mom as much as he could. As he now entered his teens he was showing considerable skill as an artist. I dabbled a little with paints, but Ron was exceptional for his age and in a different league to me. At the time, I was not aware who in his family he had taken after. I recall when Ron was young, Uncle Joe drawing him a horse which was done in matchstick style. Ron was none too pleased. From childhood he seemed to have a creative eye and obviously knew rubbish drawing when he saw it. Aunt Ruby was also useless and yet here was Ron at twelve years of age showing great skills and, within a few months, he started to win prizes for his paintings in the local horticultural and craft shows. He painted pictures of scenes around the village. A year or two later, he painted an ethereal picture of a hospital operating theatre which I have always loved. I wondered whether it was his mental impression of his own emergency operation though he would not have been awake to experience such a vision. The film "A matter of life and death" was showing at that time and he may have been inspired by the brain surgery in that film. Wherever the idea came from, it has lived with me as something extra special, hanging for over fifty years on the wall in the lounge. I have already referred to Ron's real father in an earlier chapter but it was many years later that I became aware that he had artistic merit and was the source of Ron's artistic genes.

With his wish to become a serious artist, he naturally wanted a place in an art school but he had a problem with his mathematics. I tried on several occasions to teach him maths which was a requirement for entry into art school. He would seem to understand but then, faced with a new set of figures needing the same application, his brain simply had not retained the information needed to resolve the new problem. I found it difficult to understand and at times became exasperated with him. This was obviously the worst approach and Ron would lose patience and storm from the house, his brain having suffered mathematical overload. A few days later, I visited cousin Bob's house next door to find him teaching Ron and he also was suffering the same difficulties in getting him to understand. These years during Ron's early teens led me to understand how different our brains were. I thought I could paint, but in reality compared with Ron's skill, I was rubbish. As I look at some of his paintings I envy the single brush stroke which brings a picture to life, giving it dimension and meaning. Ron became an outstanding artist in later life, exhibiting in various London art exhibitions and galleries, and I believe is still doing so.

As 1948 drew to a close, mom was in her element. A true royalist, she sat glued to the radio set listening to the broadcast from Westminster Abbey of the marriage of HRH Princess Elizabeth to Prince Philip of Greece . About a week later, she eagerly made a trip to the cinema to see newsreel of the wedding followed by a visit to W H Smith to obtain the official copy of the wedding photographs which she drooled over and it kept her occupied for some time. All her long life she followed the activities of the Royal family with a passion.

Aunt Hilda, my favourite aunt, had by this time found a job at Cadbury's in Bourneville. It was a considerable journey from Essington, but she was never one to laze around. The move appealed to me because, most weeks, she brought us a one pound (450g) bag of chocolate 'seconds'. More often than not they were Brazil nuts which had not completely coated with milk chocolate leaving part of the nut visible. These were rejected from the production line and could be purchased by the employees. It was a treat which certainly helped during the continued sweet rationing, and mom and I rationed ourselves to two a day!

CHAPTER 17

'Towards Spiritual things - c. 1948 - 51'

I had now been attending Great Wyrley Wesley Sunday school for several months. Most Sundays, after morning school, I stood at the back of the church and listened to WJ (Bill) Garratt playing incidental music on the pipe organ, prior to the main church service. I was increasingly turned on by its majesty and daydreamed that one day I might be able to play it. The best I could achieve for now was a tune on a harmonica which I had been given as a present last Christmas. Hohner musical instruments, manufactured in Germany, were beginning to appear again in music shops. I had seen them on display in a shop in Stafford Street in Walsall. My persistent pestering had obviously given mom and dad an idea and thankfully they came up with the longed-for present. I picked out a tune on the instrument quite easily and soon became quite proficient at playing tunes by ear. I clearly remember playing fluently 'There's a long, long trail a-winding' by lunch-time on Christmas day and, later in the day, the family was singing Christmas carols to my accompaniment. I had had no formal training of any kind in playing an instrument but was chuffed with this early progress and hoped that it was a first step towards conquering others, even that church organ! Well, I could dream I suppose, but I could neither afford music lessons nor was I sure that I wanted the hassle, and mom was certainly not going to fund lessons after her own experience.

She incessantly repeated the tale of her first piano lesson in Cheslyn Hay when Mr Lawrence Hawkins, set her 'The bluebells of Scotland' to learn. As soon as she reached home, she began hammering out the easily recognisable tune on the piano and in no time had the whole family singing at the top of their voices,

> "By yon bonny banks and by yon bonny braes,
> Where the sun shines bright on Loch Lomond,.....!"

The family gave their all as mom proudly pounded the ivories. Grandma and granddad were very satisfied that their hard earned cash had resulted in such a melodic sound from their daughter's fingers. I think granddad could see a burgeoning professional and was obviously excited. The following week, mom skipped her way to Cheslyn Hay to her piano lesson feeling that her piano teacher would be very pleased with her. With some pride she played her piece and felt that everyone in Cheslyn Hay must be hearing her rendition through the open windows of the music room. Alas, Lawrence Hawkins was far from pleased, not a note had been played true to the manuscript. Mom had played the tune entirely by ear.

"Miss Baker", he said sternly, "you *are* playing 'The bluebells of Scotland' but not a single note from the music in front of you! You must practice the piece again for next week."

Mom was totally demoralised and told her mom and dad that she was never going to *that man* again and, in fact, she barely touched the piano again. Nevertheless, the gene which defined that ability to play by ear was, it seems, passed to me, as I shall reveal.

Bill Garrett was a self-made man and owned a factory in Bloxwich which made electrical goods. He was a local parish councillor and drove a big car suggesting wealth but it soon became apparent to me that he was also a benefactor, particularly towards his church. In Sunday School, he tried to enthuse us with music and frequently asked for better singing if he felt pupils were not giving of their best. When it came to his address to us, he usually included interesting personal anecdotes and at times seemed to be 'name-dropping' and yet he was always fascinating to listen to. He spent his money freely on his Sunday School children, arranging coach trips to places of interest, such as to Lichfield, which would be preceded by a brief history of the city and the buildings we would see. It was not uncommon for two or three coaches of children to make a trip to Sutton Park or Trentham Gardens on Saturday afternoon, always free to us. Probably as result of his benevolence, when it came to the Sunday School Anniversary on the first and third Sundays in May, he usually attracted the largest choir in the area.

Training for the Sunday School Anniversary began about six weeks before the great day, the children attending most week-day evenings and the adult choir on Fridays. Bill Garrett's method was, for the first few evenings, to play the tunes loud enough to give everyone a chance to sing, warming up their voices, so to speak. Within a few practices, everyone had the tune and rhythm and it was now commonplace to hear groups of children singing the hymns at the top of their voices as they walked home from choir practice. Once the tunes were well known, he could concentrate on fine tuning and select his soloists as the great day neared. With about two weeks to go, Jack Carless and Albert Jones assembled the five-tiered platform above the Communion table, on which the event would be staged. During the week before the Anniversary, the adult choir attended choir practice once or twice with the children, creating a choir of up to a hundred and fifty voices. Mr. Garrett was fortunate to acquire the services of Jim Bullen of Walsall as organist for the Sunday School Anniversary whilst he himself conducted the choir. Jim Bullen arrived for the first full rehearsal during the week and, as he faultlessly played the tunes for the first time, he found a melody and beauty in the instrument that far outclassed anything Bill Garrett produced, good as he was. Jim's professionalism shone like a beacon and with his playing, the voices of the children and the adult choir were lifted to the extent that we spontaneously smiled with joy as we sang. By Friday, we were considered knocked into shape and on Sunday, 'Great Wyrley Wesley Sunday School Anniversary' could take the stage. The latter would be made ready on Saturday by aunt Nancy Baker who decorated it with the dozens of artificial flowers she had created over the winter months.

Anniversary day was always a special day in the village. In its peak years, the platform was filled with just over a hundred children and nearly fifty adult choir members. The girls wore a white dress and the boys were in white shirts with blue and white striped tie. It was a spectacular which led to seats being filled well over an hour before a service. Some years, the congregation slowly sweltered in the combined heat of a hot May day and the many bodies, packed in like sardines. The ushers made sure that no free space remained by bringing in extra chairs to fill the aisles. Those who could not be seated stood at the back or outside with the doors open. It was a day when the congregation took out their Sunday best clothes. Many women purchased new outfits for this, the Great Wyrley fashion parade, a sort of Women's Day at Ascot. Doris Jones (nee Carless), always fashion conscious, set a precedent at the 1948 Anniversary when she wore clothes based on Christian Dior's New Look which he had created to lift fashions after the drab war years. Mom invariably bought a new outfit for Anniversary day, whether I was at Upper Landywood or now at Great Wyrley Wesley, but not the New Look. She was not adventurous enough for this, but nevertheless she always looked good.

For us the singers, after an initial nervousness, the atmosphere of the day led to a desire to give our all and we felt elated and proud to be on the platform. Bill Garratt and the minister always found preachers who could hold the attention of children and adults alike. The children were always exemplary, both in their singing and in their interaction with the preachers. By the evening service, the third service of the day, our voices were certainly suffering from the day's exertion. By the final congregational hymn, "The day Thou gave us Lord is ended", we could relax and acknowledge that we had contributed to a job well done. But, singing aside, it was also a day when people gave freely to collections, between a hundred and one hundred and fifty pounds being the norm for the three services on the first day and rising over the next few years to nearly three hundred. Unfortunately, the repeat performance two weeks later, never seemed to have that same magic, possibly because we were playing to a smaller congregation and there was a little bit of 'been there, done that'.

I was a month or so short of sixteen years of age when one Sunday afternoon Grace Smith, the primary Sunday School superintendent, came into the senior class and asked if any of us would like to help with her class. Several of us followed her through to the primary school room and sat with the children, helping with the hymn singing and the accompanying actions such as twinkling fingers in 'Twinkle, twinkle, little star'. At the end of the class, Grace requested we stay behind, and it was then she asked if we would like to consider becoming Sunday School teachers. She explained that it would entail attendance at training classes during the week when we would be prepared for the following Sunday's lessons. For me it was a moment of growing up. Until now, I had been a pupil, but now I had the chance to be a teacher and along with Vernon Bullock, Grace Hall, Margaret Rowley, Dorothy Turner, Jean Gunn, Janet Bourne, Jean Turner and others, I accepted the challenge. Mom was delighted with my decision, she had always been a regular supporter of the church and I think she felt it would keep me on the straight and narrow. At the mid-week classes, we worked to the Sunday School class book issued by the Methodist Church. Grace Smith was a slave driver and, during the training, insisted that we fully understood the subject we were to teach. On Sunday, we were given a class of six or seven children and after the initial hymns and prayers, each teacher sat their group in a ring and taught the lesson of the day. Grace wandered from group to group, sitting in and listening, sometimes adding a few words herself. At feed-back during the week she would give her impressions, never being unkind to anyone, but suggesting improvements and gently goading us on. We grew fond of her ways and we all became proficient Sunday School teachers.

Vernon Bullock and I became great friends and, at his suggestion, I joined the church choir and from then on sang in the choir every Sunday evening. At choir practises on Friday evenings, we sat in the bass section of the choir and I usually found myself sitting next to Bert Rowley of Wharwell Farm. The whole of the Rowley family were in the choir, Lettie the mother and daughters Iris and Margaret. Bert had a wonderful bass voice and it was quite a shock on joining the choir to realise that I would no longer be singing the soprano air of a hymn which had been the norm. He took me in hand and explained to me the bass line of the tunes in the Methodist hymn book, following the line in my book with his finger as he sang. My voice had not yet matured and I had difficulty with the low notes, usually making do with an octave higher. After choir practice, my voice was usually hoarse as though I had severe laryngitis but I grew to love the harmony which the choir produced and the part we, the bass section, played in its creation. With Bert Rowley on one side and Percy Smith on the other, it was not long before I developed the gist of choral singing and thoroughly enjoyed it. The organ was a great help and I was soon able to recognize my line as the large bass pipes behind us sang out our melody.

September every year saw the celebration of God's bountiful harvest. Being brought up in a flourishing garden and respecting nature, I always looked forward to the Harvest Festivals at church. Mom and dad always sent plenty of produce and flowers to both Upper Landywood and Wyrley Wesley church, as did many of the congregation and other gardeners around the village.

The church was always dressed with small sheaves of cereals from the fields, garden fruits, vegetables and flowers and not forgetting a lump of coal to celebrate the harvest brought in by the miners and finally a glass of water, God's gift to life. By early Saturday afternoon the pews were covered with bundles of vegetation, flowers, fruit and vegetables which would be used for decorating the church. We also raided the hedgerows and woodlands for materials to use for the purpose. The vegetation was tied around pillars and balustrades in church interspersed with sheaves of cereal. Bunches of grapes hung down from the perimeter of the pulpit. On one occasion Grace Smith asked for bulrushes to give her design height. I cycled down to Gain's brook and squelched in some twelve inches (300mm) of mud to cut a dozen for her. Everyone put a great deal of effort into preparing the church for this special celebration. In fact, villagers seemed to come out of the woodwork to do their bit. For one display, I used my modelling skills to create a windmill with balsa wood sails, about thirty inches (75cm) in diameter. I had no electric motor and used a gramophone turntable and Meccano construction, hidden beneath the table, for the transmission to drive the windmill. The sails silently turned throughout the day and made a very nice display. Harvest Festival was another church event when we, choir and congregation, could sing with great verve and Will Garratt could shake the foundations as he made the organ rip!

"Come, ye thankful people, come! Raise the song of 'harvest home'!
All is safely gathered in, ere the winter storms begin;

There was unfortunately a problem during the sermon of the evening service, when the Meccano transmission of my windmill developed a squeak which was both off-putting to the preacher and those trying to listen to him. Since I was the only person who knew how it worked, I had to leave the choir by the back door and creep into the side door of the church to switch it off. It was just twenty minutes before the end of a whole day's display!

It was a period when I made many new friends and although I continued to meet with my old friends, Eric, Colin, David and others, usually for a chat or a game of 'Tin can nerky', I now spent far more time with my church friends.

Around this time, Will Garratt, who was forever trying to find new stimuli for the children and youth of 'his' Sunday School, asked Mr Ernie Carter (who had retired a few years earlier as headmaster of Pinfold Lane school, Cheslyn Hay) if he would consider opening a Youth Club at our church. Mr Carter had already started a boy's club at Great Wyrley Institute at the corner of Norton Lane. He had considerable experience in provisions for youth, running youth clubs and a regional youth swimming club which was showing very good results. A Youth Club was a much needed provision at Wyrley Wesley and on the opening night some twenty teenage boys attended. There was little or no equipment and Ernie had to start from scratch. Jack Carless, a Church Trustee and professional pattern maker at the Boulton Paul aircraft factory in Wolverhampton, came to the rescue in 'knocking up' a full size table tennis table. Albert Jones also helped as an intermediary between Ernie and the church for funding of other equipment such as table tennis bats, balls, net and other games.

The new table tennis table was precariously balanced on a standard six foot trestle table and novices like myself were soon knocking balls backwards and forwards over the net, learning the rules of the game from others who knew. Darts, hoop-la, board games, quizzes, talks, cycle rides and other activities were introduced and the youth club became a popular event every Saturday evening. It attracted youth of all ages up to late teenage years. Ernie Carter also made sure that we were fed. He brought currant buns, butter, cheese and tea which were sold at cost price, about sixpence (2.5p) for a filled bun. Ernie's buns usually had a slice of butter, rather than a thin spread, and a ploughman's slice of cheese. I had never before eaten cheese in a cinnamon spiced currant bun but it was absolutely delightful and along with a cup of tea, it alone was worth attending youth club for! Before long, league tables had appeared so that everyone played everyone else at table tennis or darts, all playing hard to move up the table as the weeks passed. I was, at best, average but we all improved as time passed, learning from each other the arts of spinning a table tennis ball, slamming balls, returning long shots and so on.

Ernie Carter owned a large old-fashioned brass magic lantern which projected three inch (7.5cm) painted colour slides. The large slides were loaded into a bulky wooden slide carrier and moved into the projector as required. He illustrated many talks and fictional adventures using these slides, some dating back to Victorian times. Occasionally Harold Pritchard, probably in his mid twenties, helped Ernie by feeding the projector for him. It was my first experience of illustrated lectures and the slides certainly added a degree of fascination to the talk. The talk usually lasted about thirty minutes and then we could get back again to games or perhaps a sing song or listen to a tune around the piano.

Great Wyrley Wesley also owned the field next door in Shaw's Lane and the Youth Club used it for football practice or matches, usually seven aside. The grass was not kept trimmed, except by horses, and in later years I was unfortunate enough to fracture my ankle and wrist when I tripped over a tussock of grass and was never able to play football again.

Ernie's enthusiasm to put on special events for youth of the day never seemed to wane and one Friday evening he brought most of the village's male youth together for a social evening in Great Wyrley Institute, at a shilling (5p) a head. Members of our Wyrley Wesley Youth Club were invited to join his Institute youth club for a film evening and we were delighted to do so, expecting the inevitable silent films of the time. The event was a showing of a 16mm sound film which at the time were uncommon in churches and village halls. The film, 'The man who knew too much', was a Hitchcock pre-war thriller. I remember being disappointed that it included the evil-eyed Peter Lorre who I had seen previously in 'The Maltese Falcon' at the cinema. He was a man who gave me the heebie-jeebies and I really hated him. Ernie Carter's food in the interval more than made up for Lorre. It was a great evening out with friends around my own age.

It will be noted that the youth club at Church was hitherto for boys only, since this was Ernie Carter's forte. The teenage girls had Girl Guides or Rangers, but no youth club. With the retirement of Ernie, at the ripe old age of eighty years (I think), things were to change. The Trustees of the Church appointed one of its senior members, Albert Jones, to lead a youth club for both sexes. This initially opened in the Primary room as an extension of the boy's club, and using their equipment. A few months later, Bill Garratt presented the Church with much-needed new and larger accommodation. It was a full-sized wooden barracks-hut used by the armed forces during the war years. Many barracks, four years on, became obsolete and he probably obtained it for little more than the cost of removal. It was complete with two coke-burning stoves which made it very cozy during winter months. Percy Garrett (no relation to Bill), church caretaker, kept it well stoked. The building was sited on the bowling green alongside the caretaker's garden. Jack Carless built double doors opening onto the bowling green and the building was formally opened by Mrs. Garratt. It created much more room on the Church premises and the mixed Youth Club were first to move in. The table tennis table and other games were moved over, dancing to a record player was introduced and other mixed events followed. About a year later the bowling green was converted to a grass tennis court when the Trustees agreed to purchase a professional tennis net and white line-making equipment. It was not perfect because it still had a six inch (150mm) crown, but was better than nothing and a few novices, like myself, learned the rules of the game on this court. Cycle outings were also arranged for occasional Saturday afternoons which were quite popular. A trip to somewhere like Beaudesert on Cannock Chase or even Lichfield was fairly easy. On one occasion, we decided to stretch ourselves and cycle to the Wrekin in Shropshire, about thirty miles from Great Wyrley and a sixty mile round trip! We carefully planned the route to take in places of interest such as Boscobel and Tong.

There were two ways we could cycle to Boscobel, either the boring route along Watling Street (A5) to the Bradford Arms (near Weston Park) or a circuitous route through Cheslyn Hay and Brewood. The latter was a route I knew well since I had cycled there many times, either to the Somerfield Park Summer Shows with dad or with friends to collect conkers, and I offered to lead the way, particularly as I now had a brand spanking new racing cycle which needed an airing.

This new acquisition was purchased from Keys in Walsall, next to the George Hotel. It had caught my eye whilst wandering around town during school lunch hour, a racing style silver Raleigh with Stirmey Archer gears and drop handle bars. Once I had made up my mind that this was the one and mom and dad had agreed, I was eager to take ownership. So much so that I foolishly chose to collect it at the shop and cycle home, rather than await delivery, whilst mom who had graciously tagged along to pay the bill, would return on the bus. I soon realised it was going to be a pretty scary journey because of traffic density. In fact, I did not pluck up courage to mount it until I reached the Bloxwich section of Green Lane where the road was wide and straight. I was not used to a drop-handlebar cycle, the saddle was not the correct height and the pedals were metal rather than rubber and very slippery. The first hundred yards were a nightmare. In the end I walked at least four of the six miles between Walsall and home.

Sixteen of us, boys and girls, set out for Brewood via Cheslyn Hay and along Saredon Road. We reached Calf Heath in about thirty minutes and a few minutes later entered the straight mile. When cycling alone, this was a particularly boring section of the Brewood trip since the end of the road was in sight but it seemed to take an eternity to get there. On this occasion, with about a dozen macho boys and the end visible a mile away, it begged for a race to the end. I think I came in about mid-field. An hour after leaving home, we were making our way through Brewood village and on to Boscobel House. We sat by the duck pond there, for a breather and a drink and snack. After ten minutes, everyone seemed to be in fine fettle raring to go. Cycling on down the lane, we were able to point out to first-timers the oak tree in which King Charles hid to escape the Roundheads. It required little or no pedalling to cover the next three miles down to the A41. Tong Church was our next planned stop to visit the church and grounds, where Little Nell of Dicken's fame is rumoured to be buried. We reached the Wrekin via Shifnal at about one o'clock and by now some in the group were feeling a little saddle sore, with leaden legs. We had a group chat and chose not to climb the mountain since we had to cycle the thirty mile return trip. Instead we painfully ambled a short way up the path leaving our cycles in the lane. The whole point of the trip had been to climb to the top, but our legs definitely told us otherwise.

When it came to the return journey, we chose the Watling Street as a straighter route. Dorothy Turner, one of the girls was by now struggling badly and it was obvious she could not go on. Gallant as ever, the boys took it in turns pushing her as we cycled alongside her. It meant we had to walk up the long steep hill at Oakengates. On the whole the trip was not too bad and at about five o'clock we arrived safely at Wyrley Wesley Church, most of us very tired, but happy with our achievement. There was just time to go home to freshen up before Youth Club at seven o'clock.

Every Thursday evening at Great Wyrley Wesley, the Wesley Guild was held in the Primary room, a good evening out when there was so little other entertainment. The programme for the year was circulated in September identifying the subject for the evening and the speaker or entertainer. There were essentially four categories of meeting which rotated, social, musical, devotional and citizenship.

Social evenings at the Guild were great fun, particularly when Albert Jones was compère for the evening. He had a great sense of humour and was an innate comedian with a wealth of jokes. His evenings were always a great laugh and the content very mixed. A member may present a comedy poem or a musical piece such as 'Albert and the Lion', accompanied on the piano by Margaret Rowley. Songs such as 'The laughing policeman' or 'The beau Gendarmes' were acted by male voices. Quizzes were commonplace and very much enjoyed, such as 'Guess the advert'. Some twenty advertisements, cut from magazines and newspapers, had the subject matter removed and we guessed what they advertised. So many times we had all read magazines or papers and ignored the advertisements, and now wished we had been more observant. Once during the Guild season a slot might be allocated to a short comedy play, usually read rather than played, scripts for which could be hired for a small fee. A group of us under the direction of Grace Hall rehearsed the play prior to the evening. As I developed my conjuring tricks, I gave a few demonstrations on social evenings. The social evening in later years may be allocated to a film, using the 16mm sound projector from Bloxwich Wesley Church. People took it in turns creating a programme for an evening which was more often than not well thought out and, along with refreshments generously provided by Liza Sambrook from her shop, made a fantastic evening's entertainmant.

Musical evenings could be a variety of events from the inspiring Cannock Salvation Army band and choir to a simple show put on by members. The melodic sound of the brass brought a wonderful depth to the hymns and choral music which the Salvationists sang, always drawing a rich and deserved applause. They came to us most years and it was something we looked forward to. Oliver Wood's party always provided a most entertaining group of acts. Oliver was proprietor of a grocery wholesale business in Bridgetown and uncle to Iris and Margaret Rowley. He played the violin and had a banter reminiscent of Vic Oliver, a well renowned national comedian who also used a violin during his comic act. Oliver Wood's musical party was made up of singers and instrumentalists. Iris and Margaret usually played piano duets for him. Oliver Wood also took his concert party to various venues on Cannock Chase. In later years, I performed conjuring tricks at a few of his concerts.

Wesley Guild devotional evenings were often led by an outside speaker with an interesting life or profession or by a member of our own Methodist circuit with a challenging story to tell. The idea of the evening was to stimulate discussion and learn from other people's experiences. A devotional evening could also include a quiz usually compiled by Vernon Bullock. We may be asked to identify the first line of hymns, perhaps from a line in a later verse or from a bar of music from the middle of the tune. These lightened the evening but the turn-out for devotional evenings was rarely as high as for the entertainment evenings since some saw the Guild as an evening of light entertainment and bible studies were a touch too serious. We who attended were inspired by many speakers.

The citizenship evenings were more instructive or enlightening. On two occasions I spoke about flowering plants, firstly those with unusual pollination characteristics and then the carnivorous plants which obtained their nutrients from digesting insects. I was able to demonstrate the devious methods plants use to transfer their pollen and to obtain sustenance. They sound extremely boring subjects but, at that time, they were an example of God's unique creations for life. Thursday evenings at Great Wyrley Wesley Guild were something we looked forward to. I have memories of happy occasions spent in laughter or deep thought with friends of all ages.

In late 1948 there was a Christian revival which brought a new challenge to our lives. In America Billy Graham had started evangelizing and in this country, Donald Soper, a pacifist Methodist minister of Kingsway Church in London and well known for his Sunday soapbox sessions at Speaker's corner in Hyde Park, created the OCW (Order of Christian Witness). He trained a group of evangelical preachers who toured the country much as the Wesleys had done in the eighteenth century. Several members of the Order spent a few days with us at Great Wyrley Wesley. Their aim was to get us to commit our lives anew and to renew our vows to follow the Christian teachings in the bible. In the final service, when the congregation was called forward to commit, at least three dozen Great Wyrley people did so, including myself. It was I suppose an early form of the Billy Graham meetings which hit the UK in later decades. The buffet at one of the evening meetings was fish and chips. These were collected in bulk from Evans' chip shop on the corner of Benton's Lane in the well-scrubbed large washing-up bowls from the church kitchen! It was an exceptional idea for catering for so many people for who can fail to like a freshly-cooked crisp chip and or a chip butty with the already prepared bread and butter! It was certainly different from the usual cut sandwiches. The Londoners loved it.

At this time, several of us were now mature and established Sunday School teachers. Perhaps stimulated by the OCW crusade, Grace Smith questioned whether we might also be interested in conducting adult Church services. We certainly were and a word with the minister, Rev. Stanley W. Jones, and the Church Trustees was met with a great deal of enthusiasm. Thus, in 1949, Great Wyrley Wesley Youth Group was duly founded. The initial members were Vernon Bullock, Eric Till, Jean Gunn, Margaret Rowley, Dorothy Turner, Grace Hall and myself. The training began, much as when we were coached to become Sunday School teachers. Grace Smith felt that we should use the beatitudes from the "Sermon on the Mount" in St Matthew's gospel as the subject of the first service we were to conduct. Five of us were given two verses each and we were expected to create a four-minute sermon on the topic. Jean Gunn would begin with the first two beatitudes, "Blessed are the poor in spirit" and "Blessed are they that mourn". I was given the next two, "Blessed are the meek for they shall inherit the earth" and "Blessed are they that hunger and thirst after righteousness". Margaret, Eric and Vernon were charged with the other six verses.

I did not find 'meekness' a particularly easy subject and spent a great deal of time in the school library, researching and trying to get inspiration. I managed to pull together a four minute sermon, as did the others. Jean produced some moving words which on the day visibly gained the congregation's attention and made it easy for the rest of us to follow. Dorothy and Grace Hall were to lead the prayers, read lessons and be link persons. We spent a considerable amount of time practising the service, with Grace Smith directing us and editing, so that the final version was a well polished sixty minutes. We first went live in our own church but thereafter we conducted the service in several local Methodist Churches both in our own circuit and further afield such as Reedswood Methodist Church in Walsall where we were received with great acclaim. Over a period of three or four years, the Youth Group used this principle of a group sermon on a well known topic and a link person or persons. As time passed, Janet Bourne and others joined the group and by 1950/51 several of us left. (Vernon would enter training college to become a Methodist minister, Eric would train as a local preacher, Jean would start nurse training at Wolverhampton Royal Hospital and myself medicine at Birmingham Medical School.)

The group of us became close friends and every Sunday evening, after the Church service, we collected at the home of Jean Gunn in Shaw's Lane. We sat in a circle around the front room and usually became engrossed in a topical discussion, interrupted by laughter from some witticism or other. Jean's dad, Arthur Gunn who worked at Hawkins' Tileries, industriously worked in the kitchen making sandwiches from the remains of their Sunday joint and the roast beef sandwiches were to die for. Mrs Gunn kept us topped up with cups of tea.

During the Spring of 1949, I was cycling past my *alma mater*, Landywood Primary school, when I witnessed an unusual activity. Vehicles had appeared in the field opposite (adjacent to the displaced persons huts) and, as I parked my bike and sat on the steel fence, I watched lorries with derricks drilling into the ground and pulling up long cores of earth. I was not sure what was going on but a few months later all was made manifest. Enormous excavators had appeared on site and were scraping layers of earth and creating large heaps around the perimeter of the two or three fields along the east side of Gorsey Lane. The gossip was of shallow coal-mining but, having never seen anything like it before, we could only watch and wait. The lane became a mud track as lorries and dumper trucks left and re-entered the site.

After a few weeks, a seam of coal was visible carpeting the bottom of the deep excavation. Whenever I passed the site, I had to have a nose into what was going on. I was particularly fascinated by a small diesel locomotive which pulled tubs of coal from the seam up a very steep railway track to a loading bay in the middle of Gorsey Lane. Here the track was raised so that tubs could be emptied directly into lorries waiting alongside. The tubs were triangular and pivoted at the bottom and, when a lever was pulled, the weight of the coal automatically tipped and emptied them. It was a very simply process with little manual input. The locomotive driver sat side-saddle and had to accelerate hard along the quarry floor so that the impetus gave him sufficient power to rise up to the level of the lane. Sometimes when the tubs were over-filled by the coal shovel, his engine stalled halfway up the incline and he slowly slid back to the bottom. He back tracked along the bottom of the quarry and then, with an almighty roar of his engine and great clouds of black smoke, he tried again, this time reaching the surface.

In another area of the excavation, a large dragline digger was cutting out the three to four feet (1-1.3 metres) coal seam, creating a large pile ready for removal. On the opposite side, at the base of the pile, a mechanical coal shovel with large square bucket which held about half a ton of coal, also spewed out clouds of black diesel exhaust as the driver forced his bucket deep into extracted coal. The full bucket was then swung over a waiting coal tub and driver opened a rear trapdoor to discharge the contents. As might be expected, it was a scene that captivated me and I spent hours watching them at work. The gaping chasm, full of industry, clearly revealed why there were so many small shallow mines around the village. Clearly visible was the vast seam of coal our forebears had worked. But no longer would miners have to lie on their side, cramped and hurting as they worked the seam with a pick axe and shovel. These mechanical shovels were lifting out a truckload of coal in a single scoop! It was an enlightening sight, but little did I realise that the scene before me was the beginning of the rape of the Great Wyrley countryside and would continue for decades to come.

It was inevitable as we grew older that boys and girls would get a little closer to each other and begin to pair off. This happened in the Youth Group. Eric Till and Jean Gunn became an item and I became close friends with Margaret Rowley. Also in later years, Vernon Bullock and Dorothy Turner would become a pair. We were all into our later teens and though kissing and cuddling was allowed, this was as far as such liaisons went. Margaret and I usually said good night with a session leaning against the five-bar gate adjacent to their barn. Too often we were disturbed by someone passing who would recognise us and say 'Good night!' Sexual matters were considered a blessed estate retained for marriage. It was a subject which was never really talked about and it would probably have been considered 'unseemly' to do so. Of course this went on in conversations between boys at school but one had to be seen to be more virtuous towards one's girl friend.

My sexual development and knowledge had progressed slowly, but at sixteen and a half years of age, I still had no clear idea how a baby developed inside a woman, nor how it escaped from her belly. This was never discussed in the huddles that boys found themselves in; everything but! Then on one visit to the library, I picked up and browsed a physiology book, and there it was. It was a simple diagram of a pregnant woman's abdomen showing a fully mature baby, head downwards and about to deliver through the birth canal. I was overcome and quite humbled by the picture before me. The chapter informed me how babies developed and how they came into the world. There were also new words which until now had not entered my vocabulary since they were not in common usage. My dick was really called a penis and girls became pregnant after it was inserted into their vagina and sperm introduced. The almost unbelievable story from *William* a year or two before which had started my journey of sexual enlightenment had moved to a deeper understanding. No longer would I be perplexed by comments which in earlier years had meant little to me. I could now have meaningful and more adult conversations on the subject, though penis and vagina were never at the time used in common parlance. I was still a long way from accepting the act of sex between adults as other than mucky, but then at this time I had never felt true love. The need for purity was taught as part of my Christian faith and this would not allow me to think otherwise. So many things, including masturbation (called Onanism in the Roman Catholic leaflets that I read), were considered wrong and all sex before marriage was taboo. It was going to be a year or two before the magic word 'love' became linked with sex in sermons by Rev. Stanley W. Jones, at that time our Methodist minister. I adored his words, and within a year or two I was able to accept the meaning of love, the sanctity of marriage and the deeper meaning of the sexual act.

As might be expected, sexual activities in school time was almost punishable by death! Four Queen Mary boys were found in the arboretum in congress with a girl from the High School. The incident started when one of the boys visited Bell and Webster's Chemist in Lichfield Street, to purchase a packet of Durex condoms. The manager, an Old Marian, would not sell them and informed the headmaster. Someone must have said something about happenings in the arboretum and two schoolmasters were dispatched there. The boys and the girl in Queen Mary uniforms were caught in *flagrante dilecto* (to show off my Latin skills!), and the boys were ordered to report to the headmaster's office.

At 3.00 p.m. the school stopped and everyone was told to assemble in the main hall. The boys we were told had been flogged and were subsequently expelled from school. The girl was allowed to continue her education. In fact, a conversation with Queen Mary's High School girls in later years suggested that it was never common knowledge in the school and had apparently been hushed up.

Though we teenagers at church may discuss sex, it was in a grown-up manner related to love and, as far as I am aware, never as practicing sexual lovers. My close friendship with Margaret led to a long friendship between her family, mother Lettie and father Bert and my mom and dad. They lived at Wharwell farm which was a centuries-old farmhouse. The sitting room was at the time divided by a settle alongside the open coal fireplace which was very cosy during cold winter months.

I had passed the farmhouse and barn frequently during my younger years when cycling either to the Post Office, to Matthews for shoe repairs or to Darky Lane on a nature mission, without really noticing it. On many occasions I had stopped at the water pump situated on the grass verge opposite their gateway. Set slightly back from the road, it had a rocky soak-away beneath the nozzle. From an early age I had worked the pump handle, simply to see how fast I could get the water flowing. Experience had taught me that there was an ideal pumping speed to prime it and start the column of water rising from the well. Once I could feel the weight of the column of water, I knew that I could increase speed and water would gush from the nozzle producing a torrent like a down pipe in a heavy rain storm. The pump had once been a source of water for the farm and old houses on the high ground behind but now it was looking sad and well worn and was little more than an intrigue for young children.

Bert Rowley was a road maker and repairer and laid asphalt as a business, following in his father's footsteps. One of his biggest jobs during my time with the family was building the roads throughout the Rubery Owen factory complex at Darlaston. Lettie was his bookkeeper. Bert was a joker *par excellence* and the life and sole of any party he was invited to. He frequently had my mom in stitches with his off-the-cuff remarks and actions. Sometimes tears poured down her face as she laughed uncontrollably. When having tea with us one day, he pretended to take out a glass eye and, with a rueful smile, told mom that he was putting it on the cake comport to keep an eye on his cake! No sooner had she finished wiping away the tears, than he picked up the 'eye', sucked it in his mouth, wiped it on his handkerchief and put it back in the socket! Mom couldn't get enough of Bert Rowley's antics and it was a very happy period of our lives.

Our friendship led to our families spending a holiday together at Cleethorpes on the Lincolnshire coast where we had a wonderful holiday. One day, Bert, dad and I decided to walk to a sea fort which was about a half mile from the coast and reachable across the sands at low tide. It was manned by two soldiers and they happily showed us their living quarters, the walls covered with naked pin-ups. They warned us about the speed of the tide. On the way back, we became very conscious of the rate that the tide was coming in and we found ourselves racing at quite a speed to outpace it. When we enlightened our landlady of our morning out, it turned out that we had been rather foolish landlubbers who had not checked tides and could easily have drowned. The episode really shook up Bert and for several days after we returned home, he engaged anyone who would listen about our near miss and his near handshake with his maker.

Margaret Rowley was a pianist, about Grade 6 when I first knew her, but went on to take further exams including the ABSM. She had a most wonderful touch and I spent many happy hours listening to her playing. I suppose these happy interludes led to me, more than ever, wanting to play the piano and organ. After I had conquered the harmonica I would have liked a piano accordion but mom and dad were never able to oblige. In fact there were very few available because the German factories were not yet producing them after the war. Even second-hand accordions were very expensive. Week in, week out, I perused the ads column 'Musical instruments for sale' in the Cannock Advertiser, hoping that an accordion in our price range might appear, but sadly it never did.

Watching Margaret play the piano again stimulated me to try to get a tune out of a piano. Like most people, the only tune I could play was 'Chopsticks' which she in fact had taught me. My first shot at something more occurred in the primary classroom at

Great Wyrley Wesley. After the Sunday School children had left at eleven o'clock, I sat at the piano and tried to play a chord. Singing in the choir gave me an inkling of reading music and I tried to play a harmonious four note chord. The hymn book on the piano was open at the tune 'Quam dilecta' for the hymn 'We love the place O God'. I knew the tune well, having sung it as an introit at every afternoon Sunday School class for several years. But, how do I read the music, let alone play it?

From music lessons in the first year at Queen Mary's, I knew that the lines on the right hand stave were EGBDF and the spaces FACE. Margaret had also given me the mnemonic 'All cows eat grass' (ACEG) for the spaces on the left hand stave. This was my total knowledge of the rudiments of music! Painfully slowly I was able to play the chords of the first bar of Quam dilecta, and they sounded harmonically good. I was inspired to go on and before the congregation came out of church, I was playing the first two lines of the hymn. I was very pleased with my first session and played it on the Rowley's piano later that day. There was no applause or comment and I can only presume that to such a musical family it was no more than 'chopsticks', but it certainly gave me a buzz. I had played something meaningful on the piano!

My Sunday morning sessions at the Sunday School piano became a regular thing. I had never attended the morning church service, always the two Sunday School sessions and the evening service. The problem was that I never did read a note of music and after nearly sixty years playing the piano, this still applies. I learned the chords of most scales and given the key of the piece of music I was, after several years, able to spatially read these within the staves. It has limitations in that it only works for music in chords, such as hymns. I also have to know the timing of the piece of music I am playing, since I have difficulty with this from the manuscript in front of me. Playing the bass line of many hymns helped considerably with harmonising the bass line in the choir and vice versa, so that before long I could play many tunes by ear. I am sure that having piano lessons would have been a great help but there is also a great advantage in playing by ear because it is possible to transpose keys very easily if accompanying singing.

About two years after becoming friendly with Margaret, her piano pieces for the higher exams needed a far better piano than the one currently at Wharwell farm. This meant that Bert Rowley offered the old piano to mum, knowing that I was very interested. Thereafter I was able to play a great deal of church music at home, to which mom would sing whilst doing household chores. In time I was also playing many popular songs, albeit in church-like chords, and it became very useful for sing-songs. The louder people sang, the more they obliterated the sound of any wrong notes! A few good chords to lead into a song and people at full voice will do the rest. I was now also able to fulfil my dream of being able to play a church organ and did so every Sunday in later years after taking over the Superintendent post at Upper Landywood Sunday School. I would have loved to play on the organ at Great Wyrley Wesley, but this was rightly for professionals only.

Bert Rowley liked nothing better than a sing-song and Sunday nights at Wharwell farm were always a delight when we sang music in four parts. Iris Rowley was soprano and Lettie and Margaret were altos. Bert had a natural and beautiful bass voice which filled the room. I could only marvel at the power of his voice and loved to listen and learn from him. He rarely made a mistake when singing informally and yet, singing in the church he could quickly go to pieces when the bass section sang solo. He knew that he normally held we younger bass voices together and presumably saw himself singing solo if we failed, something he always dreaded. I could feel his body next to me beginning to shake as the bass 'solo' approached. Suddenly that hitherto majestic voice had lost its power, momentarily conquered by fear. The other regular stalwart in the bass section was Percy Smith, a more strident bass voice, but accurate and reliable and he always came to the rescue. For a brief period that melodious roundness of the bass line had died. Nevertheless, Bert was soon back on form when the four parts came together again, his body relaxing and his vocal power booting up to normal.

Christmas was fun when members of the choir toured Great Wyrley and Landywood, singing carols in four parts. We generally called at the homes of the older members of the church congregation, some of whom now had difficulties getting to church, but we also visited homes where we might expect a good donation towards church funds. With the latter in mind we also sang at Harrison's club in Wharwell Lane and the Labour Club on Walsall Road, singing two or three carols, receiving both warm applause and donations. As well as the standard Christmas carols; 'O come all ye faithful', 'Silent night', 'Hark the herald angels sing' and 'While shepherds watched (Sweet Chiming Bells)', our forte was 'Hark the glad sound' and other carols arranged by Cornelius Whitehouse, one-time stalwart of Salem Methodist Church in Cheslyn Hay. His tunes were fun to sing and, for us, had jolly bass lines which we could belt out. In early years on such a tour, Bert would put his arm round my shoulder singing the bass line close to my ear, so that I could pick up the note, and then conduct the beat with his free hand. It was a great tutorship and I have always been thankful for his guiding hand. I felt great uplift in later years when I was able to commit full voice to the carols and a very strong feeling for the Almighty, particularly the new Christ child. On the occasional frosty December night, the lanterns we carried shone through our breath as it condensed into cumulus clouds around the group and ice particles condensed on the scarves around our faces. On such clear nights the stars always seemed brighter than ever and the brilliant planet Jupiter could easily have been the 'Star in the East' which had heralded the birth of the new Child. We were celebrating this wondrous event and we gave everything in our joyous exclamation. An occasional mince pie and a cup of tea, sometimes a glass of sherry (even for a Methodist!), was always welcome and lubricated our voices as we moved from house to house.

CHAPTER 18

'Sixth form - c. 1949 - 51'

At school, in June 1949, I knew I had performed much better in my second take of School Certificate and was now expecting to enter the sixth form after the long vacation where I would study Physics, Chemistry and Maths, my best subjects. Or at least, this was my intention, but during the last fortnight of the school year, 'Chad' (Mr Chadburn) came into the classroom and said,

"Will those who are studying biology in the sixth form please go immediately to the girls school (Queen Mary's High School for girls) next door."

I had not even considered this subject and I had certainly not been given details of the course next door. Obviously those who were working towards medicine or other life sciences as a career had been given details since biology was a requirement for a university place. Since I was considering an electrical engineering degree at university, I needed Physics and Mathematics and would continue Chemistry.

Chad's words had an electric effect! Having spent many years very close to nature, without even thinking, I followed the half dozen boys who were filing out of the classroom. It was a spontaneous decision made in what can only be described as a flash of inspiration and it was to change the rest of my life. Within months, biology would become my strongest subject and I grew very passionate about it.

In that preliminary gathering we met Miss Eld, 'Piggy' was her nick name, who outlined the next two years. It sounded great. In essence, she told us, the course would be divided into botany and zoology each with both theoretical and practical components and would also include field studies. Somehow, I immediately knew that I had done the right thing and I returned to the boy's school in a very happy frame of mind.

Come mid-August, the postman delivered the exam results and I had managed a decent School Certificate result. Geography my new subject for the re-take brought me a distinction to add to the science subjects. I was really looking forward to the Sixth form and studying biology, physics and chemistry.

On our first day at Queen Mary's High, we joined the girls also taking biology at sixth form level, in the laboratory. We were each provided with our own microscope for the duration of the course. Tony Wiggin brought in a Victorian brass binocular microscope which was about twice as large as the standard issue and obviously a statement of one-upmanship. Incidentally, in later years he became biology master at Queen Mary's boy's school. Piggy Eld proved to be an outstanding teacher and I could not get enough of her. She was forthright and had a considerable understanding of her subject. Coverage of the syllabus was important to her but she also took us down avenues of the latest research on a given subject.

Physics was taught by Mr Chadburn, again an outstanding master and teacher who, through his neat use of the blackboard, was able to clarify the most difficult physical topics. It must have been very difficult for him because one half of his class was studying mathematics and were therefore fully conversant with calculus, important in the theory of physics, whereas we, the biologists, had no such knowledge. And yet he gave extra time to us and explained the same theory in the terms that we could understand. He never baulked when he was waxing lyrical in calculus and we told him that we did not understand. It may seem repetitive but I say again, he was outstanding. I meticulously copied his blackboard notes and often annotated my notes in the margin whenever he gave some modern analogy to explain a theory, particularly where this 'aside' had helped me to understand. My carefully constructed notes later proved to be ideal for examination revision and my marginal notes and cartoons somehow allowed me to visualise and re-live the moment that Chad had stood before us and explained that topic.

Chemistry, hitherto my strongest subject and taught by Maggie Mason, was now taught by a master of Australian origin whose name eludes me. He was late middle-aged and obviously had some years in the subject behind him, but he never really had full control of his class. In fact, we were able to use chemicals which we had no right to use without full supervision and which were positively dangerous, particularly those on the top shelf in the store room which did not appear to have been opened for decades and which inquisitive teenagers simply had to open. Nevertheless, he was a good chemistry master and we learnt a lot. The course was covered comprehensively and we became very competent in the laboratory.

For the first time since I had entered the school in 1943, I was thoroughly enjoying every lesson. Gone were those dreadful subjects that I had abhorred in earlier years! The syllabuses were certainly much more difficult but it was like being in heaven. Experimentation in all three laboratories took us to very advanced levels. Chemistry was quite analytical. We analysed unknown substances and were expected to deduce what they were. In Physics, experiments in light, sound and thermodynamics were to a very high level of accuracy. I look back with trepidation at some of the chemicals we were using at the time. Concentrated acids were dangerous enough, but aqua regia and hydrofluoric acid (used for cleaning glass) were exceptionally destructive of anything they came in contact with but we were now sixth formers and considered responsible. In Biology, we prepared plant tissues with cut throat razors and stained them for microscopy. We dissected a frog, rabbit and dogfish to learn their anatomy. Obviously all were backed up by demanding theoretical issues, but I adored it!

During this time, mom asked a favour of me on behalf of members of Upper Landywood Church, where she attended evening services. They asked if I would consider taking over their Sunday School. It had apparently not been successful since Philip West had had to retire and passed away. A few children still attending from around the village were currently being taught by Mrs Harper, a member of the church, from Long Lane, Essington. (She was mother of Betty Harper, who had been in my class at Landywood School.) Unfortunately she had other commitments and was having difficulty giving consistent time to the Sunday school. Other church members were at times left to soldier on and did not feel qualified to do so. At this time I was fully trained by Grace

Smith and accepted the challenge. Another advantage was that I was by now playing hymns fairly well on the piano at home and could therefore provide accompaniment, where they were currently managing without. I had attended the Sunday school for several years and knew the church well and knew that music was provided by a large two-manual harmonium.

I suppose about a dozen children attended my first school at 11 a.m. on the first Sunday morning. There were no Methodist Church teacher's preparation books there and hence I was obliged to construct my own services which included children's hymns, prayers, readings and a story, usually based on some human endeavour, with a Christian theme. I found the organ quite exhilarating and very soon had it tamed. With knee swells fully extended and plenty of fast pedaling, it had enormous power and an excellent tone. I was thankful for the knowledge I had gleaned from pedaling the harmonium at Colin Parson's home when younger. I was a little limited in that some hymns I could play and others not, but had a repertoire of about twenty which allowed me to get by. With the organ as accompaniment, the children always sang very well and seemed to enjoy singing. After a few months, obviously word had got around and attendances were frequently nearer to two dozen. We had two Sunday School services, morning and afternoon, which meant that during this period I could only attend the Sunday evening services at Great Wyrley Wesley but also continued to attend the week-day meetings there. It was a period when I was also working hard for my higher exams but I succeeded in finding time for both. (I continued to conduct the Sunday Schools at Upper Landywood until my commitments at Medical School in the mid 1950s demanded more week-end work, by which time some of the children were now teenagers. The school was then taken over by Jim Alden who had moved from Hilton Lane to live in the new houses in upper Street's Lane.)

During my first year in the sixth form, we in the Air Training Corps joined the Junior Training Corps (army) and became the Queen Mary's Combined Cadet Force. We were also introduced to an enthusiastic new RAF officer in Mr Dickson who had recently started at Queen Mary's. I was now promoted to the rank of corporal as a drill instructor, training first year air and army cadets. This new authority led to me growing in stature. I suppose I had control of a 'band of men', albeit initially thirteen year old boys, and I gave my all to my new job. It eventually led to me rising through the ranks over the next two years, sergeant and eventually flight sergeant. As the latter, I was fortunate enough, on at least two occasions, to command the whole of the parade, during the Commanding Officer's inspection. It was an awesome experience to hear the explosive blast of about two hundred boots on tarmac as they came to attention - on my command!

In the classroom, we worked hard towards attaining 'A' levels in the General Certificate of Education (which at this time had replaced Higher School Certificate). With such intensity of study, I suppose it was inevitable that sometimes anarchy would overshadow decorum. Let's instead call it light relief from the more serious matters, for this was how we saw it when we rummaged on the top shelves of the store room in the chemistry laboratory and found new reagents. These finds led to us creating substances we were not supposed to. Our Australian chemistry master, unlike his strict predecessor, seemed to think that no harm could come from allowing sixth formers into the store room, but he hadn't reckoned on inquisitive minds. On two occasions following our rummages, we created substances which were certainly not part of the Chemistry syllabus. The most dangerous, I suppose, was nitrogen tri-iodide, an explosive compound very simply made using an ammonium salt and iodine and filtering the solution. The dark residue on the filter paper was nitrogen tri-iodide which was stable whilst wet, but foolishly we took the residue back to the classroom to dry over a radiator during a double physics lesson with Chad. Tony Wiggin sat closest to the paper and, about half way through the lesson, he thought he heard it crackling and turned round frantically signalling to us. Whilst Mr Chadburn was writing on the blackboard, Tony lifted his desk and walked it into a space about six feet away. Fortunately the school bell rang and in the gap between the twin lesson, he ran out of the classroom with the filter paper and soaked it in a hand basin to prevent further problems.

The lesson resumed, but every time Chad walked from his desk to the blackboard, there was a resounding crack under his feet. The explosive had obviously scattered as Tony ran out with the dry filter paper. Chad tolerated this for a while and then turned to us, his face looking extremely stern.

"I can only assume that someone has been making nitrogen tri-iodide", he said gravely, "On this occasion I shall simply say that should it occur again, I shall not overlook it and someone could be expelled from school!"

We blushed and then the colour drained from our cheeks, in rapid succession. My heart was madly pounding. How close was that? After the lesson we could only admire Chad for the fair way he had treated us. He had probably done the same thing at our age, but knew how dangerous this explosive substance was and had given us fair warning which we respected. We never manufactured it again.

Our other illegal substance was phenyl iso-cyanide, a compound with a nauseating and obnoxious smell. It was finding old sealed bottles of phenyl hydrazine on the top shelf which led to this one. Why had these been ordered by Maggie Mason but never used? It was a conundrum which needed further investigation. We searched through a textbook to see what it might be used for and came up with the manufacture of phenyl iso-cyanide. On removing the sealed stopper of one bottle of phenyl hydrazine we were blasted, like a bottle of champagne, with a very pungent vapour ten times worse than smelling salts, which half blinded us. A mixture of several chemicals led to the manufacture of phenyl iso-cyanide which had a terrible smell which made us retch and was like nothing I had ever smelled before. Bad egg gas (hydrogen sulphide) had nothing on it! The product was carefully stored in a corked test tube awaiting a quarry and the chance for use arose in an unusual place.

As a nation, we were still rationed for many items required for daily living, though as I entered the sixth form, at least clothes rationing was taken off the list, which certainly cheered up mom. Sweets and chocolates remained on the list, along with meat and petrol. We had a three month respite at this time with sweets, but within three months they were put back on the list! The meat ration was in fact worsening and we were each allowed about ten pence (4p), equivalent to about four to six ounces (100–180g) of reasonable meat per week. It would have needed a family with about a dozen ration books to buy a leg of lamb! This ration fell even more over the next year or so! We were thankful that we had a pig to support our small ration. Petrol was rationed and also this year increased in price by tuppence halfpenny (1p) to just over two shillings (10p) per gallon.

1949 was also the year that the Wolves beat Leicester City 3-1 in the FA Cup. Most of my friends were Wolves supporters and we were elated. The queue outside Burkes' newspaper shop was about thirty feet (10m) long when I cycled down to collect dad's copy of Express and Star Sports newspaper. People were waving the paper in the air, displaying the headline, 'IT'S OURS'! I am sure we all read every letter of the match coverage several times over.

During the summer vacation, the Air Force section (of the school Combined Cadet Force) attended the annual camp at RAF Hullavington in Wiltshire (on the Salisbury Plain). Groups from several schools were camped in parallel lines of six-man tents. Our line was adjacent to a rather stuck-up school from Surrey and they proved a little hard to swallow. It was not uncommon to come back from the NAAFI and find we had to re-pitch our tents and collect our belongings which were strewn around the field. Our first revenge attack was phenyl iso-cyanide, a test tube of which I had taken wrapped in clothing in my case. We carefully sprinkled some the obnoxious stuff into their straw-filled pillows and palliasses. Unfortunately it did not have the desired effect. Yes, they noticed a foul smell but put it down to body odour or something and set about refilling their beds with fresh straw! Our hope to see them retching and bringing back their evening meal, was never fulfilled!

Our second chance for revenge came a day or so later. We played cricket with them most evenings after work, using as wickets the red fire extinguishers, placed in pairs at regular intervals in the aisles between rows of tents. Two of us had previously had a nose inside one of them by unscrewing the brass cap, revealing a glass acid capsule which was broken by the plunger to create carbon dioxide foam when it mixed with the contents.

The weather was very hot and after marching from venue to venue, we looked forward during the evenings to a rest and a pint of still (lime juice) in the NAAFI. It was here that we hatched a plot which would involve removing of the acid capsule from one of the pair of extinguishers we used as wickets. This we did during the next afternoon and come the early evening we played cricket as usual with the Surrey contingent, choosing to bat first. During his innings our opening bat 'accidentally' clouted the plunger of doctored extinguisher and pointedly remarked, "That was lucky, thank God it was a dud!" Thereafter each of us at some point during our innings gave the plunger a smack and pulled it out again.

We changed innings and took our place on the field. Early on in their innings our wicket keeper 'carelessly' knocked over the pair of extinguishers whilst pretending to stump someone, all according to plan! He replaced them, switching them in the process! It was around their fourth man that gave the plunger a clout! Within a second or two, a jet of foam covered them, but even worse it sprayed their commanding officer's open tent. Unfortunately he had laid out his dress uniform for a do in the officer's mess that evening and it was well and truly enveloped by about twelve inches (30cm) of foam! We tried very hard to keep a straight face as they buzzed around like Spitfires in a dog fight, struggling to turn the spray away from the CO's tent and then nervously discussing who was going to break the bad news to him. They had not seemed to grasp that they had been set up!

A highlight of this particular annual camp was a flight in a Lancaster bomber (of Dam busters fame). We were making our way from RAF Lyneham, nearby, to RAF Cranwell in Lincolnshire to see the passing-out parade of new RAF officers. It was a distance of 200 miles and each of us sat in the various seats used by the wartime crews since there were no formal seats. Some sat in the gun turret positions. I was asked to occupy the bomb-aimers position. There was no seat, simply a pad on which I could lie on my trunk, but I had a bird's eye view of the country as we passed over it. Although wearing an overcoat, we were flying at about 10,000 feet and it was very cold. I was absolutely frozen which took away some of the enjoyment but I convinced myself that very few teenagers will have had this the experience and this made my shivering body a little more bearable. We attended the passing out parade at Cranwell and returned in the same Lancaster to Hullavington. This time I swapped positions to allow someone else to get the view below but was unable to get a gun turret position which must have been fun! Our next flight from Lyneham was in an Avro York transport plane, a rather bulky beast with fuselage almost touching the ground. It was only a short flight over the English Channel and back and I presume this plane was used because it could seat about half of those at annual camp. I was sitting about six feet from its truly enormous wheels and, during landing, I was gob-smacked at the immense streak of dense smoke and flames from rubber as we touched the landing strip. In all it proved to be a camp of great comradeship and we learned a considerable amount about the Royal Air Force.

Since I had proved to be a good shot on our range at Moss Close, I was chosen during autumn to represent the school at Hawarden near Chester. Five or six schools were represented there and we were shooting at targets at a thousand and fifteen hundred feet (300metres and 500metres) using standard .303 army rifles. The problem was, on the day of the contest, the range was covered by dense sea mist which allowed only occasional glimpses of the target, and it was almost impossible to say whose target had come into view. We were on our bellies on a sodden grassy knoll firing in our own time and every slight waft of wind which gave a brief sight of a target was accompanied by a volley of shots from the six rifles on the firing line. My final score was appalling due, I told myself, to the fact that my bull's eyes were on someone else's target, optimistically assuming that I had actually hit the target at these distances! The train journey home was extremely miserable, partly because I felt that I had let the school down and also due to the fact that I was sporting a very wet bedraggled uniform.

I was fortunate to go on another school trip in May 1950, this time a biology field trip to Flatford Mill, at East Bergholt in Suffolk. Being John Constable country, it was stimulating to see the somewhat damp and decaying Willy Lot's cottage, depicted in Constable's 'Haywain' and to stand at the point where he had stood to paint it. We were accommodated in the mill house which housed about twenty biology students in two dormitories and had a lecture and study room. The boy's beds were on the upper floor and the girls on the lower. There were fairly wide cracks between the floor boards of our dorm which proved quite revealing when some of the more extrovert girls prepared for bed, certainly to a group of testosterone-charged boys. Just a brief flash of a naked breast led to audible gasps from we voyeurs and we struggled with the crotches of our trousers to make room for rapidly tumescing penises which craved more space. We looked at each other incredulously, not believing our luck, but the lights below were immediately switched off, damn it! Our stay at the mill was to be a week of hard work and study but might there at least be some light relief at the end of each day? These were the whispers between us as we made ready to sleep. It was not to be, it seems that the girls had either spotted their revealing ceiling, perhaps a chink of light, or had been tipped off, and thereafter they were more careful where they undressed.

Work in the field was quite intense, plotting botanical transects and quadrats of areas of countryside around Flatford mill, recognising and correctly labelling each plant at regular intervals. Back at base, the field work was meticulously written up with appropriate diagrams. There were then discussions in groups at the end of the day with specialist tutors. A trip to the local marshes and to Orford Ness to see the large variety of waterfowl was inspirational and I was staggered by the vast numbers of sheld ducks, which were never seen around home. One trip was sadly marred when on the mudflats we noticed a swan with a severe compound fracture of its wing after flying into overhead power lines. The son of the warden, who was leading the expedition, went back to his jeep and returned with a shot gun. A shot on the move from fifty yards scored a direct hit at the back of the head and the swan was put out of its misery. We thought the swan was going to be left to scavengers, but the marksman had other ideas. He dragged the corpse back to his van and on the last evening we had roast swan for our evening meal. It was not the most flavoursome meal and rather tough, but it had not had time to hang and the chef was probably not used to preparing swan. It was a talking point for some time because of the novelty and in view of the laws relating swans.

On the last evening we held a party in Willy Lot's cottage playing the usual party games since there was no music. 'Spinning the bottle' has always brought boys and girls together and someone was placed on the light switch to allow the couple to kiss in darkness. Invariably the lights were turned on at the height of a passionate snog and a hand ferreting in clothing, to the raucous howls from the rest of the party. I had my moment and then spun the bottle which fixed on Margaret Aldridge. As we clinched, the lights went out. A few moments later, the door of the cottage burst open and standing there in her dressing gown and holding a paraffin lantern like Florence Nightingale was Piggy Eld, our biology mistress. She was very angry by what she saw and ordered us all back to our beds. She made no comment next day as we mounted the coach for home but for some time thereafter I felt a little sheepish in her presence.

As part of our continuing development, Chad insisted that we must all deliver a lecture to Science Sixth during our second year, on any topic of our choice. By now I had been preparing and delivering sermons as part of the Church Youth Group and was not particularly phased by this thought. One of the first lectures of the year was given by Philip Gray and his chosen subject was colour photography. At this point in time, it was virtually impossible to obtain Kodak colour film and, even then, only at a price. Philip's father had been able to acquire the film and had taken some outstanding colour images of everyday things, particularly garden flowers which seemed to have three dimensions. I was stunned by the sheer beauty of these images and Philip set about explaining the underlying science and processing of Kodachrome film. It was an outstanding start to the year's lectures and set a level we must all strive to achieve.

I searched the library for an interesting subject which would cover new ground for my peers and eventually stumbled on the world problem with malaria. I read in depth and found the work done by Manson and Ross some fifty years earlier on the life cycle of the malaria parasite particularly enlightening. It clearly explained how the disease was spread to man by the anopheles mosquito. I was able to draw posters as lecture aids since I did not have slides. Luckily the lecture went well and the subject seemed to be enjoyed by everyone. Chad, in debriefing me, told me that he was surprised by my authority in front of a class as he had always considered me a somewhat reserved person. He had obviously not seen me on the parade ground! Nevertheless, this coming from him, whom I revered, gave great impetus to my persona.

I thoroughly enjoyed the advanced physics taught by him and it explained many issues I had previously wondered about. One modern topic not in our syllabus still puzzled me, the power of the atomic bomb. This had a year or two earlier devastated two cities in Japan and it had proved so overwhelming that Japan had conceded. The power of the bombs was very much at the forefront of media articles in the first few years after the war, and particularly the ethics of atomic bombs. At the time it was largely hush-hush. I had heard of 'chain reaction' but did not really understand. I then managed to find a book in Walsall public library which explained the design of the bomb. As I read on, it seemed beyond comprehension that two pieces of uranium, weighing a few pounds each, could be smashed together to create an explosion which caused such devastation, an explosion thousands of times bigger than that created by the largest bombs dropped on German targets, such as battleship Turpitz. The reason for the chain reaction was not fully explained and still eluded me but it was a frightening thought for the future of mankind.

Whilst on the subject of explosions, the family at this time experienced another bombshell when uncle Bob found himself a new lady, thought to be an associate from his workplace. It was not sufficient for him to secretly visit her at her home near Brewood, or even in his car down some leafy lane, instead he chose to move her into the front room of the bungalow. He had always been an introvert individual, keeping his private life to himself and mom knew he had always gone out of his way to make sure that she never knew what was going on, but this fiasco was the last thing she expected. Aunt Sarah was understandably very distressed by this cuckoo in her nest. She had lived her life serving her husband to the best of her ability, at times frightened of him. She could never be considered an attractive woman and certainly never purchased new clothes to raise her image, whereas the new lady was attractive and did dress to kill. In view of her lifelong subservience and fear, aunt Sarah could never have challenged him. He had offended her in public on too many occasions. Grandma and mom were incensed by these events and were feeling deeply for aunt Sarah's heartbreak. Grandma, the matriarch, had obviously had words with granddad and the next thing we were aware of was granddad banging on the front window with a house brick, shouting at the woman to leave the house immediately. In the process a large pane of glass was broken and it must have seemed to the lady like a vigilante attack. Uncle Bob was at work at the time. When he returned home and heard and saw what had happened, he set about taking his newly found lady home to Brewood. I am not aware of what was said and I suspect under normal circumstances uncle Bob would have put up a fight with granddad, but the lady was probably frightened out of her wits by what might happen if she stayed there. It seemed to do the trick and normality was restored. Uncle Bob appeared to have cowered to granddad's attack and I think that was the end of the relationship.

A month or so later, perhaps as an act of retribution by the Almighty, he was smitten with very painful piles. Dr Middleton came to see him at home and diagnosed large prolapsed and thrombosed haemorrhoids (piles). The sight was apparently so fascinating to a medical man that he immediately returned home to collect his son Baron, in his final years at Medical School, to see the bunch of 'juicy black grapes' projecting from uncle Bob's backside. The latter agreed that an eager Baron Middleton could examine him and both medics concluded that it was job for the hospital, where he spent the next week or so.

After these episodes he put his energies into his bungalow, spending most of the winter removing rotten wood from his bay windows. I was very impressed by the job he made. New pieces of timber were expertly let in to replace the decay, all carefully dowelled and glued. An antique furniture restorer would have been very proud of his workmanship. His next project was to enhance his front garden with square concrete plant holders on pedestals, set at the corners of the lawn. He designed and built them himself, creating the wooden mould in which they were cast. They looked very attractive, particularly when planted with geraniums. Mom fell for them hook, line and sinker, and next year decided she would like something similar on our front. I knew I could make them but told her I was concerned because he would obviously charge us with copying, which would of course be true. However, after thinking about it, I relented because he was not my favourite uncle and it would give him something else to chunter about. After some thought, I designed and constructed pentagonal concrete planters on pedestals (rather than square) which would hold more compost. I think when he saw my design, he realised it was technically more complex, and essentially moaned to grandma on one of her visits that, whatever the shape, I had copied his idea. I was not proud of this but mom thought her planters were great and I suppose that was all that mattered!

Margaret Rowley and I were an item for about two years and I had become quite close to her family. I visited Wharwell farm regularly and also visited Margaret's uncles and aunts. Her mother, Lettie, was a kind lady but also authoritative. This may have come from her lineage in the Wood family. Her brother Oliver was managing director of a wholesale grocery business in Bridgetown and lived in the large house on the corner of North Street and Walsall Road with a warehouse in the grounds. I referred to him earlier with regard to his concert parties around Cannock Chase venues. Parties at his house were great fun and his house had the added advantage of a snooker room with full-sized table, my first experience of the game, which Bert Rowley taught me. Oliver and Lettie's sister, aunt Ruby Wood, lived in Norton Canes and Margaret and I occasionally cycled there to visit her. She had taught Margaret to play the piano in her early years. I have already said that I never had music lessons, but there is little doubt of the enormous impact the family had on me, which led to some semblance of playing the piano and organ all my adult life. On one occasion, I was playing on Margaret's piano when I could just about knock up a tune. Lettie was upstairs resting in bed with a virus illness. I was suddenly aware of banging on the floor above me and a booming voice letting me know that I was playing the last bar wrong! I presume it was grinding on a thick head associated with her fever. My association with the family was an extremely enjoyable period of my life.

With regard to our relationship, Margaret decided to go her own way in the summer of 1951. She felt that since I would be going to Leicester in the autumn, we would spend a great deal of time apart and should not be tied to each other. In reality, I think she had recently met her future husband, Keith Barnett, and was smitten. In other words, I was being dumped! The separation did hurt and I shed a few tears but I knew I would be spending time away from home for at least three years and had to be realistic. At the time I had feelings for Jean Gunn since we often went to school together and had similar interests. We were both aware of our closeness but it was no more than that. She was at the time in a strong relationship with Eric Till and I did not feel it would be gentlemanly to take my feelings further. She was going on to Nursing School at Wolverhampton Royal Hospital for a career in nursing. Since I had been praised by Piggy Eld (biology mistress) for the quality of my dissections of animals, I promised Jean that I would get a rabbit and dissect it to demonstrate animal anatomy to her. It would help in her study of human anatomy in nursing school. First of all, I had to get a rabbit.

At the time I knew of Janet Bourne as someone around church but we had never really spoken to each other. In fact she had been around since Landywood school days, though in a class two years younger. We were never in the same group, she had her friends and I had mine. It was mom who pointed out what a nice girl she was and after reflecting on the times I had noticed her, I set about trying to strike up an acquaintanceship. I was not sure how to set about it. I could I suppose have joined in a conversation in the youth club but decided instead on laying in wait and innocently crossing her path, as it were. I waited at the top of Jones' Lane where I had a view of the Walsall bus stop and her grandma's, Liza Sambrook's, shop. Janet came out of the house and I crossed the road and casually struck up a conversation with her. She agreed to go for a walk down Jones' Lane and it was the beginning of a long relationship (we have been together about sixty years in all). Janet was also going on to study Radiography in Walsall hospitals and it seemed sensible to demonstrate animal anatomy to her also. During the school holiday we spent an afternoon searching the hills around the Grove pit for a rabbit, without success. In the end I used a domestic rabbit for an anatomy demonstration for Jean but Janet is still waiting!

All of us remained close friends for several more years at Wyrley Wesley, mostly now at week-ends only, continuing with the Youth Group, Youth Club, choral singing and so on. Eventually some several years later we were obliged to go our separate ways as we qualified in our professions.

In August 1951, I received good news. I had passed my 'A levels' with excellent grades. Although I had a place in Leicester University to study Pharmacy, I suddenly realised that it was not what I wanted to do. Piggy Eld had remarked how excellent my animal dissections were and felt that I would be better looking at medicine or surgery as a career. I decided, therefore, to wait another year and try for a place in these subjects. Friends Bram Davis and Philip Gray were going to Birmingham Medical School this year. I spoke to Miss Eld who agreed to teach me advanced Zoology and Botany for the year. In the CCF I told Mr Dickson of my arrangements and he was happy to let me continue as Staff Sergeant and hoped I might make Warrant Officer during the year. I was happy to do the extra year and started work. On my first visit to Miss Eld, she came up with an idea. Often people given university places fail to obtain the necessary grades, why didn't I approach Birmingham to see if they had a place for this year. I did so and was immediately called for interview. I was given a place to study medicine immediately and joined Bram and Philip.

At church, it was around this time that a stranger appeared on the scene. I had heard about Peter Turner, son of William (Bill) Turner our Sunday School superintendent, from Miss Liddle during my years at Landywood school, as I have mentioned earlier. He had spent most of his early life in Coleshill hospital. Peter suffered from osteogenesis imperfecta, he was to tell me later, and in his early life many of his bones had fractured with only minor stresses. Although his bones had strengthened with age, his legs had been severely damaged by the multiple childhood trauma. He turned up to church on a truck, not dissimilar to those we used to build, but driven by an overhead pedal crank and chain which he pedaled with his hands. It was a great example of what could be created for mobility, before wheelchairs for the disabled became more commonplace. Peter was able to get around the village like an F1 driver and became a very active member of both church and, in later years, village life, where he became a local councillor.

CHAPTER 19

A eulogy to the local countryside as it was

The chronicle of my early life is almost complete. I have already described the countryside at some length but, even at the expense of repeating myself, it will bear fuller description.

At the outset, I am sad; saddened that the generations that have followed have not witnessed their countryside as I knew it. My 'Song of Spring', conveying the lyrics of my early life, had a joyous melody but, come early 'summer', there was crashing discord. Mechanical excavators were ripping the heart out of the area and in seconds (it seemed) the hedgerows, fields and streams, brimming with nature, were gone. Later still, the change in farming with the use of herbicide, meant that areas spared of opencast mining were also in trouble.

Not everything had been rosy. Some meadows in my early life did contain a small shale heap here and there, reflecting shallow coal mining, but it had not significantly changed the general flora and fauna. Land scarred in this way was already being reclaimed by new vegetation, and even by rabbits for their warrens. Some areas were more seriously damaged where shale had been spread over natural soil, thereby creating semi-barren fields. Such were the Coalpit field in Cheslyn Hay, a field between Hazel Lane and Jones' Lane and Whitehouse's field adjacent to Street's Lane in Upper Landywood. The surface of these fields was too poor for productive farming and they lay fallow, awaiting the time when nature might reclaim them. Other monuments to our past which scarred the area (referred to earlier) were the brick domes over unfilled mine shafts, the mountains of shale and the unused mineral lines. These might be considered blots on the canvas but around them was a natural landscape which an artist like Constable would have been proud to paint.

The level of opencast mining in the 1950s and 1960s was as defiling as any rape. The vital structure of the earth, which had taken millions of years in creation, was lost forever, sadly replaced by a mishmash of earth from deeper layers. Gone were the superficial sponges and clay layers which for thousands of years had fed clear running streams. Gone were the hedgerows and mature trees, to be replaced by third rate fencing. Gone were the myriad of creatures that lived in the haven that was.

As I have walked or driven the patch in subsequent years, the sight of essentially barren fields and sterile fences has hurt terribly. Coal was without doubt needed after World War II to revitalise industry and get Britain moving again, but opencast mining of the type then practised, was sheer recklessness. The violation had started opposite Landywood school, my school, and thereafter spread like wildfire throughout the adjacent countryside. An area desecrated very badly was Jones' Lane as enormous caterpillar land scrapers removed layer after layer of the earth from some eight to ten meadows and cereal fields and piled it in heaps around the perimeter. It was very much part of my playground and was now gone. Let me walk you down the lane as it was.

At the top of Jones' lane on Walsall Road, the Memorial Gates named men from the village who served and died fighting in World War I, forever remembered annually with a parade along Walsall Road and a Remembrance Service. The gates, which were normally locked, were the entrance to nicely laid-out gardens and the drive extended down towards the recreation ground.

On the left, a few yards down the lane, was the gate to the playing field which we also used as access to the recreation ground in the far corner of the field. Opposite this was an elongated meadow sometimes used as a football field, surrounded by unkempt tall hawthorn hedges and a bird's paradise. On a chilly morning, hundreds of beaded necklaces, the result of dew on spider's webs, stretched between boughs already hanging heavy with a bountiful supply of red berries. It was the field used from 1951 for Bank Holiday shows. It had replaced the field used for this purpose after the war on the corner of Hilton Lane and Landywood Lane, behind Bullock's cottage. The fields were the termination for carnival parades, where the judging of entrants took place. A parade would start a distance away and slowly progress via several lanes through the village. Usually two or three vehicles, lorries or farm carts, had been decorated in a theme and were interspersed in a parade of individuals dressed in DIY costumes. In the early years after the war, children dressed as war figures, Churchill, squander bugs, members of the armed forces (using dad's uniform) and so on. Various categories, embracing young to old were judged and received a prize, about three shillings (15p) for the winner down to one shilling (5p) for third place. At both showgrounds, there were side shows, but the latter also had a track laid out for races and a large marquee which housed the village horticultural and crafts show.

Dad usually supported the local show by sending produce to the horticultural section, but good as his flowers and vegetables were, so much was sold at the door that the residue rarely met the standard for a prize. There were always 'professional' showmen who exhibited around the Midlands and invariably won the top prizes. Year in, year out, the same names would appear on the red winner's ticket. It was impossible for the average village gardener to find, for instance, six identical tomatoes. They would need to be collected from several greenhouses to meet perfection. The professionals were able to do this, as I described with Tom Farrington's dahlias, hence their frequent wins. Granddad's long runner beans won on one occasion and I managed to win first prize with three white gladioli which was a reasonable result when showing alongside the 'pros'.

It was in the crafts' section of the same marquee in 1953, a year or two after my chronicle ends, that cousin Ron exhibited his early art work and started to win prizes. In the same show, I entered a swan, using a framework of wire-netting and decorating it with white Esther Reads (double marguerites) which I think took first prize.

At most shows, during the afternoon, various events had been organised, races (including the inevitable three-legged, egg and spoon and sack races for various categories and ages) and also professional displays. My prowess in these races over the several years of village shows amounted to winning one egg and spoon and one sack race! The 1953 show was possibly the last held in this field before the National Coal Board took up residence when I think the main event was a motor cycle display.

Further down Jones' lane on the left was the red clay tennis court and pavilion which had probably been built in around 1920, presumably by Harrison's Mining Company. It was a very professional looking court and had obviously been used by skilled and amateur players in the 1920s and 1930s. Jim and Elsie Sambrook (children of Liza, of the shop) and Dr Reggie Tomkinson (Cheslyn Hay GP) were active members. By the beginning of the war it was used only rarely and then not at all as tennis racquets and rubber balls became difficult to obtain. Serious tennis never seemed to take off again after the war and the pavilion and court lay fallow until the National Coal Board destroyed it during opencast mining.

Harrison's cricket ground, just below it, also had quite a large pavilion and a field the size of an average village cricket pitch. A few seats and benches were available but we mostly sat on the grass. It was a reasonably professional looking ground, well maintained in my early years and used for several years after the war until the rape of Jones' lane.

Further down the lane, several fields on my right across to Jacob's Hall Lane were used for arable farming, all surrounded by good hedgerows for wildlife which included large trees. Hedgerows throughout the village were a mix of hawthorn, hazel, elder, blackthorn, holly and oak with scattered briars and dog roses. The commoner trees were oak, ash, elm, beech, sycamore and birch. On the opposite side of Jones' lane was a very large wheat field followed by an area of scrub land, levelled shale and clinker from earlier mining. The latter extended down to Slackey (Hazel) Lane and was surrounded on all sides by a forty two inch (1.1 metre) fence of metal railings, typically used around areas of superficial mining over the previous century. There were several such fences around, including Street's Lane, representing now aborted mining activity in the villages. The land within only grew more resilient plants such as ox-eye daisy, ragwort, groundsel and willowherbs, though the latter looked very anaemic compared with their tall healthy siblings in more fertile areas down the lane. These flowers were scattered amongst tussocks of hardy grasses and saplings of common hedgerow shrubs, such as hawthorn, blackthorn and gorse. Ground tracking bramble fruited with quite tart blackberries.

About three hundred yards (280m) further on (in those days), Jones' Lane was joined by Jacob's Hall lane and a little way up the latter, Darky lane, a favourite haunt of mine. Continuing along the lane we pass the fast running stream which we usually called Mac's (Gain's) brook running beneath a low bridge with brick parapets. The land adjacent to the stream was marshy and grew a wealth of marshland flowers, and was alive with all types of flying insect, including large dragon flies, damsel flies and butterflies. Water creatures abounded, particularly sticklebacks, crayfish, water snails, crested newts, frogs, caddis fly larvae and so on. I spent many a happy hour lifting large stones and trawling this stream. Beyond this was the bridge beneath which the hawser driven tubs ran between the Sinkin' and the Grove pit on the edge of Pelsall common and the linesman's hut adjacent.

At the bend in Jones' lane, we can walk straight ahead through the gipsy gardens (Gain's lane) or bear right towards Little Wyrley and the Grove pit. The gardens were so called because the wide area along the first hundred yards (100m) of the lane periodically accommodated about a dozen gipsy caravans, each housing a large family. Smoke issuing from the chimneys and outdoor braziers sometimes created a stinky fog in the lane.

Women could be seen cooking or boiling clothes on the braziers. Others stripped bark from hazel sticks and men split them and shaped them with sharp knives to create washing-line pegs. Two halves of a peg were bound together by a thin strip of metal (one eighth inch (3mm)) cut from used food cans, wrapped around and held by a single tack. Gipsy women regularly toured houses, asking sixpence (2.5p) for a bundle of a dozen pegs or an artificial chrysanthemum, again created from hazel sticks and dyed various colours. Mom always bought something because she was concerned that the lady might put a curse on her. When young and alone I was terrified to cycle past the gipsy gardens and would only do so when there were two or three of us. Mom had impressed on me not to go there since gipsies were known to kidnap young boys and this warning stuck with me for a long time!

Just beyond the gipsy gardens, on the right, is a meadow which in Spring has the largest array of lady smocks around and mom always gasped when she saw them in bloom. Then to the Watling Street (A5) which I frequently crossed and cycled on into Norton Canes village and beyond.

I chose to walk down Jones' lane but the picture I have described is representative of most lanes on my patch, including Street's lane where I lived, and I found great happiness in life's gifts around me. I suppose I was fortunate to have learned to enjoy them at an early age from Miss Liddle and it was enhanced later when I formally studied Botany and Zoology, allowing me to understand the in-depth secrets of living things. Let me therefore outline nature's bounty around the villages of Landywood, Great Wyrley and Cheslyn Hay.

In studying botany, one of the commoner practical tests was to lay out a transect of a piece of land by stretching a taut string between pegs and recording the plant present every three inches (75mm) along the line. A similar analysis of an area was a quadrat where the plants growing in a pegged out square yard (square metre) were plotted. We learned these techniques at Flatford Mill and continued them at home in the meadows, hedgerows or wasteland and there was great joy when we plotted a plant unknown to us. We then had to make a methodical search of a textbook on British Flora, using the characteristics of the plant, the arrangement of its leaves, the shape of the leaves, the number of sepals beneath the flower head, the number of petals, stamens and so on, in order to identify the species. This need to identify a plant was not simply confined to the 'classroom', I became interested in any new species that I came across on country walks, a practice which has continued throughout life.

Although in my teenage years I did not maintain a diary of the local flora, I believe the following list to be a fair representation of those I witnessed in and around villages prior to the 1950s.

Aconite, woodland winter	Broom
Arum (lords and ladies)	Broomrape
Balsam	Bryony
Bindweed, large and small	Buttercup, various
Bird's foot trefoil	Campion, red, white and bladder
Bittercress, hairy	Celandine, lesser
Blackberry	Charlock
Blackthorn	Chervil
Bluebell	Chickweed

Coldsfoot	Orchid, spotted
Corn cockle	Pansy, wild
Cow parsley	Pignut
Cowslip	Plantain, various, including common water
Cranesbill, various	Poppy, field
Crowfoot, water	Pondweed, common
Daisy, common field and ox-eye	Primrose, wild
Dandelion	Ragged robin
Dead Nettle, red and white	Ragwort
Dock various, including water	Rose, wild dog
Fat hen	Scabious, field
Forget-me-not	Scarlet Pimpernel
Foxglove	Shepherd's purse
Garlic mustard	Silverweed
Gorse	Sorrel, common woodland
Ground elder	St John's wort
Groundsel	Speedwell, common
Harebell	Stitchwort, greater
Hawkbit	Strawberry, wild
Heather and ling	Thistle, various
Honeysuckle	Toadflax, yellow
Horsetail	Tormentil
Iris, yellow flag	Willowherb, rosebay and greater
Knapweed, common	Toadflax, upright yellow and creeping
Knotweed, Japanese	Vetch, various
Lady's smock	Violet, dog
Mallow, common and lesser	Water cress
Marsh kingcup	Water mint
Meadow sweet	Water lily, yellow
Nettle, common stinging	Wood anemone
Nightshade, black	Wood sorrel

I have not given the Latin names for the wild flowers but for logging purposes we used their Latin name - *Lamium album, Lamium purpureum* (white and red dead nettle), *Epilobium augustifolium* (rosebay willowherb) and so on. The list is not complete since it does not include grasses and ferns which we did not study in depth. Errors may also have crept in but I offer the list as a reasonably honest representation of local flora, most of them extremely common.

The floral cycle began in early spring with snowdrops, followed by winter aconites and a little later in the woodlands, lords and ladies, sorrel, bluebells and rhododendron (praecox). Beneath the hedgerows, the first to burst into life were large clumps of greater stitchwort some patches as large as six feet in diameter. We called them cuckoo flowers and very quickly they were adorned with 'cuckoo spit', the frothy excretion of the froghopper. As a child, I was led to believe that it was genuine cuckoo spit since it coincided with the arrival of the cuckoo in April. It certainly created an unsightly mess on the carpet of fresh white flowers.

Most hedgerows around us sprang into flower as the blackthorn burst its buds which, later in the year, would provide an abundance of sloes. Following this in late April, hawthorn blossom (may) appeared along with the blossom of the crab apple trees. A week or two later the umbelliferous clumps of white flowers covered the elder bushes. As I walked or cycled the lanes, year by year, I knew each of the bushes and usually greeted them as they displayed their new floral adornment. I suppose my favourite was always the dog rose, which we called the Alexandra rose, after its symbolic use annually (like the poppy of Remembrance day) on the collection day for hospitals and other charities (instituted by Queen Alexandra, wife of King Edward VII). A large bush, often some eight feet across, would in mid-summer display hundreds of beautiful pink rose buds which, as the sun rose in the sky, gaped open to reveal pink blushed white petals and seemingly hundreds of red stamens. In late summer, these same bushes were covered with bright orange hips, the source of Rose Hip syrup during the war years.

Even the shale heaps had their day. A somewhat tantalising spring flower which grew on the mounds was the coldsfoot which for a week or so clothed the drabness in a carpet of bright yellow before darkening to old gold. Like blackthorn, the flowers preceded the leaves and always intrigued me. Where yesterday there was nothing, walking the same path today, bright yellow flowers surround me! Sadly once the flowers had died back, the leaves appeared which were quite large pale greyish green and rather ugly in comparison to the flower. From a distance the greyish leaf masses were almost invisible against the grey shale and simply accentuated its drabness. A few weeks later, the mounds would again display a coat of gold as ragwort took over, interspersed, where the clinker had weathered, with yellow toadflax and groundsel. Occasionally, decayed clinker might also be the compost for a spotted orchid or two, particularly along the canal towpath by the Grove pit. Generally, these orchids grew in the meadows.

Nothing was ever quite as spectacular as the meadows in June when wild scabious, ox-eye daisy, knapweed, buttercup, dandelion, clover, bird's foot trefoil, cat's ear, hawkbit, poppies and other colourful but less common flowers were at their youthful best, popping their heads above surrounding grasses of various types. Insects were at peak activity, humming ecstatically as they worked the flower heads, whilst butterflies flitted silently from flower to flower and leaf to leaf. Standing out against the rich colours were hundreds of Burnet moths, jet black with bright red spots. There were also as many red-brown click beetles, looking very ungainly as mating pairs took to the air, when I walked through and disturbed the grass. In the wheat fields, poppies and charlock produced a heavy peppering of bright red and yellow. In the marshy areas, celandine and lady's smocks were followed by kingcups, forget-me-nots, catmint, yellow irises, reeds, rushes and eventually bulrushes. In the streams, the marsh plants grew at the margins and white water cress flowers matted the faster flowing areas. Under the hedges were many field flowers already mentioned, but most bizarre and not uncommon was broomrape, a curious erect leafless stem of creamy brown flowers which, before studying botany, I would stand and look at very closely and think to myself, 'what are you, are you a flower or some kind of fungus?' I was fascinated by it and, as the years cycled by, I treated it as a returning but, as yet, unresolved friend. In later years, I learned that they were parasitic plants growing mainly on vetch and clover.

As I have intimated, birds were of significant interest to me and I collected their eggs for several years. Whilst today, with the significant reduction in bird numbers, I would look on this hobby with horror, in my early teens birds of many species were extremely common. I am listing birds which I saw in the local countryside and have put an asterisk (★) by those from which I was able to collect an egg.

Blackbird ★

Carrion crow ★

Chiff chaff

Coot ★

Collared dove

Cuckoo ★★★

Finches, bullfinch, greenfinch ★, goldfinch and chaffinch ★

House martin ★

Jackdaw ★

Jay

Kestrel ★

Kingfisher

Lapwing ★

Linnet ★ (we called them seven-coloured linnet)

Magpie ★

Mallard ★

Moorhen ★

Owl, barn ★ and tawny

Partridge ★

Pheasant ★

Pipit, tree ★ and meadow ★

Reed bunting ★

Robin ★

Rook

Skylark

Snipe ★

Sparrow hawk

Sparrow, hedge (dunnock) ★, house ★ and tree ★

Starling ★

Swallow ★

Swan ★ (The egg was a gift and some years old)

Swift ★

Thrush, mistle ★ and song ★

Tit, blue ★, coal ★, great ★ and long-tailed ★

Wagtail, pied ★ and yellow ★

Whitethroat ★

Willow warbler ★

Woodpecker, green and spotted

Wood pigeon ★

Wren ★

Yellow hammer ★

Egg collecting around the villages was a hobby which necessitated walking tens of miles around the perimeters of fields and, for ground nesters, criss-crossing most of them. It was easier to spot a nest in a hedgerow from beneath since they were well camouflaged against predator birds from above. Gorse patches, where pipits, finches, yellow hammers and wrens mostly nested, were never easy, particularly in short trousers. One of the commonest birds to nest in the gorse patches was the yellow hammer, with easily recognised eggs. They looked as though the bird had taken a purple biro and scribbled on her mottled pale cream eggs. For this reason they were referred to as 'scribblers'. Only by sitting quietly and partially hidden and watching birds come and go, was I led to their nests.

Many birds nested in trees, some not easy to climb, but I was obliged to do so if I was going to collect an egg. It was fairly difficult to extract an egg from nests built in a tree cavity with a small hole as access and I created a long-handled spoon (an apostle spoon bound to a stick) for the purpose. The larger birds, nesting in or near the canopy were only difficult insofar as branches became thinner and therefore weaker and I sometimes felt terribly insecure, but I usually succeeded. I have previously described my ordeal with a kestrel near the top of a tree.

Nests in reed beds in the many marshes and along the canalside were reasonably easy to access. I always treated the kingfisher as something special. Even though I was aware of a couple of nests in the canal embankment between Baker's bridge and Long lane, I was never drawn, to raid one. In fact I think it would have destroyed the nest and I only ever saw those two pairs of the birds. The commoner water birds, coots, mallard, and moorhens had nests in the reeds which were quite easy to spot. The swan's nests were always elevated and on open view but I was taught that they were the king's birds and was never tempted to try for an egg. In any case they could be quite unpleasant if anyone approached the nest. The swan's egg in my collection, was quite an old egg and was given to me by a friend of dad's. Snipe's nests were very common in the reeds in the 'valley' field and I simply had to take off my shoes and paddle to a nest.

I tried many times to find a skylark's nest as described earlier, but never succeeded. Partridges and lapwings (peewits) were extremely common and easy to find, the former often with more than a dozen eggs under a hedgerow in a wheat field and the latter fairly easy to see in the meadows as the parents could be seen sitting on the eggs. During the autumn, a flock of as many as two hundred peewits would collect and forage in Cooper's field opposite our bungalow, no doubt collecting to migrate, and making an almighty cacophony.

Of all the birds I had the pleasure to observe, the cuckoo was the enigma. Like the striking of Big Ben at the midnight hour on New Year's eve, the first call of the cuckoo was the signal for early summer. Year after year it returned to the large oak tree in the field above our house announcing itself to all who might listen, but hoping that a mate would respond. At the first call we smiled at each other, recognising that an acquaintance had returned. We immediately broke into the ditty,

The cuckoo comes in April,
Sings its song in May,
It changes its tune in the middle of June
And then it flies away.

It may have been a seasonal reminder to us but would mean hard work for many small birds now nesting. The hatchling of the cuckoo is enormous and it was beyond belief to see a meadow pipit feeding a bird some four times larger than itself. A cuckoo chick flew onto Uncle Bob's lawn one afternoon and I watched a pair of dunnocks working their butts off trying to meet the requirements of the ravenous machine. How cruel is nature, I thought, and had a strong urge to go out and bump it off to relieve the exhausted 'parents'! I collected three cuckoo eggs over the years from different nests which were easy to detect because they were larger than any other in the nest. I considered that I was doing the host birds a service in removing the cuckoo egg and, for this reason, was not unhappy to have three in my collection.

The eggs of birds nesting around houses, farm outhouses and pit buildings were not difficult to collect. My first eggs were probably those of the house sparrow and starling because, whenever they nested in granddad's eaves, he pulled the nests out. His argument was that they brought fleas to the house and their droppings made an almighty mess of the house and yard. Swallows and house martins were very common. A barn owl nested every year in the 'barn' along Landywood Lane. A robin and wren frequently nested around granddad's garden, the former nesting once in an empty paint can in the garden shed.

My collection of just over forty bird's eggs was subsequently given to Miss Liddle and kept in the nature cupboard as a museum piece. Birds were so numerous that people did not really raise an eye-brow at the hobby and Miss Liddle was very happy to accept the gift. If anything, bird losses were more affected by boys, usually teenagers, who felt that it was fun to pull a nest from the hedgerows, throw stones at nests in trees or even worse, drop a stone in a nest full of eggs. I felt utter disgust when one day I walked over Baker's bridge across the canal and looked down to see a large stone had been dropped onto five eggs in a blackbird's nest. I remember feeling utter despair for the human race.

The other hobby I have mentioned was butterfly collecting, which certainly gave me plenty of exercise. The interesting fact is that most were seen and caught within some 400 metres of home and the majority of them in the fields of Caddick farm. These were normal meadows of the day, some grazed and some used for hay making. The flowers seemed to attract local butterflies and I am fairly sure that I collected a specimen of every species in the area. My collection finally displayed fifteen different butterflies.

Brimstone	Red admiral
Common blue	Small copper
Large white	Small heath
Large tortoiseshell	Small tortoiseshell
Marbled white	Small white
Meadow brown	Wall
Orange tip	White admiral
Peacock	

Apart from my hobbies, I spent hours watching insects or tracing where a grasshopper chatter was coming from. I sat patiently watching spiders build a web, wondering where the endless spinning yarn was coming from. I examined moths and their caterpillars though did not collect them. At around eight years of age I saw a privet hawk moth caterpillar which was so large that I ran into the house to get cousin Ron to show him the large snake on the drive, my hands gesticulating something at least two feet long! When I returned with him, it had reduced to about three inches (75mm), but was still the largest caterpillar I had ever seen!

The fields and meadows of Landywood, Great Wyrley and Cheslyn Hay were my Elysian fields as I have already said. They shaped my whole life. Its destruction was a massive loss for local residents, but fortunately there are still many similar untouched areas throughout Britain which can be visited and where nature is thriving. Thankfully lessons have been learned about the destruction of large tranches of the countryside so that even motorways are today wonderful havens for wildlife. I know Mother Nature will eventually return my childhood playground to normality, and to be fair, is already doing so. However, three generations will not have witnessed the setting for my 'Song of Spring', and that is sad.

EPILOGUE

Keats asked, 'where are the songs of Spring?' I hope my 'lyrics' have answered this question. You will have gleaned that Spring for me was a most enjoyable part of my life, but what about summer and autumn?

As a result of my love of nature I studied biology and went on to study medicine at Birmingham Medical School. After qualifying, I was a House Officer at St Chad's Hospital for a year prior to joining the army for two years of National Service. I was stationed for a long time in Warwickshire and got pleasure from the flora and fauna there. During this time I married Janet Bourne, granddaughter of Mrs Eliza Sambrook, whose shop I have described. We were lucky to produce four wonderful children.

After meeting Janet, who trained as a radiographer at Walsall Hospitals, I became hooked on diagnostic Radiology and specialised in the subject, requiring a further five years training in Birmingham hospitals to gain the appropriate qualifications.

In 1965 I was appointed consultant radiologist at Dudley Road Hospital in Birmingham and in 1975 moved to Walsall where I worked until my recent retirement (2011), both as Unit General Manager to Walsall acute hospitals for a period and then as Medical Director.

Mom died in 1997 and dad in 2001, but prior to this, we visited them weekly and hence I have been able to watch the villages grow. I continued to sing in the choir at Great Wyrley Wesley Church until around 1975. Perhaps my last contribution in that year was to write a hymn to celebrate the fiftieth anniversary of the Walsall Road church, a church that had moulded me and in my youth had been a hive of activities, music and worship. It is dedicated to all who have worked so hard over the years to build the edifice where they worship God and promote Christianity.

Hail, O Anniversary day,
Fifty years of harmony!
We and forbears, in full voice,
Permeate this edifice.
Echoes ringing
Of past singing,
Swelling out in full refrain,
Covenant with God again.

Fifty years of Sunday School,
Childhood's nurture bountiful.
Christ-like seeds can germinate,
Lordly harvest emanate.
Children's voices!
Each rejoices
And, with teachers, all acclaim,
Covenant with God again.

Fifty years of meetings, where
Business, fellowship and prayer
Have, in concert unity,
Proclaimed Christianity.
Members sharing,
Clergy caring,
Trustees, stewards, leaders hymn,
Covenant with God again.

Fifty years, and so lives on
Wyrley Wesley bastion!
Let's give thanks and homage pay
For safe refuge to this day.
Praise with fervour
Christ our Saviour!
Loud our voice, and in His Name,
Covenant with God again

Having thoroughly enjoyed the Spring, summer and autumn of life, I now look forward to a mild winter.

One final thought, what about that steam locomotive that I always dreamed of building? Winter is certainly giving me more free time and sure enough the construction of "Jessie" is well underway. She is a 0-4-0 saddle tank shunting locomotive in seven and a quarter inch gauge. I need at least five years to complete it, but will my winter be long enough? Who knows?